I0812262

Believers Church Bible Commentary

Douglas B. Miller and Loren L. Johns, Editors

BELIEVERS CHURCH BIBLE COMMENTARY

Old Testament
Genesis, by Eugene F. Roop, 1987
Exodus, by Waldemar Janzen, 2000
Judges, by Terry L. Brensinger, 1999
Ruth, Jonah, Esther, by Eugene F. Roop, 2002
Psalms, by James H. Waltner, 2006
Proverbs, by John W. Miller, 2004
Isaiah, by Ivan D. Friesen, 2009
Jeremiah, by Elmer A. Martens, 1986
Ezekiel, by Millard C. Lind, 1996
Daniel, by Paul M. Lederach, 1994
Hosea, Amos, by Allen R. Guenther, 1998

New Testament
Matthew, by Richard B. Gardner, 1991
Mark, by Timothy J. Geddert, 2001
Acts, by Chalmer E. Faw, 1993
Romans, by John E. Toews, 2004
2 Corinthians, by V. George Shillington, 1998
Ephesians, by Thomas R. Yoder Neufeld, 2002
Colossians, Philemon, by Ernest D. Martin, 1993
1-2 Thessalonians, by Jacob W. Elias, 1995
1-2 Timothy, Titus, by Paul M. Zehr, 2010
1-2 Peter, Jude, by Erland Waltner and J. Daryl Charles, 1999
Revelation, by John R. Yeatts, 2003

Believers Church Bible Commentary

1 & 2 Timothy Titus

Paul M. Zehr

HERALD PRESS
Scottdale, Pennsylvania
Waterloo, Ontario

Library of Congress Cataloging-in-Publication Data
Zehr, Paul M., 1936-
1 & 2 Timothy, Titus / Paul M. Zehr.
p. cm.—(Believers church Bible commentary series)
Includes bibliographical references and index.
ISBN 978-0-8361-9492-0 (pbk.)
1. Bible. N.T. Pastoral Epistles—Commentaries. I. Title. II. Title: First and Second Timothy, Titus.
BS2735.53.Z44 2010
227'.83077—dc22

2009052968

Library of Congress Control Number: 2009052968
International Standard Book Number: 978-0-8361-9492-0
Printed in the United States of America
Cover by Merrill R. Miller

15 14 13 12 11 10   10 9 8 7 6 5 4 3 2 1

To order or request information please call 1-800-245-7894 or visit www.heraldpress.com.

To the in-service pastors and students preparing for Christian ministry in my classes over the years, from whom I have learned much about the personal character, calling, and work of pastoral ministry.

Abbreviations

1QS	Rule of the Community (a Dead Sea Scroll)
ABD	*Anchor Bible Dictionary*. Edited by David Noel Freedman. 6 vols. New York: Doubleday, 1992.
alt.	quotation slightly altered for good style in English
art.	article
BDAG	Bauer, W., F. W. Danker, W. F. Arndt, and F. W. Gingrich. *A Greek-English Lexicon of the New Testament and Other Early Christian Literature*. 3rd ed. Chicago: University of Chicago Press, 2000.
ca.	circa, approximately (esp. with a date)
cf.	*confer*, compare
CW	*The Complete Writings of Menno Simons*. Translated by Leonard Verduin. Edited by J. C. Wenger. Scottdale, PA: Herald Press, 1956.
d.	died
DPL	*Dictionary of Paul and His Letters*. Edited by Gerald F. Hawthorne and Ralph P. Martin. Downers Grove, IL: InterVarsity, 1993.
e.g.	*exempli gratia*, for example
esp.	especially
et al.	*et alia*, and others
GNT	Greek New Testament
i.e.	*id est*, that is
IDB	*Interpreter's Dictionary of the Bible*. Edited by G. A. Buttrick. 4 vols. Nashville: Abingdon, 1962.
KJV	King James Version
lit.	literally
LXX	Septuagint
ME	*The Mennonite Encyclopedia*. Vols. 1–4 edited by H. S. Bender et al. Vol. 5 edited by C. J. Dyck and D. D. Martin. Scottdale, PA: Herald Press, 1955-59, 1990.
NA	Eberhard Nestle and Kurt Aland, eds. *Novum Testamentum Graece*. 27th rev. ed. Stuttgart: Deutsche Bibelgesellschaft, 1993.
NEB	New English Bible
NIV	New International Version
NJB	New Jerusalem Bible
NRSV	New Revised Standard Version
n.s.	new series
NT	New Testament
OT	Old Testament
QS	Qumran Scrolls (Dead Sea Scrolls)
REB	Revised English Bible
RSV	Revised Standard Version
s.v.	*sub verbo*, under the word
TBC	The Text in Biblical Context
TDNT	*Theological Dictionary of the New Testament*. Edited by G. Kittel and G. Friedrich. Translated by G. W. Bromiley. 10 vols. Grand Rapids: Eerdmans. 1964-76.
TLC	The Text in the Life of the Church
TNIV	Today's New International Version
UBS*GNT*	United Bible Societies. *The Greek New Testament*. Edited by Barbara Aland, Kurt Aland, Johannes Karavidopoulos, Carlo M. Martini, and Bruce M. Metzger. 4th rev. ed. Stuttgart: Deutsche Bibelgesellschaft, 1993.

Contents

Titus

Series Foreword

The Believers Church Bible Commentary Series makes available a new tool for basic Bible study. It is published for all who seek more fully to understand the original message of Scripture and its meaning for today—Sunday school teachers, members of Bible study groups, students, pastors, and others. The series is based on the conviction that God is still speaking to all who will listen, and that the Holy Spirit makes the Word a living and authoritative guide for all who want to know and do God's will.

The desire to help as wide a range of readers as possible has determined the approach of the writers. Since no blocks of biblical text are provided, readers may continue to use the translation with which they are most familiar. The writers of the series use the *New Revised Standard Version*, the *Revised Standard Version*, the *New International Version*, and the *New American Standard Bible* on a comparative basis. They indicate which text they follow most closely and where they make their own translations. The writers have not worked alone, but in consultation with select counselors, the series' editors, and the Editorial Council.

Every volume illuminates the Scriptures; provides necessary theological, sociological, and ethical meanings; and, in general, makes "the rough places plain." Critical issues are not avoided, but neither are they moved into the foreground as debates among scholars. Each section offers explanatory notes, followed by focused articles, "The Text in Biblical Context" and "The Text in the Life of the Church." This commentary aids the interpretive process but does not try to supersede the authority of the Word and Spirit as discerned in the gathered church.

The term *believers church* has often been used in the history of the church. Since the sixteenth century, it has frequently been applied to the Anabaptists and later the Mennonites, as well as to the Church of the Brethren and similar groups. As a descriptive term, it includes more than Mennonites and Brethren. *Believers church* now represents specific theological understandings, such as believers baptism, commitment to the Rule of Christ in Matthew 18:15-20 as crucial for church membership, belief in the power of love in all relationships, and willingness to follow Christ in the way of the cross. The writers chosen for the series stand in this tradition.

Believers church people have always been known for their emphasis on obedience to the simple meaning of Scripture. Because of this, they do not have a long history of deep historical-critical biblical scholarship. This series attempts to be faithful to the Scriptures while also taking archaeology and current biblical studies seriously. Doing this means that at many points the writers will not differ greatly from interpretations that can be found in many other good commentaries. Yet these writers share basic convictions about Christ, the church and its mission, God and history, human nature, the Christian life, and other doctrines. These presuppositions do shape a writer's interpretation of Scripture. Thus this series, like all other commentaries, stands within a specific historical church tradition.

Many in this stream of the church have expressed a need for help in Bible study. This is justification enough to produce the Believers Church Bible Commentary. Nevertheless, the Holy Spirit is not bound to any tradition. May this series be an instrument in breaking down walls between Christians in North America and around the world, bringing new joy in obedience through a fuller understanding of the Word.

The Editorial Council

Author's Preface

My interest in 1 & 2 Timothy, Titus emerged out of teaching and pastoring. In my early years of ministry I discovered a need to expand my understanding of the role of the pastor in the congregation and in the community. I also became aware of my need to increase my pastoral skills. Serving as pastor for more than 20 years and guiding pastors as bishop for 25 years strengthened my resolve to help pastors grow in the Christian ministry.

I learned much about the character, conduct, and content of the pastor's message and work through Paul M. Miller, with whom I teamed in Supervised Pastoral Education for several years. Paul taught me the importance of the letters to Timothy and Titus. His wise teaching on "how one ought to behave in the household of God" (1 Tim 3:15) and encouragement to "carry out your ministry fully" (2 Tim 4:5) enriched many pastors. While developing in-service pastoral training programs, Ralph Lebold and John Esau taught me the importance of the pastor as person and the role of the pastoral office and work in the congregation.

In graduate school I gave attention to a philosophy of pastoral education as I worked on a curriculum guide for training in-service pastors. It was here that I came to an awareness of three major questions. What kind of person should the pastor be? It is the question of being. What should the pastor know? It is the question of knowledge. And what must the pastor do? It is the question of skills needed for pastoral ministry. I discovered in my personal life and in the lives of many pastors that growth in these areas of ministry is not only possible but also necessary. Paul told Timothy, "Put these things into practice, devote yourself to them, so that all may see your progress" (1 Tim 4:15).

In preparing this commentary on 1 & 2 Timothy, Titus, I perceived that these letters are not as much about pastoral work as they are about clarifying one's theology and applying it in the context of the Christian ministry. Theology informs the practice of ministry. In these letters Paul's ultimate concern is sound [healthy] doctrine and teaching. What is the content of our preaching and teaching? Healthy teaching and preaching makes a healthy church. Healthy theology lines up with the theological content of the earliest witnesses of Jesus known as apostolic teaching. Healthy theology centers in preaching and teaching about Jesus Christ and the Christ-way of living. How well is our preaching and teaching applied to the various issues faced by the church in its contemporary setting? Healthy Christian teaching speaks to politics, philosophy, religion, and the social and cultural practices of the people. It invites people to Christ for salvation and for living.

Several persons have read some parts or all of this commentary manuscript at various stages of its preparation. For their constructive feedback I thank Samuel Thomas, Daniel Dietzel, George R. Brunk III, Pamela Rutt, Luann H. Martin, and Jacob W. Elias.

Loren L. Johns, NT Editor for the Believers Church Bible Commentary series, provided encouragement, pointed me to sources of information, and strengthened the readability of these pages. The Editorial Council (in my absence) gave valuable feedback on ways to improve the manuscript. Any shortcomings and mistakes in these pages belong to me and not to the persons who read the manuscript and gave me constructive feedback along the way. To all of these persons I owe much gratitude. I also thank Amy Gingerich of Herald Press for guiding this manuscript through publication.

Finally, I thank my wife, Mary, for her constant encouragement and prayer support in preparing this commentary.

Introduction

Lively scholarly interest in 1 & 2 Timothy and Titus is evident with the publication of a dozen commentaries on these letters in the last fifteen years as well as in the Society of Biblical Literature meetings.

Contemporary Christianity is called upon to explain and apply the meaning of the gospel in a postmodern culture. How shall the contemporary church deal with philosophical, social, and cultural differences as it applies the gospel in today's world? What is the task of the ordained ministry in contemporary culture? How shall Christians apply the ethical dimensions of the gospel in our day? How do we move beyond Christianity as a belief system to the actual living out of Christian faith in a postmodern society?

Upheaval in the church regarding pastoral conduct in recent years has shattered some parishioners' confidence in pastoral leadership. The letters to Timothy and Titus speak to the pastor as a person. The pastor's proclamation of the gospel is enhanced or diminished by the pastor's own example of living out the Christian faith. Paul holds right belief (orthodoxy) and right living (orthopraxy) together in the letters to Timothy and Titus. His admonition to Timothy is relevant today: "Set the believers an example in speech and conduct, in love, in faith, in purity" (1 Tim 4:12).

Written in the second half of the first century, the letters to Timothy and Titus provide glimpses into ways the early church worked at discerning how to apply the meaning of the gospel of Jesus Christ within its own social, cultural, economic, philosophical, political, and religious setting. Shall the church simply follow the prevailing social, cultural, and political practices in order to be relevant? Or shall the church confront the culture and adopt an alternative way of living?

Paul's letters to Timothy and Titus demonstrate that the church can carry out its mission in the midst of prevailing culture and at the same time maintain its true faith. These letters demythologize imperial religion and proclaim God as the true Savior of the world.

While presenting the centrality of the gospel, the church also asks how Christian ethics apply to family relationships and employer-employee relationships. The letters to Timothy and Titus wrestle with these questions as the author tries to maintain the true gospel of Jesus Christ in the church's mission in Ephesus and on the island of Crete. No longer are the major questions of circumcision seen, as in Paul's earlier writing in Galatians. Nor is the question of meat offered to idols up for discussion, as in 1 Corinthians 8 and Romans 14. Instead, the churches in Ephesus and Crete face new issues.

Ephesus, known as the gateway to Asia, was located at the eastern edge of the Aegean Sea. Its major harbor and trans-Anatolian highway enriched its economic and cultural life. Its religious life comprised several traditions, including the Ephesian deity at the temple of Artemis. Throughout the city were shrines to Cybele, the Phrygian mother goddess, and to Zeus, the male deity. The Egyptian mystery rites were present in the temple of Serapis. Most prominent was the imperial temple dedicated to Augustus Caesar and his successor Roman emperors. Thus the growing Christian church in this important city faced religious syncretism and needed to clarify its faith in God and in the gospel of Jesus Christ over against other competing religions. Paul works at this by setting forth the centrality of the gospel through several confessional statements (1 Tim 2:5-6; 3:16; 2 Tim 1:9-10; 2:8-13).

In addition, Paul warns people whose teachings are unacceptable and whose behaviors are unfaithful. Paul presents the character qualities desired in leaders of the church. He offers Timothy personal instruction and encouragement. In 2 Timothy the apostle encourages young Timothy in his leadership role. Just as Paul endures suffering, so Timothy is to endure suffering and faithfully carry out his task of leading the church. Timothy is to follow Jesus Christ as the prime example of faithfulness in the midst of suffering and death. The relationship between present suffering and future glory leads Paul to cite a "sure saying" in 2 Timothy 2:11-13.

On the island of Crete, a young church is growing and needs leaders. The Cretans were known for their exaggerated oratory, which extended as far as self-deprecation: one of their own bygone poets described them as "always liars, vicious brutes, and lazy gluttons" (Titus 1:12). In addition, they were known for drinking too much wine and pursuing sexual pleasures. Some of this culture rubbed off on the Jewish people in Crete, which led to arguments and contentions over the Cretans' founding myths and the interpretations of their traditional laws. With both Jews and Gentiles coming to Jesus as the Messiah, these arguments intensified. In giving guidance to the church and Titus its leader, the apostle Paul calls attention to the centrality of the gospel in confessional statements in Titus 2:11-14 and 3:4-7.

A mission theme also characterizes 1 & 2 Timothy and Titus. Timothy and Titus continue the missionary legacy of Paul, the great first-century missionary. This missionary theme is present in the confessional statements and in nearly all of the sayings. Timothy and Titus communicate the gospel cross-culturally in the language of the Greco-Roman world. As Paul spoke about God at Athens in the presence of an unknown god (Acts 17:22-34), so the author of these letters talks about God as Savior in contrast to the Roman emperor *[Names for God and the Imperial Cult, p. 357]*.

Already at Thessalonica, Paul was accused of "acting contrary to the decrees of the emperor, saying that there is another king named Jesus" (Acts 17:7). Now in 1 & 2 Timothy and Titus, the Christian gospel directly confronts imperial religion. Not only is God called Savior in contrast to the Roman emperor, but language used when the Roman emperor visited cities in the empire is now attributed to God's work in Jesus Christ. As the early church adjusted some ethical practices, such as what foods to eat and the practice of circumcision, so Paul in Titus gives moral instructions and makes adjustments for young women, young men, and slaves as the Christian church establishes itself on the pagan island of Crete.

In short, each letter expresses salvation in slightly different ways, indicating the individuality of each letter. At the same time, salvation is laid out consistently with Paul's theology elsewhere. But it is described with distinctive terminology carefully chosen to communicate the gospel in a Greco-Roman context. It is not a purely Gentile context; Jewish elements are clearly seen (1 Tim 1:6-11; Titus 1:10-11; 2 Tim 2:10; 3:14-15). And Timothy and Titus must deal with some Jewish "Gnostic" or proto-Gnostic elements. Gnosticism was condemned by church leaders in the second century as an unfaithful understanding of salvation through esoteric knowledge, although some hints of it can be detected already in the first century (1 Tim 4:1-5; 6:3-5; Titus 1:10-16; 3:9-11; 2 Tim 2:16-18, 23; 3:1-9; 4:3).

Since its early years, the Christian church has claimed 1 & 2 Timothy and Titus as authentic, accepted, canonical letters. Although the authorship question is debated, the church has embraced these letters as Scripture *[Authorship, p. 325]*. Central to the author is the importance of *sound doctrine* (healthy teaching) based on true faith in Jesus Christ and its implications for godly living. As the church hammered out Christian theology and ethics in the latter half of the first century, it needed to clarify this healthy teaching over against unhealthy teaching, for the good of the church. (I use the words "unhealthy teaching" and "unhealthy teachers" in this commentary to suggest unacceptable deviation from "sound" [healthy] teaching as discerned by the author of these letters. *Sound* teaching is a medical adjective used in a theological sense for healthy teaching that is consistent with the gospel of Jesus Christ; see notes on 1 Tim 1:10-11.) Properly understood, the content of 1 & 2 Timothy, Titus is relevant and presents healthy teaching for the contemporary church.

Letters to Timothy and Titus or Letters to Individual Delegates?

Interpreters face two questions. First, what is the relationship between 1 & 2 Timothy, Titus and the undisputed Paulines? (Undisputed Paulines are the letters whose authorship by Paul is seldom disputed; disputed Paulines are the letters whose authorship some scholars dispute.) Missing in the letters to Timothy and Titus is the common Pauline terminology of justification by faith, the cross, and the body of Christ, which are prominent in Galatians, Romans, and the Corinthian letters. In addition, about 175 words in the letters to Timothy and Titus are not found in other Pauline writings.

These differences in terminology have led some scholars to conclude that Paul did not write these letters. However, other Pauline themes are present in these letters, such as God, Christ, salvation, Holy Spirit, church, and eschatology. Five "faithful sayings" appear in these letters, marking a theological tradition that was handed down (1 Tim 1:15; 3:1; 4:8-9; 2 Tim 2:11-13; Titus 3:8). Several confessional formulations point to Paul's view of salvation (1 Tim 2:5-6; 3:16; 2 Tim 1:9-10; 2:11-13; Titus 2:11-14; 3:4-7). Differences in terminology, such as "God our Savior" and "godliness" may suggest that the author was writing for a larger Greco-Roman audience in addressing these letters to Timothy in Ephesus and Titus in Crete. Furthermore, Paul used different secretaries in his writing. Knowing the author is helpful in interpreting a given New Testament (NT) book, but it was not necessary for canonization and acceptance by the church as authentic Scripture.

Second, what is the relationship between these three letters? In 1703 D. N. Bardot used the term *pastoral* for Titus, and in 1726 P. Anton called all three letters to Timothy and Titus "pastoral epistles." Today many scholars place these three letters together as one body of writing and call them pastoral epistles. Indeed, 1 & 2 Timothy and Titus work with pastoral issues, but they do so in the context of larger theological and ethical issues.

A flat, thematic interpretive approach to these three letters obscures the diverse literary and theological issues within and between them. One recent writer has suggested we drop the phrase pastoral epistles since it has become a restraining device, suggesting instead that we interpret each letter separately (Towner 2006: 88). Unlike the undisputed Paulines, which are addressed to churches, 1 & 2 Timothy and Titus, along with Philemon, are addressed to individual persons. The letters are arranged in the canon according to length, beginning with the longest and ending with the shortest.

Significant differences distinguish each letter. Second Timothy shares some themes and language with 1 Timothy and Titus, but it is more personal in tone and includes detailed historical references and greetings to fellow workers (e.g., 2 Tim 4:9-12). Timothy is exhorted to follow Paul's model of faithfulness in the midst of suffering and not to be ashamed of the gospel or of Paul (2 Tim 1:8, 11-13; 2:3, 8-10; 3:10-17; 4:5-7). Second Timothy includes both personal paraenetic (advice in the form of exhortation) and testamentary (farewell discourse) forms of literature (2 Tim 4:6-18). Most scholars agree that 2 Timothy is the most Pauline of the three epistles.

First Timothy and Titus have a common interest in God as Savior, character qualities for church leaders (1 Tim 3:1-13; Titus 1:5-9), and household behavior (1 Tim 2:8-15; 5:3-25; 6:1-2; Titus 2:3-10). First Timothy and Titus are distinguished from 2 Timothy by these common features and by a literary form called *mandata principis* (commands and exhortations from a superior). Nevertheless, significant differences exist between 1 Timothy and Titus. They are written to different co-workers. Timothy is in Ephesus, where imperial religion is strong, the influence of Artemis of the Ephesians still lingers, and where elders need special attention (1 Tim 5:17-25). Because of adverse teaching creeping into the church, Timothy is instructed to choose a bishop (the word occurs only in the singular in these three letters) and deacons carefully (1 Tim 3:1-13). Moreover, Timothy is instructed to correct the influence of unhealthy teaching (1 Tim 1:3-4, 18-20; 6:3-5, 20-21). The church at Ephesus began during Paul's second missionary journey (Acts 19:1-41) and now needs midcourse corrections. Timothy, as a confidant of Paul, is told what changes to make in the church at Ephesus.

The letter to Titus deals with leadership for a young mission church on the island of Crete. The Cretan church exists in a context of behavior that is morally and culturally suspect. Some unhealthy teachings affect this church (Titus 1:10-16; 3:9-11). For the first time, Titus is to appoint elders in each town. Personal greetings and instructions to fellow workers are also included (Titus 3:12-13). While both 1 Timothy and Titus include instructional material and emphasize correction of unhealthy teaching, each addresses distinct historical and theological settings.

Given these similarities and differences, this commentary will interpret these three letters both vertically and horizontally. Each letter will be introduced as a separate letter, with literary, historical, and authorship analyses. This vertical reading will set forth the uniqueness of each individual letter and its message. A vertical method of interpreting each individual letter will result in some repetition of material in this commentary, since the letters cover similar themes, each with its own historical and theological nuances. However, because the letters do have some relationship to each other, they will be interpreted horizontally for the purpose of noting their common themes. Essays in the back of the commentary highlight some of these themes. Read this way, the letters to Timothy and Titus are a cluster of writings like the Corinthian and Thessalonian correspondence *[Order and Historical Sequence, p. 358]*.

Occasion and Purpose

First Timothy is addressed to Timothy, "my loyal child in the faith" (1:2), whom Paul left in Ephesus as his personal delegate to stop the influence of unhealthy teaching in the church. According to 1 Timothy 1:3, Paul was on his way to Macedonia when he first instructed Timothy "to remain in Ephesus so that you may instruct certain people not to teach any different doctrine." In the undisputed Paulines, the apostle dealt with teachers from Jerusalem who insisted on circumcision. In 1 Timothy, promoters of unhealthy teaching have combined Hellenistic Judaism with its allegorical interpretation of the OT and other forms of Hellenistic religious syncretism, including emperor worship.

In contrast to the religious, social, and political life of the culture of Ephesus, Timothy is commanded to set forth a divinely organized pattern of life, God's ordering of reality (*oikonomia theou*), as stated in 1 Timothy 1:4. The emperor took to himself the role of savior, the role of father or householder, and regarded the empire and its inhabitants as his household.

First Timothy is written to help the church understand that all of life is subject to the will of God. Not only does this mean a rejection of deviant, unhealthy teaching, but house churches are also to be a microcosm or paradigm of a world obedient to God's ordering (Towner 2006: 69). Both right doctrine and right living are emphasized. Timothy must know how to behave in the household of God, which is the church of the living God, the pillar and bulwark of the truth (1 Tim 3:15).

Church leaders need character that is consistent with living according to the will of God. Thus Timothy is exhorted to correct deviant teaching, give healthy doctrinal teaching, and choose leaders with godly character so that the church can be God's household in society. The church models Christian behavior in its care of widows (1 Tim 5:3-16). Behavior of men and women in worship and slaves at work are part of the church's witness of God's grace (2:8-15; 6:1-2). As such, the church will be a visible expression of God's redemptive presence in the midst of Greco-Roman Ephesus. Timothy is commanded to carry on the work of public ministry in his life, his preaching, and his teaching (4:11-16).

Titus was left on the island of Crete to set in order what had not yet been done at that time: to appoint elders in the various congregations across the whole island (Titus 1:5). Here also unhealthy teachings appeared. Some deviant teachers are "of the circumcision" (1:10). Titus is instructed to silence them. In light of the reputation of the Cretans as liars, the letter to Titus opens with a lengthy introduction that emphasizes God's eternal life and that God never lies (1:1-3). God's eternal life is seen in the gospel of Jesus Christ and condemns elements of the value system of the Cretan culture.

In contrast to the prevailing Roman culture of imperial religion, the letter includes two major confessional statements in 2:11-14 and 3:4-7. These confessional statements present God's saving work through Christ, which calls for a different way of thinking about grace, epiphany, salvation, household living, and divine beneficence when compared with the pagan gods and the emperor.

In comparison with 1 Timothy, the letter to Titus has fewer second-person imperatives, suggesting less urgency. Titus must deal with opponents forthrightly so the church can move forward in its life and mission. Salvation in Jesus Christ brings about good works, which now must characterize these young Christians (1:8, 16; 2:7, 14; 3:1, 8, 14). Christ died to create a people who are zealous of good works (2:14). Young Christians in Crete are invited to Christlike living within their household for the sake of outsiders (2:5, 7-8, 10; 3:1, 8).

Relationships and character traits within Christian households (2:1-10) must become such that persons outside the Christian faith will stop rejecting the gospel and actually find it attractive (2:5, 10).

Second Timothy is the most Pauline of the three letters. Paul's circumstances have changed. He is in prison a second time and knows that death is imminent. Thus the letter contains elements of Paul's last will and testament (4:6-8). Concerns about unhealthy teachings reappear, and Timothy is directed to deal urgently with them.

The letter alternates between comments on Paul's own life and advice to Timothy about Christian ministry. It exhorts Timothy to loyalty and willingness to suffer for the gospel. Paul presents himself as a model for Christian ministry as he recalls previous experiences of mission endeavor with Timothy at his side (3:10-12). Timothy is not to be ashamed of the Lord or of Paul (1:8). As a good missionary and church leader, Timothy must now stir up the gift God has given him for leadership in the church by relying on the power of God (1:6-7). Timothy is exhorted to carry out his ministry fully (4:1-5).

In contrast to the emperor's supposed role as savior for the kingdom's inhabitants and his occasional formal appearance, Timothy is to focus his ministry on the grace and loving-kindness of God, as seen in the appearing of Christ in the world, through whom God brought salvation, life, and immortality through the gospel (2 Tim 1:9-10). This gospel, centered in the historical and resurrected Jesus Christ, includes a future bodily resurrection, which some deny (2:16-18). Timothy is to hold to the standard of sound teaching he heard from Paul and to guard the deposit of faith given to him (1:13-14). A sure saying calls attention to the faithfulness of God (2:11-13).

Finally, the warmth of Paul's relationship with Timothy is seen in Paul's request that Timothy come to him soon—before winter (2 Tim 4:9, 21). Many personal greetings and notes at the end of the letter suggest Pauline authorship as he recalls his comrades in the faith and places where they serve.

Authorship and Date

Authorship and date remain difficult problems for the interpreter of the letters to Timothy and Titus *[Authorship, p. 325]*. No one knows for sure who wrote 1 & 2 Timothy or Titus, or when they were written. Scholars who believe that Paul wrote these epistles date them in the last two or three years of his life. Other scholars believe they were written by an unnamed writer after Paul's death, toward the end of the first century, and that the letters speak to the post-Pauline period of the church as it faced new issues in its development within the Greco-Roman world.

Scholars also debate how many authors wrote the letters to Timothy and Titus. Some hold to one author for all three letters. Others suggest two authors—one for 1 Timothy and Titus, and a second for 2 Timothy. Yet others propose three separate authors—one for each letter.

It is easy to observe that 1 Timothy and Titus differ significantly from 2 Timothy. Second Timothy is more personal and Pauline in tone and content than 1 Timothy or Titus. Titus and 1 Timothy seem to combine Pauline theological themes and non-Pauline themes, such as godliness, the church as the household of God, church leaders, and household behavior—themes that fit best into a post-Pauline period between AD 65 and 85. If a secretary gave expression to Paul's ideas, that could account for the language and syntax differences from the (earlier) Pauline letters. We know Paul used different secretaries in writing his epistles, so it is not impossible that a secretary or amanuensis (one who writes down the words of another) wrote the letters to Timothy and Titus.

So what can we make of the authorship debate? First, the authenticity and authority of the letters to Timothy and Titus does not rest on Pauline authorship. Hebrews, for example, is authentic Scripture even though we do not know who wrote it. Second, the letters to Timothy and Titus were early recognized as authoritative Scripture—long before the canon was recognized as a canon. Third, the letters to Timothy and Titus were written *before* the writings of Clement of Rome (ca. AD 96), Ignatius (ca. 115), and Polycarp (ca. 117). Fourth, the letters to Timothy and Titus speak in "Pauline" language, meaning in terms with which Paul would have been comfortable. To say that these letters speak in Pauline language does not tell us *how* the letters came from Paul, but it does assert Paul's major influence over them. And fifth, some scholars in the last twenty-five years have raised serious questions about assumptions underlying the view of non-Pauline authorship.

In this commentary I examine questions of authorship and date as I introduce each letter. I also look for evidence that Luke may have taken Paul's thoughts and put them into words *[Authorship, p. 325]*.

I use the NRSV as the primary English translation in this commentary. When I use other English translations, I identify them *[Abbreviations, p. 6]*.

1 Timothy

Introduction to 1 Timothy

Timothy and Ephesus

A flourishing church arose during Paul's stint of missionary work in Ephesus, the provincial capital of the western province of Asia Minor (Acts 19:1-41; 20:17, 31). Ephesus was located in the Lycus River valley, near a seaport on the Aegean Sea. Land and sea routes intersected with this city, making it a financial, communication, and travel hub to other parts of the empire—both to the east and to the west. During the first century, the population of Ephesus reached nearly 250,000 people, making it the fourth-largest city in the Roman Empire after Rome, Alexandria, and Antioch of Syria.

According to Acts 20:4, Timothy was with Paul as the apostle left Ephesus and set out for Jerusalem. He traveled with Paul as far as Troas. Later Timothy was with Paul in Rome during his house arrest in the early 60s. Paul wrote, "But Timothy's worth you know, how like a son with a father he has served with me in the work of the gospel" (Phil 2:22). Later Paul sent Timothy to Ephesus to provide continuing leadership for the church in this great city. Because of Timothy's experience of working at Thessalonica and Corinth and serving as a traveling companion with Paul, the apostle trusted his ability to lead the church at Ephesus. Paul needed someone who knew both Judaism and Greco-Roman religions to guide that church, which existed amid religious syncretism. Timothy met these requirements.

Type of Literature

First Timothy offers instruction for church leaders. The purpose of the letter is to teach true doctrine and correct those who are teaching wrong things in Ephesus. For example, Paul begins by commanding his loyal child, Timothy, to correct persons who are teaching a different doctrine (1:3-4). In contrast, Titus is given responsibility in the church at Crete to appoint elders of integrity. These two foci show the similarity between 1 Timothy and Titus while also revealing a difference in their emphases. Second Timothy calls attention to the personal relationship between Paul and Timothy and provides insight into the final years of Paul's life. Thus the literary content of 1 Timothy and Titus is instructional and apologetic, while 2 Timothy is more personal and self-revealing.

The kind of literature found in 1 Timothy is much like Hellenistic mandate letters (*mandata principis*) in which a higher official sent commands to subordinates. The letter moves back and forth between negative and positive exhortations. As a mandate letter, 1 Timothy gives instructions on how to guide the church at Ephesus. The form of the letter gives the reader insight into its tone. First Timothy is a serious letter dealing with urgent issues in the church at Ephesus. Both inductive and deductive forms of argument involving the use of paradigms are found (1:11-17, 19-20; 4:12). Paul moves from the stronger arguments to the weaker ones as he points to his own example as a guide for Timothy to follow. Ethical exhortations permeate this letter. For example, note the first-person singular verbs (1:3; 2:1, 8, 12; 5:14, 21), the second-person singular verbs (5:1, 3, 7, 11, 19-20, 22), and the third-person singular and plural verbs (2:11; 3:10, 12; 5:4, 9, 16-17; 6:2). "Must" and "ought" verbs occur in 1 Timothy (3:2, 7, 15). First Timothy also includes traditional material such as confessions, Scriptures, and trustworthy sayings.

A close literary analysis shows Lukan traits in 1 Timothy. In the birth narratives of Luke the angel says, "To you is born this day in the city of David a Savior" (Luke 2:11), and 1 Timothy 1:1 calls God *Savior*. Similar phrases are found in Acts and in 1 Timothy (Acts 14:15 and 1 Tim 3:15; 4:10; Acts 24:3 and 1 Tim 4:3-4; Acts 3:17 and 1 Tim 1:13). Ben Witherington III finds 861 examples of compound words in Luke-Acts and 135 examples of compound words in the letters to Timothy and Titus (Witherington 2006: 175). Furthermore, we see an interesting thematic link between Luke-Acts and 1 Timothy. Luke emphasizes economic justice, as does 1 Timothy (Luke 1:53; 12:13-21; 18:18-25; 19:1-10; Acts 8:14-24; 1 Tim 3:3, 8; 6:5, 9-10, 17-19). When Paul talks about an honorarium for elders in 1 Timothy 5:17, he quotes the words of Jesus as recorded in Luke 10:7. Salvation is emphasized in Luke (Luke 1:47; 19:9-10; Acts 4:12) as well as in 1 Timothy (1:1, 15; 2:3-4; 4:10). Groups of people mentioned in Timothy are also mentioned in Acts, such as widows (Acts 6:1; 1 Tim 5:3-16), deacons (Acts 6:1-6; 1 Tim 3:8-13), elders (Acts 14:23; 15:2, 22; 20:17; 1 Tim 5:17-25), overseers/bishops (Acts 20:28; 1 Tim 3:1-7), slaves (Luke 19:12-27; 20:10-11; 1 Tim 6:1-2), and women of high standing (Acts 17:4, 12; 1 Tim 2:9-10).

Authorship

Paul identifies himself as the sender of the letter and describes his experience of salvation in Christ (1 Tim 1:1; 12-17). The apostle's voice comes through in some of the confessional material. But the term "body of Christ," so prominent in the undisputed Pauline writings, is not found in 1 Timothy. Instead, the church is the household of God (3:15). The phrase in Christ, prominent in Paul's undisputed letters, appears sparingly (1 Tim 1:14; 3:13). And the noun *godliness* does not appear in the other Pauline letters, though it appears several times in 1 Timothy (2:2; 3:16; 4:7-8; 5:4; 6:3, 5-6, 11), 2 Timothy (3:5), and Titus (1:1), as well as in Acts (Acts 3:12). Many words in 1 Timothy are not found in other NT writings yet are familiar in the Greco-Roman world, leading some NT scholars to question Pauline authorship. Of the three letters, 1 Timothy may be the least Pauline in writing style.

I am inclined to propose a combination of Paul and Luke in composing 1 Timothy (contra Aageson 2008: 114). Traditionally, the author of Luke-Acts has been identified as Luke, a companion of Paul and a Gentile medical doctor. If correct, this Luke would have been familiar with the vocabulary of the Greco-Roman world. The literary ties noted above between Luke-Acts and 1 Timothy may indicate that "Luke composed these documents from Paul with more direct wording from Paul at some junctures, and in some places with less. . . . The voice is the voice of the apostle to the Gentiles, but the hand is the hand of a Gentile Christian named Luke" (Witherington 2006: 176).

I think Luke may have been Paul's secretary and that he combined Pauline material with his own material. I use the name *Paul* as author with this modification. The date of writing can range from AD 65 to 80-85. It is more likely that it was written in the mid- to late 60s, although a later date, during the post-Pauline period, is a possibility *[Authorship, p. 325]*.

Contents

Paul calls attention to God's way of ordering life (1 Tim 1:4). God's economy is tied to godliness. This is a divine order to which members of the household ought to conform in faith (Aageson 2008: 35). Household behavior can no longer continue according to the Greco-Roman status quo. Instead, men, women, widows, slaves, and rich persons are called to godliness (2:8-15; 5:1-16; 6:1-2, 17-19). Paul takes common household patterns of behavior and adjusts them to fit the life of the church as the new household of God (3:15). This household-of-God image becomes the organizing structure around which he instructs, exhorts, and makes theological claims. Paul does not view the church as withdrawn from the world, nor does the church ignore the context in which the gospel is proclaimed. Instead, the gospel is contextualized within the Greco-Roman culture, which enables the missionary task of the church to move forward in Ephesus.

Godliness is a major theme in 1 Timothy (2:2; 3:16; 4:7-8; 6:3, 5-6, 11). It is tied to believing in Christ (3:16) and is acceptable before God our Savior (2:3). *Godliness* requires the discipline of training and is opposed to those who teach and follow unhealthy views (4:7-9). It is connected with sound teaching, in contrast to those who teach otherwise (6:3-6). Paul says, *I am writing these instructions to you so that, if I am delayed, you may know how one ought to behave in the household of God, which is the church of the living God, the pillar and bulwark of the truth* (3:14-15). Both right doctrine (orthodoxy) and right living (orthopraxy) are promoted in 1 Timothy. Timothy is commanded to do public ministry both by how he lives and by his preaching and teaching (4:11-16).

In contrast to Roman imperial religion, which identified the emperor and other government officials as savior, God is *our* Savior, who desires everyone to be saved and to come to the knowledge of the truth (1 Tim 1:1; 2:3-4; 4:10). God is the living God, who gives life (4:10; 6:13). In 1 Timothy 2:5 the oneness of God is explicitly stated, indicating a tie to Paul's monotheistic theology in earlier writings (Rom 3:30; 1 Cor 8:4; Gal 3:20). The oneness of God is tied to Christ Jesus, who is the mediator between God and humanity (1 Tim 2:5-6). Christ Jesus came into the world to save sinners, including Paul (1:15). Christ is the foundation of the two confessional statements (2:5-6; 3:16) and of eschatology (6:14).

Three faithful sayings occur in 1 Timothy. The first centers on Christ, who came into the world to save sinners (1:15). The second speaks of the integrity and importance of leadership in the church (3:1). And the third returns to salvation and speaks of godliness as that which holds promise for both the present life and the life to come (4:9).

Unhealthy teachings were present in the Ephesian church. Paul warned against opponents in Acts 20:30, and here too he is confronting the church in Ephesus with the importance of sound teaching. The unhealthy teachings addressed by Paul include meaningless talk, Jewish misinterpretation of the Law (1 Tim 1:6-11), abstinence from food, and asceticism (4:1-5). A final form of deviant behavior is using religion as a means of financial gain (6:5). As in Luke-Acts, Christian conversion includes economic conversion (Luke 19:1-10; Acts 8:14-24). Thus, rich persons are exhorted to use their money to do good and to be rich in good works, generous, and ready to share (1 Tim 6:17-19). To counteract the effect of these unhealthy teachings in the church, Timothy is instructed to teach sound (healthy) doctrine and moral behavior that conforms to the truth of the gospel.

Timothy is charged with responsibility to correct present church leaders and to choose new leaders who show godly character traits (1 Tim 1:18-20; 3:1-13; 5:17-25). Paul calls for upright moral character for bishops, deacons, and elders. Qualities desired in church leaders are character traits and Paul does not specify the duties, liturgical responsibilities, or hierarchical roles later attached to these offices in 1 Clement (ca. AD 96) and the letters of Ignatius (ca. 115). Thus, 1 Timothy reflects an earlier period in the development of church organization and was most likely written before AD 96. Paul wants church leaders to teach and to live godly lives because God is saving the world through their life and work.

OUTLINE

Salutation, 1:1-2
The Church Leader's Life and Teaching, 1:3-20
Prayer and Behavior in the Household of God, 2:1-15
Character Traits for Leaders in the Household of God, 3:1-16
The Leader's Duties in the Household of God, 4:1-16
Managing the Church as the Household of God, 5:1-6:10, 17-19
Final Instructions for Timothy, 6:11-16, 20-21

1 Timothy 1:1-2

Salutation

PREVIEW

First Timothy begins with a standard form of salutation found in most letters in the Greco-Roman period: name of sender, name of addressee, and blessing on the addressee. This form occurs as well in other Pauline letters. In the greeting Paul identifies his call as apostle by command of God and from that calling gives commands to Timothy, his loyal child, on how to lead the church (1:1-2). The God who has commanded Paul is none other than God our Savior.

OUTLINE

The Sender, 1:1
The Addressee, 1:2a
The Blessing, 1:2b

EXPLANATORY NOTES

The Sender 1:1

Paul is an apostle *according to the command of God* (1:1). The authenticity of his message here, as in Galatians, is based on the authenticity of God's command and calling. Paul is commissioned by none other than the eternal God. He is a member of the apostolic circle, through whom divine revelation came to the first-century church. Under the command of God, the apostle is under obligation to carry out the order laid upon him. The term *command* was used of royal commands that must be obeyed. "Apostleship involves responsibility; the apostle is a [person] under orders from God" (Kelly: 40). Since Paul is under command from God, his instructions to Timothy likewise take on authority in the church.

Paul's apostolic command is from *God our Savior* and from *Christ Jesus our hope* (1:1). We speak of Jesus as our Savior, but Paul surprisingly calls God "our Savior." Salvation is a past event (1:15; Titus 3:5) with a present reality (2 Tim 1:10). It also includes a future dimension (1 Tim 2:15; 4:16). God our Savior extends into a "faithful saying" in 1 Timothy 4:10, where it is aligned with godliness. Godliness is a central theme in 1 Timothy *[Godliness, p. 346]*. What one believes and how one lives are inseparable. In contrast to those who teach unhealthy doctrine and live ungodly lives, Timothy is to give special attention to godliness because moral behavior enhances the credibility of one's beliefs. Stated another way, the lack of godliness among some indicates their belief is faulty. The character of God as Savior (2:2-3) and the saving activity of Jesus Christ (2:5-6; 6:12-13) give content and meaning to piety. Both piety and its goal of eternal life are grounded in God as Savior (Sumney: 158). *God our Savior*, therefore, opens up a major theological theme in 1 Timothy *[Names for God and the Imperial Cult, p. 357]*.

Paul is an apostle of Jesus Christ and belongs to Christ. His apostolic command came both from God our Savior and Christ Jesus our hope. More than wishful thinking, hope implies a sure future because its substance and foundation rests in Christ. The word group for *hope* occurs eight times in the letters to Timothy and Titus (1 Tim 1:1; 3:14; 4:10; 5:5: 6:17; Titus 1:2; 2:13; 3:7). Hope is both present and future. The widow sets her hope on God in the present time, as does the rich person (1 Tim 5:5; 6:17). The eschatological dimension of hope arises as believers *wait for the blessed hope and the manifestation of the glory of our great God and Savior, Jesus Christ* (Titus 2:13). Since our hope is *set on the living God, who is the savior of all people* (1 Tim 4:10), hope and salvation go hand in hand. God is the grounding and the object of our hope, which is realized through Christ Jesus (Collins: 23). Both salvation and hope rest in God and in Christ Jesus, who is the source of the command that authenticates Paul's apostleship.

The Addressee 1:2a

The second part of the salutation expresses the Christian standing of the recipient, Timothy, and his relationship to Paul. In earlier Pauline writings, Timothy is a young co-worker related to Paul as an older mentor or patron. It is like a father-son relationship (Philem 10). Bonds of affection led Paul to use the intimate kinship term *child* when referring to Timothy (1 Cor 4:17; Phil 2:19-22). Paul qualifies the relationship further by calling Timothy *my loyal child in the faith* (1 Tim 1:2a). This social relationship between sender and receiver is one of implied sonship. Timothy is a child of Paul in the faith and therefore an heir.

As spiritual son, Timothy is Paul's successor and carries Paul's authority to the Ephesian church. His loyalty as a true child in the faith distinguishes him from those who depart from the faith. The word *faith* occurs twenty times in the six chapters of 1 Timothy. This frequent use indicates faith's importance in the letter. As a child in the faith, Timothy qualifies as Paul's successor to lead the church at Ephesus.

The Blessing 1:2b

Grace, mercy, and peace from God the Father and Christ Jesus our Lord (1:2b) embodies much of the standard greetings in the Pauline letters. *Grace* (*charis*) replaces the word "greetings" (*chairein*, as in Acts 15:23) in the typical Hellenistic letter. *Peace* picks up the traditional Jewish greeting of "shalom." The combination of *grace* and *peace* is universal in Paul's greetings to the churches (Rom 1:7; 1 Cor 1:3; 2 Cor 1:2; Gal 1:3; Eph 1:2; Phil 1:2; Col 1:2; 1 Thess 1:1; 2 Thess 1:2). This combination indicates a general greeting that includes both Jewish and Gentile readers. It becomes a more specific Christian greeting, however, as Paul adds *from God the Father and Christ Jesus our Lord*. The source of greeting is always God and Christ Jesus and the relationship that they have to the recipients of this grace and peace.

Unlike Paul's greetings elsewhere, the word *mercy* appears here. The word *mercy* might indicate the influence of a theology stressing mercy since Paul also received mercy (1 Tim 1:13). Paul considered Timothy's Jewish background in using this word. Timothy needed God's special favor because he felt himself to be in difficulty and needed sympathy, tenderness, and comfort for the task of leading the Ephesian church. The threefold wish (grace, mercy, and peace) indicates that Paul wants Timothy to experience the blessing of laboring in the power and protection of God. "The wish itself is an indication that the salvation of God, by which these things become accessible to his people, is very real and present for the writer" (I. H. Marshall 1999: 358).

THE TEXT IN BIBLICAL CONTEXT

God Our Savior

The phrase *God our Savior* occurs five times in the OT and only eight times in the NT, six of which are in the letters to Timothy and Titus (Luke 1:47; 1 Tim 1:1; 2:3; 4:10; Titus 1:3; 2:10; 3:4; Jude 25). In the first-century Greco-Roman world, the term *savior* (*sōtēr*) was used in emperor worship and was applied to various mythical figures and emperors, including the infamous Nero. Inscriptions found at Ephesus indicate that the term was used for both emperors and local patrons (Baugh: 335). "At Ephesus an inscription to Julius Caesar said that he was 'god made manifest, of Ares and Aphrodite, the common savior of human life'" (Witherington 2006: 104). In AD 25 Tiberius declared that he was a mortal and that divine honor belonged to Augustus, the real savior of humankind. The title *divus* appeared on a denarius of Tiberius and a papyrus from AD 37, which called him "son of god." Philo notes that while Jews could not worship Caligula, many did regard him as a savior and benefactor. Both Claudius and Titus were called "savior of the world." In contrast to the prevailing Greco-Roman custom, the Bible presents God as Savior.

Paul speaks of God from the Jewish tradition in language that the Greco-Roman world understands. Paul polemically states that only God is Savior—not the emperor or the patrons. Salvation was the purpose of Jesus' coming into the world (1 Tim 1:15)—a salvation effected through his death and resurrection (2:6). It is offered to all people (1 Tim 2:4; 4:10; Titus 2:11), but only those who believe can call God "our Savior" (1 Tim 1:1; 2:3; 2 Tim 1:10; Titus 2:10).

In the OT, God is called Savior many times. In Exodus 14:13, when the children of Israel stand by the Sea of Reeds with the Egyptian army coming toward them, Moses says, "Do not be afraid, stand firm, and see the deliverance (*sōtērian*, LXX) that the LORD will accomplish for you today." It is God, not Moses, who saves the people at the sea (Exod 15:1-21). In the OT, "to save" often means to rescue or deliver someone—usually the children of Israel or an individual—from enemies. The Passover celebrated the reality that God delivered the people of Israel from their enemies. Later a writer of the Psalms cries out to God to "save" from enemies (e.g., 6:4; 7:1; 22:21).

Several passages in Isaiah speak of the saving God. "Surely God is my salvation; I will trust, and will not be afraid, for the LORD GOD is my strength and my might; he has become my salvation" (12:2). "For I am the LORD your God, the Holy One of Israel, your Savior" (43:3). "I, I am the LORD, and besides me there is no savior" (43:11). Salvation in Isaiah was quite this-worldly and political, as seen in the promise of a new Davidic king (9:2-7; 11:1-10) and of a new exodus as God comes to restore the people (40:1-11). Other OT prophets looked beyond the immediate situation and talked about a future dimension to God's saving work in different language. For example, Jeremiah speaks of a new covenant (31:31-34), and Ezekiel describes new life in the symbolic language of dead bones coming alive (37:1-14).

In the NT, Jesus Christ is Savior. "She will bear a son, and you are to name him Jesus, for he will save his people from their sins" (Matt 1:21). "For the Son of Man came to seek out and to save the lost" (Luke 19:10). In the Gospels, salvation comes by repentance from sin and faith in Jesus Christ. At times salvation comes through the healing ministry of Jesus. In John, salvation is described in the language of eternal life. By believing in and accepting Jesus, one has eternal life (John 3:16; 1 John 5:12). In the Pauline epistles, salvation is described with four metaphors: justification, redemption, reconciliation, and adoption. Throughout the NT, salvation comes through the ministry and atoning death of Jesus Christ on the cross (Rom 3:21-25; 2 Cor 5:19, 21; 6:2). God's love and grace provide the foundation for this saving work of Christ (Rom 5:8; Eph 2:8). Salvation brings reconciliation and peace through Jesus Christ (Rom 5:10-11; Eph 1:9, 20; 2:11-22; Col 2:20). And salvation encompasses a new covenant relationship with God in Jesus Christ that is both internal as it cleanses the sinner (Heb 9:14) and eternal in its dimension (9:15).

Beyond the phrase *God our Savior*, the letters to Timothy and Titus also speak of Jesus bringing salvation. Salvation was the purpose of his coming (1 Tim 1:15) and of his death (2:6). Salvation is offered to all people (1 Tim 2:4; 4:10; Titus 2:11), including Paul as a sinner (1 Tim 1:15). Though available for all, only those who believe (4:10) can claim God as Savior (1 Tim 1:1; 2:3; Titus 2:10; cf. 2 Tim 1:10). Moreover, the letters to Timothy and Titus speak of salvation accomplished by Christ in the past tense (1 Tim 1:15; Titus 3:5), in the present tense (2 Tim 1:10), and in the future tense (1 Tim 2:15; 4:16; 2 Tim 2:10; Titus 3:7). Salvation in three tenses recalls Paul's earlier letters, where he says Christians "were saved" (past tense) in Romans 8:24, Christians "are being saved" (present tense) in 1 Cor 1:18, and Christians "will . . . be saved" (future tense) in Romans 5:9-10 (cf. also 1 Pet 1:3-5). Finally, in the book of Revelation, Jesus is Savior as Christians sing, "Worthy is the Lamb that was slaughtered to receive power and wealth and wisdom and might and honor and glory and blessing" (Rev 5:12).

THE TEXT IN THE LIFE OF THE CHURCH

The Wholeness of Salvation

Salvation holds a prominent place in the history of Christian thought. Orthodox teaching proclaims Christ as Savior. Medieval theology emphasized the sacraments as the means of receiving God's grace and thereby experiencing salvation. Protestant reformers promoted justification by faith as the central NT theme in salvation. Sixteenth-century Anabaptists generally agreed with the Protestant reformers that all people have sinned and need salvation, that salvation is provided through the death of Christ on the cross, and that this salvation becomes effective only if and when people respond in faith. In Anabaptist thought, the saving work of Christ is based on more than his death on the cross. The whole Christ saves by his life of faithfulness to God, by his death, and by his resurrection.

Anabaptists, Protestants, and Catholics differ in their views on the nature of grace and the human response to Christ's work. In Catholic thought, salvation depends on more than accepting a series of doctrinal propositions. In reaction to Catholicism, Martin Luther taught justification by faith alone and not by works. Anabaptists called for committing the whole person to Christ. Repentance for them was genuine only when it included amendment of life. Discipleship belongs integrally to the work of salvation. Good deeds do not bring about salvation; they are an extension of the gracious work of God in the life of the believer.

Grace works within new Christian believers, releasing them from the condemnation of sins through forgiveness, transforming them into new persons in Jesus Christ and enabling them to walk in a new life of Christian discipleship through the work of the Holy Spirit. Grace is universal in that God offers grace to all people. Salvation is preached to all, with the invitation that God will save whoever repents and believes. God offers grace to all people and gives each one freedom to choose or reject God. The choice between life and death is the responsibility of the one to whom grace is offered.

Anabaptists tend toward a holistic view of salvation. They do not separate soul from body in the salvation process. The Gnostics thought the body was evil or irrelevant and the soul was good; therefore God saves souls and not bodies. For Anabaptists, salvation encompasses the whole person and affects the entire life. This Anabaptist view of salvation rejects a separation between justification and sanctification and between an invisible and a visible church. Since people who experience salvation are visible, they become part of a visible community of Christian believers, the church. Salvation is certainly personal, but it is not a private matter. We are reconciled to God and to one another in Jesus Christ and become part of the visible community of faith, the church. Thus salvation includes incorporation into the body of Christ, the church.

1 Timothy 1:3-20

The Church Leader's Life and Teaching

PREVIEW

First Timothy 1:3-20 is one unit of thought. Paul commands Timothy not to teach any different doctrine from the *divine training that is known by faith* (1:4). Such instruction has love as its goal and is characterized by *a pure heart, a good conscience, and sincere faith* (1:5). God's way of ordering and saving the world stands in contrast to the opposing teachers. These teachers needed correction because they thought they were teaching the law, when in reality they were deviating from it. Recognizing the problem, Paul calls attention to the divine and true intention of the law in 1:8-11 and says that healthy teaching *conforms to the glorious gospel of the blessed God* (1:11).

Moving from the negative to the positive, Paul calls attention to grace, drawing on his own experience of salvation in Jesus Christ (1:12-17). In doing so, Paul contrasts his own new self with those who are teaching unhealthy doctrine. He also calls attention to the first of five faithful sayings in the letters to Timothy and Titus: *Christ Jesus came into the world to save sinners* (1:15).

Finally, Paul returns to the importance of faithful teaching and exhorts Timothy to exercise himself in fighting the fight of faith with good conscience in leading the church at Ephesus. Timothy must recognize that two persons, Hymenaeus and Alexander, have shipwrecked their faith and need discipline (1:19-20). Paul declares that Hymenaeus and Alexander can no longer receive the blessing and care of the church body. Hopefully, they will learn not to blaspheme and will return to Christ and the church through repentance and renewed faith. If God can save Paul, the foremost of sinners, God can also save Hymenaeus and Alexander if they repent—even after they have been expelled from the congregation and turned over to Satan.

OUTLINE

Instructions to Timothy to Teach True Doctrine, 1:3-7
True Teaching Conforms to the Gospel, 1:8-11
Paul, the Foremost Sinner, Experiences God's Mercy, 1:12-17
Fighting the Good Fight of Faith, 1:18-20

EXPLANATORY NOTES

Instructions to Timothy to Teach True Doctrine 1:3-7

Paul waits until 1:12 to give thanks to Christ and then moves directly into an exhortation, indicating the seriousness of this communication with Timothy and the church in Ephesus. As resident teacher in Ephesus, Timothy is commanded not to teach or allow others to teach heterodoxy but to teach according to God's plan, which is known by faith (1:4). This section contains four divisions: the historical context (1:3a), Paul's command and a description of the problem (1:3b-4), the purpose of the command to teach true doctrine (1:5), and the urgent need to correct the deviant teachers (1:6-7).

I urge you is a technical term expressing a strong urge, an appeal to someone, a strong request (BDAG: 765). While Paul moves from place to place in missionary work, Timothy is to remain in Ephesus for a specific purpose, to confront those who teach falsely and to set forth true Christian teaching. Paul's reference to Macedonia may indicate that he has been released from house arrest in Rome and later made a fourth missionary trip through Asia Minor and Macedonia. Or it may simply mean that Paul was leaving Ephesus and going on to Macedonia. At any rate, Paul is elsewhere and commands Timothy to stay in Ephesus.

As the provincial capital of Asia, Ephesus was important commercially and religiously. Its harbor made possible the commercial activity of the city and the province. Ephesus was the home of the huge temple of Artemis (Diana), which was known as one of the Seven Wonders of the World. The cult of Artemis was a religious movement in Asia Minor unrelated to Judaism and Christianity. The church matured through two years of Paul's teaching (Acts 19:8-10, 20). Paul did not want to see this active church destroyed by deviant teaching; hence, he wrote to Timothy *so that you may instruct certain people not to teach any different doctrine* (1:3b).

These teachers, though not directly named, were likely traveling teachers, though they may have been elders in the Ephesian church. Paul calls them *teachers of the law* (1:7). Two such teachers are named and excommunicated in 1:19-20. They taught a different doctrine (*heterodidaskaleō*, 1:3) and thus, like the Galatian teachers, promoted "a different gospel" (Gal 1:6) *[Unhealthy Teaching, p. 366]*. "It is not that the teaching of the opponents was merely different; it is that their teaching was essentially different and therefore wrong" (Mounce: 19). Apparently their teaching combined some aspects of Judaism with Hellenistic and early Gnostic ideas. It included misinterpretations of the law, myths, allegorical reinterpretations of the Old Testament, and fanciful interpretations of genealogies (Mounce: lxix-lxx). The unhealthy teaching included asceticism by forbidding marriage (1 Tim 4:3; 5:14) and advocating abstention from food (4:3), licentiousness, and a low view of the physical world. These elements were later to form a cohesive system of thought in second-century Gnosticism. In short, their teaching was similar to the errors at Colossae and Corinth, which mixed Jewish teaching with speculative superstition and magic (Mounce: lxxv).

Conversely, Paul commands Timothy to teach *divine training* (*oikonomia*) that is *known by faith*. God's way of ordering things is understood by faith. "The right ordering of the community would certainly be included in Paul's understanding of the divine order, but 1 Timothy's understanding of what is to be received 'in faith' above all includes God's way of creating and saving the world" (Johnson 2001: 164). This divine training is known within the context of Christian faith, which distinguishes the Christian community's underlying principle of existence from human management and speculative ideas. The deviant teacher's speculations are contrary to God's way of ordering society and especially the household of God. Johnson suggests that the economy of God may be the central underlying theological theme in 1 Timothy (147-54). This commentary prefers an integration of the theological themes of godliness and the economy of God with God our Savior. Household behavior will be viewed in the context of the larger purpose of God's work of saving the world.

In contrast to these teachers, Timothy is commanded to teach with a goal of *love that comes from a pure heart, a good conscience, and sincere faith* (1:5). Paul makes love a goal and calls attention to its highest value when compared with faith and hope (1 Cor 12:31; 13:13). Healthy teaching encourages love for God and love for other persons. The aim is not mere conformity to a set of behavioral norms, but a deep and abiding inner human disposition that places one's relationship with God and other persons at the center of teaching.

Love springs out of a pure heart, a good conscience, and sincere faith. *Heart* is the biblical designation for the seat of human reflection and decision. A pure heart symbolizes right relationship with God. *Heart* represents the whole human person to the depth of one's being (Collins: 28).

The concept of a good conscience comes from the Hellenistic environment. It means the moral consciousness that God gives to people (Rom 2:15; 2 Cor 4:2). In the letters to Timothy and Titus, the term *conscience* is always accompanied by a descriptive adjective: good conscience (1 Tim 1:5, 19), clear conscience (1 Tim 3:9; 2 Tim 1:3), seared conscience (1 Tim 4:2), and defiled (*corrupted*) conscience (Titus 1:15) *[Conscience, p. 338]*. A good conscience contrasts with the seared conscience of evildoers. It indicates moral integrity and is similar to a pure heart. But although "the heart is the origin of desires, the conscience functions to direct, evaluate, and control behavior along lines set by given norms" (I. H. Marshall 1999: 370). Sincere faith comprises the third force behind true love. Insincere faith is no faith at all. Sincere faith is genuine, a faith filled with integrity, an honest faith that fully trusts in God. Thus sincere faith, a good conscience, and a pure heart comprise love, which is the aim of Timothy's instruction.

Some people have deviated from these (1 Tim 1:6-7). Paul now states a reason for opposing the other teachers. These teachers deviated from the qualities of love listed above. Instead of moving toward the goal of the commandment, they miss the mark of the desired qualities of love. In their desire to be teachers of the law, they have actually been misinterpreting the law by meaningless talk and using the law wrongly. Their wrong use of the law indicates they do not understand the law at all. A major concern arises precisely here. Elders and church leaders must bring their teaching and character into alignment. Timothy is commanded to teach true doctrine while living with a pure heart, a good conscience, and a sincere faith (v. 5). These teachers have deviated from this standard by their meaningless talk and lack of understanding the law. "They want to be something they are not. They are therefore identified as intellectual imposters" (Johnson 2001: 166). Their meaningless talk and lack of understanding indicate that they know neither the language nor the content of the Law.

True Teaching Conforms to the Gospel 1:8-11

Paul further criticizes the teachers in verses 8-11 and shows why they do not conform to the glorious gospel. Their view and practice of the law are illegitimate. They use the Torah as a source of myths and genealogies or for ascetic practices. The law itself is good when used legitimately (1:8). These teachers are not using the law legitimately, but if corrected, they may change their pattern of life and use it legitimately in the future. Paul does not say that the proper use of the law itself is gospel. Rather, a proper use of the law leads one in the direction of the gospel. Thus, the law is good. The participial phrase *knowing this* (1:9 GNT) implies that the law is good if used appropriately. With this, Paul lays out the appropriate purpose and use of the law as God's word against sin. He presents a vice list similar to other vice lists in the epistles (Rom 1:29-31; 13:13; 1 Cor 5:10-11; 6:9-10; 2 Cor 12:20-21; Gal 5:19-21; Eph 4:31; 5:3-5; Col 3:5, 8; 1 Tim 6:4-5; Titus 3:3; 2 Tim 3:2-5). These lists of vices are similar to those in the Hellenistic world (Malherbe: 138-41). Paul focuses attention on types of persons rather than types of sins and how their sinful behavior compares to the Decalogue *[Vice Lists, p. 368]*.

The first three couplets (in 1 Tim 1:9) are offenses against God. The first couplet, *lawless and disobedient*, suggests that these would-be teachers of the law in Ephesus talk *about* the law but misuse it. Instead of teaching the true Law, they teach a figurative, allegorical, or symbolic interpretation of the law. Their unruly behavior and teaching misses the good intention of the law. A second couplet, *the godless and sinners*, refers to persons who lack the common goal to live a good life, even in the Hellenistic world (Collins: 122-26). Lack of godliness appears with the term *sinners* and is used elsewhere in the NT for both Jews and Gentiles who do wrong in the sight of God. In contrast, Paul urges Timothy and church leaders to live godly

1 Timothy 1:9-10	**Exodus 20, Deuteronomy 5**
Those who kill fathers and mothers	Honor your father and mother (Exod 20:12; Deut 5:16)
Murderers	You shall not kill/murder (KJV/NRSV: Exod 20:13; Deut 5:17)
Fornicators, sodomites	You shall not commit adultery (Exod 20:14; Deut 5:18)
slave traders	You shall not steal (Exod 20:15; Deut 5:19)
Liars, perjurers	You shall not bear false witness (Exod 20:16; Deut 5:20)

lives. The third couplet, *the unholy and profane*, refers to those who have defiled themselves by their lack of religion and opposition to the sacred. The vices listed may be a summary reference to the first precepts of the Decalogue or perhaps a direct violation of the fourth commandment, to keep the Sabbath (Exod 20:8-11; Deut 5:12-15). The remaining vices are an interpretation of commands five through nine of the Decalogue (see chart).

Those who kill father or mother disobey the fifth command in an extreme way. Murderers disobey the sixth command. Fornicators and sodomites break the seventh command. *Fornicators* is a more general term and covers a wide range of sexual sins. The term translated *sodomites* (*arsenokoitēs*, 1 Tim 1:10) is a compound word derived from *arsēn* (male) and *koitē* (marriage bed), both of which occur in the LXX of Leviticus 18:22 and 20:13. The term may have been coined by Paul since it occurs only here and in 1 Corinthians 6:9 in the NT. It appears several times in the early church fathers (D. F. Wright: 128-46). BDAG defines *arsenokoitēs* as a male who engages in sexual activity with a person of his own sex (135). Jerome D. Quinn and William C. Wacker hold that it is not limited to an older man having sex with a younger man (a pederast), but includes consenting adult males having sexual relationships with each other (88, 100-1).

According to Robert A. Gagnon, the larger New Testament theology of human sexuality (cf. Rom 1:24-27) suggests that the term cannot be limited to abusive homosexual activity but applies to all same-sex intercourse (327). However, some scholars hold an alternative view, suggesting that the Greek term should not be equated with homosexuality as we know it today. Homosexuality may reflect a genetic disposition in which one is born with a homosexual orientation. What the Bible condemns is promiscuity. This alternate view says that monogamous covenantal same-sex unions may be permissible. While discussion between these two views continues (Grimsrud and Nation: 2008), pastors search for healthy ways to provide pastoral care for persons struggling with their sexual identity. Despite the modern controversy over the meaning of the word and its interpretation for today, Paul condemns it here and in Romans 1:26-27 (Hays 1986: 184-215). Fornicators and sodomites break the commandment in the Decalogue not to commit adultery. Slave traders are those who have sold persons captured in war or who have kidnapped people, both of which dramatically break the commandment against stealing. Liars and perjurers obviously break the command against bearing false witness. The purpose of the law, if interpreted and used legitimately, prevents such behaviors and condemns persons who commit these sins.

To make sure nothing is missed, Paul adds, *And whatever else is contrary to the sound teaching that conforms to the glorious gospel of the blessed God, which he entrusted to me* (1 Tim 1:10b-11). *Sound* (*hygiainousē*, related to "hygiene"; cf. 1 Tim 1:10; 6:3; 2 Tim 1:13; 4:3; Titus 1:9, 13; 2:1-2, 8) is a medical metaphor pointing to *healthy teaching* that conforms to the gospel. Healthy teaching includes both doctrinal content and behavior. "Healthy teaching leads to proper Christian behavior, love and good works; the diseased teaching leads to controversies, arrogance, abusiveness, and strife" (Fee 1988: 46).

Paul, the Foremost Sinner, Experiences God's Mercy 1:12-17

In 1 Timothy 1:3-7, Paul lays out the basic problem and instructs Timothy to stop the unhealthy teaching. In 1:8-11 the opponents have been misusing the law. Now in 1:12-17, Paul turns from observance of the law to a focus on himself as an example of God's work of salvation through grace and mercy. Paul's personal example provides a clear contrast to the teachers who adhered to Jewish myths based on the law.

Some commentators see this section as a digression from the thought that Paul conveys in 1:8-11 and picks up again in 1:18-20. But these verses highlight the contents of the chapter from the perspective of Paul's personal experience. Here Paul talks about mercy and his vocational calling, both of which refer back to the salutation (1:1-2). Paul appeals to his own experience as evidence of the transforming power of God. If God can call and change a person like Paul, who has so violently opposed the gospel, God can transform anyone. The section begins with a thanksgiving (v. 12), interrupted in this letter until now, and ends with a doxology (v. 17). Between is Paul's own testimony of God's work in his life.

I am grateful to Christ Jesus our Lord. Many times Paul thanks God in his epistles, but here *Christ Jesus our Lord* is the object of thanksgiving. Paul thanks Christ Jesus for strengthening him, judging him faithful, and appointing him to Christ's service. Paul is talking about his conversion in the past rather than the continuing work of Christ in his life. *Strengthening* refers to Paul's initial call to ministry and the Christ-given ability to perform apostolic tasks. God has strengthened him and entrusted him with the apostolic task because God has reckoned him trustworthy. God entrusts his gospel to those whom he has made trustworthy. The term *service* (*diakonia*) appears several times in Luke-Acts and now is applied to Paul, who is appointed to God's service.

As in 2 Corinthians 5:18-19, Paul is commissioned for a special work by none other than Christ Jesus our Lord. This commissioning is all the more remarkable because at the time of conversion Paul was living a wicked life, which he describes with three terms: *blasphemer, persecutor, using violence.* Paul's persecution of the church (Acts 8:1; 9:1-4) was blasphemy against God and violence against God's people (Collins: 37). As a blasphemer, Paul abused and slandered Jesus as God's son and Messiah. As a persecutor of the church, Paul acted in opposition to God and denied what God had done through Christ. His violent, insulting behavior stemmed from pride and arrogance (I. H. Marshall 1999: 391).

Paul's abusive life stands in contrast to the change that Christ instilled in him. With a strong adversative form of *but,* Paul calls attention to the *mercy, grace, faith, and love* that came by Christ Jesus. Literally, he received God's mercy. God showed this violent man steadfast love and kindness. God's mercy came to Paul despite his violent actions in defense of the law because he acted in unbelief and ignorance of Jesus Christ. Paul does not mean that God owed him mercy. Rather, he reflects on the OT distinction between unwitting disobedience and purposeful sinning (e.g., Num 15:22-31). "His former conduct is not thereby less culpable or grotesque, but for Paul this distinction at least explains why he became an object of God's compassion rather than his wrath" (Fee 1988: 51). Amazingly, God's grace *overflowed* to him (1 Tim 1:14). This compound verb appears only here in the NT and is similar to Romans 5:20, which says, *Where sin increased, grace abounded all the more* (lit., "superabounded"). Paul acknowledges that God's grace overflowed to him beyond measure while in sin. It came with the faith and love that are in Christ Jesus.

The saying is sure (1 Tim 1:15). Having acknowledged his own experience of grace, Paul interjects a striking formula known as a *faithful saying* (KJV). Five "faithful sayings" appear in the letters to Timothy and Titus and nowhere else in the NT in quite the same form (1 Tim 1:15; 3:1; 4:9; 2 Tim 2:11; Titus 3:8; but cf. John 4:37; Rev 3:14; 19:9; 21:5; 22:6). "Faithful sayings" have a solemn ring and in each case introduce or follow a citation, probably drawn from early catechetical or liturgical material, which Paul wishes to emphasize *[Faithful Sayings, p. 344]*. The formula used to introduce the saying (*Here is a trustworthy saying*; 1 Tim 1:15 NIV) indicates that it is a "received" tradition that bears official validation. Paul wants to relate his own experience as a demonstration of Christian truth by quoting a saying that is accepted by the church as a whole. In other words, Paul's conversion is confirmed by a traditional saying that "indicates what has been said rests on a firm basis of church teaching and is in line with it" (I. H. Marshall 1999: 397). The faithful saying affirms that Christ Jesus came into the world to save sinners.

Paul recognizes that Christ came into the world to save him, the *foremost* of *sinners*. His use of the verb *I am* with the personal pronoun (*I myself am*; emphatic in GNT) highlights the extent of Paul's recognition of his sinfulness. Just as the tax collector asked God, "Be merciful to me, a sinner!" in the parable of the Pharisee and the tax collector in Luke 18:13, so Paul recognizes his sinfulness and need of mercy. Paul never forgets that salvation is for sinners. The more he perceives the magnitude of God's grace, the more he consciously reflects on his own previously sinful state. He describes his sinfulness not simply as a matter of sequence, but also as "chief" or *foremost* because in his persecution of the church he was actually persecuting Christ (Acts 9:4-5). In short, Paul believes that if God can save him, given who he was and what he did, there is hope for all persons. The extremity of Paul's sinfulness forthrightly demonstrates God's mercy and grace to save any sinner.

But for that very reason I received mercy (1 Tim 1:16). Again Paul uses the strong adversative *but,* indicating the importance of what he is saying. He received mercy and grace not only as a backward-looking statement about his sinfulness, but also as a forward-looking statement of God's reason and purpose in saving him. In saving Paul, Christ was displaying patience, making him an example for others to believe in Christ in the future. This work of God's grace and mercy is not merely shown to him; it is also shown *in* him so others will see it and believe. Paul has experienced God's grace as an individual, but that grace was not hidden. His conversion became visible to many persons. And because Paul was always conscious of his sinfulness, the grace of Christ continued to be displayed in his life.

Paul's thanksgiving focuses on his own experience and mission rather than the experience of those whom he addresses. It includes more than a statement of Christian doctrine. Paul uses the trustworthy saying to point out his own experience of salvation and grace. Thus the thanksgiving is self-revealing: it recounts Paul's change from a persecutor to a believer in Christ through whom Christ is displaying his patience so that others can see it and believe in Christ for eternal life.

No wonder he concludes with a doxology (v. 17)! What began as thanksgiving and moves to a personal testimony of God's abundant grace fittingly ends in a hymn of praise. Glory and honor are not for the Roman emperor or the local politician, who has a limited period of rule, but for the King of all ages. Is the doxology addressed to

Christ as King? If so, he declares Christ to be "the only God," thus uniting Christ and God. More likely Paul means God as King (note that he calls God our Savior in v. 1). This King is incorruptible, distinguishing him from mortal creatures. This King is invisible, in contrast to the visibility of earthly kings (1 Tim 3:16). Reflecting the Jewish Shema (Deut 6:4), Paul speaks of *the only God*. God does not die like other kings. His reign is eternal. People give God glory and honor as they praise him for who he is and what he does forever and ever. The *Amen* anticipates the Ephesian church's affirmation of the doxology, which is similar to the Aaronic blessing given in the synagogue (Num 6:24-26; 1QS 2.10).

Fighting the Good Fight of Faith 1:18-20

Paul returns to 1:3 and his reason for writing: so that Timothy might instruct certain people not to teach any different doctrine. He reiterates that instruction in 1:18. By following these instructions, Timothy will fight the good fight with *faith and a good conscience*. These instructions agree with the prophecies made earlier about Timothy. In 1 Timothy 4:14 Paul calls attention to Timothy's gift, which the elders recognized when they laid hands on him. And in 2 Timothy 1:6 Paul reminds Timothy of God's gift granted to him when Paul laid on hands. Whether the prophecies made about Timothy and/or his ministry took place at the time of his appointment to give leadership to the church at Ephesus is not clear. In either case, Timothy must now follow Paul's instructions and fight the good fight of faith. While struggling against opponents of the gospel, Timothy also struggles with spiritual forces of evil. Timothy must continue to fight this battle against the teaching of error while exercising faith and a good conscience (1 Tim 1:19; 6:12; 2 Tim 4:7).

Some persons at Ephesus have already rejected conscience and have suffered a shipwreck in their faith. The term *rejecting* indicates a deliberate rejection of conscience. The words used suggest a "positive spurning of conscience rather than mere carelessness" (Kelly: 57). By rejecting *conscience*, Hymenaeus and Alexander have chosen to relinquish their faith. Hymenaeus appears in 1 Timothy 1:20 and in 2 Timothy 2:17-18, where he denies the resurrection. We do not know if these occurrences refer to the same person. Alexander is mentioned in Acts 19:33-34 as a Jew shouted down by the mob at Ephesus. In 2 Timothy 4:14-15 (NIV) his name appears as a *metalworker* who did great harm to Paul. In any case, Hymenaeus and Alexander have chosen to leave the faith.

So devastating is their sin that Paul describes them as persons *whom I have turned over to Satan* (1 Tim 1:20). To "turn over to Satan" means to excommunicate them from the community of faith (Bassler 1996: 47). As in 1 Corinthians 5:2, 5, where a member of the church is handed over to Satan, so here at Ephesus the discipline of two members takes place. The phrase "hand over to Satan" means to put out into Satan's sphere (Fee 1988: 59). Outside of the fellowship of God's people, an erring brother or sister does not receive the spiritual care and protection of the Christian community and is thus vulnerable to Satan (cf. Col 1:13-14). This is not simply or primarily a matter of punishment, since a redemptive concern is expressed: that these two persons *may learn not to blaspheme*. As elsewhere in the letters to Timothy and Titus, Paul wants to silence opponents of the true Christian faith so that they may turn from their evil ways and experience restoration in the church (2 Tim 2:25-26; Titus 1:13).

THE TEXT IN BIBLICAL CONTEXT

When Leaders Lack Integrity

The lack of integrity among leaders stands out as a key concern in the letters to Timothy and Titus. No less than twenty-seven persons are named, nineteen with good character and eight with evil character. These eight lack integrity and inflict disgrace upon God's people (Hymenaeus, 1 Tim 1:20 and 2 Tim 2:17-18; Alexander, 1 Tim 1:20 and 2 Tim 4:14; Phygelus, 2 Tim 1:15; Hermogenes, 2 Tim 1:15; Philetus, 2 Tim 2:17-18; Jannes, 2 Tim 3:8; Jambres, 2 Tim 3:8; Demas, 2 Tim 4:10). In 1 Timothy 1:3, Paul instructs Timothy to uphold true Christian doctrine and godly living, in contrast to those who teach error and live ungodly lives (1 Tim 1:5-7). This command is in keeping with the broader biblical teaching calling for the integrity of leaders.

The OT consistently opposes false teaching and ungodly character by leaders of God's people. Aaron brought disgrace upon God's people by making and worshiping the golden calf (Exod 32:21-29), which resulted in the death of about three thousand people. Miriam, the sister of Moses, led a choir in singing a triumphal song to the Lord after crossing the Sea of Reeds, but was punished with leprosy when she opposed Moses at Hazeroth (Num 12:1-15). False priests stood condemned for leading the people astray (Jer 2:8, 13; Amos 7:10-17). False prophets were confronted for their evil deeds (1 Kings 18:1-40), as was David himself (2 Sam 11). Jeremiah condemned false prophets, who prophesied out of "the deceit of their own minds" (14:14), spoke their own words rather than the Lord's, and led people astray with lies (23:30-32). Micah condemned prophets for falsehood when they sought to use the prophetic role for material gain (3:5-7). Jeremiah condemned shepherds who did not inquire of the Lord, resulting in scattered sheep (10:21). He sounded the death knell for false shepherds (25:34-38) and condemned those who led people astray (50:6). Ezekiel condemned shepherds for lack of concern for the sheep and using their role only to feed themselves (34:1-6). Ezekiel said, "Thus says the Lord GOD, I am against the shepherds; and I will demand my sheep at their hand, and put a stop to their feeding the sheep; no longer shall the shepherds feed themselves. I will rescue my sheep from their mouths, so that they may not be food for them" (34:10).

Jesus spoke harsh words to scribes and Pharisees who did not teach the true message of God or live upright lives. In Matthew 23, Jesus pronounces seven woes upon them. In John 10, Jesus describes himself as the good shepherd, in contrast to other shepherds, who were like a thief or a hired hand and did not care for the sheep (10:10, 12). In the Sermon on the Mount, Jesus says, "Beware of false prophets, who come to you in sheep's clothing but inwardly are ravenous wolves. You will know them by their fruits" (Matt 7:15-16a; cf. also Mark 13:21-22; Acts 20:29-30).

Distinguishing between true and deceitful teaching was a major task of the early church. When the gospel reached Samaria, a magician by the name of Simon heard the good news of the kingdom of God, believed, and was baptized. When Simon offered money so that he could have power to give the Holy Spirit by laying on hands, Peter strongly rebuked him: "You have no part or share in this, for your heart is not right before God" (Acts 8:21). When some of the people in Lystra turned to Christianity at the message of Paul and Barnabas, they wanted to honor Barnabas as Zeus and Paul as Hermes. Unlike Simon in Samaria (8:9-10), Paul and Barnabas refused to be the objects of worship (14:15). Even Peter came under discipline by the apostle Paul for his two-faced behavior regarding eating with Gentile Christians (Gal 2:14). In 2 Corinthians 11:5 Paul speaks out against the so-called "super-apostles" (2 Cor 11:13). In certain things, however, the church gave room for differences of conscience and did not condemn people who thought and acted differently (cf. Rom 14; 1 Cor 8). And sometimes the early church carefully worked through differences of understanding in interpreting the meaning of the gospel, as in the case of circumcision at the Jerusalem conference (Acts 15).

THE TEXT IN THE LIFE OF THE CHURCH

The Human Condition in Biblical Perspective

The faithful saying that *Christ Jesus came into the world to save sinners* (1 Tim 1:15) was common knowledge among early Christians and may have been a confessional statement in the early church. How did the Christian church follow this teaching over the centuries?

During and after the reign of Constantine (AD 306-337), it became easier for the church to ignore the moral imperatives of discipleship. Except for a few ascetics, less emphasis was given to holy living. Early in the fifth century, Pelagius expressed concern about the standard of moral life in the church. He reacted to the influence of Manichaeism and its interpretation of Romans 5:12 regarding the effect of Adam's sin upon the human race. Pelagius said there is no hereditary transmission of sin through reproduction but humans sin voluntarily by following Adam's example.

Augustine of Hippo reacted to Pelagius's view and said sin was hereditary. Its transmission from one generation to the next was associated with sexual reproduction. He justified infant baptism on the assumption that infants inherit a sinful nature from birth and therefore must be baptized to remove this original sin. Augustine believed that God responds to us in our sin by grace, but this grace is conditioned by God's decree of predestination, in which God wills some to be saved and provides irresistible grace for them.

Thomas Aquinas based his thought on the creation of humans in the image and likeness of God. In Aquinas's dualistic view, humans can reason and therefore have a natural knowledge of God. In addition to rational knowledge, supernatural revelation has made known God's salvation and grace. Martin Luther said that both the image and likeness of God in creation were corrupted by the fall. Therefore humans are totally depraved. John Calvin likewise rejected a distinction between the image and likeness of God and saw both as corrupted by the fall. Even the human will is depraved. One cannot choose to do what is good and turn to God even if one wants to do so. Turning to God comes only through God's irresistible grace. Calvin went so far as to say that some are predestined to be saved and others are predestined to be damned.

Anabaptists disagreed with other sixteenth-century reformers on the extent of the fall, particularly with regard to the presence of the divine image in human beings. They saw some of the divine image within humans and believed that God could appeal to that divine image to turn a person from sin to Christ for redemption. They did not deny the reality of sin or the inheritance of sin from Adam and Eve. But they did not agree that the tendency toward sinning was inevitable. They had a stronger theology of the real, transforming power of the Holy Spirit. Thus they rejected the idea of the bondage of the will and predestination.

Infants do not yet know the difference between good and evil (cf. Isa 7:15-16). Thus Anabaptists rejected infant baptism as a means for the removal of sin and talked about infants and children being "safe" rather than "saved." They said each person is responsible before God for one's own sin. What condemns people is their choice to live in sin when they know better.

This grace of God in Jesus Christ transforms those who acknowledge sin and accept Jesus Christ as Lord and Savior. The powerful and effective grace of God brings the whole person under the lordship of Christ, freeing the person from the power of original sin. The work of the Holy Spirit opposes the tendency toward evil deeds and helps the believer walk in an obedient life of Christian discipleship.

Anabaptists take sin seriously and see it as having both personal and corporate effects. Salvation brings about the release and transformation of the individual from sin; it also shields the Christian believer from the corporate environment of sin as one enters into the body of Christ, the church, which is God's new creation and order of life. Grace therefore treats not only past sins and the symptoms of sin; it also treats the cause of sin. "Grace is more than pardon for human sins and shortcomings; grace also is transformative, re-creative power. Popular Protestant understandings of sin and grace tend toward a never-ending *cul de sac* of grace: we sin, we ask forgiveness of God, God forgives. Sin, however, is not the last word where God's grace and Spirit are active. Regeneration and new life in Christ are possible (2 Cor 3:17-18; Eph 2:8-10, esp. v. 10)" (Kauffman, *ME* 5:825).

The Integrity of Christian Leaders

A strong connection exists between the leader's personal integrity as a minister of the gospel and the credibility of the gospel message itself. If sinful persons are to believe the gospel, the human person giving the gospel message must be trustworthy.

In the Schleitheim Confession of 1527, the Anabaptists said, "We have been united as follows concerning shepherds in the church of God. The shepherd in the church shall be a person according to the rule of Paul [1 Tim 3:7], fully and completely, who has a good report of those who are outside the faith" (art. 5; in Yoder 1977: 13).

The Wismar Articles of 1554 include these words: "No one is to undertake of himself to preach or admonish from church to church unless he be sent or ordained thereto by the congregation or the elders" (art. 9; in *CW:* 1042).

In response to the need for greater moral integrity among ministers, seminaries in North America are giving more attention to the pastor as person and to character formation as essential to the integrity of one's ministry. Spiritual formation and the pastor's own sense of being are now an integral part of preparation for the pastoral ministry. Pastors must be ethical in their practice of Christian ministry and attend to their own moral character. Most Christian denominations, including believers church denominations, have ethical guidelines for pastors (Thomas: 106-27). As pastors practice spiritual disciplines and maintain high moral and ethical standards in their life and work, they will be effective in Christian ministry.

1 Timothy 2:1-15

Prayer and Behavior in the Household of God

PREVIEW

Men, women, bishops, and deacons should *know how one ought to behave in the household of God, which is the church of the living God, the pillar and bulwark of truth* (1 Tim 3:15). After warning unhealthy teachers in chapter 1, Paul turns to the behavior of men and women in the church in chapter 2. The section begins with a call to prayer for all, including government leaders (2:1-4). This call to prayer is followed by a confessional statement (2:5-6). In this confessional statement, God's work of salvation in Jesus Christ is the basis for Paul's missionary calling (2:8) and provides an undergirding theological reason for Christian moral behavior. Salvation in Christ affects the way men and women relate to each other and behave in the church. The section goes on to describe how men should behave in the church (2:8) and concludes with teaching on how women should behave in the church (2:9-15).

OUTLINE

Prayer for All, Including Government Leaders, 2:1-4
Confessional Statement, 2:5-7
Men's Behavior in the Church, 2:8
Women's Behavior in the Church, 2:9-15

EXPLANATORY NOTES

Prayer for All, Including Government Leaders 2:1-4

Paul urges readers of this epistle to pray for all people. The verb *I urge* or *I am requesting* is the preferred reading (Metzger 1994: 572). This verb, coupled with the word *therefore/then*, indicates that Paul is building his request on what precedes in chapter 1. In responding to the teachers who have been causing serious problems in the church, Paul has excommunicated two persons (1:19-20); now he gives Timothy instructions on how the church is to conduct its life (2:1–3:16).

Prayer for all people is essential because God desires that *all* persons *be saved* (v. 4 NIV). The Greek word *anthrōpos* (human being) includes both men and women. This prayer contrasts with the thought of the later Gnostics, who held that persons who had more insight than others would be saved. Limiting one's prayers for salvation to only a few persons is theologically deficient because God's salvation is for all. Paul calls attention to the inclusiveness of the gospel by using the term *all* three times in verses 1, 4, and 6. Prayers are said on behalf of *all* people (v. 1), God desires salvation of *all* people (v. 4), and Jesus has given himself as a ransom for *all* (v. 6). Paul proclaims this gospel to the nations, *Gentiles* (v. 7).

First of all signifies a priority of importance. Prayer may not take priority in sequence or time, but it is first in importance because it is connected to God's work of salvation for all persons. Several kinds of prayer are named one after another: *supplications, prayers, intercessions, and thanksgivings*. Paul uses a rhetorical device, *repetitio*, which groups synonyms to drive home his main point. The point is that all prayers and types of prayers should be for all the people God wants to save.

Four kinds of prayers are listed. First is *supplications*, or *requests* (NIV), a general term for a petition for God to act on behalf of the people. It is a statement of need. Second is *prayers*, a general term for prayer or a place of prayer. It is used in the NT only of prayers addressed to God. Third, *intercessions* are petitions offered to a superior often on behalf of others. Elsewhere in the NT or LXX, the term is found only in 1 Timothy 4:5 and 2 Maccabees 4:8. Paul does use the cognate verb, *to intercede*, when speaking of the Holy Spirit's intercession (Rom 8:27) and Christ's intercession for the saints (Rom 8:34; cf. Heb 7:25). Finally, through *thanksgivings* God's people reflect on the past and thank God for response to their prayers. God's people pray with anticipation about the present and future, believing that a faithful God in the past will answer their contemporary prayers.

Prayers are offered *for everyone*, including *for kings and all who are in high positions* (1 Tim 2:2). Prayers for everyone include the unhealthy teachers in the Ephesian church. It includes prayers for enemies, as Jesus taught (Matt 5:43-48), and praying for governing rulers, whether they are friend or foe. It includes prayers for the Roman emperors and for regional leaders, such as Herod Antipas. As in Luke-Acts, the term *kings* (*basileis*) is used widely for many persons under the Roman imperium as well as Caesar (Quinn and Wacker 2000: 177). In keeping with his Jewish faith, Paul advocates praying for the governing authorities. The phrase *all who are in high positions* indicates that prayers are to ascend to God, not just for the king, prime minister, or president. The phrase encompasses all who govern, including the emperor, provincial officials, and local magistrates. Such prayers had a long history in Judaism. This practice of prayer differs from the Gentile practice. Prayers in 1 Timothy 2:1-2 are raised *for* the emperor, not *to* the emperor, as in the imperial cult, which divinized the emperors. The four kinds of prayers given in verse 1 exclude idol worship, which some Ephesians were expressing in the imperial religion.

Paul offers two reasons for these Christian prayers. First, *so that we may lead a quiet and peaceable life in all godliness and dignity*. Paul hopes that through their prayers, the Ephesian Christians will not be under suspicion of disloyalty to the governing authorities and can practice Christian living without disturbance. Christians live in *godliness and dignity*. These two terms represent the Hellenistic counterpart to the Hebraic terms for holiness and righteousness. The Ephesian Christians are not to be boisterous, but through quiet demeanor (not silence) and upright behavior, the Christian church will survive and grow in the Roman Empire, despite its expanding civil religion.

Paul repeats *one God* in verse 5, which Jews confessed for centuries (Deut 6:4). Thus only one Savior (*sōtēr*) is confessed, in keeping with the basic Christian confession "Jesus is Lord" (Rom 10:9; 1 Cor 12:3; 2 Cor 4:5; Eph 4:5; Phil 2:9-11). In Paul's day the Roman imperial cult was active. By the end of the first century, cities in Asia, including Ephesus, wanted to become the keeper (*neōkoros*, Acts 19:35) of this cult. Earlier at Thessalonica (Acts 17:7) and Ephesus (Acts 19:23-34), Paul ran into opposition from those involved in imperial religion. Now he calls upon Timothy and the young church at Ephesus to pray for the governing authorities so that the Christian church will survive and grow amid polytheistic religion.

Second, they are to pray because *this is right and acceptable in the sight of God our Savior, who desires everyone to be saved and to come to the knowledge of the truth*. This is the most important reason for praying. More than survival is at stake. We present our prayers in the heavenly court, face-to-face with God, like a person presenting a petition before an earthly judge. God wants to save everyone (1 Tim 2:4; 4:10; Titus 2:11; cf. 2 Pet 3:9).

Prayers for governing authorities extend beyond a peaceful life for Christians. Prayers are offered to God, who is in the business of saving everyone. We pray for governing authorities because we have a missionary God. In our prayers we request that governing authorities not get in the way of the saving work of God for all humankind. The gospel is universal in scope (2:5-6); it is not for an elite few.

The phrase *who [God] desires everyone to be saved* calls for further explanation. A universalist view holds that God saves every person, regardless of a person's response. This view is problematic because of what Paul said at the end of chapter 1, when delivering two persons to Satan. A second view is that God saves all but the worst sinners. Later rabbinic Judaism would hold this view, but Paul's statement that *he* is the worst sinner (1:15) disallows it. A third view is that God is saving all the elect, those predestined to be saved. A better interpretation is that God desires that all people should be saved, whether or not they respond to his gracious offer (I. H. Marshall 1999: 426-27). The point is that God's salvation is universal, over against the unhealthy exclusiveness of the proto-Gnostic view. God is saving all, whether Jew or Gentile. And God even desires the salvation of those who do not accept this gracious offer. In short, sinful persons cannot blame God for their condition, since God desires that they be saved. If persons are not saved, it is because they have refused to respond to God's gracious offer of salvation in Christ Jesus.

And to come to the knowledge of the truth suggests that salvation has its cognitive side (1 Tim 3:15; 4:3; 2 Tim 3:8; 4:4; Titus 1:1). One hears and accepts the gospel message itself. Salvation comprises the main theme of the confessional statement that follows.

Confessional Statement 2:5-7

Building on God's desire to save all persons (2:4), Paul uses what may have been an existing confessional statement held by the early church. It is typical of a Pauline compressed salvation statement (Rom 3:21-26; 5:8-10; 1 Cor 8:6; 2 Cor 5:19-21; Gal 1:4; 2:20; Eph 5:2; Phil 2:5-11; Col 1:15-20; 1 Thess 5:9-10; 1 Tim 3:16; Titus 3:4-7). The confessional/liturgical statement emphasizes three themes: the uniqueness of one God, the person of Christ as mediator, and the redemptive work of Christ.

For there is one God calls attention to Israel's basic belief in Yahweh, which was recited again and again in the Shema: "Hear O Israel: the

LORD is our God, the LORD alone" or "the LORD is one" (Deut 6:4). Throughout their life spans, devout Jews recite this passage. In response to the proto-Gnostics, who thought they possessed special favors from God, and other Jews, who thought God belonged exclusively to them, Paul clarifies that there is only one God. Paul actually builds salvation precisely on the oneness of God. If God is to be more than a tribal deity, God must be one for all humans (Johnson 2001: 197). If there were many gods, there could be many ways of salvation. But since there is only one God, there is only one way of salvation. Paul's theology in 2:4-5 is in keeping with his other writings on one God, through whom salvation comes for both the Jew and the Greek (Rom 3:29-30; 1 Cor 8:6; Gal 3:20; Eph 4:6; 1 Tim 1:17). There is not one gospel for the Jews and another for the rest of humankind (the Gentiles) because there is only one God for all people.

There is also one mediator between God and humankind, Christ Jesus, himself human (1 Tim 2:5). A mediator (*mesitēs*) is one who acts as a go-between, linking two parties. The mediator is a negotiator, one who "establishes a relation which would not otherwise exist" (*TDNT* 4:601). The confession assumes universal sinfulness, so all of humanity needs outside help to experience reconciliation with God. The translation "between God and men" (NIV) is inadequate since the Greek term *anthrōpos* means both men and women.

Jesus Christ is the mediator. Paul refers to Christ's humanity and not his maleness in defining his mediator role. As mediator, Christ is not an emperor for whom deity is ascribed, as in pagan religion, but the divine one who has become human. Christ Jesus is mediator not because he is Lord, but precisely because he is human. This emphasis on Christ's humanity reflects the Adam-Christ imagery of Romans 5:12-21, in which Christ becomes the representative of the new humanity in the new order of redemption. Jesus Christ represents both parties—God and humanity—and is the only one who can reconcile them. Jesus speaks for God to humans in divine revelation, and he speaks to God on behalf of humans as intercessor. There is only one mediator because Jesus Christ alone is sufficient to meet the need. Jesus established a new covenant between God and humanity in this mediator role (Heb 9:15).

Who gave himself a ransom for all (1 Tim 1:6). The one mediator, the human Christ Jesus, gave himself for our redemption. Mark 10:45 looks forward to Jesus giving himself, and Paul looks back at the cross as Jesus' self-giving act within human history for our redemption. The reflexive pronoun indicates that Jesus was not forced to give himself, but freely offered himself on our behalf. The idea of giving himself is found in Jesus' own teaching (Mark 10:45) and elsewhere in Paul (Gal 1:4; Titus 2:14). In verse 6, however, Paul stresses that redemption is *for all.* As prayers are for all and as God desires that all be saved, so Jesus gives his life for all; without Jesus' giving himself, no one can be saved and prayer would be meaningless. As the one God wills the salvation of all, the one mediator gives himself for all (Johnson 2001: 197).

Two terms catch our attention. First, Jesus gave himself on behalf of all. Paul makes a prepositional change from "instead of" (*anti*) in Mark 10:45 to a preposition meaning *on behalf of* (*hyper*), implying *for* all people. This preposition expresses representation. Elsewhere Paul uses this preposition along with the reflexive pronoun *who* in describing Christ's self-offering (Rom 8:32; Gal 1:4; 2:20; Titus 2:14). Second, Christ gave himself as a ransom (*antilytron*). Human life offered as a ransom is rooted in the literature that arose in response to the Maccabean crisis in the second century BC (2 Macc 7:37-38; 4 Macc 6:27-29; 17:21-22). Christ's death involved paying a price to bring about ransom or freedom. Such freedom from the power of sin is gained only when the price is paid. Because the cost of giving up his life on behalf of all was so great, to exclude any person from the offer of salvation is unthinkable. Throughout the paragraph, the emphasis is on the potential redemption made possible in Christ Jesus for all people. We pray for *all*, including governing authorities, because God wants to save *all* and the human Jesus Christ, who is the mediator, gave his life a ransom for *all.* Both God and Christ desire nothing less than the salvation of *all.* First Timothy 2:1-7 is missionary through and through.

Paul indicates that *this was attested at the right time* (v. 6). This idiomatic phrase stands in apposition to the preceding clause. Its difficulty is seen by various attempts to add to it by later scribes. The shorter and more difficult reading adopted by Nestle-Aland seems more authentic, despite the difficulties of translating this idiom. A similar idiom appears in 1 Timothy 6:15 and Titus 1:3. Who or what is the subject of the witness in 1 Timothy 2:6b—Paul's appointment as a herald, or Christ's death? In light of what precedes the idiom and what follows, both give witness. But the idiom calls attention to the crucial moment, the moment of opportunity, chosen by God for the manifestation of salvation. The death of Christ stands in history as the opportune time for God's convincing witness of his desire to save all of humankind.

For this I was appointed a herald and an apostle, . . . a teacher (2:7). Paul was appointed to proclaim the good news of salvation for all humankind, salvation through the cross of Jesus Christ. The words *I was appointed* restate what Paul wrote in 1:12, that his ministerial status comes directly by divine initiative. Paul's appointment to preach the gospel to all the nations, both Jews and Gentiles, substantiates God's desire to save all persons and thus lays an obligation on the readers of this letter to pray for all. The weight of Paul's appointment finds expression in the triad *apostle, herald, teacher.* In 2 Timothy 1:11 the triad appears again. The three terms describe different but related aspects of Paul's ministry. *Herald* and *teacher* embrace and interpret *apostle* (Collins: 63).

The term *herald* means a proclaimer, one who announces the good news to those who have not yet heard it. In secular society the herald made public announcements. He announced a ruler's decisive victories, the freeing of slaves, the beginning of public games, the orders of the king, and the king's arrival. A herald in the ancient world was like the announcer who enters the room of a joint session of the United States Congress before the State of the Union address and shouts, "Mr. Speaker, the President of the United States." The herald needed a loud voice and the ability to repeat strictly what he had been told (Mounce: 92).

As a herald-apostle under divine appointment, Paul announces publicly the good news of what God has done to those who have not yet heard it. As such, the apostle moved from place to place as a missionary in the Greco-Roman world, announcing the good news. Paul is also a teacher. Teaching was prominent in the Pauline churches, is expected of church leaders (1 Tim 3:2; 5:17; 2 Tim 4:2), and is not limited to office (2 Tim 2:2; Titus 2:3). In the traditions of early Judaism, a revered person's teaching was passed on to succeeding generations. As a *teacher of the Gentiles,* Paul passes on values to the next generation. He openly declares that the gospel is for all. Both preaching and teaching arose out of Paul's divine appointment to the apostolic office. At the end of his life, Paul looks back and recognizes that God has given him strength to carry out this apostolic commission *so that through me the message might be fully proclaimed and all Gentiles hear it* (2 Tim 4:17).

Paul underscores his authority as an apostle by stating *I am telling the truth, I am not lying* and insisting that his teaching is *in faith and truth.* The authenticity of Paul's gospel rests upon the authenticity of his person and his apostolic calling. With fidelity and veracity, Paul has carried out this apostolic preaching and teaching ministry. The integrity of the herald and teacher enhances the authority of the spoken and written word. For Paul, faithfulness and truthfulness support the evidence that his ministry and authority have originated in God. Some of the teachers at Ephesus have questioned Paul's apostleship to the Gentiles, implying that the gospel is only for Jews. But Paul boldly confronts those who contest his mission by saying that he continues to speak the truth and continues not to lie as he preaches and teaches the gospel message. For Paul, apostleship and the gospel for the Gentiles belong indissolubly together (I. H. Marshall 1999: 434).

The universality of the gospel is the underlying theme of 1 Timothy 2:1-7. The one God of both Jew and Gentile desires all humankind to be saved and come to the knowledge of the truth. God send his Son, Jesus, as mediator between sinful humanity and God. The human Jesus Christ gave himself as a ransom for all. Since God did this, Paul will announce the good news to all.

Men's Behavior in the Church 2:8

The quiet and peaceful life of 1 Timothy 2:2 is carried a step further and applied to men in the church. In the previous section *all* persons are instructed in prayer. Now Paul speaks specifically about *men's* prayers by using a specific plural noun (*tous andras*), meaning the male gender.

To all the house churches in Ephesus, Paul directs his instructions for men to pray in every place. Men are to pray in the usual Jewish posture: *lifting up* washed *hands.* "According to the Talmud, Rabbi Joshua ben Levi taught that one who does not lift his hands in prayer is not to raise his hands in blessing" (Collins: 66).

Far more serious than posture is the attitude with which men pray. Men are to pray *without anger or argument.* Open hands are the opposite of clenched fists, which indicate anger or resentment. Apparently some of the teachers in Ephesus are known for having an angry and argumentative attitude. Several times anger and argumentative speech are condemned (1 Tim 3:3, 8, 11; 5:13; 6:11; 2 Tim 2:24; Titus 1:7; 2:3; 3:2). In calling for a right attitude in prayer and worship, the apostle applies the teachings of Jesus (Matt 5:21-26). If "pious Jews waited an hour before reciting the Eighteen Benedictions so that their hearts might be totally directed toward God" (Collins: 66), then Christian men must also examine their attitude when coming to prayer and worship. A profane attitude in prayer is worse than an improper posture. Elsewhere Paul writes, "Do everything without murmuring and arguing" (Phil 2:14). Holy hands lifted up and open to God suggest total commitment to God, the opposite of expressing anger and questioning God. Much attention has been given to teaching on women's behavior in worship in 1 Timothy 2:9-15, but far too little is said about men's behavior in worship. Might this indicate men's reluctance to examine themselves?

Women's Behavior in the Church 2:9-15

First Timothy 2:9-15 is a key passage in discussions about women's leadership roles in the church. An enormous number of writings have appeared, both from writers who favor women as pastors and from those who oppose women as pastors and elders. Interpretations range from a hierarchical view of men above women, deemed necessary for "a world estranged from God" to "believe that God was in Christ reconciling the world to himself" (Köstenberger, Schreiner, and Baldwin: 11-12), to an egalitarian view based in part on the idea that Paul was countering the negative influence of the cult of Artemis upon the church at Ephesus (Mickelsen: 232-44). Hermeneutical differences easily divide scholars working on this passage. Rather than going into detail on these various interpretations of the text, I will present my own observations based on the literary setting, the social and cultural setting, exegetical insights, and what Paul means by the phrase *saved through childbearing.*

First, the literary setting. First Timothy 2:9-15 is part of a larger literary unit dealing with unhealthy doctrine in the church (1 Tim 1:3). Some of the women in Ephesus were apparently attracted by unhealthy teaching, and Paul seeks to correct the situation. First Timothy addresses women's behavior in worship (2:10-15), appropriate pastoral behavior toward older and younger women (5:2), desired qualities in women deacons (3:11), the need to support widows in the service of the church (5:9-10), correction of some behavioral patterns of younger widows (5:11-15), and responsibility toward poor widows (5:3-8, 16). Paul also warns against widows going from house to house, speaking things they ought not say (5:13). He indicates that some have turned away to follow Satan (5:15). Perhaps as much as 60 percent of 1 Timothy deals with deviant teaching. It would be misleading not to interpret 2:9-15 within this larger context.

The sinful teaching that Paul addresses here includes forbidding marriage, advocating abstinence from certain foods, and claiming that the resurrection has already taken place (1 Tim 4:3; 2 Tim 2:18). It has affected both men and women who *deviated from* or *renounced* the faith, *missed the mark,* or *wandered away* from the goal of Paul's instruction (1 Tim 1:4-6; 4:1: 6:21; 2 Tim 1:15; 4:4). Some church leaders may in fact *fall into disgrace and the snare of the devil* (1 Tim 3:6-7). An emerging division between teaching and lifestyle is evident in that some have rejected *a good conscience* (1 Tim 1:5, 19; 4:2; Titus 1:15), some hold to an *outward form of godliness* while *denying its power* (2 Tim 3:5; Titus 1:16), and some are lured into a false security by *imagining that godliness is a means of gain* (1 Tim 6:5; see also 3:3, 8; 6:10; 2 Tim 3:2; Titus 1:10). Unhealthy teaching includes *meaningless talk*, *disputes about words*, and *profane chatter* (1 Tim 1:6; 6:4, 20; 2 Tim 2:14, 16). Such talk is swamped by inherent contradictions in *what is falsely called knowledge* (1 Tim 1:4; 6:4, 20; 2 Tim 2:23; Titus 1:10; 3:9). It arises out of deception (1 Tim 1:7; 4:1; 2 Tim 3:13, Titus 1:10) and indicates that some have been caught in *the snare* and captivity of *the devil* (1 Tim 6:5; 2 Tim 2:15-26). Some women have accepted unhealthy teaching to such a degree that, in their desire to learn, they have not been able to comprehend *the truth* (2 Tim 3:6-7) and have followed *old wives' tales* (1 Tim 4:7).

One can see clear literary parallels between 1 Timothy 2:8–3:13; 1 Timothy 5:1–6:2; and Titus 2:1-14. These literary parallels indicate that God's salvation is also for women. In 1 Timothy 2:3-4, God desires that both men and women be saved. Timothy is to honor the faith that his mother and grandmother taught him (2 Tim 1:5).

Second, the larger social and cultural setting of the Roman world provides insight into 1 Timothy 2:9-15. From about 44 BC onward, women in some circles of the Roman Empire claimed a bold new freedom (Winter 2003: 21). Certain scholars refer to the emergence of a "new woman" at this time. Some philosophers and Roman rulers spoke against the liberation of women because they worried that it would bring about a breakdown in family morality. The women of high standing who became Christians in Thessalonica (Acts 17:4) and Beroea (17:12) may have included some of these newly liberated women in the Roman Empire.

These "liberated" women exercised significant social, financial, and sexual freedom. Some of them were lax in their commitment to sexual faithfulness in marriage and in some cases practiced adultery freely. In Corinth their influence affected some Christian women to the degree that they removed their head veil in the worship service (1 Cor 11:1-16). Paul asks these Corinthian women to keep the veil on because removing it associates these Christian women with promiscuous, liberated women in society. Bruce W. Winter writes, "If, according to Roman law, 'she was what she wore' or in this case what she removed from her head, then this gesture made a statement in support of the mores of some of her secular sisters, the new wives, who sought to ridicule the much-prized virtue of modesty which epitomized the married women" (Winter 2003: 96).

According to 1 Timothy 2:9, Christian women (*gynaikas* without the article functions generically and means women in general) are to adorn themselves in ways that reflect Christian virtues of modesty and holiness. The newly liberated women in Ephesus appeared with special braided hairstyle, gold, pearls, and expensive clothing. The sculpture and literature of the period make it clear that women often wore their hair in elaborate arrangements, with braids and curls piled high and decorated with gems, gold, and/or pearls. Witherington imagines a "scene in an evening Christian worship meeting in a relatively small space with many lamps lit. In this situation, hair-styles featuring reflective items such as gold or pearls would be a regular distraction from the proper focus of worship" (Witherington 2006: 225). In contrast, Christian women are to appear in more culturally acceptable clothing so that the Christian message itself is not misinterpreted by the larger society.

Winter's research suggests that the Christian woman's modesty was set against the antithetical behavior of the promiscuous wife in public. The public perception of Christian wives was a critical matter in the community; it would play into the hands of the enemy of the early Christian movement in Ephesus if they dressed like high-class prostitutes. The dress code was prescribed in 2:9b because it sent signals of a lack of moral respectability and sexual availability to those at banquets, at other social gatherings, or in the public spaces that women frequented, including theaters. Thus 2:9a seeks an adornment of the female virtues of modesty and self-control, coupled with good deeds, rather than the wrong attire. Because in Roman society you were what you wore, the concerns in this new community of Christians were that the values of the "new woman" could intrude into the gatherings in Christian homes; hence the concern for preventative measures in 1 Timothy 2:9-15 (Winter 2003: 121-22). After reviewing several inscriptions and epitaphs regarding women in Ephesus, Witherington concludes, "It seems clear that part of Luke and Paul's rhetorical strategy is to praise women in the same terms with which the women in the inscriptions are praised, but for behaving in more specifically Christian ways with the Christian community" (Witherington 2006: 220).

Another cultural factor was the cult of Artemis in Ephesus. "Artemis of the Ephesians," honored in the great temple in Ephesus, was a female image that exalted the female. Artemis was thought to pursue the male gods in the Greco-Roman world, and she and her female adherents were considered to be superior to men. Following this line of thought, R. C. Kroeger and C. C. Kroeger suggest that 1 Timothy 2:12 could be rendered, "I do not allow a woman to teach or proclaim herself author of man" (192). The cult honored Artemis as mother goddess, source of life, and the one who nourished all creatures and was herself the power and source of fertility in nature. In the festivals the priestess of Artemis would pursue a man, pretending that she was Artemis pursuing a male god. Witherington cites several inscriptions of women serving as priestesses in the temple of Artemis (Witherington 2006: 218-21).

R. C. Kroeger and C. C. Kroeger try to match 1 Timothy 2:13 with several references to the Artemis cult that claimed woman to be the originator of man (37-55). As Philip H. Towner points out, some of the Kroegers' interpretation is questionable, since some of the cited references in Greco-Roman literature come in later Gnostic sources (Towner 2006: 221 n. 88, 232 n. 128). Paul corrects the false teaching that women are superior to men by saying that *Adam was formed first, then Eve*. In fact, Paul says Eve *was deceived* (1 Tim 2:13-14), indicating that the female cannot claim superiority. Christian women in Ephesus need not look to Artemis as their protector for safe travel and protector through the childbearing process, as did other non-Christian Ephesian women (Pierce and Groothuis: 220). Since Christians are facing the excesses of a new class of liberated women as well as the cult of Artemis in Ephesus, one can readily understand Paul's call for adornment of the heart in the Christian virtues and his negative response to the cult's view of women's superiority.

Third, exegetical insights. Although Paul uses the plural noun *women* in verses 9 and 10, he changes the noun to the singular *woman* in verse 11. Normally the singular Greek noun *woman* (*gynē*) refers to a married woman, and indeed the context implies this (e.g., 1 Tim 3:2; Titus 1:6). But the singular noun without an article can also function generically and refer to women in general. Women are not merely encouraged to learn: they are *commanded* to learn. They are to learn in quietness and submission to their teacher. The passage describes how women are to learn and does not command absolute silence or subordination to men in general (Witherington 2006: 226). The phrase *She is to keep silent* (*She must be silent*, NIV) is more correctly translated as *She is to keep quiet*. The primary meaning of the Greek term *hēsychia* is "quietness." Both Paul and other NT writers use this term or its cognate forms this way (1 Thess 4:11; 2 Thess 3:12; 1 Tim 2:2; Luke 23:56; Acts 11:18; 21:14; 1 Pet 3:4). Both men and women are to lead a quiet and peaceful life in 1 Timothy 2:2. Women are to learn in quietness (*hēsychia*) in 1 Timothy 2:11 and to keep quiet (*hēsychia*) in 1 Timothy 2:12. Four times in 1 Timothy 2 Paul calls for quiet and peace instead of disputing. When Paul and other NT writers want to write about "silence," they use a different Greek word, *sigaō* (Rom 16:25; 1 Cor 14:28, 30, 34). The learning context in 1 Timothy 2:11-12 suggests that Paul is talking about maintaining the reverence and quietness necessary for learning to take place.

Submission to the teacher fits a learning context. In the first-century world, women were not as well-educated as men. To dominate the worship time with questions or comments would have disrupted the meeting. Thus Paul commands the women to learn in a manner conducive to learning. Rather than being totally silent and under the authority of men, women are commanded to learn by listening attentively. The thought is not so much of silence as it is acceptance without demurring (I. H. Marshall 1999: 453). First Timothy 2:11-12 refers not to how a wife is to be submissive to her husband but how a godly wife is to respond to Christian instruction (Winter 2003: 113-14). Negatively, she is to exercise quietness instead of extensive talking. Positively, she is to learn.

Given the first-century setting, the woman is not *to teach or to have authority over a man.* Some interpret verse 12 to mean that even now a woman cannot exercise a teaching or governing role over men in church and therefore cannot be a pastor. Unfortunately, the Greek word *authenteō* was translated as "rule over" or "exercise authority over" another (cf. NIV, NJB). Some church leaders have employed this translation to insist that a woman is not to have authority over men in the church. A closer examination of the Greek construction in 1 Timothy 2:12 does not support this view *[Authenteō, p. 333]*. One may interpret *authenteō* in a neutral way, suggesting that Paul is prohibiting any kind of teaching that places a woman over a man. Or one may interpret *authenteō* in a more negative domineering sense (cf. "usurp authority over," KJV), as we see in a papyrus letter from 27 BC (Witherington 2006: 227). Paul is not condemning all women's teaching of men, but rather a certain *kind* of teaching by women.

Instead of following the work of Knight (1984), Moo (1981), and Köstenberger, Schreiner, and Baldwin (1995), I prefer the negative interpretation of *authenteō*. The command is clear: a woman is to be quiet. She is not to be silent, but to exercise a demeanor that is conducive to learning, as suggested in the previous verse. The use of the two infinitives in the given word order suggests that a woman is not to teach and domineer a man (perhaps her husband), but give herself to a learning demeanor, since most women were not educated in the first-century world. The entire context of verses 11 and 12 is negative. Paul is correcting problems in worship and in verse 12 corrects the abuse of power and teaching privilege in the worship setting at Ephesus.

Given the context of the verse, it seems most likely that some women in Ephesus, perhaps encouraged by the unhealthy teachers, were trying to gain an advantage over the men by teaching in a domineering, dictatorial fashion. The men became angry and disputed what the women were doing so that their prayers were hindered by anger or argument (v. 8). Paul wants to correct inappropriate behavior on the part of both men and women. So the apostle instructs men to put aside the anger that was affecting their prayers and instead exercise quietness of demeanor. And Paul encourages Christian women not to use the public worship setting as a place to domineer men, but to go about the task of learning in a gentle, quiet demeanor.

To prohibit teaching by those who are seeking to domineer, Paul is saying, "Let a woman learn in a quiet and submissive fashion. I do not, however, permit her to teach with the intent to dominate a man" (Pierce and Groothuis: 223). Paul is not excluding women from teaching in the church nor is he excluding women from teaching men in the church. I agree with Witherington that "there is no universal and unqualified prohibition of women teaching and preaching in this text" (Witherington 1988: 122).

Given the Ephesian context when 1 Timothy 2:9-15 was written, Paul is correcting a situation that was detrimental to the spread of the gospel. As I. Howard Marshall says, "The quiet demeanor and recognition of authority which are to characterize the learner are contrasted with teaching in a manner which is heavy-handed and abuses authority. . . . It is, therefore, more likely the verb characterizes the nature of the teaching rather than the role of women in church leadership in general" (1999: 460).

Paul begs both men and women to exercise the kind of demeanor that does not bring disrepute upon the church. At the same time Paul encourages women to learn and grow in their knowledge of Christian faith. In so doing, Paul speaks directly to the problem in Ephesus of women trying to assume the mantle of teaching before they have learned the apostolic message properly, women who may have been misled by deviant teachers (Witherington 2006: 231). Interpreted in this way, 1 Timothy 2:9-15 fits well the larger context of 1 Timothy 2:1–3:16, with its emphasis upon how one ought to behave in the household of God so that the gospel is unhindered as set forth by the confessional statements in 2:5-6 and 3:16.

Fourth, we have yet to examine what Paul meant when he said, *Yet she will be saved through childbearing.* In 2:13 the apostle looks back at creation (Gen 2:7, 22) and in 2:14 the fall (Gen 3:1-13). He cites the creation not to talk about order to guide the church's view of men and women but to explain his reaction to false teaching. Paul is selective in how he uses the creation account and does not quote from the first account in Genesis 1:27, where God created man and woman together and equally. Because the apostle's concern is about women in Ephesus who are deceived by deviant teachers, he uses the account of Eve's deception in Genesis 3 for instructional purposes rather than to set forth an order in creation. The word *for* implies further explanation. Paul is prohibiting women from domineering men not because Eve was formed after Adam and sinned first. True, Eve was deceived by Satan (Gen 3:13b; Rom 7:8; 2 Cor 11:3), but Adam likewise sinned without being deceived! In the Geneses 2 narrative, Eve was not yet created when God gave the original prohibition to Adam. Nothing is said here about women being more susceptible by nature to deception than men (Witherington 2006: 229). Elsewhere, Paul makes it clear that sin passed on through Adam, who represents fallen humanity (Rom 5:12-21; 1 Cor 15:22), when he could have placed the blame on Eve. The point Paul makes is that Eve was deceived just as women in Ephesus are in danger of being deceived by deviant teaching (1 Tim 5:14-15). This teaching includes forbidding marriage and bearing children (1 Tim 4:3).

Some see *saved through childbearing* as a reference to Eve and/or Mary the mother of Jesus, who gave birth to the one who would bring God's salvation. It is more likely that Paul is instructing the women to turn away from deviant teaching that rejects women's domestic role by avoiding marriage and even terminating pregnancy by abortion (Winter 2003: 110-12). Read this way, the text says that women will experience salvation in Christ in the context of their normal domestic pattern of living, including giving birth to children. The issue is not salvation *through* (by means of) the pain of childbirth. Nor does one obtain salvation by avoiding marriage, childbirth, and aborting pregnancy, as the unhealthy teachers implied. Instead, one has salvation in Christ while following (during) the normal domestic life in the first-century world. Thus, 1 Timothy 2:13-14a ties into what is stated in verses 11-12.

Moreover, this salvation will become reality for the Ephesian women, *provided they continue in faith and love and holiness, with modesty*. Notice that the noun changes from the singular to the plural (*they continue*), which moves attention away from Eve to the Ephesian women, who will experience salvation by continuing in these four virtues. An alternate interpretation takes the plural to mean both husband-father and wife-mother, with Adam and Eve as antecedents in the preceding verse, thus meaning that both parents are responsible to rear children and not just to bear children.

The four virtues named (*faith, love, holiness, modesty*) were commonly upheld in Greek literature (Waters: 703-35). Kenneth L. Waters Sr. suggests that the passage may be interpreted metaphorically to mean that the four virtues are children. Thus, childbearing in 1 Timothy 2:15 is a metaphor for virtue bearing, placing the emphasis on childrearing. Both men and women are to practice these virtues and are saved in this way (Waters: 727-31). Although this metaphorical interpretation is questionable, 1 Timothy 2:15 is not talking about receiving salvation through (by means of) the pain of childbirth. Instead, Christian women are to turn away from the present deviant teaching and continue in domestic life and in faithfulness as they practice the virtues of faith, love, holiness, and modesty. By continuing in these virtues, they, like men, will be saved.

In summary, 1 Timothy 2:9-15, though difficult to interpret, as the recent debate indicates, invites the reader inside the first-century church at Ephesus as it struggles against deviant teaching; we can observe how Christian teaching was applied in that historical and cultural setting. The passage is not an attempt to lay down a rule for how men and women are to relate to each other in the church across the centuries. Paul does not give full support either to a hierarchical view or to an egalitarian view. Instead, the passage suggests that women and men complement each other and that neither is to "exercise authority over" the other in a hierarchical way. By emphasizing learning in quietness, Paul turns women's attention away from both the unhealthy teachers infiltrating the young Christian church at Ephesus and the Jewish and Greco-Roman practices of not educating women.

THE TEXT IN BIBLICAL CONTEXT

Salvation for All

God desires everyone to be saved and come to the knowledge of the truth (1 Tim 2:4). God's desire to save all is stated directly and indirectly in the larger biblical context. Already in the covenant with Abraham, we read of God's desire that all the families of the earth be blessed (Gen 12:3). In the early chapters of Exodus, God's saving purpose is clearly stated: "so that you may know I am the LORD," or "so that the Egyptians shall know that I am the LORD." Jonah likewise preached in Nineveh, a Gentile city, so they would know the Lord. Israel's role in the world was to be "a light to the nations" (Isa 11:9; 42:6; 49:6). Through the prophet Ezekiel, God said, "For I have no pleasure in the death of anyone" (18:32). In like manner Peter writes, "The Lord is not slow about his promise, as some think of slowness, but is patient with you, not wanting any to perish, but all to come to repentance" (2 Pet 3:9).

Salvation for all rests upon the foundation of the oneness of God in both the OT and the NT (Exod 20:1-3; Deut 6:4; 1 Tim 2:5a). The oneness of God means that God is God both of the Jews and Gentiles and provides one salvation for both (Rom 3:30). There are not two gods or more, two salvations or more, or two peoples of God or more. There is only one God, one salvation, and one people of God (Eph 4:4-6). This oneness of God distinguishes the biblical teaching about God from polytheism in the ancient Near East as seen in the OT and in the Greco-Roman world of the first century. No distinction can be made between Jew and Gentile because "the same Lord is Lord of all and is generous to all who call on him" (Rom 10:12). The prophet Malachi asks, "Have we not all one father? Has not one God created us?" (Mal 2:10; cf. Acts 17:26-27). Anything less than one God and one salvation leaves the world in a state of religious confusion, with a truncated gospel and the gospel reduced to a racial, ethnic, and tribal religion.

Moreover all persons have sinned and are therefore in need of God's grace (Rom 3:23; 5:12, 18). Through grace, God makes redemption possible for all persons who have sinned. Where sin increased, grace increased all the more; literally "superabounded" (Rom 5:20 NIV). Over and over the Bible asserts that the atoning death of Christ is for all people.

Other NT texts speak of God's election and calling (Rom 8:29; 11:28-32; Eph 1:3-14). These texts speak of God's gracious offer of salvation to all and can be placed alongside human freedom texts, which place responsibility on individuals to choose to accept or reject God's salvation. In Romans 5:12-21, Paul teaches salvation for all who accept it "by faith" (5:1). As sin and death are universal, so grace and life are universal in the sense that they are available to all. As all sinned, so Christ died for all. Other NT texts indicate that human persons are responsible and can be saved only if they believe in Christ and his atoning work at the cross for their salvation. Thus, the NT claims both the universal and the particular in regard to salvation. John E. Toews writes,

> There is universal salvation because Christ defeats the powers of Sin and Death, and there is particular salvation, because salvation is only through Christ. The universal does not deny the particular, but affirms it, and the particular needs the universal to be authentically and divinely

> transformative. God's grace is universal and humans are responsible to respond to that grace. (Toews: 413)

God is Sovereign; God functions out of God's own being and comes to us in grace with the offer of salvation. As free persons, we can and do respond to God either by accepting his work of redemption in Christ Jesus or by turning it aside. We pray for all persons, knowing that God desires for everyone to be saved and to come to the knowledge of the truth. We believe that Christ Jesus gave himself a ransom for all and that all are invited to accept God's gracious offer of salvation.

Women in the Church

The closest parallel to 1 Timothy 2:9-15 is 1 Corinthians 14:34-35. Whereas 1 Timothy 2:11-12 speaks about "quietness" (*hēsychia*), 1 Corinthians 14:34 speaks about "silence" (*sigaō*). Paul wrote the Corinthian passage to a church that utilized women's gifts in praying and prophecy (1 Cor 11:2-16). Paul wrote 1 Timothy 2:9-15 in a context where some Christian women were given special roles in the church (1 Tim 3:11; 5:9; 2 Tim 1:5; Titus 2:3-5). But in 1 Timothy we see more warning against women going astray through unhealthy teaching than we do in 1 Corinthians. Both passages rest on Jewish teaching regarding the order of creation. Both passages must be interpreted in their sociocultural context. Jewish women were generally unlearned. Philo held that women were easily deceived (Collins: 71). Without the opportunity to study Scripture, women in many parts of the first-century church were not qualified to teach. Newly liberated women were causing major social and domestic problems in the Roman Empire. In some settings they were bringing disrepute upon the church (Winter 2003: 77-122). Paul desired orderly worship in the midst of freedom in Jesus Christ, which was a different kind of freedom. Thus, Paul's teaching on "silence" in 1 Corinthians 14:34-35 and "quietness" in 1 Timothy 2:11-12 should be understood within its respective historical contexts rather than as a general rule for all the churches throughout time.

Paul makes use of an interpretation of Genesis 2:18-25, emphasizing that Eve was created after Adam. Paul K. Jewett notes that all of the Pauline texts supporting female subordination appeal to the second creation narrative, which, in the thought of Paul's day, served as the basis for the doctrine of subordination and for placing restrictions on women (Jewett: 119). However, this is a misguided interpretation of Genesis in terms of meaning and importance. Adam and Eve were equals in creation. Both were created in the image of God (Gen 1:27), and Eve was a suitable helper as Adam's partner, not as an inferior (2:18). In Genesis 1:26-27 we learn that God created Adam and Eve in the image of God and created *them* male and female, indicating equality of role. In 1 Corinthians 11:11-12, Paul states that both order in creation and order in birth need to be taken into account when considering male and female roles in the church. In creation, man is first, and woman comes from man; in birth, woman is first, and man comes from woman. Neither is independent of the other. In the OT, such women as Miriam, Deborah, Huldah, and Esther led God's people.

Jesus honored women and included them in his ministry. Five women are listed in his messianic pedigree (Matt 1:3-16). Jesus conversed with the Samaritan woman when it was not socially acceptable (John 4:1-42). In contrast to traditional teaching that favored men in marriage, Jesus' ministry is consistent with women and men serving as equal partners in the marriage covenant (cf. Mark 10:2-9, 42-45;). He ministered to women and healed them (Matt 15:28; Luke 7:36-50; 8:40-42), used female terms to describe himself (Matt 23:37; Luke 13:34), and taught women (Luke 10:38-42). Women honored Jesus by anointing him before the crucifixion (John 12:3-8), being present at the crucifixion (Matt 27:55-56; Mark 15:40-41; Luke 23:48-49; John 19:25), and staying at the crucifixion when others left (Luke 23:48-49). Women were the last persons to leave the cross and the first persons to bear witness of the resurrected Lord. One cannot push the fact that Jesus chose twelve men as disciples too far because women also followed him, provided the financial resources needed for his ministry (Luke 8:1-3), and bore witness to the resurrection.

In the book of Acts, Luke gives special attention to Christian women, including husband-wife teaching teams, women teachers, women prophets, and women deacons. The church in Philippi met in Lydia's home (16:40). As Witherington says, Luke "takes care to reveal to his audience that where the Gospel went, women, often prominent, were some of the first, foremost, and most faithful converts to the Christian faith, and that their conversion led to their assuming new roles in the service of the Gospel" (Witherington 1988: 157).

Basic NT teaching on women in the church is found in Galatians 3:27-28. As F. F. Bruce writes, "Paul states the basic principle here; if restrictions on it are found elsewhere in the Pauline corpus, as in 1 Cor 14:34f. . . . or 1 Tim 2:11f., they are to be understood in relation to Gal 3:28, and not vice versa" (Bruce: 190). The old orders in creation and especially in the fall are replaced with a new order of redemption in Christ. This new order of redemption does not mean that a man becomes a woman, or a woman becomes a man, or that gender is eliminated. Instead, the order of redemption changes the way men and women relate to each other, just as it changed the way Jews and Gentiles related to each other. The Jerusalem Council clarified that a Gentile does not need to become a Jew in order to be saved. In like manner, Paul openly declares that a woman does not need to become a man in order to be included in the new covenant. And it logically follows that if a Gentile Christian can be a leader in the Christian church without becoming a Jew by way of circumcision, so also a woman can become a leader in the Christian church without becoming a man by way of surgery. This is the essence of the gospel!

Moreover, Paul speaks freely of women's involvement in the church. Women as well as men exercised the gifts of prophecy and teaching (1 Cor 11:4-5; 12:29; 14:26; Eph 4:11; Col 3:16). We know over fifty men by name in Paul's writings. And we know many women by name in these same Pauline writings. Of the twenty-six Christians named in Romans 16, seven are women to whom Paul gives some title or compliment. In fact, one woman named Junia is identified as an apostle (16:7). What is surprising, given the first-century culture, is that Paul mentions thirteen women as co-workers:

Apphia, Philem 2
Chloe, 1 Cor 1:11
Euodia, Phil 4:2
Syntyche, Phil 4:2
Nympha, Col 4:15
Lydia, Acts 16:13-15
Phoebe, Rom 16:1
Priscilla, Rom 16:3
Junia, Rom 16:7
Tryphaena, Rom 16:12
Tryphosa, Rom 16:12
Persis, Rom 16:12
Mary, Rom 16:6

Four of these women led house churches (Lydia, Chloe, Nympha, and Apphia). Four "worked hard [*kopiaō*] in the Lord" (Rom 16:6, 12). These four are Mary, Trophaena, Tryphosa, and Persis. The phrase "worked hard in the Lord" refers to Paul's apostolic ministry and work of leaders in the churches in his day. He specifically calls Priscilla/Prisca, Euodia, and Syntyche co-workers. He calls Phoebe a *diakonos,* which means "minister" as well as "deacon." It is the normal NT Greek word used when referring to a minister of the gospel. And he calls Junia an apostle (Rom 16:7). There is no evidence of any man with this name in all of ancient literature. This name was not changed from a female name to a male name until the thirteenth century AD by Giles of Rome (1247-1316). Junia was a female apostle.

In addition to these women in Paul's epistles, we discover the following in the book of Acts: women prophesy at Pentecost (2:16-18), Sapphira is as culpable as Ananias (5:11), women as well as men are martyred (9:1-2), Dorcas has a significant role in the church and is specifically called a "disciple" (9:36-43), the disciples meet in Mary's home (12:12), women of standing apparently become Christians (17:4, 11-12, 34; cf. also 13:50), and four daughters of Philip prophesy (21:9).

Interpreting 1 Timothy 2:9-15 within the larger biblical context leads to the conclusion that Paul is dealing with a local situation in the church at Ephesus. First Timothy 2:9-15 is not a universal prohibition against women teaching men, nor is it a reason to exclude women from pastoral ministry. Instead, it is a limited and particular restriction on the guidelines for women's involvement in the church of Jesus Christ, guidelines found elsewhere in the NT. Paul does not want the gospel hindered or the church brought into disrepute by unacceptable behavior on the part of some women who follow deviant teaching or are not socially acceptable in the Greco-Roman setting at Ephesus. Read this way, 1 Timothy 2:9-15 is not normative for the church today in any direct, straightforward way. Apparently the second-century church did not understand it as a timeless prohibition of women's ministry, since Pliny's letter to the Roman Emperor Trajan in AD 112 refers to "two slave-women who are ministers" in his report about Christians in the province of Bithynia.

THE TEXT IN THE LIFE OF THE CHURCH

Freedom of the Will

On April 1, 1527, Balthasar Hubmaier wrote a treatise on the *Freedom of the Will* to Count George of Bradenburg-Ansbach, a follower of Luther. On May 20, 1527, Hubmaier wrote a second treatise on the same subject to Duke Frederick II, stating Anabaptist ideas on human freedom (Pipkin and Yoder: 426-91). Hubmaier's writings became foundational in distinguishing Anabaptism from Catholic, Lutheran, and Reformed views on original sin and the freedom of the will in responding to God's grace and salvation. In the second treatise, Hubmaier identifies 1 Timothy 2:4 as the revealed will of God.

In the early 1600s, Jacob Arminius turned away from aspects of Calvinistic theology and emphasized human freedom. Between the times of Hubmaier and Arminius, the brilliant Geneva theologian John Calvin went beyond Augustine in explaining his views on predestination, election, and salvation. Followers of Arminius, preferring the name Remonstrants, promoted human freedom.

Arminianism differs from the historic five points of Calvinism: total depravity, unconditional election, limited atonement, irresistible grace, and the perseverance of the saints (or eternal security). Arminius taught that inherited human depravity leaves the will free and humans responsible for their own destiny through the human choice of faith or unbelief. Calvin taught that the human person is fully depraved by Adam's sin and therefore does not have the freedom of choice. Arminius said that predestination is conditional, based on God's foreknowledge, and not upon an arbitrary decree. Calvin taught unconditional election—that it is entirely of God. He even held to double election: some are predestined to salvation and some are predestined to damnation. Arminius said that Christ's work of redemption is for all, not just the elect, even though not all people accept redemption in Christ and therefore fail to lay hold of the benefits of the cross. Calvin said that Jesus died only for the elect, not for everyone. Therefore the atonement is limited. Arminius said that grace can be rejected by humans in their exercise of free will. Thus it is possible that one may become a Christian and later turn away from Christ and thereby reject God's grace and goodness. Calvin said that grace is irresistible. And once one is saved in Christ, one can never again become lost. Arminius emphasized the keeping power of Christ. He did not deny the omnipotent power of God, but he did not go so far as to make God the author of sin and of the eternal damnation of humans. Instead, he emphasized the importance of the response of faith as the basis for the operation of God's grace in one's life. Calvin held to the perseverance of the saints: a person once saved can never go astray because one is eternally secure. Arminianism and Calvinism have had a significant influence on Western theology for four hundred years, and they continue to be debated.

Historically, the believers churches have never accepted Calvinism nor have their confessions of faith promulgated the five points of Calvinism. Sixteenth-century Anabaptism predated the Calvinist-Arminian controversy. These early Anabaptists were influenced by Erasmian humanism, which emphasized human freedom and responsibility within the context of God's sovereignty and salvation by grace. This view took human depravity and the primacy of divine grace seriously without denying the freedom of the will.

Anabaptists resisted Augustine's attempt to ascribe all choice to God and little to humankind. They believed that Augustine's view sanctioned the status quo and tended to equate Christianity with it.

The Anabaptists called for a radical change in behavior, which assumed some capacity for what people experience as genuine choice (Finger 2004: 511). God first moves toward humans in grace, which makes possible a human response of faith in Christ. In this, God is consistent with Godself. God is a God of love, who does not violate human freedom to say yes or no to grace. God respects human freedom so that all who respond in faith enter into covenant relationship with God, based on love and commitment both from God's side and the human side. "We love because [God] first loved us" (1 John 4:19). Because God desires that everyone be saved and Christ gave himself a ransom for all (1 Tim 2:4, 6), human beings are invited to respond positively to God's grace and salvation. This is the good news of the gospel.

1 Timothy 3:1-16

Character Traits for Leaders in the Household of God

PREVIEW

In light of God's desire to save all and the importance of behavior in the church, Paul turns to address leaders for the church. Of all the desired qualities one looks for in a leader, character ethics are of utmost importance. This section begins by outlining the moral character of bishops (3:1-7), then moves on to the moral character of deacons (3:8-13).

Paul states the purpose of the letter in 3:15, which indicates why the moral character of leaders is important. The section concludes with a hymnlike confessional statement (3:16).

OUTLINE

The Moral Character of Bishops, 3:1-7
The Moral Character of Deacons, 3:8-13
The Purpose of the Letter, 3:14-15
Confessional Statement, 3:16

EXPLANATORY NOTES

The Moral Character of Bishops 3:1-7

The saying is sure (3:1a): of the five "faithful sayings" in the letters to Timothy and Titus, this one is the most debated *[Faithful Sayings, p. 344]*. Much of the debate centers on whether the "faithful saying" precedes (in 2:15) or follows (in 3:1b) the declaration in 3:1a. The NEB follows a textual variant in a few Western sources and translates the phrase as "This is a popular saying." But this is unlikely (Metzger 1994: 573) and could reflect a scribe's frustration about whether the saying refers to what precedes or what follows.

Most faithful sayings relate to salvation. For this reason, some NT scholars, including editors of the UBS*GNT* (4th ed.) and the NA (27th ed.) texts, apply the saying to 1 Timothy 2:15, which speaks of salvation. This interpretation is unlikely since 2:15 does not have the characteristics of a saying and 3:1 does, despite its noncreedal content (Fee 1988: 79). One can argue that 1 Timothy 2:1-15 has an underlying salvation theme. But from a literary viewpoint, the faithful sayings normally arise around a "quotation-commendation formula," which is not present in 1 Timothy 2:15 (Knight 1979: 4-22).

R. A. Campbell argues that the faithful sayings have four elements: introductory formula, parenthetical reinforcement, the saying, and further qualification (1994b: 77-80). On this basis, Campbell argues that the faithful saying in 1 Timothy 3:1 is misplaced and should be applied to the confessional statement in 1 Timothy 3:16 (Campbell 1994b: 80-84). Though attractive, Campbell's solution is questionable since there is no manuscript evidence for it. Though arguments for applying the faithful saying to what precedes or what follows 3:1a are almost evenly balanced, I think it most likely that the *faithful saying* is what follows in 3:1b.

The *faithful saying* formula calls attention to the credibility of the gospel and the credibility of the person who proclaims that gospel. A church leader's credibility is tied directly to the trustworthiness of the gospel and vice versa. This combination calls for a *faithful saying*. Credibility enhances the leader's authority. Church leaders stand for a credible cause or message: the gospel. But a credible cause by itself is not enough. The church leader needs a credible character or personality consistent with the gospel. Thus 1 Timothy 3:1-7 is about the leader's character virtues rather than leadership tasks. However, a bishop's work in itself is a *noble task* (3:1). "The position of overseer is such a significant matter, a noble task, that it should indeed be the kind of task to which a person might aspire" (Fee 1988: 79).

The bishop office developed rather late in the NT. The term *bishop/*

overseer (*episkopos*) occurs several times in the LXX in reference to the Levites and their care of the place of worship (Num 4:16; 2 Chron 34:12, 17; 2 Esd 21 [Neh 11]: 9, 14, 22). Leadership in the early church followed the synagogue model, which had elders. As need arose, deacons were added to the synagogue model of leadership. In Acts 20:28 some of the elders in the Ephesian church are called "bishops/overseers" (*episkopoi*), and in Philippians 1:1-2 both "bishops and deacons" are named. Bishops did administrative or supervisory work, while deacons did service ministries. In the Hellenistic world, the term *bishop* was used to describe those who held various official positions in respect to their office and work (*TDNT* 2:611). An *episkopos* is a supervisor, superintendent, and overseer (Johnson 2001: 212). In 1 Peter 2:25 Christ is called "bishop/guardian/overseer." However, the term is never applied to traveling ministries in the NT church, such as apostles, prophets, and teachers (*TDNT* 2:615). In Titus 1:5-7 Paul talks about the qualities desired for *elders* (*presbyteroi*), in the plural, and then calls attention to *a bishop* (*episkopos*) in the singular. In the letters to Timothy and Titus, the term *bishop* is always used in the singular, and the term *elder* almost always appears in the plural.

What is the relationship between a bishop and elders? One view is that the terms are interchangeable, since the term *elder* is derived from the Jewish synagogue and the term *bishop* is derived from Hellenistic circles. With different shades of meaning, the bishop was considered to be the leader of the circle of elders, the first among equals (Bartlett: 168). Another view is that elders gave attention to teaching while the bishop gave attention to supervision and management. We are talking about a time in the development of the church before the rise of the monarchical bishop. The gradual transition from charismatic leaders to more formal church offices eventually led to the monarchical bishop. As house churches emerged in Roman cities, elders provided for each individual house church's teaching. One highly respected elder who was exemplary in managing the household was chosen to supervise, oversee, and teach in several house churches, each with their respective elders. The distinction in tasks is significant, since Paul calls the bishopric "a noble task."

Paul lays out a catalog of fifteen virtues desired in a bishop. Character determines a bishop's effectiveness in Christian ministry and has a direct bearing on the integrity of the gospel in the Greco-Roman world. The catalog begins with *above reproach* (3:2). This is a far-reaching overall virtue that covers the whole list in a general way. This virtue applies also to widows (5:7) and to Timothy himself (6:14 GNT). It means irreproachable in observable conduct (Fee 1988:

80). The bishop is to be blameless. As J. N. D. Kelly says, "He should present no obvious defect of character or conduct, in his past or present life, which the malicious, whether within or without the church, can exploit to his discredit" (75).

A bishop is to be *the husband of but one wife* (NIV). Not only the bishop, but also the deacon (3:12), the elder (Titus 1:6), and the enrolled widow (1 Tim 5:9) are given similar instruction regarding marriage. What does this restriction mean? Several options are possible:

1. It could mean that the bishop must be a married person.
2. It could mean that although other men in the Ephesian church were allowed to practice polygamy, a bishop could not.
3. It could mean that the bishop must have one wife at a time, but if divorce shatters the marriage, he must choose another wife.
4. It could mean that divorce and remarriage are prohibited for the bishop.
5. It could mean that if the bishop's wife dies, he is prohibited from marrying a second time.

This last option ties into the marital restriction on widows in 1 Timothy 5:9, in contrast to the younger widows, who were encouraged to marry. Read in its historical context, the first option is unlikely because the letters to Timothy and Titus presuppose that the male church leader is already married. Given the low state of family morality in the first-century world, the second and third options are unlikely. One could interpret the phrase to mean that if the church leader is divorced, he should not remarry. In its historical setting, "husband of one wife" perhaps meant that in the event of the spouse's death, the bishop should not remarry. Certainly it calls for integrity and fidelity to the marriage covenant. And fidelity to one's spouse is an important ingredient of the leader's credibility. Infidelity to the covenant commitment to one's spouse in marriage often destroys the fabric of trust that is essential for effective and credible church leadership (Johnson 2001: 224).

Temperate or *sober* means to be clearheaded, to control one's appetites and passions. In the metaphorical sense, it refers to sound judgment. This virtue also applies to women (1 Tim 3:11) and to older men (Titus 2:2). The term may relate to the prohibition on drunkenness that follows in 1 Timothy 3:3. However, it is used to describe Timothy's freedom from every form of excess and uncontrolled passion in 2 Timothy 4:5. Controlling one's personality in an upright manner through disciplined living enhances the bishop's effectiveness among the people.

Sensible or *self-control* calls attention to one's inner character, while *respectable* speaks of one's external deportment. The overseer is to be well-mannered and orderly. His appearance and projection of the self in a well-mannered and orderly way prevents distraction from the bishop's work and message. Hospitality was an important virtue in the first-century church since the overseer provided meals and lodging for many traveling missionaries, for persons who carried messages from church to church, and for the needs of members of the congregation.

An apt teacher refers not so much to a character trait as to a desired skill. While the earlier charismatic period of the church included teachers who traveled from church to church (1 Cor 12:28-29), the overseer was now taking responsibility for teaching in the congregation (1 Tim 5:17; 2 Tim 2:24; Titus 1:9). A bishop is responsible to correct unhealthy teaching and to instruct Christian believers in the truth of God's word and the gospel.

Not a drunkard (1 Tim 3:3) refers to one of the vices common in antiquity. The overseer need not abstain from wine (5:23). But like the deacon (3:8), the overseer must control his appetite so that drunkenness does not overtake him (Titus 1:7; cf. Eph 5:18).

The next three virtues call attention to the overseer's attitude: *not violent, but gentle, not quarrelsome*. The Greek means not a giver of blows. Unhealthy teachers were characterized by strife and quarrels (1 Tim 6:3-5; 2 Tim 2:23-26; Titus 3:9). Insecurity increases the possibility of falling into the snare of arguing and lashing out at others. An overseer is an emotionally healthy person, with confidence in the gospel message and in himself. An impatient overseer can easily hand out rough treatment to immature members of the church. *Not a lover of money* characterizes the overseer in contrast to the teachers who use religion as a means of financial gain (1 Tim 6:5-10). Teachers in antiquity often faced the money temptation (Johnson 2001: 215). Greed dare not characterize any Christian, much less the overseer who, as head of the household, handles the church's finances (Titus 1:7). Using religion for financial gain was severely condemned in the early church (Acts 8:14-24) and is a vice that church leaders must carefully avoid today. Church leaders do well to pray regularly, "Remove far from me falsehood and lying; give me neither poverty nor riches; feed me with the food that I need, or I shall be full, and deny you, and say, 'Who is the Lord?' or I shall be poor, and steal, and profane the name of my God" (Prov 30:8-9).

In 1 Timothy 3:4-5, Paul instructs Timothy on household management. In the first century the paterfamilias was the head of the household. Other household members, including children, were submissive to the head of the household. This patriarchal family structure created problems in the church when a wife and/or slaves became Christians and the head of the household did not. In some cases the whole household (father, mother, and slaves) became Christians (Acts 16:25-34). Often when the father became a Christian, others likewise became Christians and a house church began. Church buildings arose centuries later. An overseer was normally chosen from one or more house church groups. The ability to manage one's own household well was positive evidence that the one chosen as overseer could manage the church as the household of God (1 Tim 3:15; Titus 1:7). One incapable of managing his own household is likewise incapable of managing the church, as the implied negative answer to the question indicates *[Household Behavior, p. 355]*.

Moving beyond household management, the overseer *must not be a recent convert* (1 Tim 3:6). He cannot be a neophyte, a recent seedling newly planted in the Christian community (Collins: 84). Instead, maturity in the faith is required (5:22). Choosing a newly converted person as an overseer places a person in a role for which he is not ready. The neophyte's head can swell and become *puffed up with conceit* (lit., *filled with smoke*) without the benefit of a mature mind and judgment, plunging the recent convert into the same condemnation as the devil.

Finally, the virtues are brought to a close with an emphasis on the overseer's reputation in the larger (non-Christian) community. *He must be well thought of by outsiders* (3:7). Persons outside judge the church by the character and conduct of its leaders. Unethical and unwise conduct can easily disgrace a church leader and become a *snare of the devil*, who seeks to slander the church. To prevent slander from the non-Christian community, the church must choose an overseer with a good reputation in the community at large. These virtues end on a note in verse 7 much as they began in verse 2. A bishop who is above reproach with persons outside the church aids the church in its mission of promoting God's salvation in the world.

The Moral Character of Deacons 3:8-13

With the word *likewise*, the writer turns to another group of leaders in the church: deacons. The plural noun *deacons* comes from a general term meaning one who waits at a table or serves. The term is applied to Jesus as servant (Mark 10:45) and to various kinds of Christian workers. It is used for a special group of leaders in Philippians 1:1. In the letters to Timothy and Titus, the Greek root behind *deacon* is used both as a noun and as a verb, referring to Christian servants and to ministry in the sense of service (1 Tim 1:12; 3:8, 10, 12-13; 4:6; 2 Tim 1:18; 4:5, 11). Timothy is a servant of Jesus Christ (1 Tim 4:6), but here in 1 Timothy 3:8, 12, the term refers to people with a special role in the church alongside overseers. In Acts 6:1-6, persons were chosen for a special work different from that of the apostles: serving the needs of the Hellenistic widows. In the early church, the term *deacon* was used first as a function, then gradually as a position, and eventually as an office. Sometime after the letters to Timothy and Titus the deacon function and position developed into a full office in the church, as we discover in the second century.

Paul does not emphasize the duties of deacons, but like bishops, speaks of their *character* (1 Tim 3:8-10). The desired character traits of deacons are similar to those of overseers, as listed earlier in the chapter. Though a bishop must possess the ability to teach (v. 2a), deacons are not given this requirement. Instead, the deacon is to hold fast to the deep truths of the Christian gospel (v. 9) and *first be tested* (v. 10a) before being chosen for this task.

The list of desired qualities begins with the qualifier *serious*. Similar to the overseer who is above reproach (v. 2), deacons need inward character, a dignified and serious manner of life that outwardly engenders respect from others. This virtue is followed by three prohibitions. First, *not double-tongued* means deacons must not be duplicitous. They are not double talkers who say one thing while thinking another or who say one thing to one person and something different to the next (Kelly: 81). As go-between persons in the Christian community, deacons dare not yield to the vice of duplicity, which destroys the trust people give them to carry out their service. Second, *not indulging in much wine* speaks against the excessive use of wine, which leads to drunkenness and disqualifies one from this work. Paul applies this prohibition to other church leaders as well, such as bishops and women deacons. Third, deacons are *not greedy for money*. Again, this prohibition is similar to one applied to the bishop (1 Tim 3:3; Titus 1:7), in contrast to the teachers who were greedy for gain (1 Tim 6:5-10; Titus 1:10-11). This prohibition underscores the need for faithfulness and honesty in handling the church's financial matters (I. H. Marshall 1999: 490).

In 1 Timothy 3:9, Paul states a positive trait desired of deacons:

Hold fast to the mystery of the faith with a clear conscience. The mystery of the faith refers to the totality of truth given by divine revelation: the gospel of Jesus Christ. Deacons hold fast to the faith with a conscience purified by God. They hold the faith in full transparent honesty and integrity. To assure the church of this ability, deacons are *first to be tested.* The use of the imperative both in holding fast and in being tested indicates the importance of the deacon's integrity. The term *tested* means to be scrutinized, much as the Athenian court screened candidates for public office (Collins: 89). Through a testing and screening process, persons who are blameless or have *nothing against them* (NIV) can be chosen as a deacon.

The term *likewise* in verse 11, as in verse 8, marks the introduction of another group of persons in the church. Some hold that verse 11 refers to the wife of a deacon, while others think Paul is speaking of women deacons. I agree with the latter view, which is consistent with Paul's argument in 1 Timothy 5:9, 11-12. The Eastern church ordained women as deacons (Madigan and Osiek: 2005). Titus 2:3 implies that older women were given a special teaching role in the church. Although 1 Timothy 3:12 says male deacons should have one wife, nothing is said in 3:11 that these females are their wives. Furthermore, it would be unusual for Paul to speak of the qualities of deacons' wives when he is completely silent about the qualities of bishops' wives. Finally, Phoebe is called a deacon by Paul in Romans 16:1, and Pliny the Younger, who investigated Christians for the Roman emperor, wrote about two Christian slave women in AD 112, whom the Christians called deacons or ministers.

Like male deacons, female deacons are to be dignified and serious. Female deacons are not to be slanderous or double-tongued. They are to be *temperate*, applying moderation in the use of alcoholic beverages (Titus 2:3), as with male deacons and overseers (1 Tim 3:3, 8). Finally, female deacons are to be *faithful in all things.* They are to be trustworthy and loyal in character and in faithfulness to the gospel. These qualities stand in stark contrast to unfaithful women in 1 Timothy 5:11-15 and 2 Timothy 3:6, who give in to unhealthy teachers in the Ephesian church.

In verse 12 Paul returns to male deacons and adds two more qualities. Like overseers, male deacons are to be *married only once,* the husband of one wife. For a fuller discussion of the meaning of this phrase, see the comments on 3:2, above. A man who is faithful in marriage is more likely to attain and inspire trust within the church (Johnson 2001: 229). Again, like the overseer, deacons are to *manage their children and their households well.* Good household management was a virtue in the Greco-Roman world. This virtue is now applied to the church as the household of God (3:15). If indeed the household is the church, or a microcosm of the church, evidence that one can manage the church well can be found in how one manages one's household. In short, the qualities necessary for service in the church will be evident in the home (Mounce: 205).

Paul concludes this section on deacons by giving two positive comments regarding those who serve well. First, they *gain a good standing for themselves.* Paul places personal responsibility upon the deacon to serve well. In doing so, one's earned authority increases one's influence and reputation in the believing community. Second, they gain *great boldness in the faith that is in Christ Jesus.* Faithful service always builds one's confidence in God and in the assurance of salvation in Christ Jesus. It works both ways. Faithful service increases one's confidence in one's own identity and ability to serve in the eyes of the Christian community. At the same time it increases one's confidence in Christ Jesus.

The Purpose of the Letter 3:14-15

Having laid down behavioral qualities of men, women, bishops, and deacons in the church, Paul now arrives at a summary of his purpose for writing this letter to Timothy. First Timothy 3:14-15 builds a bridge between the first part of the epistle, with its emphasis on prayer and ministry, and the second part, with its practical dimensions. It also provides the theological basis for the second part of the epistle, with its rules and regulations. And it counteracts the unhealthy teaching that threatens the church.

Paul writes so that, if he should be delayed in visiting Timothy at Ephesus, Timothy might know *how one ought to behave in the household of God.* Paul wants to visit Timothy and the church at Ephesus in order to clarify right belief and behavior. Such clarification is necessary due to the rise of teaching and conduct that has betrayed the truth. The church's carelessness in upholding the truth has called for Paul's immediate response. If he is delayed in coming, the letter will help the church to correct the unhealthy teaching immediately.

Paul describes the church in two word pictures that were vivid in the minds of the Ephesians: temple and family household. "With these two images, family and temple, Paul expresses the two urgencies of this letter: his concern over proper behavior among believers vis-à-vis the deviant teachers, and the church as the people entrusted to uphold and proclaim the truth of the gospel" (Fee 1988: 92). Ephesus was guardian of the great wonder of the ancient world, the temple of Artemis (Diana). It was immense—four times the size of the Parthenon in Athens: 425 feet long, 220 feet wide, and 60 feet high. It had 127 pillars, of which thirty-six were overlaid with gold, jewels, and intricate carving. The household, consisting of parents, children, slaves, and the extended family, was the basic social unit in Greco-Roman society.

Paul uses word pictures to describe *the household of God, which is the church of the living God, the pillar and bulwark of the truth.* By using a term familiar with daily living in households, Paul leads the hearers of this letter to better theological understanding of the church as God's house *[Ecclesiology, p. 340]*. Elsewhere, Paul describes the church as the house of God (Eph 2:19-22) and temple of God (1 Cor 3:16-17; 2 Cor 6:19; Eph 2:21). Just as God dwelt among the people in the ancient tabernacle (Exod 25:22), in the temple (1 Kings 8:10-11; 2 Chron 5:13-14), and in Jesus Christ (John 1:14), so now the church is the house of the living God, where God dwells in splendor and holiness. In contrast to the image of Artemis in the pagan temple, the living God dwells in the church. Believers belong to the church of the living God, in contrast to those who identify with the lifeless image of Artemis. The church as household is the pillar and bulwark of the truth. The Greek term for *pillar* refers to something that provides support. The term *bulwark* means *foundation* (NIV). Together these terms call attention to truth as the foundation and support of the church as the temple of the living God. "If the church is founded on truth, the manner of life of its leaders and other members must be appropriate; equally, if the church upholds the truth, it cannot do so if it is not in sound condition" (I. H. Marshall 1999: 498).

If Ephesians shouted, "Great is Artemis of the Ephesians" (Acts 19:28, 34), Paul is here heralding a new shout that repudiates the pagan claim: *The mystery of our religion is great.* There is no denying it: the truth is beyond controversy, as the Greek term *homologoumenōs* implies. This term is translated *without any doubt* (NRSV), *great beyond all question* (REB), and *beyond all question* (TNIV). By *mystery*, Paul means that the redemptive plan of God, which has been secret, is now fully revealed in Jesus Christ (Eph 3:5-6). This *mystery of our religion* is nothing short of the living person, Jesus Christ. This mystery of religion, Jesus Christ, is worth shouting about because it is a revelation of a living person whom one can experience in a personal way, in contrast to the Greek understandings of gods and of Artemis. This greatness of the Christian religion is declared in a hymnlike confessional statement (3:16).

Confessional Statement 3:16

Paul adds a hymn to the summary of verse 15 that states the confessed faith of the early Christians. In literary terms, it is a series of six short lines, each of which begins with a third-person singular verb with similar-sounding endings. Each verb is followed by a prepositional phrase introduced by "in" and a noun (except for the third line, which omits the preposition). This is a hymn about Christ. In the preferred reading, the opening word "who" (*hos*) refers to Christ rather than God. The term *God* does not appear in an uncial manuscript before the eighth or ninth century (Metzger 1994: 573-74). The hymn begins with a relative pronoun, as do the christological hymns in Philippians 2:6-11 and Colossians 1:15-20.

How is the hymn arranged? Several options are possible. First, the hymn may proceed chronologically, with the six lines following the story of the Christ's incarnation, ministry, and exaltation. Second, the hymn may have three couplets of two lines each. In this arrangement, one line speaks of the earthly reality and the second line speaks of a heavenly reality in an A-B, B-A, A-B pattern. George W. Knight III suggests that the first section presents Christ's work accomplished, the second his work made known, and the third his work acknowledged (Knight 1992: 183).

1A (Earth) manifested in the flesh
1B (Heaven) vindicated in spirit
  2B (Heaven) seen by angels
  2A (Earth) proclaimed among the nations
    3A (Earth) believed on in the world
    3B (Heaven) taken up in glory

Third, the hymn may be a chiasm: A, B, C, C′ B′ A′ *[Chiasm, p. 334]*. In such an arrangement, the "A" sections provide chronological bookends for Jesus' ministry, contrasting flesh and glory. The "B" sections contrast the spirit world with the human world. And the "C" sections contrast the invisible witnesses to the incarnation and glorification with visible witnesses (Mounce: 217).

A was revealed in flesh
  B was vindicated in spirit
    C was seen by angels
    C′ was preached among the nations
  B′ was believed in the world
A′ was taken up in glory

A fourth and perhaps better arrangement is to view the hymn as having two stanzas of three lines each (as in NRSV). The first stanza speaks of Christ's earthly ministry, concluding with a word of triumph and glorification. The second stanza speaks of the ongoing ministry of Christ through the church. In this arrangement the lines are in parallel arrangement: lines 1 and 4, lines 2 and 5, and lines 3 and 6. Christ appeared in the flesh and is preached to the nations (lines 1 and 4). Christ was vindicated in the spirit and is therefore the object of faith (lines 2 and 5). His vindication was witnessed by angels, and as a result of people's belief, Christ is glorified throughout the world (lines 3 and 6). This two-stanza arrangement fits well the broader context of the epistle, since the first stanza describes the mighty works of Christ: incarnation, resurrection, and ascension. The second stanza shows the church's response to Christ through the preaching of the gospel so that people can come to faith and thus give glory to Christ. We may diagram this arrangement as follows (cf. NRSV):

[Jesus] Who	
1A was revealed in flesh,	(incarnation)
1B was vindicated in spirit,	(baptism)
1C was seen by angels,	(victorious ascent)
2A was proclaimed among Gentiles,	(early preaching)
2B was believed in the world,	(ensuing faith)
2C was taken up in glory.	(present reign, enthronement)

We now examine each line of this wonderful Christ hymn. *He was revealed in flesh* is an affirmation of the incarnation (John 1:14; Rom 1:3; Phil 2:7-8). It focuses attention on Jesus' work in salvation history *[Christology, p. 335]*. Jesus was a real man (1 Pet 3:18). As used in this verse, *flesh* refers to ordinary human existence. As a complement to the flesh, *vindicated in spirit* may point to the divine and human elements of Jesus. More likely the phrase refers to God's vindication of Jesus' life and death by raising him from the dead (Rom 1:4). Christ's resurrection was God's vindication of Jesus in the presence of the hostile powers that put him to death. And God placed him in a realm where the Holy Spirit is the operative agent. *Seen by angels* may refer to the earthly witnesses of the resurrected Lord, who have proclaimed the message of the resurrection. In this interpretation the word *angelois* simply means messengers. The preferred way of interpreting the phrase places the angels in the heavenly realm, where they worship the glorified Christ (Phil 2:9-11; Col 2:15; Heb 1:6). In this spiritual realm, the heavenly hosts, especially angels, are subject to the resurrected, ascended Lord and worship him.

Proclaimed among the Gentiles refers to the period of time after the resurrection and ascension of Christ, when the early Christians preached Jesus Christ to the known world. Timothy also preaches the good news of Christ (2 Tim 2:1-2; 4:2). *Believed in throughout the world* speaks of the results of the worldwide proclamation of Christ and its universal acceptance. Lines 4 and 5 in this hymn speak of the church's missionary task of proclaiming the saving work of God. *Taken up in glory* calls attention not only to the ascension and the place where Jesus now is, but also the manner of his exaltation. Jesus was taken into the realm of divine glory, and he is in the presence and radiance of God. The risen Christ shares in the glory that belongs to the only God (1 Tim 1:11, 17; 2 Tim 2:10, 4:18; Titus 2:13). The word *glory* in the NT often symbolizes the resurrection of Jesus. Christ dwells in glory as the resurrected and ascended Lord, and this provides eternal evidence of Christ's triumph over the powers of evil.

In summary, 1 Timothy 2:4-6 begins with a confessional statement declaring God's desire to save all people. This saving work of God calls for prayers for all, including government leaders; for Christian deportment in worship by both men and women—conduct that does not turn people away from the gospel; and for choosing persons with integrity to lead the church (3:1-13). Now Paul concludes with a summary statement in 3:15 on the church as the household of God. The section climaxes with a joyful hymnlike confession about the incarnate life, death, resurrection, ascension, and glorification of Jesus Christ, whom the church proclaims to all peoples.

THE TEXT IN BIBLICAL CONTEXT

Leaders for God's People

The stringent qualities for leaders in 1 Timothy 3 call attention to the importance of leadership for God's people. Jesus led as servant and said:

> You know that among the Gentiles those whom they recognize as their rulers lord it over them, and their great ones are tyrants over them. But it is not so among you; but whoever wishes to become great among you must be your servant, and whoever wishes to be first among you must be slave of all. For the Son of Man came not to be served but to serve, and to give his life a ransom for many. (Mark 10:42-45)

Jesus the servant was not passive. Servant leaders lead, but they do not lord it over others. Following the ascension of Christ, the apostles led the church. While Peter and Paul were prominent apostles, they were also subject to other apostles, as seen at the Jerusalem conference (Acts 15:1-29). And Peter was corrected when he made mistakes (Gal 2:11-14).

With the coming of the Holy Spirit, the character of Christ was manifested in the church and in its leaders through the fruit and gifts of the Spirit, which enable the church and its leaders to carry out the mission of Christ (Ellis 1989: 34). In the earliest period of Christianity, leadership and charismatic gifts were closely related. Later, leadership offices began to emerge. By the second century, these offices were fully developed. God's Spirit was poured out on all flesh so that both sons and daughters might actively participate in ministry (Acts 2:17). Paul openly declared that just as one cannot discriminate on the basis of race, neither can one discriminate on the basis of gender in the Christian church (Gal 3:27-28). Thus the early church recognized and accepted women as prophets (1 Cor 11:5), deacons (Rom 16:1), and apostles (16:7). Leaders in God's church, whether male or female, are accountable to each other. Through the Holy Spirit's presence and work in their lives, leaders express the character of Christ and give themselves to the mission of Christ.

As the church expanded through mission, Paul and Barnabas chose elders for each fledgling congregation (Acts 14:23). In his farewell address to the elders of the church of Ephesus (20:17), Paul says, "Keep watch over yourselves and over all the flock, of which the Holy Spirit has made you *overseers*, to shepherd [or pastor] the church of God that he obtained with the blood of his own Son" (20:28). In this chapter the terms *elders* (*presbyteroi*) and overseers or *bishops* (*episkopoi*) are used interchangeably. This interchange in terminology raises several questions: Who are elders and what do they do? Who are overseers and what do they do? What is the relationship between elder and overseer?

Following the Jewish synagogue model and the household model in the Greco-Roman world, the church chose older, mature persons of wisdom as elders for the house churches in the NT. The plural *elders* is a collective term. In Greek literature, bishop (*episkopos*) is a classical term for one who supervises or who has an oversight function (Collins: 328-29; Johnson 2001: 212). In the letters to Timothy and Titus, the term *bishop* always appears in the singular. It is unlikely that *elder* and *bishop* are interchangeable terms, with *elder* coming out of the Jewish synagogue tradition and *bishop* coming out of the Greek world. The terms *elder* and *bishop* could apply to different roles and work in the church and therefore refer to two separate groups of persons. In this view, the bishop was chosen from among the elders.

The bishop or overseer may have provided supervision for several house churches in a given city, while the elders provided leadership for a given house church (Campbell 1994a: 176-209). David L. Bartlett is probably right in suggesting that bishops were a subset of the council of elders—a leader of the circle of elders, first among equals (168).

A transition took place as the number of congregations grew. The oversight role expanded. By the second century, the bishop office was fully developed. In this historical context, the bishop and elders of a given household of God, or a group of households within a given town, received direction from both elders and a bishop. Despite uncertainty about the terminology, the work of the elders and bishop was clear: they taught true faith and rebuked those who went astray (1 Tim 1:3; 3:2; 5:17-20; Titus 1:9). In addition, the bishop had supervisory responsibilities like those of the father of the household (Bartlett: 170). The bishop provided the ministry of oversight.

Deacons served a different role in the church. They are listed in the plural in the letters to Timothy and Titus, as well as in Acts 6:1-6 and Philippians 1:1. The word *deacon* (*diakonos*) means one who serves in a general way and is applied to both male and female persons in the church (Rom 16:1; 1 Tim 3:11). The diaconate was a service ministry in the Christian church. In the letters to Timothy and Titus, Paul emphasizes the spiritual character, the *being* of the deacons, rather than describing their duties (1 Tim 3:8-10, 12-13).

Household of God

In 1 Timothy 3:15 Paul uses household imagery to describe the church. Within the larger biblical context, one finds reasons for this historical and theological understanding of church.

House-of-God imagery is found in the OT. Jacob dreamed that the living God of Abraham and Isaac stood beside him, affirming the covenant promise. When Jacob awoke, he said, "Surely the LORD is in this place—and I did not know it! . . . How awesome is this place! This is none other than the house of God, and this is the gate of heaven" (Gen 28:16-17). The phrase "house of God" suggests the immanence of God: God lives within and can be experienced in the domestic language of house.

One term for tabernacle, *mishkan*, means dwelling and indicates God's desire to be near the people. At the ancient tabernacle, Israel experienced the living God, who maintained both awesome holiness in transcendence and grace-filled immanence. The term *mishkan* fittingly describes God's dwelling in the midst of the people as the way God revealed Godself, how the people perceived who God is, and how the children of Israel worshiped God in this ancient structure. When Israelite families brought their firstfruits offering to the Lord, they brought it into the house of the Lord their God (Exod 23:19; 34:26). Under King Solomon, the temple was constructed (1 Kings 6:14), and some of the articles of furniture from the ancient tabernacle, including the ark of the covenant, were placed inside the new temple. This new structure was dedicated to the Lord (1 Kings 8:1-66). Raymond F. Collins says, "The motifs of assembly and dwelling place come together in the biblical notion of the 'house of God.' There God dwells; there God's people come together to meet God" (102).

After the temple was destroyed, the children of Israel struggled with the meaning of the absence of God's house. The prophet Ezekiel wrote about a vision of a new temple (Ezek 40:1–48:35). Upon their return from exile, the children of Israel rebuilt the wall of Jerusalem and a smaller temple, which eventually was also destroyed. During the intertestamental period, the Jews dispersed throughout the Mediterranean world and began synagogues as places of worship. Finally, King Herod and his successors rebuilt and expanded the temple between 19 BC and AD 66. Herod's temple became the center of Jewish activity during the first century and was known as the house of God. It was destroyed by the Roman army in AD 70.

Jesus began his public ministry in the synagogue in Nazareth (Luke 4:16-21). Much of Jesus' conflict with the Jewish hierarchy took place in the temple area of Jerusalem. With indignation Jesus said, "Stop making my Father's house a marketplace!" (John 2:16b). Moreover, the early Jesus movement maintained that the dwelling of God was not in Herod's temple, but instead was in Jesus. John wrote, "The Word became flesh and made his *dwelling* among us. We have seen his glory, the glory as of the one and only Son, who came from the Father, full of grace and truth" (John 1:14 TNIV, with stress added).

Following the resurrection and ascension of Jesus Christ, the early disciples gathered in an upper room in Jerusalem and experienced the coming of the Holy Spirit on the day of Pentecost. In response to Peter's sermon, about three thousand persons became believers in Jesus. They met daily in the temple (Acts 2:46a) but broke bread in houses (2:46b). Using the building metaphor, Paul told the Corinthian Christians that they were "God's building" (1 Cor 3:9b) and "God's temple," since the Holy Spirit dwells in them (1 Cor 3:16). Paul described the church as the body of Christ and as the household of God. Peter likewise called the church "the household of God" (1 Pet 2:5; 4:17).

Whenever Paul and Barnabas entered a new city, they went to the synagogue first. If rejected in the synagogue, Paul went to a house in the area and proclaimed the word of God (Acts 16:40; 18:7-8). As a result, many house churches arose from the early missionary expansion of the church. Paul often referred to "the church in your house" (Rom 16:5; 1 Cor 16:19; Col 4:15; Philem 2). The house is where church happened, and the Christian household became the life setting for the New Testament letters (Collins: 104). For several centuries, Christians met in houses. The earliest reference to a church building is found in Clement of Alexandria about AD 200 (Ellis 1989: 141). Not until the fourth century, when Emperor Constantine began building basilicas, were buildings constructed for the sole purpose of Christian worship (Gehring: 1).

New Testament house churches had rooms large enough to hold 40 to 45 people (Banks: 35). At Ephesus one excavated dwelling measured 4,500 square feet (Ellis 1989: 140). The following places with house churches are named in the NT:

- Caesarea: Cornelius (Acts 10)
- Cenchreae: Phoebe (Rom 16:1-2)
- Colossae: Apphia (Philem 2), Philemon (Philem 1)
- Corinth: Titius Justus (Acts 18:7), Crispus (Acts 18:8), Chloe (1 Cor 1:11), Stephanus (1 Cor 1:16; 16:15-17), Gaius (Rom 16:23), Erastus (16:23)
- Ephesus: Onesiphorus (2 Tim 4:19)
- Jerusalem: Mary, John Mark's mother (Acts 12:12; cf. 1:13-26; 2:46; 5:1-11)
- Laodicea: Nympha (Col 4:15; cf. Rev 3:20-22)
- Philippi: Lydia (Acts 16:40), the converted jailer (16:25-34)
- Rome: Prisca/Priscilla and Aquila (Rom 16:3), Philologus and Julia (16:15), Hermas (16:14), Aristobulus (16:10), Narcissus (16:11), Paul (Acts 28:16-31).
- Thessalonica: Jason (Acts 17:1-10)
- Troas: Eutychus (Acts 20:7-12)

The transfer of church from synagogue to houses is unique to the early Christian movement. Despite opposition, the house church became a way of defining ecclesiology and theology. It became the setting where Christian faith and the social/cultural life of the first- and second-century Roman world both clashed and came together. House churches provided for accountability, intimacy, worship, and fellowship. House churches included diversity of age and socioeconomic standing.

The letters to Timothy and Titus imply that the church has a close tie to Roman household life. The church's overseer is much like the manager of a household. Women and slaves are identified and function in the church much as in the Roman household. But there are also major differences:

- The Roman household served the pagan gods of the house manager, but the Christians claimed that only Jesus is Lord.
- The Roman household manager often had immoral sexual relationships with female slaves and other women, but the Christians practiced sexual fidelity between husband and wife.
- In the Roman household, slaves and women were subject to the master in daily work and religious life, but Christians experienced freedom in Christ to the degree that both slaves and women could lead worship services, even with the master and household manager present.
- The householder in the Greco-Roman world provided administrative leadership for the house, but the Christian householder (*episkopos*) provided both administration and careful Christian teaching.
- Although the letters to Timothy and Titus instruct them to respect general social norms for the sake of the church's mission, they also urge godly discernment in living out their new freedom in Christ (cf. Gal 3:28).

Christians were ridiculed because their behavior patterns were not acceptable in the Roman households of the day. Such ridicule had a negative effect upon the church's evangelistic efforts. On the one hand, Christian behavior was modified for the sake of mission. On the other hand, the acceptance of persons from various social and economic levels into the Christian church as the household of God undermined the social, racial, gender, and economic stratification of the day. The church as household of God provided an opportunity for Paul to reflect seriously on the theological meaning of the church as the house of God, both in regard to the church's order and structure and in regard to its mission. Thus Paul uses "household of God" for both descriptive and prescriptive purposes (Verner: 182). Describing the household of God in the likeness of the Greco-Roman household helped Christians to understand order and relationships. Through the use of purpose clauses, the apostle directed the church in its mission as it confronted unsound teaching and ridicule and as it carried out its evangelistic mission within pagan Roman society. As a result of these two foci, change eventually came in the church's social, cultural, and economic structures *[Household Behavior, p. 355; Contextualizing the Gospel, p. 339]*.

THE TEXT IN THE LIFE OF THE CHURCH

Officeholders in the Church

In the *Teaching of the Twelve Apostles* 15 (*Didache*, ca. AD 100), we read, "Therefore appoint for yourselves bishops and deacons worthy of the Lord, men who are humble and not avaricious and true and approved, for they too carry out for you the ministry of the prophets and teachers. You must not, therefore, despise them, for they are your honored men, along with the prophets and teachers" (M. W. Holmes: 267). Like 1 Timothy 3:1-13, this statement calls attention to the qualities of the person chosen to lead the church, suggesting that some self-proclaimed prophets and teachers lacked these qualities and therefore harmed the church.

By the middle of the second century, monarchical bishops existed in all regions of the church. Tying the monarchical bishop with apostolic succession raised the dignity and power of the bishop office. The theological interpretation of apostolic succession provided for these church offices gave immense power to the church from the third to the sixteenth century. Both in Eastern Orthodoxy and Western Catholicism, apostolic succession created a major division in authority between the ordained offices in the church and the laypeople. The sixteenth-century Reformation rejected apostolic succession and placed a new emphasis on the role of the laity.

Sixteenth-century Anabaptists upheld church offices but rejected apostolic succession. In 1527 the Anabaptists agreed in the Schleitheim Confession:

> We have been united as follows concerning shepherds in the church of God. The shepherd in the church shall be a person according to the rule of Paul, fully and completely, who has a good report of those who are outside the faith. The office of such a person shall be to read and exhort and teach, warn, admonish, or ban in the congregation, and properly to preside among the sisters and brothers in prayer, and in the breaking of bread, and in all things to take care of the body of Christ, that it may be built up and developed, so that the name of God might be praised and honored through us, and the mouth of the mocker be stopped. He shall be supported, wherein he has need, by the congregation which has chosen him, so that he who serves the gospel can also live there-from, as the Lord has ordered. But should a shepherd do something worthy of reprimand, nothing shall be done with him without the voice of two or

> three witnesses. If they sin they shall be publicly reprimanded, so that others might fear. But if the shepherd should be driven away or led to the Lord by the cross, at the same hour another shall be ordained to his place, so that the little folk and the little flock of God may not be destroyed, but be preserved by warning and be consoled. (art. 5; in Yoder 1977: 13-14)

Menno Simons, leader of Anabaptists in the Netherlands, wrote in his *Foundation of Christian Doctrine*: "For no one can serve in this high and holy office conformable to God's will, except he whom the Lord of the vineyard has made capable by the Spirit of His grace" (*CW*: 162). Menno went on to say, "It is undoubtedly proper that if anyone teaches and reproves others, he should first himself be rightly taught and blameless, as Paul teaches: If a man desire the office of a bishop, he desireth a good work" (*CW*: 170).

First Timothy 3:11 may refer to a deacon office for women in the church. In 1632 Mennonite leaders in Holland stated in the Dordrecht Confession (art. 9) that the congregation "should ordain and choose honorable old widows to be deaconesses, that they, with the deacons, should visit, comfort, and care for the poor, weak, ill, distressed, and needy people, as also widows and orphans, and help to alleviate the needs of the congregation to the best of their abilities: 1 Timothy 5:9-10; Romans 16:1-2; James 1:27" (Kauffmann and Miller: 9, alt.). German and Dutch Mennonite churches preserved the deaconess office for many years. Regrettably, the term *deaconess* was changed to *servants* in the German and English translations. As a result, most English-speaking Mennonites did not call or ordain women as deacons. An exception was the Middle District of Virginia Mennonite Conference, where deaconesses were ordained over a hundred-year period from about 1860 until 1962 (Lehman: 1).

Many confessions of faith in the Anabaptist traditions speak of an office of ministry. Often these confessions cite 1 Timothy 3:1-13 and Titus 1:5-9 on the importance of the spiritual life of the person chosen for the Christian ministry. In some areas and conferences, leadership ministry in the church has expressed itself in a threefold way, yet with varied terms: bishop/overseer/*Ältester* (elder), minister/preacher/pastor, and deacon/elder.

1 Timothy 4:1-16

The Leader's Duties in the Household of God

PREVIEW

Building on the confessional statements (1 Tim 2:3-6; 3:16) and on the idea of the church as the household of God (3:15), Paul instructs Timothy on how to care for the household. Faithfulness in conducting the life of the church according to God's ordering (1:4b) means that household members are not free to do as they wish, nor are they merely to follow the prevailing culture. As leader of the church in Ephesus, Timothy carries primary responsibility for the life of the household. Hence, the leaders' duties are outlined in chapter 4.

Timothy's duties begin with instructions on how to respond when deviant and sometimes sinful teaching confronts the church. In 4:1-5 the apostle outlines the problematic teaching. It consists of two major prohibitions: not eating certain foods and forbidding marriage. Paul notes that this teaching comes from the devil.

A transition from the previous subsection to Timothy's quality of life as a servant of Christ appears in 4:6. He must instruct the brothers and sisters in the church at Ephesus with sound teaching. Using an athletic metaphor, Paul argues from the lesser to the greater in setting forth godliness as the goal of personal discipline. The disciplined life of godliness is far greater than the disciplined athlete who runs a footrace. Godliness points to a life of salvation. This is life in the living God, which is supported by a sure saying. The subsection ends in 4:10, with an emphasis on God, the Savior of all people, particularly those who believe in Jesus.

First Timothy 4:11-16 calls attention to Timothy's public ministry. Paul gives ten imperative commands about the duties of the minister of the gospel. If Timothy follows these commands, he will save both himself and the young church in Ephesus.

OUTLINE

Sinful Teaching and the Church, 4:1-5
Training in Godliness, 4:6-10
The Leader's Duties in the Church, 4:11-16

EXPLANATORY NOTES

Sinful Teaching and the Church 4:1-5

Early Christians understood that the latter days arrived with the crucifixion, resurrection, and ascension of Christ, and with the coming of the Holy Spirit (Acts 2:17-21, 29-36; 3:11-26). Early Christians understood that some would renounce the faith in the latter times (Mark 13:5-8; Acts 20:29-31; 2 Thess 2:3, 9-11). In 1 Timothy 4:1-5, Paul speaks to members of the Christian community in Ephesus who are susceptible to unsound teaching and are beginning to desert the faith. He makes a distinction between Christians who go astray and persons who lead them astray. Paul calls persons who lead others astray *hypocritical liars* (4:2 NIV) who have paid attention to *deceitful spirits and teachings of demons* (v. 1). Several times in the letters to Timothy and Titus, Paul warns against the deceitful conduct of unhealthy teachers (2 Tim 2:16-18; 3:13; 4:3-4). The term *spirit* is now changed to the plural, with the adjective *deceitful* added, which distinguishes the seductive spirits from the Holy Spirit. Both in the Dead Sea Scrolls and in *The Testament of the Twelve Patriarchs* God's people were led astray by deceitful spirits (1QS 3.22; *Testament of Reuben* 2.1). The origin of such teaching is none other than Satan himself. As hypocritical liars, these teachers, who wore a false face, made an outward show but inwardly were deceitful. They are marked with a stigma, indicating that they belong to Satan, the devil. In addition, their conscience is seared and no longer condemns what they formerly knew was immoral *[Unhealthy Teaching, p. 366]*.

Believing that the resurrection had already occurred (2 Tim 2:18), some teachers are rejecting marriage and certain foods. Paul dealt with both topics in his early writings: first in regard to marriage and Jewish dietary laws (1 Cor 7–8; Rom 14:6), and then in response to proto-Gnostic influences on the early church (Col 2:16, 21-23). At Ephesus the problem had expanded to the degree that persons were being led astray.

Paul's response to these teachings comes directly from creation (1 Tim 4:3-4). God created both food and sex. To the man and the woman, God said, "Be fruitful and multiply" (Gen 1:28), and to both the man and the woman God said, "Eat" (Gen 2:16). To reject food and sex is to reject the creating God (Johnson 2001: 248). God gave both food and sex in creation *to be received with thanksgiving by those who believe and know the truth* (1 Tim 4:3).

Christians who have an experiential knowledge of the truth contained in the gospel receive food and marriage with thanksgiving. Their status as believers does not prevent them from eating or engaging in sexual relationships as husband and wife. These gifts from God find joyful acceptance in a thanksgiving prayer before and sometimes also after meals in the Hebrew-Christian tradition.

Evil use of food and sex is not only a cosmological matter, it is also a moral matter, since what was created for good is turned into evil. Luke Timothy Johnson says, "It is, therefore, not sexual activity as such that must be proscribed, but the corrupt misuse of human sexuality. It is not food that most be avoided, but the evil disordering of human appetites" (Johnson 2001: 248). Used appropriately, both food and sex are *sanctified by God's word and by prayer* (v. 5). Thanksgiving prayers recognize the prior action of God and that God has sanctified food and sex in creation.

Paul responds to this teaching with three arguments. First, God created food and marriage. Second, Christians receive food and sex from the creator God with thanksgiving. And third, through the gospel and prayers of thanksgiving, Christians use food and sex in a holy manner. Prayer does not necessarily sanctify food and sex, but through prayer the community acknowledges and activates what God has declared to be true (Towner 2006: 299). Thus Paul confronts this teaching directly and refutes it with a logical argument. Collins writes, "Using an enthymeme, a rhetorical syllogism in which one of the premises is assumed rather than stated, he affirms the goodness of what the deviant teachers reject: Everything created by God is good; the things that 'some' are rejecting were created by God; hence, these things are good and are to be received with prayer and gratitude" (114).

Training in Godliness 4:6-10

In moving from the negative of 4:1-5 to the positive of 4:6-10, Paul calls attention to the character of the Christian leader. Timothy is to *put these instructions before the brothers and sisters* (v. 6). He is to care for himself as well as the congregation. Caring begins with modeling Christian character in the presence of the whole congregation by concentrating on *the words of the faith and of the sound teaching that you have followed.* Timothy will continue to nourish himself and not just rely on teaching from the past. Nourishment includes the words of the faith, the content of the gospel, and the truth expressed in the gospel. Nourishment also includes teaching an objective body of truth, which we call Christian doctrine. In contrast to the *teachings of demons* (1 Tim 4:1), Timothy must nourish himself on the good *deposit* of Christian doctrine (2 Tim 1:14 NIV). The goodness of Timothy's teaching depends largely on what he himself has learned and how he continues to nourish his life as he gives attention to the gospel and Christian doctrine.

Here Paul suddenly changes metaphors. He moves from the metaphor of nourishment and pedagogy to an athletic metaphor as he instructs Timothy to train himself in godliness. At the same time, Timothy is to stay away from *profane myths and old wives' tales* (1 Tim 4:7). *Profane myths* were empty words, babbling—the opposite of holy speech. *Old wives' tales* was a patriarchal, cultural expression used in Greco-Roman culture to deride women. This culturally prejudicial term was used to ridicule uneducated women.

As an athlete trains the body in the gym, so Timothy is to train himself in godliness (4:7-8). Paul uses a rhetorical appeal—one that we often see in later rabbinic rhetoric—to emphasize the importance of godliness (Collins: 122). He argues from the lesser to the greater by acknowledging some benefit in bodily exercise. Athletes disciplined themselves through careful diet and energetic exercise to prepare for the Greek races. Even if the athlete won the race, the benefit was temporary. In contrast, *godliness is valuable in every way, holding promise for both the present life and the life to come* (v. 8). Though bodily exercise may benefit the athlete a little today, godliness has a lasting benefit for life in the present and also in the age to come.

The word *godliness* (*eusebeia*) appears only five times in the rest of the New Testament, but in the letters to Timothy and Titus it appears many times (1 Tim 2:2; 3:16; 4:7-8; 6:3, 5-6, 11; 2 Tim 3:5; Titus 1:1) *[Godliness, p. 346]*. True godliness entails genuine faith, the truth, and its visible expression in life (Fee 1988: 104). Paul also contrasts godliness with godless myths and religious asceticism. He likens asceticism (1 Tim 4:1-5) in the name of religion and bodily exercise (v. 8) to athletes' training for the Olympic Games. At best, bodily exercise is limited to this world. But godliness has to do with the essence of faith and one's response to the living God. Godliness affects both present and future life.

The saying is sure and worthy of full acceptance (4:9). This is the third trustworthy saying formula in 1 Timothy (cf. 1:15; 3:1). Here the question is whether the trustworthy saying is tied to 4:10, which follows the saying, or whether it refers back to verse 8b, which precedes the saying. For two reasons I interpret the trustworthy saying as referring back to the words *holding promise for both the present life and the life to come* in 8b. First, verse 8b itself talks about salvation. Second, the transitional term *for* in verse 10 indicates a reason for or confirmation of the preceding thought (Knight 1992: 202).

Godliness that holds promise *for both the present life and the life to come* is explained in several distinct ways; it involves human struggle, it is based on hope in the living God, and it is God's gift of salvation. First, Christians *toil and struggle* as they train themselves in godliness. Toil is tedious and requires much energy, often wearing people out to the point of exhaustion. Christians struggle (*agōnizomai*, 4:10) to achieve godliness, much as an athlete trains for the Olympic race.

The author of 4 Maccabees uses the word *struggle* (*agōnos*, "contest") for the athlete who contends in the arena until suffering a martyr's death (4 Macc 11:20). Toil and struggle are not for personal fulfillment, but for the sake of the gospel. Salvation in the present life and the life to come is too important to be lazy and too significant not to withstand the forces of opposition against it. Second, *we have our hope set on the living God.* The tense of the verb indicates that our hope is firmly fixed on the living God, in a continuing *state* of hope, not just a single *act* of hope. Our hope is in an active, living God (Luke 20:38; 1 Tim 4:10). Only a living God can impart life to come (1 Tim 4:8). The resurrection of Jesus Christ affirms this living God (1 Cor 15:15). Third, this living God is *the Savior of all people, especially of those who believe.* Again Paul emphasizes God as Savior. As stated in 1 Timothy 2:4, 6, the saving work of God in Jesus Christ is for all people. Salvation for Paul is not a universalism in which everyone is saved. Although it is universal in that Christ gave his life as *a ransom for all* (1 Tim 2:6), receiving salvation requires human response to Jesus Christ. The God who wants to save all also wants each *to come to the knowledge of the truth* in Jesus (2:4).

The Leader's Duties in the Church 4:11-16

In 4:11-16, Paul then turns to Timothy's public life and ministry in the church. A distinct literary style with no less than ten imperatives indicates the beginning of a new section. In these verses, the imperatives are as follows:

11 insist on
11 teach
12 let no one despise your youth
14 do not neglect the gift that is in you
15 put these things into practice
15 devote yourself to them

12 be an example	16 pay close attention to yourself
13 give attention to	16 continue in these things

All of these imperatives are present tense, implying that Timothy's response should be one of continuing action in his ongoing ministry. They are summarized in verse 16: *Pay close attention to yourself and your teaching; continue in these things, for in doing this you will save both yourself and your hearers.* The paragraph begins with *these things*, a term that occurs three times in this chapter (4:6, 11, 15). *These things* refers to the matters to which Timothy is to give personal attention and about which he is to teach in the congregation.

The first imperative indicates that Timothy is to insist on these things as an authoritative church leader. He must forthrightly command the teachers to cease teaching falsehood while he continues to teach true, healthy doctrine. In short, Timothy must exercise vigorous spiritual leadership in evangelism and nurture. This charge occurs several times in the letters to Timothy and Titus (1 Tim 5:7; 6:2b; 2 Tim 2:2, 14; Titus 2:15).

Let no one despise your youth (1 Tim 4:12). As a young church leader, perhaps in his early thirties, Timothy lives in a culture that honors the wisdom of older men. Timothy is commanded, third, not to allow anyone to look down on him because of his age or timidity (1 Cor 16:10-11; 2 Tim 1:6-14). Against the prevailing custom of the day in Ephesus, the Christian community must know that Timothy has Paul's authority to teach these things even to older persons, despite his youthfulness. With a strong adversative *but* (*alla*), Timothy is commanded, fourth, *to set the believers an example.* He must model Christian belief and behavior.

Five qualities make up the example that Timothy is to model for the church. The first two qualities are exterior and the last three are interior. Timothy's outward life is to exemplify Christian behavior *in speech and conduct.* Paul wants Timothy to model Christian character through daily conversation and conduct and through teaching in the congregation. By modeling Christian character in speech and in conduct, Timothy's message will have integrity and authority. Conversation and conduct are followed by three interior qualities: *love, faith,* and *purity.* Some manuscripts add "in spirit," but the better reading omits it (Metzger 1994: 574). *Love* and *faith* are common Pauline virtues (found in earlier epistles as well as in 1 Tim 1:5). Love is fraternal charity, giving oneself for the good of others. Faith means fidelity, trustworthiness, faithfulness. Paul could add hope as the third virtue, but here the third interior quality is purity. *Purity* may refer to sexual chastity (1 Tim 5:2). If so, we see here an implicit correction of some persons (1 Tim 5:11-15; 2 Tim 3:6). Purity also means integrity of heart (1 Tim 5:22). These three interior qualities give authenticity to the young leader's public ministry. Leaders like Timothy who model what they preach and teach are not intimidated by older persons and cultural norms, despite their youthfulness.

Until I arrive (1 Tim 4:13) reveals Paul's plan to visit Ephesus (cf. 3:14). Here Paul lays out Timothy's work in the meantime. This phrase lends support to Pauline authorship of 1 Timothy and asserts the apostle's authority despite his absence. Several public activities in the congregation comprise Timothy's work. He is to *give attention to the public reading of scripture, to exhorting, to teaching.* These public activities focus attention on the use of Scripture. Elsewhere in the letters to Timothy and Titus Scripture is given high importance in the life of the church (2 Tim 3:15-17). The Scriptures are the foundation for Timothy's preaching and teaching. Public reading of Scripture was common in Jewish synagogues and early Christian communities. Without printed Bibles, the public reading of Scripture held a significant place in the worship service. The leader then explained the meaning of the Scriptures and applied them to life. Teaching included catechetical instruction in Christian doctrine and ethics. It, too, is found in Paul's epistles (Col 3:5-17; Eph 5:1-20). By obeying this fifth imperative, Timothy will lead the congregation in these public activities based on Scripture.

A sixth imperative is *Do not neglect the gift* [*charisma*] *that is in you* (1 Tim 4:14). A charisma is a gracious endowment that enables a person to carry out a special function in the Christian community. In the letters to Timothy and Titus, *charisma* is used only of the gift that comes from God through the laying on of hands, whether by the elders or Paul or both (Quinn and Wacker: 391). Paul specifically commands Timothy to exercise this God-given *charisma* for the good of the church.

The apostle reminds Timothy that this gift was recognized and affirmed *through prophecy with the laying on of hands by the council of elders.* Three elements come together in this passage: the word of prophecy, the gift, and the laying on of hands as affirmation of that gift. Although in 2 Timothy 1:6 Paul alone laid hands on Timothy, we see reference here in 1 Timothy 4:14 to a group of elders that has laid hands on him. In the OT, hands were laid on certain persons to convey a blessing. At other times the laying on of hands indicated the passing on of authority (Num 27:18-23; Deut 34:9). Laying on of hands accompanied the voice of the Spirit in the midst of the body of believers as Paul and Barnabas were consecrated for missionary work (Acts 13:1-3). Similarly, the voice of the Spirit through prophecy (1 Tim 4:14) has indicated that a gift is present in Timothy, which the group of elders have affirmed and consecrated for service in the church. Laying on of hands here is not passing on authority as much as it is recognizing the authority already present in Timothy's gift. Laying on of hands is the response of the congregation to the gift that the Spirit has already made visible and active in Timothy's life. As such, Timothy receives the affirmation and support of the elders, becoming a preaching and teaching elder as a result of this gift *[Ordination, p. 359]*.

The seventh and eighth imperatives closely follow in verse 15. *Put these things into practice, devote yourself to them, so that all may see your progress.* The commands are brief and sharp. Total and complete commitment is required. There is no room for halfhearted ministry here. Timothy must give himself fully to these things. The word *progress* was used by the ancient Stoics to indicate advances by a novice in philosophy and ethics. Paul uses the same term for the spread of the gospel (Phil 1:12). If Timothy devotes himself to these things, the congregation will observe his progress and cease regarding him as an inexperienced person or discounting his authority (Kelly: 109). When a congregation observes progress in a pastor, it soon affirms and supports that pastor. If growth and progress are not forthcoming, the congregation will no longer provide the necessary support, regardless of the pastor's years of experience in Christian ministry.

A summary of Timothy's charge comes in the ninth and tenth imperatives in verse 16. *Pay close attention to yourself and to your teaching; continue in these things.* In this verse the personal and public sides of Timothy's ministry come together. The verb tense indicates continuous action: Timothy must give sustained attention to his own spiritual life so that he exemplifies Christian character and so that his teaching expresses the sound, healthy doctrine that will confront unhealthy teaching and build up the congregation. What is at stake is nothing short of salvation itself. *For in doing this you will save both yourself and your hearers.* The term *for* introduces a purpose clause and states the goal of the preceding directive. If Timothy fulfills the charge, he will save both himself and those who listen to his preaching and teaching. He need not fear failure in Christian ministry as long as he devotes himself to these things. He need not fear that the gospel is unable to overcome the influence of unhealthy teachers. Instead, Timothy finds confidence in the gospel message of Jesus Christ and devotes himself to the work of preaching and teaching this message. This section of 1 Timothy 4 ends with concern for the gospel and people's salvation (1 Tim 4:10, 16). Paul could not be clearer: God is Savior of all.

THE TEXT IN BIBLICAL CONTEXT

Food and Marriage

Some persons in Ephesus claimed that the resurrection had already occurred and therefore one was released from the physical body and the present age (2 Tim 2:18). If the resurrection is past, then Jesus' teaching that there is no marriage in the resurrection should apply now (Matt 22:30). In short, some teachers held to an over-realized eschatology that perpetuated a negative view of the temporal world, thus rejecting certain foods and sexual relationships. In 1 Timothy 4:1-5, Paul condemns this teaching since it misinterprets the resurrection and misunderstands the theology of creation.

Throughout the Bible unholy sexual relationships are condemned. The prophets forthrightly condemned the sexual orgies of Baal religion. Gluttony too is a serious sin (Deut 21:20; Prov 23:21; Matt 11:19). However, sexual relationships within marriage and eating food in moderation are affirmed. Jesus taught, "From the beginning of creation, 'God made them male and female.' For this reason a man shall leave his father and mother and be joined to his wife, and the two shall become one flesh.' So they are no longer two, but one flesh" (Mark 10:6-8). In Mark 7:19, Jesus declared all foods clean, in contrast to the prevailing Jewish dietary laws. The Jerusalem Council offered guidance to Gentile Christians regarding food and marriage (Acts 15:20, 29). Paul took part in early Christian discussions about food and sex, condemning neither, but expressing concern that one not offend other brothers and sisters over matters of conscience (Rom 14:13-23; 1 Cor 7:12-16; 8:1-13). The author of Hebrews wrote, "Let marriage be held in honor by all, and let the marriage bed be kept undefiled; for God will judge fornicators and adulterers" (13:4).

In contrast to the view of the Ephesian teachers, Jesus taught an eschatology affirming that the kingdom of God is now and that it is also future ("already, but not yet"). Likewise, the resurrection is now (Rom 6:4; Col 3:1) and it is future (Rom 8:18-25; 1 Cor 15:12-28; Phil 3:20-21; 1 Thess 4:13-18). As Christians live between the now and the not yet of God's reign, they affirm a theology of creation that embraces nourishment and the enjoyment of food, as well as the joy of celebrating marriage in the sexual union between man and woman.

Present Life and the Life to Come

Paul alludes to the salvation theme by including *the present life and the life to come* as part of a "faithful saying" (1 Tim 4:8-9). In the Bible, salvation is eschatological in both the present and the future. The OT prophets spoke of the coming latter days. These latter days would be the days of the Messiah and the outpouring of God's spirit. Peter interpreted the life, death, and resurrection of Christ and the outpouring of the Holy Spirit as evidence that the latter days had arrived (Acts 2:17-21, 35-36; 3:11-26). He openly stated, "All the prophets, as many as have spoken, from Samuel and those after him, also predicted these days" (3:24). The phrase "kingdom of God" appears at strategic points in the book of Acts as the gospel breaks into new cultures (1:3, 6; 8:12; 14:22; 19:8; 28:23, 31).

In Johannine theology, future life in Christ has already broken into the present. John presents an inaugurated eschatology. This inaugurated eschatology is not the over-realized eschatology that some in Ephesus held to by saying that the bodily resurrection is past rather than future. Paul's inaugurated eschatology emphasizes new life in Christ now and the fullness of that new life in the future. He uses several phrases to describe the present life in Christ and the future life.

- The kingdom of the Son now; the kingdom of the Father in the future (Col 1:13-14; 1 Cor 15:20-28).
- Participation in new creation order in Christ now, in the new Adam, but lived out in the context of the old order (Rom 5:15, 17, 20; 1 Cor 15:22, 45; 2 Cor 5:16-17).
- Raised with Christ now, with a future bodily resurrection based on believers being united with Christ in his resurrection (Rom 6:4; 1 Cor 15:20, 23, 29-57; Eph 2:4-6; Col 3:1; 1 Thess 4:13-18).
- The Holy Spirit as evidence (*arrabōn*) that we belong to Christ now, and the guarantee that we will experience the fullness of God's presence in the future (2 Cor 1:22; 5:5; Eph 1:13b-14).
- Leaving the old self behind and experiencing the new self in Christ (Rom 6:6; Eph 4:22-24; Col 3:9-11).
- Christians have already experienced the new life (2 Cor 2:16) yet look forward to the inheritance of eternal life (Gal 6:8). Christians have already been saved (Eph 2:5) yet still await an ultimate salvation (Rom 13:11).
- The Christian's resurrection body will be transformed so that it may be conformed to the body of his glory (Phil 3:21).

In keeping with Paul's theology, the letters to Timothy and Titus mention eternal life (1 Tim 1:16; 6:12; Titus 1:2; 3:7), real life (1 Tim 6:19), life in Christ Jesus (2 Tim 1:1), and Christian hope (Titus 1:2; 3:7). Indeed, the pursuit of godliness is of great value because it holds promise both for the present life and the life to come (1 Tim 4:8).

Public Ministry

Credibility in leadership builds on credibility of character. Paul commands Timothy to set the believers an example in five areas: speech, life, love, faith, and purity. Personal failure prevented Moses from entering the Promised Land (Num 20:12). David was prevented from building a house for God because he shed blood as a warrior (1 Chron 28:3). In contrast, Jesus lived in full obedience to the will of God. His example became the measure for determining right and wrong behavior in the early Christian church (Phil 2:5; 1 Pet 2:21-25; 1 John 2:6).

Timothy's public ministry had a threefold focus: public *reading of Scripture*, *preaching*, and *teaching* (1 Tim 4:13 TNIV). Several psalms call attention to the importance of God's word (Pss 19:7-10; 119:97-105). Reading Scripture was part of synagogue worship. In the synagogue at Nazareth, Jesus began his public ministry by reading from Isaiah (Luke 4:16-20). Early Christian communities listened as Scripture was read in their worship services (Acts 13:15, 27; 15:21; 2 Cor 3:14; Col 4:16). Public Scripture reading was common in biblical times because most persons did not have access to the Bible.

Teaching followed the rabbinic method of education. In postexilic Judaism, rabbis taught the meaning of God's word to groups of disciples. Jesus taught "as one having authority, and not as the scribes" (Matt 7:29). Jesus taught by parables and by public discourse. Paul taught in Corinth for eighteen months (Acts 18:11) and in Ephesus for two years (Acts 19:8-10). Teaching was a gift of the Spirit in the early church (Rom 12:7; 1 Cor 12:28; Eph 4:11).

Paul commands Timothy to engage in the public acts of ministry: reading Scripture, preaching, and teaching. In addition, he is to live in faithfulness to God. Timothy is to be an example for the believers (1 Tim 4:12) and to *pay close attention* both to himself and his teaching (4:16). By devoting himself to these activities, others will see his progress (4:15). By carrying out public ministry in this manner and living a devout life, Timothy stands within the larger biblical tradition of public ministries.

THE TEXT IN THE LIFE OF THE CHURCH

Food and Marriage

About a hundred years after Paul wrote this text, Irenaeus wrote about the Gnostics' opposition to marriage (*Against Heresies* 1.24.2; 1.28.1). The patristic texts and the apocryphal *Acts of Paul* clearly indicate that issues surrounding sex and marriage were debated among second-century Christians.

Some Christians in the third and fourth centuries practiced asceticism. In medieval Europe, rejection of marriage became the hallmark of priests. Poverty, chastity, and obedience are major themes in the Rule of Francis of Assisi in late medieval monasticism.

Protestant Reformers in the sixteenth century rejected asceticism. Leaders of the Lutheran, Reformed, and Anabaptist movements married and had children. Christians' prayer before (and after) meals today indicates that food is to be received with thanksgiving.

Some Christians have taken on spiritual disciplines from the medieval church, including singleness and fasting. For many Christians, these disciplines are not based on the view that the resurrection is past. Instead, these disciplines are practiced for spiritual enrichment. The greater problems Christians face in contemporary culture are sex outside of marriage and obesity.

Godliness Is Valuable

Athletes—such as tennis stars Venus and Serena Williams and basketball legend LeBron James—spend countless hours in training. The writer of 1 Timothy says, "Physical training is of some value" (4:8). In comparison, missionary martyr Jim Elliott said, "He is no fool who gives what he cannot keep to gain what he cannot lose!" (Elisabeth Elliot: 174).

Two movements in the history of the believers church illustrate the value of godliness. One movement was the Anabaptist missionary endeavor. In the sixteenth century, Anabaptist leaders willingly challenged the Corpus Christianum by rejecting infant baptism and forming small believers church communities. They rejected the principle of territoriality and believed that the earth belongs to the Lord. Many Anabaptist men and women obeyed the missionary mandate of Christ regardless of the costs. The result was an effective missionary movement long before the modern missionary movements of the nineteenth and twentieth centuries. Anabaptists believed that God's offer of salvation for everyone was realized both in the present life in Christ and in the future life. As both men and women shared the gospel with neighbors, fellow workers, and others, these Anabaptists became a church of martyrs (Shenk: 24). Their godliness expressed in missionary efforts created a free church movement separate from the state and contributed a believers church to the new world.

A second movement in the pursuit of godliness arose in the German Pietism of the late 1600s and early 1700s. August Hermann Francke (1663-1727) and Philip Jacob Spener (1635-1705) sensed that an overemphasis on doctrinal orthodoxy—with its primary stress on right beliefs rather than on right living and right relationship with Christ—had brought decline in the church. Francke and Spener called for an experiential, biblically centered, and ethically minded Christian movement that emphasized a personal relationship with Christ. Francke and Spener arranged small groups for Bible study, prayer, and devotion to the Lord. This was the beginning of the German Lutheran Pietist movement. The Moravian Church and Wesleyan Methodism later grew out of the larger Pietist movement. In 1708, eight persons led by Alexander Mack (1679-1735) united in a covenant of the cross of Jesus Christ as a church of Christian believers. As these eight persons pursued godliness, they embraced believers baptism, the church as a Christian community separated from the state church, and a desire to live by the teachings of Christ. With such commitments, these eight persons identified themselves as Anabaptists by way of the Pietist movement (Durnbaugh: 120-30). From these eight persons came the Church of the Brethren.

1 Timothy 5:1–6:10, 17-19

Managing the Church as the Household of God

PREVIEW

Paul writes an extended paragraph on widows as part of a larger segment in which he gives instruction on three groups of people in the church: widows (1 Tim 5:3-16), elders (5:17-25), and slaves (6:1-2). The grammatical transition from the previous section (4:6-16) shows that the present paragraphs are part of the instructions to Timothy and are theologically tied to understanding the church as the household of God (3:15). The instructions regarding these three groups of people center on how members of the household are to conduct their lives for the good of the church and its mission in the world. Paul identifies each of these groups by name and by the term *honor* (verb: *timaō*; noun: *timē*) in 1 Timothy 5:3, 17; 6:1. While Paul gives these instructions directly to Timothy, he intends Timothy to pass on some of them to the widows and some to the entire church.

Paul then gives instruction regarding money and the church (6:2b-10; 17-19). On the negative side, love of money can be a source of evil (6:2b-10). On the positive side, Christians can uses riches for the good of the church and for building up heavenly treasure (6:17-19).

OUTLINE

Older Men in the Church, 5:1-2
Widows in the Church, 5:3-16
Elders in the Church, 5:17-25

Slaves in the Church, 6:1-2a
Money and the Church, 6:2b-10, 17-19

EXPLANATORY NOTES

Older Men in the Church 5:1-2

Speech in the Christian community is graced in a manner descriptive of family relationships involving fathers, mothers, brothers, and sisters. A fragmentary household code prescribes proper conduct toward older and younger men and toward older and younger women. In the church, one is to speak to an older man as if he were one's father. The command, *Do not speak harshly to an older man,* forbids speaking sharply to a man above fifty years of age. The Greek word used here can be translated *elder* or *older man.* Its context indicates that Paul has an "older man" in mind. *Speak harshly* refers to strong rebuke that is on the verge of violence. Timothy is instructed to exhort (NIV) older persons with a gentle spirit.

Widows in the Church 5:3-16

Widows received special attention in the NT church. Luke-Acts contains more references to widows than any other NT document. The sixteen references include Anna (Luke 2:37), the many Israelite widows (Luke 4:25-26), the Christian widows in Acts 6:1, and the widows in Joppa (Acts 9:36-41).

Paul mentions three kinds of widows in 1 Timothy 5:3-16. First are the older, destitute widows who do not have supporting family members and thus need financial assistance from the church (5:3, 5, 9-10, 16b). Second, some widows have family members who can provide for their financial support (5:4, 8, 16a). And, third, the younger widows attracted to the opposite sex include some idle widows who have become involved in sin (5:11-15).

Christian widows faced difficulties in the first century. Males dominated the Roman household and took sexual advantage of slaves, widows, and even daughters, without recrimination. Some slaves and females became Christians in households led by male masters who had not become Christians. This created tension for those slaves and females as they tried to negotiate cultural expectations in the context of the call to Christian holiness. Roman society did not practice polygamy as a way of providing a living for females, nor did it provide an accepted role for single widows younger than fifty years old; they were expected to remarry. The Augustan laws and related measures "penalized unmarried men from the ages of twenty-five to sixty and unmarried women from twenty to fifty who did not have children and did not marry if they were divorced or widowed" (Winter 2003: 137).

Men were often seven to eight years older than women when they married. Since women married shortly after puberty, in their midteens to upper teens, this age gap was largely accountable for the large number of widows in the Roman Empire (Winter 2003: 137-38). As many as 30 percent of women in the ancient world were widows. According to Roman practice, after the death of a husband, a widow was expected not to remarry for at least ten months to give time for mourning. But she was encouraged to remarry within two years of the death of her husband, lest she experience financial and inheritance penalties (Winter 2003: 138).

Paul says that the church is to honor older, destitute widows. He calls them "real" widows, who do not have adequate finances or family to care for them. The verb *honor* (*timaō*) in 5:5 and the noun *timē* in 5:17 mean to respect and take financial responsibility for another person. *Honor* appears in the fifth commandment: "Honor your father and your mother" (Exod 20:12; Deut 5:16). Care for widows was a common duty in the OT. The NT Christian community also cared for widows (Luke 2:37; Acts 6:1-6; 9:36, 39, 41; James 1:27). First Timothy 5:5 says that a *real widow, left alone,* needs help from the church. Not only has her husband died; she also has no other family members to take care of her. Therefore she *has set her hope on God and continues in supplications and prayers night and day*. The verb tense indicates continuing action in setting one's hope on God, rather than a single act of prayer. Real widows' prayers indicate reliance on God alone and include both praise and a cry for help in the likeness of Anna's prayers in the temple (Luke 2:37). Their needs contrast with those of widows who have children and grandchildren to care for them (5:8, 16) or widows who live for pleasure (5:6).

A second group of widows lives for pleasure (5:11-15). They may think they are living a life of freedom, but self-indulgence in pleasure, luxury, and sensual activities indicate that they are living in death. By living immoral lives, these widows have cut their ties to real, eternal life in Jesus Christ. Paul gives specific commands to keep the witness of the church from being compromised by widows involved in scandalous behavior (v. 7). At stake is the church's integrity. At the same time, the church is called upon to provide financial support for widows who are without other means of support.

If a widow has living children or grandchildren, her family should take financial responsibility for her rather than the church. The family is to care for widows who are relatives (5:4, 8, 16). Paul gives two reasons for assuming this responsibility. First, *whoever does not provide for relatives, and especially family members, has denied the faith and is worse than an unbeliever* (5:8). And second, *let the church not be burdened, so that it can assist those who are real widows* (v. 16). The first reason is tied to the witness of the church. According to civil law, families are to care for their widows. If non-Christian families care for their widows as a cultural or legal practice, but Christian families do not, both the family and the church open themselves to criticism from pagan citizens.

Throughout 1 Timothy, Paul calls for the kind of proper Christian behavior that will not bring the witness of the church into disrepute by outsiders (2:2; 3:1-7; 5:14; 6:1). If Christian believers care less for widows than nonbelievers do, Christians would be worse than those who do not even make a profession of faith. With these scathing words, Paul condemns believers whose practice is inconsistent with living out the faith within their household, since it breaks their religious commitment.

The second reason, found in verse 16, is based on the reality that the church is not able to provide care and financial support for all widows. For financial reasons, the church must restrict its responsibility to *real widows* (5:3, 16b), who have no living family care and support.

Paul then turns to a third group: younger widows who have lost their husbands during their childbearing years. In contrast to the older widows, who present a financial problem, these younger widows present a moral problem. Paul identifies three ascending moral concerns:

1. Their sensual desires alienate them from Christ (v. 11).
2. Their idleness leads to sinful speech in the community (v. 13).
3. Some have turned away to follow Satan (v. 15).

A moral concern emerged because some widows in the church have become sexually active in the interval between the start of widowhood and remarriage. Some younger Christian widows have also married non-Christians and are feeling social pressure to give up their faith. "Social customs of the time dictated that a wife follow the religion of her husband. . . . Were a Christian widow to marry a non-Christian and succumb to the social pressure to follow the gods of her husband, she would have abandoned her faith in Christ" (Collins: 141). Given Christian teaching on marriage and remarriage elsewhere in the NT (e.g., 1 Cor 7:39), it is likely that some younger widows did marry unbelievers, incurring condemnation (1 Tim 5:12). And non-Christians were beginning to question the credibility of the Christian faith.

The second moral concern is idleness. Paul equates idleness to misuse of time as younger widows are *gadding about from house to house* (v. 13). They are not merely idle, but also gossips and busybodies, saying what they should not say. If a younger widow has no children, the demands of running a household are lessened and make visiting other households attractive. Likely some of the younger widows fall into meaningless talk. Going *from house to house* implies a lifestyle of instability and flightiness (Johnson 2001: 267). Speech turns to gossip, and these widows become busybodies. As a result, some younger widows have found themselves saying things *they should not say* (v. 13b). Younger widows soon become like the teachers whose talk is foolish (1:6), empty (6:20), and inappropriate (1:6-7; 4:7; 6:3-4). Perhaps some of these younger widows are participating in deviant teaching (cf. 2 Tim 3:6-7).

The involvement of some of the widows in sin is borne out by 5:15, which expresses Paul's third moral concern: the turning of some *to follow Satan*. The verb *turned away* in the letters to Timothy and Titus describes both the unhealthy teachers and those whom they have deceived. In meaning, it is closely tied to other verbs related to leaving the Christian faith. Paul *turned* Hymenaeus and Alexander *over to Satan* in 1:20, and now in 5:15 Paul says that some younger widows have *turned* themselves over willingly to Satan.

Paul responds to these three moral concerns in verse 14. He uses the verb *I wish* (GNT) followed by four infinitives: *I wish* young widows to remarry, to bear children, to manage their households, and to give the adversary no occasion to revile believers. Unlike the unhealthy teachers (4:3), Paul does not oppose marriage or remarriage after the death of a spouse. Following the customary practice of younger widows remarrying, Paul restricts marriage to fellow Christians (cf. 1 Cor 7:39), thus preventing the problem of a believer leaving the faith and following the pagan gods of a non-Christian husband in her second marriage, or the pressure or temptation for her to do so.

Noteworthy is Paul's infinitive *to manage* (their households; 5:14 GNT). Paul mentions household management elsewhere in the letters to Timothy and Titus as a male responsibility (3:4, 12, 15), but he uses it in 5:14 with reference to the management role of Christian women. Unlike the women who were gadding about from house to house, Paul encourages younger widows to remarry and to enjoy the freedom of domestic life. Paul does not want to give the adversary any occasion to revile. Here again is concern for authentic Christian witness as the church proclaims salvation. Holy living and mission are tied together. Apparently non-Christians have been criticizing the church at Ephesus. The immoral behavior of some widows has been bringing disrepute upon the church (5:14b). Paul instructs Timothy regarding the indiscretions of younger widows, in part to address the larger missionary task of the church. To survive, the church in Ephesus needs to live authentically and to proclaim salvation in Jesus Christ with integrity.

In contrast to younger widows, Paul gives different instructions for older widows. Children and grandchildren should care for widows, and the church should provide support for widows who have no family to take care of them. In addition, some widows are to *be put on the list* (5:9). Younger widows are not allowed on this list (5:11), some of whom have *violated their first pledge* (5:12b). *First pledge* likely refers to a faith commitment to Christ, from which some have turned away to follow the unhealthy teachers.

The verb *katalegō* in 5:9—translated *put on the roll* (NEB), *enrollment* (NJB), *put on the list* (NIV, NRSV)—appears only here in the NT. It is a technical term used for some kind of official list (Fee 1988: 119). In Hellenistic literature the word is used for the conscription of soldiers into the army, for reception into the circle of the gods, and for acceptance into the body of the Roman senate (Johnson 2001: 264). What list is Paul talking about? One possibility is that there was a definite order of widows with a leadership role in the church. A qualification for placement on this list is that the widow's marriage situation (wife of one husband) must correspond to the rule for overseers (1 Tim 3:2), deacons (3:12), and elders (Titus 1:6). The activities of widows on this list suggest work that they did in the past rather than work they are invited to do in the future.

A second possibility is that Paul is making a distinction between widows who should be supported financially by the church and other widows who are supported by family members, or who, in the case of younger widows, should remarry. In this view, only some older destitute widows without family are to be supported by the church. But this answer leaves one with other questions, such as who takes care of older widows who have no living family members but do not meet some of the criteria given for being placed on the list. For example, how does the church respond to a destitute older widow who has married a second time and become a widow again? And what about widows who are not attested for their good works? Or widows who do not have children? Or who have not helped the afflicted? Or those who have not devoted themselves to doing well in every way? Younger widows are not to be placed on the list on the assumption that they will marry again.

Eight conditions restrict the list to certain kinds of widows. The first two conditions describe her status in society at large: sixty years old (ten years beyond age fifty, up to which society expected widows to remarry; see above) and the wife of only one husband. The remaining six conditions point to her Christian character (1 Tim 5:10):

1. She is *well attested for her good works.*
2. She *has brought up children* (either her own children or orphans or both).
3. She has *shown hospitality*, treating traveling Christians graciously.
4. She has *washed the saints' feet* (a menial act normally performed by slaves and thus a symbol of humble service).
5. She has *helped the afflicted* (i.e., has given aid to someone in need).
6. She has devoted herself to *doing good in every way.*
7. Such *good works* are found in both godly women (1 Tim 2:10) and godly men (2 Tim 2:21; 3:17; Titus 1:16; 3:1).

In summary, Paul instructs Christian widows (by way of Timothy) in the context of the first-century culture regarding marriage practices. This context also includes the existence of liberated women in the Roman Empire, who were a concern to Roman leaders and writers. Paul's instruction for the church in 5:3-16 contains elements acceptable to Roman society as a whole and includes Christian instruction that surpasses common practice in Roman society. His instructions for young widows are an attempt to turn them away from a lifestyle that has been bringing a reaction against the Christian movement. In short, Paul gives four commands. First, provide financial support for older widows who are alone and financially destitute (5:3). Second, enroll certain older widows (5:9). Third, avoid younger widows who have strayed away from the faith (5:11). And fourth, instruct younger widows to remarry (5:14).

Elders in the Church 5:17-25

From behavior in the household of God (3:15) to instructions on the treatment of household members, the author moves on to address elders. The word *honor* in verse 17 ties the passage to the larger section. As widows are the object of honor in 5:3-16, so now elders are the object of honor in 5:17-25. An underlying concern is the influence of unhealthy teaching on the elders at Ephesus. The passage speaks about both honoring and disciplining elders. Faithful elders are distinguished from unfaithful elders, who need discipline. Since some elders need to be replaced, Paul instructs Timothy about choosing elders with great care, since some people's sins, or good deeds, are not immediately evident.

Elders should be *considered worthy of double honor, especially those who labor in preaching and teaching* (v. 17). The early church assumed the synagogue model, with a group of elders giving local leadership (Acts 11:30; 14:23; 15:2) even as the apostles gave overall leadership to the church. In Acts 20 the terms *elder* (*presbyteros*, v. 17) and *bishop* (*epis-*

kopos, v. 28) are used interchangeably, which may indicate that some elders are assigned a bishop or overseer role. Some of these elders, especially bishops, labor in preaching and teaching (1 Tim 5:17; Titus 1:9). Some interpreters distinguish between ruling elders and teaching elders, but this is not the emphasis in this passage. In 1 Timothy 5:19-21, Paul distinguishes elders who rule well (in preaching and teaching) from elders who need discipline.

Elders who labor in preaching and teaching are worthy of a double portion of honor. Does this mean they are given twice as much money as the widows? The leading Greek-English lexicon for the study of the New Testament (BDAG) says that *timē* in 1 Timothy 5:17 should be translated as "honorarium" or "compensation." In commenting on this verse, fourth-century leaders Chrysostom and Ambrosiaster both assumed that Paul was speaking about financial compensation (Gorday: 204). On the other hand, Paul warns that money can become a church leader's downfall (3:3, 8; 6:5, 10, 17). It may well be that we should not push the distinction; both honor and financial compensation may be in view. In any case, elders who work well and labor hard are to be held in high esteem and given sustenance by the Christian community they serve. For the church leader who does well and is not greedy for gain, a double portion of respect and stipend does not cause a problem (Mounce: 309). But a church leader who is lazy and greedy for money is neither worthy of honor nor financial remuneration.

Paul supports financial remuneration for elders by quoting Scripture in 5:18. The first citation is taken from the Septuagint translation of Deuteronomy 25:4, also cited in 1 Corinthians 9:9. In contrast to the cruel farmer who does not feed an ox properly, a good farmer allows the ox to eat from the grain on which it is trampling on the threshing floor. In keeping with the rabbinic pattern of arguing from the lesser matter to the greater matter, Paul says that if animals are to be fed from their work, how much more should working preachers and teachers be supported (Collins: 145)! The second citation comes from the words of Jesus in Luke 10:7 (cf. Matt 10:10). The underlying significance of 1 Timothy 5:17-18 is not that the person who preaches and teaches is worthy of double honor because of the position held in the church. It is not the office but the work of preaching and teaching that is important in the life of the church. When preaching and teaching are done well by persons of integrity, double honor is given so that they can schedule the necessary time to give their best efforts to preaching and teaching.

Not all elders at Ephesus are worthy of double honor; some have begun following unhealthy teaching (1:19-20). Accusations against some elders have come to Timothy's attention. The negative imperative of 5:19 indicates that Timothy should stop receiving unsubstantiated accusations. On the one hand, Paul instructs Timothy to protect elders from malicious and unsubstantiated accusations. On the other hand, if and when discipline is needed, Timothy must exercise it impartially, without favoritism (vv. 20-21). In short, Timothy must work *without prejudice* and *partiality*. Charges against a church leader must first of all be substantiated. Evidence for the accusation must first be established by two or three witnesses, based on the biblical principle of multiple witnesses (Deut 17:6; 19:15) and Jesus' teaching on how to work at discipline in the church (Matt 18:16; cf. also Heb 10:28). Truth is established by credible multiple witnesses. Upon receiving an accusation against a church leader that is substantiated by two or more witnesses, Timothy is to confront that person about their wrongdoing. If the elder refuses to repent, discipline moves to the next level: rebuke *in the presence of all*. This second step is taken only if they *persist in sin* (1 Tim 5:20). The verb tense for *persist* indicates continuing action. Apparently Timothy has spoken to some elders, but they have persisted in sin. Although this kind of discipline may feel harsh, it is done for two reasons: (1) the erring elder may yet repent (2 Tim 2:25); and (2) the rest of the congregation may stand in fear as they are motivated to avoid similar sinful behavior (Collins: 148).

The public setting for rebuke follows the principle of Deuteronomy 19:17-18. Peter and the early apostles publicly rebuked Ananias and Sapphira in Acts 5:1-11. Later Paul rebuked Peter publicly when he did not act consistently with the gospel (Gal 2:14). Rebuking opponents is the responsibility of a bishop like Timothy (2 Tim 4:2; Titus 1:9, 13; 2:15). When discipline is needed for leaders who persist in sin and when done publicly, it can prevent others from practicing the same sin while providing spiritual healing for the congregation that has been deceived by their leader. Timothy must not accept false accusations against any elder; but if an elder is guilty of sin and persists in it even after admonition, that elder is to be publicly rebuked.

To assure fairness of treatment for each elder, Paul reminds Timothy that he is leading the church *in the presence of God and of Christ Jesus and of the elect angels* (1 Tim 5:21). Timothy works both in the presence of the Christian community in Ephesus and in the presence of the divine Godhead. Paul uses the phrase "in the presence of God" several times (Rom 14:22; 1 Cor 1:29; 2 Cor 4:2; Gal 1:20). In the letters to Timothy and Titus, he adds *Jesus Christ* to this formula three times (1 Tim 5:21; 6:13; 2 Tim 4:1). The phrase adds weight to Paul's statement. By adding the elect angels, Paul implies that the whole heavenly tribune stands as witness to his words. It is also a reminder that God's judgment is completely impartial. In the hard work of discipline, Timothy dare not distinguish between friend and foe. An elder who is not guilty of sin is not to be condemned. If an elder is guilty and persists in sin, the bishop and the church dare not carelessly overlook the situation. Church discipline in the presence of God and the Christian congregation is too serious to be prejudiced one way or another. It requires nothing short of honest, serious, hard work.

In light of the problematic teachers in the background, Timothy may have publicly rebuked and dismissed some elders caught up in unhealthy teaching. These dismissed elders must now be replaced with new elders. Timothy is instructed to choose carefully and without haste (1 Tim 5:22), lest someone be ordained who will promote false doctrine and live a sinful life. *Do not be hasty in the laying on of hands* (NIV) is correctly interpreted by the NRSV translators as a reference to ordination. Timothy also had experienced the laying on of hands when he was chosen (1 Tim 4:14). The laying on of hands in a commissioning ritual such as ordination or in a ritual of forgiveness is not to be done hastily, lest Timothy become guilty of participating in the sins of others. If Timothy keeps people in office who are sinning (5:20) or if he does not pay attention to moral character in choosing elders, Timothy is participating in their corruption (Johnson 2001: 281). To maintain Christian integrity as a leader, Timothy must keep himself free from sin in dealing with others so that he can deal honestly with sin if and when he must do so. He must be slow to commission new elders because, as verses 24-25 indicate, the sins of some take time to surface, while others' good character may be seen only over a period of time. Care is needed in choosing elders lest sins show up later.

One way the unhealthy teachers have expressed themselves is through abstinence and ascetic teachings (4:3-4). Timothy may have abstained from wine and followed the abstinence teaching of the teachers by drinking only water, which in his case created health problems, perhaps because it was impure. So Paul instructs him not only to keep himself pure and free of sin, but also to take care of his physical health by taking a little wine. Stomach problems were common in the ancient world, and Greco-Roman doctors prescribed a little wine. The Talmud indicates that Jewish elders also believed that wine was the primary medicine (Collins: 149). For health reasons, Timothy is to avoid the ascetic practice and the Nazirite rejection of wine (Num 6:1-4), which Paul apparently considers unhealthy teaching.

Paul summarizes this section on elders by reminding Timothy that some sins come into the open before the judgment while other sins come into the open only at the judgment. Similarly, some people's good works are clearly seen now, while others' good works become visible only later. In both cases, sins and good works cannot be hidden forever. For this reason, Timothy should exercise caution in disciplining elders and in choosing new elders.

Slaves in the Church 6:1-2a

Slaves comprised a third group of persons in the household of God who needed instruction. In the Roman world a small percentage of people were very rich. Persons serving in the Roman Senate and the equestrians made up the privileged classes of people and numbered less than 1 percent of the population (Bell: 187). Most persons were patrons or clients. Patrons provided for the well-being of clients by providing jobs, food, shelter, and so forth. In some wealthy households, even some of the slaves had clients, who hoped that they would influence their owner to secure favors for them (Bell: 192). Slavery was not limited to poor persons in Roman society, nor was it based on race. Roman law did not formally recognize slave marriages. Slaves were considered property. David A. de Silva suggests that fully 25 percent of the Roman population were slaves (de Silva: 141), while another writer thinks that slaves may have constituted a majority in society (Collins: 152).

Persons became slaves if their country was conquered by another country. Criminals, persons who defaulted on their debts, and those born into slave families were all considered slaves in the first century. Some slaves served in high levels of administration, while others worked in domestic and fieldwork. Though Aristotle defined a slave as a "living tool" (*Nicomachean Ethics* 8.11; de Silva: 142), Stoics and Christians recognized the humanness of slaves (Bell: 194).

Paul's instructions on slaves connect to those regarding widows and elders in the church through the use of the term *honor*. In the Pauline mission, slaves became Christians and participated in the household of God. A Christian slave owner could go to the worship service in his household and see his slave(s) in the gathering. The slave may even be leading worship. On the one hand, Christian slaves needed instruction on how to conduct themselves in a social and cultural context with its own expectations about what slaves could or could not do. On the other hand, the church understood that freedom in Christ meant that the slave was a brother or sister in the congregation (Gal 3:28). Therefore the church had to learn how to live out its life of freedom and faithfulness to Christ in the midst of a culture that generally treated slaves poorly. The church could withdraw from society, or it could simply accommodate itself to society, both of which would destroy its life and mission.

Paul instructs Christian slaves about how they should live in two kinds of settings within the larger culture. First, he instructs slaves who have non-Christian masters (6:1). Second, he instructs slaves who have Christian masters (6:2). With both, Paul is concerned about the mission of the church (6:1b, 2b; Titus 2:10b) *[Contextualizing the Gospel, p. 339]*. As with widows (1 Tim 5:7, 14-15) and elders (5:20), the behavior of Christian slaves has a direct effect upon the mission of the church (6:1b). Paul's teaching on slaves here in 1 Timothy 6:1-2 is similar to other NT household codes (Eph 6:5-9; Col 3:22–4:1; 1 Pet 2:18-25), with two major exceptions. First, in 1 Timothy, Christian masters are not told how to treat slaves (Verner: 140-41). And second, a major distinction is made between the way slaves treat non-Christian masters and Christian masters. This distinction is significant because the religion of the master of the household often determined the religion of the whole household, including the slaves.

Let all who are under the yoke of slavery regard their masters as worthy of all honor (6:1a). The phrase *under the yoke of slavery* refers to Christians who live under the power and rule of a master. It is the normal phrase used for being under a tyrant, or in slavery, and calls attention to its burdensome character (I. H. Marshall 1999: 629). The exhortation to attribute honor to a non-Christian master indicates that Christian slaves who have found freedom in Christ likely want to be free of their masters. If slaves show disrespect and even rebel against their masters, their attitude becomes diametrically opposed to the social practice of the day. To prevent major conflict within that social and cultural context, slaves are exhorted to show respect to their masters. Disrespect to masters will bring disrepute upon the church and clash with the commonly accepted cultural practice.

Respect toward non-Christian masters is emphasized with a purpose clause: *so that the name of God and the teaching may not be blasphemed* (6:1b). Respect and honor may lead some masters to Christ. In words reminiscent of Romans 12:21, "Do not be overcome by evil, but overcome evil with good," Paul exhorts Christian slaves to align their attitude toward masters with the mission of the church. Paul considers the success of the gospel to hold more importance than the immediate abolition of slavery in Roman society, for if the gospel reaches many in Roman society, slavery itself will eventually be abolished. A similar statement in Titus 2:10 says that slaves are to live in submission to their masters *so that in everything they may be an ornament to the doctrine of God our Savior*. Lack of submission can bring the Christian message into disrepute, while submission to non-Christian masters enhances it (Bassler 1996: 104). Since God desires that everyone be saved (1 Tim

2:4), Paul apparently thinks it best not to be too disruptive of Roman society or to bring slander upon the church. Instead, Paul believes the mission of the church should lead the way. As more citizens became Christians, the institution of slavery may be eliminated. The church at Ephesus cannot afford a reputation that denies Christian teaching and blasphemes the name of God.

Next, Paul addresses slaves who have Christian masters (6:2). The Christian slave and the Christian master are brothers (NIV) and sisters in Christ. Does this mean that the master-slave relationship should also change? Paul says that *those who have believing masters must not be disrespectful to them* (6:2a). The term *be disrespectful* means to hold or show contempt toward another. Some Christian slaves think that since both master and slave are fellow members in the church family, they no longer need to be subordinate to their masters (Verner: 143). The Christian gospel was a radical leveler in Greco-Roman society, and communities of faith were hard-pressed to negotiate the implications of the gospel in terms of social roles. The fact that a slaveholder was a Christian could not become an excuse for the slave to take advantage of the master's religion to further one's own cause. On the contrary, the slave should offer willing service all the more, since servanthood brings a benefit. Paul argues from the lesser to the greater by saying the slave *must serve them all the more*. Even the master who is a Christian is still the master, and the slave is still the slave. Moreover, the service of an obedient slave results in a *benefit*. The word *benefit* means good deed, benefit, service, or benefit of service. Knight indicates that this term was used in the first century to describe the actions of one in authority who was a benefactor toward one under him (Knight 1992: 247). Thus a Christian slave's willing service for a Christian master bestows good on the master. The master in response returns that good to the slave by providing a good living for the slave.

Paul has deliberately picked up the language of honor and shame common in the ancient world (1 Tim 6:1-2) [*Honor and Shame*, p. 354]. But he reverses it. In the ancient world only masters could be benefactors. Masters as benefactors are worthy of honor (Johnson 2001: 290). But here Paul places the slave in the position of being the benefactor! A slave's service represents a position of strength and brings honor not only to the master, but also to the name of God and the Christian teaching. By slaves treating the master as beloved, both master and slaves can be brothers and sisters together in Christ and enjoy life together in the church. Both master and slaves exercise what it means to serve a higher authority (i.e., Christ) and become slaves of Christ. This Christian attitude greatly enhanced the Christian mission within

Roman society with its cultural and social stratification, while also giving the church freedom to live as Christians.

Money and the Church 6:2b-10, 17-19

After instructing Timothy on how the church should treat widows, elders, and slaves, Paul calls attention to the unhealthy teachers one more time. Paul contrasts their teachings, belief, and behavior (6:3-10) sharply with Timothy's belief and behavior (6:11-16). The teachers' own spiritual decline reaches a low point when they use religion as a means of financial gain. In contrast, rich Christians are to use their money in a godly way (6:17-19). In both cases, financial gain is evaluated from the perspective of eternity.

Paul begins by instructing Timothy to *teach and urge these duties.* These words constitute a transitional phrase that summarizes what Paul has said previously about widows, elders, and slaves, and the indictment of the unhealthy teachers who teach otherwise.

With a conditional sentence in verses 3-5, Paul assumes that the opponents are not teaching true doctrine. Paul uses "if" in the protasis (the conditional clause; v. 3 NIV; *whoever*, NRSV) and implies "then" in the apodosis (the statement based on the supposition; vv. 4-5) to indicate the kind of work the promoters of deviant teaching do. *Whoever teaches otherwise* (*heterodidaskalei*, v. 3) expresses their teaching by their behavior (vv. 4-5) and motivation (vv. 6-10). Though Paul does not fully describe their teaching, he contrasts it with sound (healthy) teaching. It *does not agree with the sound words of our Lord Jesus Christ and the teaching that is in accordance with godliness* (v. 3). *Sound* (*hygiainousin*, related to "hygiene") is a medical term and qualifies *words*, thus pointing to *healthy teaching* (cf. 1:10). The indictment on the opponents is that neither unhealthy teaching nor unhealthy practice corresponds to the words of our Lord Jesus Christ. They are not teaching according to the gospel and the way of Jesus. Sound words about Christ and teaching according to godliness bring together the content of the gospel in the first expression and the effects of the proclamation of the gospel in the second expression (Mounce: 337).

In rejecting the true gospel, some of the Ephesians are showing themselves to be conceited and to know nothing (6:4). The term refers to a swollen-headed person who knows nothing (Kelly: 134). They crave controversy, from which envy and strife arise. When these traits are present, slander, suspicions, and irritable speech follow. Such an unhealthy atmosphere destroys Christian community. In addition, their sickness robs them of the truth and leads to a depraved mind (cf. 2 Tim 3:8 NIV). The vice list that follows contains several items that Paul mentions in Romans 1:29-31, which portray a depraved mind among the Gentiles. So degrading is their sinful attitudes that their minds no longer think properly. They regress from empty pride to ignorance to disputing with words.

Wrangling (1 Tim 6:5) could be translated "constant disputations" and may suggest, according to Collins, the possibility of some violence (156). Evil desires proceeding from a corrupt mind lead to thinking that religion is a means to material gain (6:5b; 2 Tim 3:2). The teachers are using religion for financial gain in a manner similar to the way that merchants in Ephesus made money by selling items identified with Diana of the Ephesians (Acts 19:23-27).

Paul counters the teachers' greed by stating why godliness is not a means of financial gain. Real gain is *godliness combined with contentment* (1 Tim 6:6). The term *contentment* means self-sufficiency, rather than living in luxury or being greedy for wealth (*TDNT* 1:466-67). Contentment means being satisfied with what one has. In short, godliness provides all that we need. The gain is in contentment rather than in using religion for selfish ends.

For we brought nothing into the world, so that we can take nothing out of it (v. 7). The word *for* suggests the reason we should not selfishly seek wealth: we cannot take it with us when we leave this world. These words are similar to Job's words: "Naked I came from my mother's womb, and naked shall I return there" (1:21). Verse 7 is also similar to the words in Ecclesiastes: "As they came from their mother's womb, so they shall go again, naked as they came; they shall take nothing for their toil, which they may carry with their hands" (5:15). Likewise, Jesus taught that one cannot take riches into the next world (Luke 12:16-21).

It is difficult to know how to translate the conjunction *that* or *because*, which connects the two clauses in the middle of verse 7. Does it mean that birth and death are similar, with nothing on either end of life? Or does the conjunction suggest that as we came into the world without anything, so also we leave the world without anything? It is translated in various ways: *so that* (NRSV), *and* (NIV, NJB), and *for that matter* (NEB). Many take it in the weakened sense and translate it as *and*. Perhaps it is best not to translate the conjunction literally. Further explanation comes in verse 8: *But if we have food and clothing, we will be content with these.* These words echo the teaching of Jesus in the Sermon on the Mount (Matt 6:24-34). Contentment with food and clothing produces gain in godliness, which is not to say that religion is a means of financial gain.

In verses 9-10, Paul returns to the sin of greed. The persons in Ephesus about whom Paul is concerned do not recognize the danger in their selfish desire for riches. The teaching on riches here in 1 Timothy 6:9-10 agrees with Jesus' teaching on riches in Luke 16:19-31 and the rejection of Simon the magician by Peter and John in Acts 8:9-24. Paul in effect says the desire *to be rich* plunges one into a deceiving *temptation* and leads one into the devil's snare. Once *trapped* in the snare, selfish *desires* escalate to the point where one falls *into ruin and destruction* (1 Tim 6:9). The all-consuming sinful desire to become rich ends up sinking one into the depths of moral decline. Three steps lead the greedy person to destruction. First is the lure of *temptation* by Satan, second is the trap that catches one in many *senseless and harmful desires*, and third is plunging headlong *into ruin and destruction.* Collins writes, "The imagery of sinking is consistent with that of the pit into which the money-lovers fall, that is, the pit of ruin and destruction" (158).

For the love of money is a root of all kinds of evil (v. 10a). This phrase is a commonly held proverb, which Paul uses to strengthen the argument of verse 9. The philosophic moralists believed that there are root vices. The term *root* is used in proverbial sayings with reference to results either good or bad (I. H. Marshall 1999: 651). Here its proverbial meaning is bad. Paul does not mean that the love of money is the only root of all evil, but that it is one root among several that bring evil. Proverbs are often inexact and overstated, hyperbolic. Here the proverb indicates the danger of loving money. It is a trap that leads to many other sins. *In their eagerness to be rich* (10b), the teachers *have wandered away from the faith* and have inflicted pain upon themselves in their unfulfilled desire for riches.

Paul does not end teaching about money on a negative note. Instead, he turns to the positive and speaks about the good way in which money can be used in the church. In 6:17-19, Paul turns to faithful Christians who are wealthy and are not guilty of greed. He puts things in perspective by comparing life in this world with eternal life, as he did previously in a faithful saying (4:8b-10). In 6:17-18, Paul gives six admonitions, built around five imperatives. After commanding the rich *not to be haughty* or to *set their hopes on . . . riches*, Paul calls attention to the riches that God provides and lists four positive ways rich Christians can use their wealth. Paul contrasts the present and the future as he begins with those who are presently rich and ends with those who store up treasure as a good foundation for the future. He contrasts setting one's hope on earthly riches with placing one's hope in God (6:19). Paul plays with the root word *rich* (*plou-*, related to "plutocrat") by using the term in four different ways, all of which sound similar in Greek: a plural personal noun, the *rich*; an objective noun, *wealth*; an adverb, *richly*; and a verb, *to be rich*.

For the fifth time in this epistle, Paul charges or commands (*parangellō*) Timothy (1:3; 4:11; 5:7; 6:13, 17). Knowing that a rich person may face certain temptations, Paul (through Timothy) commands rich persons *not to be haughty or to set their hopes on the uncertainty of riches* (v. 17a). The uncertainty of riches is often mentioned in the OT wisdom literature and in the teaching of Jesus (Prov 11:28; Eccl 5:13-17; Luke 12:16-21). Wealthy people face the danger of becoming proud of their riches by thinking that riches give one security in life. The wealthy look with disdain on those with less wealth, thereby creating social divisions. Arrogance and pride easily engulf the rich. The Bible consistently teaches that human wealth is transitory and unreliable (Luke 12:13-31; James 1:9-11; 4:13-17; 5:1-6). So Paul exhorts rich Christians to set their hope *on God who richly provides us with everything for our enjoyment* (1 Tim 6:17b). God is the benefactor, and we are recipients of his benefits. God richly provides for us (Pss 104:27-28; 145:15-16; Matt 6:25-33). God's provisions are full of grace. They are not limited to financial benefits. God's rich provisions are meant to bring us enjoyment. As recipients, we are not to confuse the gift with the Giver, but we are to place our hope in God.

On the more positive side, Paul gives wealthy Christians four commands on how to use riches with an awareness that all one has is a gift from God. The four commands are *to do good, to be rich in good works,* [*to be*] *generous, and* [*to be*] *ready to share* (1 Tim 6:18). Wealthy Christians can do good deeds with their money. How can the wealthy be rich in good works? By helping the church care for needy widows and by providing financial support for those who preach and teach (5:3, 17). Generosity and the readiness to share demonstrate a willing and generous spirit. In all these ways, the rich use their wealth for the benefit of others, and their actions correspond to God's way of providing richly for us. This teaching parallels what Jesus says in Luke: one should hope in God and not in riches (12:22-34; 18:29), use wealth for doing good (12:33; 14:12-14; 18:22), and store up treasure for eternal life (12:16-21; 18:22). Zacchaeus experienced economic conversion and shared his wealth with others (19:1-10). In like manner, 1 Timothy 6:17-19 teaches a positive use of riches, the opposite of using greed for financial gain (6:6-10).

In carrying out these four commands, wealthy Christians store up treasure for the future and take hold of real life—eternal life (v. 19). Paul encourages Timothy to pursue this eternal life. The use of the term *real* underscores the difference between present life in this world based on fleeting wealth and life that only the eternal God can give. As William D. Mounce says, "By being generous, the rich are not losing their wealth. Rather they are laying it away in heaven, and by doing so, they are establishing a firm foundation for eternity, for life that is truly life" (368).

THE TEXT IN BIBLICAL CONTEXT

Care of Widows

In the OT, three groups of persons are given special care: the orphan, the stranger, and the widow. Ancient society allowed a young woman two roles: she could be an unmarried virgin in her father's house, or a faithful and child-producing wife in her husband's home.

The prophets voiced stern condemnations against the mistreatment of widows. According to Malachi 3:5, God will bring swift judgment upon those who mistreat the alien, the orphan, or the widow. According to the Law and the Prophets, the widow as a member of the covenant community must receive the same merciful treatment that is given to the sojourner (migrant, alien) and the fatherless (orphans; Deut 14:29; 24:17; Amos 2:8; Zech 7:10). When grain and grapes were harvested, some were left for the hungry widow, the stranger, and the orphan (Deut 24:19-22). The Levite, the sojourner, the fatherless, and the widow are to be given a tithe of the produce in the third year (Deut 26:12; 27:19).

God will sustain the fatherless children and preserve the widows if they put their trust in God (Jer 49:11). God is declared to be "father of orphans and protector of widows" (Ps 68:5). He watches over the strangers and upholds the orphan and the widow (146:9). Jesus reaffirmed God's concern for the widow by speaking with anger about those who "devour widows' houses" (Luke 20:47). And James writes about pure religion that cares for orphans and widows in their distress (1:27).

In the early church, the same concern about widows in the Jewish Christian community was extended to the Hellenistic Christian community (Acts 6:1-6). First Timothy 5:3-16 identifies three groups of widows. First are the older, *real*, destitute widows, who have no other means of financial support (5:3, 5, 9-10, 16b). Second are younger widows, who are encouraged to remarry (5:11, 14). And third are middle-aged or older widows who have family members to take care of them (5:4, 8, 16). From the first and third groups of widows emerged a special list of widows who were enrolled and given a ministry role in the church (5:9; see notes for 1 Tim 5, above). This special order of widows is recognized by some of the early church fathers, such as Ignatius (*To the Smyrnaeans* 13.1).

Elders

Elders have a long history in Israel and in the Christian church. As parents exercised authority in the family, so elders exercised authority in the clan, tribe, and local community (*TDNT* 6:655). In Exodus 18:13-27,

Jethro told Moses, his son-in-law, to choose able, God-fearing, and trustworthy people who would not take a bribe to help manage the children of Israel. In Numbers 11:16-30, Moses chose seventy elders upon whom the Spirit of Yahweh rested to help give spiritual oversight to the children of Israel. During the intertestamental period, a "council of elders" (*gerousia*, senate) arose and became a ruling body of Jews, with its seat in Jerusalem during the Seleucid Period for Judah (early second century BC). Out of this ruling body emerged the seventy-one-member Sanhedrin (council/court). In synagogues, one person was chosen as "the ruler of the synagogue." He took care of the building and selected persons to read the OT Scripture and conduct the worship service. By the first century AD, each Jewish community had its council of elders or presbytery, which gave general administrative oversight of the Jewish communities and represented the Jews in relationships with the Roman authorities (Shepherd: 73).

Over time, Jewish elders added comments to the OT known as "the tradition of the elders" (Matt 15:2; Mark 7:3-5). This commentary on Scripture often was given as much authority as the OT law itself. Jesus confronted the elders and corrected their interpretations by calling attention to the true meaning of the Law. Six times in the Sermon on the Mount, Jesus stated, "You have heard that it was said. . . , but I say to you. . . ."

Early Christianity naturally assumed this Jewish eldership model. The Jerusalem church had elders (Acts 11:30; 15:2, 4, 6, 22-23; 16:4; 21:18). Paul and Barnabas ordained elders in the mission churches in Asia (14:23). Paul met with the Ephesian elders during his final journey to Jerusalem. In Acts 20 the term *elder* (*presbyteros*, v. 17) is changed to *bishop* (*episkopos*, v. 28), a Greek term used for administrators. There are deacons and bishops in the church at Philippi (Phil 1:1). Titus is exhorted to appoint elders in every town (Titus 1:5). Elders who do well in preaching and teaching in Ephesus are worthy of double honor (1 Tim 5:17), are disciplined only after two or three witnesses present evidence against them (v. 19), and are to be chosen carefully (v. 22). In 1 Timothy 3:1-7 Paul gives the spiritual qualifications for a bishop.

A gradual transition took place within the NT from an earlier charismatic form of leadership (1 Cor 12:4-31) to office gifts (Eph 4:11-12) and finally to the full development of offices. In this transition we see a combination of lay leadership gifts alongside office gifts. Many agree with Lightfoot's classic theory that the episcopate arose out of the presbytery in a gradual process whereby one of the elders was chosen as bishop. Thus, all bishops formerly were elders, but not all elders became bishops.

By the time of Ignatius (ca. 115), the threefold order of bishop, elder, and deacon as ordained offices was prominent (e.g., Ignatius, *To the Magnesians* 2; *To the Smyrnaeans* 8.1; *To the Trallians* 3.1; 7.2). Already in about AD 96, Clement of Rome spoke of a succession of "tested men" to replace the bishops and deacons so that there would not be strife over the title of bishop (*1 Clement* 42.4-5; 44.1-3; Shepherd: 74). What Clement of Rome hinted at later became known as apostolic succession, in order to establish a clear line of authority for the church.

Slavery

In the biblical world and the world of the ancient Near East, slavery was unlike the slavery practiced in the New World of the West (Dandamayev: 58). In biblical times, slavery was not tied to race. Slavery was an economic institution, much like unjust employer-employee relations in the modern world: an institutionalized classism.

We see slavery in all periods of antiquity among the Egyptian, Mesopotamian, Hittite, and Persian societies. In the Greek tradition, an enslaved person was considered inferior by nature and thus fortunate to have a Greek master (Dandamayev: 66). Aristotle taught that some ethnic groups were by nature suited to be slaves (*Politics* 1.1255a.20; Bell: 193) and defined a slave as a "living tool" (*Nicomachean Ethics* 8.11; de Silva: 142). Sources of slavery included captives taken in war battles, persons who could not pay their debts, persons born as children of slaves, and the sale of children of free persons into slavery. Slaves were bought and sold, deposited as security, included in dowries, and transferred by inheritance. Ancient laws prohibited slaves from leaving their master. A slave who escaped and was caught had to return to the master. Children born to a female slave were considered to be the property of her master.

According to the OT, a person could be held in slavery for only six years (Exod 21:2; Deut 15:12; Jer 34:14). If a Hebrew slave was married when he became a slave, his wife was set free with him at the end of the six-year period (Exod 21:3; Lev 25:40-42). When freed, the slave could go back to his family (Lev 25:39-41). If the slave decided not to go free, but become part of the master's family, the master would pierce the slave's ear with an awl, which marked the slave for life (Exod 21:6; Deut 15:16-17). If a Hebrew sold himself to a resident alien (such as to pay a debt), that alien was required to set him free as soon as he or a relative could pay for his redemption (Lev 25:47-52). If the slave could not redeem himself through hired labor, he continued to work until the year of Jubilee, when he and his children were to be set free (25:53-54). According to the Deuteronomic law, a Hebrew may sell oneself to another Hebrew and work for six years; in the seventh year the master is to release that slave and give the freed person gifts for establishing a household. After all, six years of slave labor was worth far more to the master than that of a regular hired man (Deut 15:13-14, 18).

Female slaves were often treated as a commodity. A female was leased for work, given as a pledge, or handed over as dowry. Male members of a household understood that they could use a female slave's body for her physical strength in work or for sexual exploitation. On the year of Jubilee, all slaves were to be freed (Lev 25:40-43). Release from slavery by the hand of God became a metaphor for divine redemption. "Remember that you were a slave in the land of Egypt, and the LORD your God redeemed you" (Deut 15:15).

Slavery in Palestine was a domestic and economic way of life. Slaves worked alongside their master in the field, were treated like members of the family (in some senses), and participated in the religious observances of their master, including Sabbath rest.

Slavery in the NT must be interpreted in the context of the Greco-Roman world. First-century slavery was largely an economic way of life. The education of slaves was encouraged, and many slaves carried out highly responsible social functions. Slaves took part in religious and cultural life, much the same as freeborn persons. Most urban and domestic slaves anticipated emancipation by the age of thirty (Bartchy: 66).

Children became the primary source of slaves. Many persons sold themselves into slavery to pay debts, to climb socially, and to find a more secure life than some free persons had (Bartchy: 67). Erastus, the city treasurer of Corinth (Rom 16:23), was likely a slave who had sold himself to the city to the age of forty and then was allowed to go free. The city honored Erastus for his years of service by placing a marker on the street in front of the main theater with his name on it. As a Christian, Erastus was one of the more prominent members of the Christian church in Corinth. Unfortunately, some infants in the Roman world were rejected by their fathers and left at the edge of town to die. Often these infants were picked up by slave traders or other persons who could not have children (Bell: 240). This practice is not mentioned in the NT, but it was a known practice in the Roman world. Owners of slaves not only expected a slave person to work, but they also believed that they had free access to a female slave's body. Thus, slaves were regarded as sexually available by masters and their sons. The NT often speaks against sexual sins, which surely included the sexual exploitation of slaves.

Slaves who became Christians belonged to larger Roman households. When this happened, tension arose between Christian slaves and non-Christian masters, since Christianity required a change in morality *[Household Behavior, p. 355]*. An account of the Christian influence upon slavery is found in the book of Philemon. Onesimus, a runaway slave, became a Christian under Paul's missionary work. Paul works with the tension between Onesimus's world of slavery and his new Christian world. The apostle writes to Philemon and instructs him to treat Onesimus "as a . . . beloved brother" (16). Onesimus cannot be Philemon's brother on Sunday and just a slave the rest of the week. A new Christian relationship must be forged between the two. From the book of Philemon, it is clear that a new social reality is beginning to arise as the Christian message breaks into the Roman world.

Money

The OT law required a tithe of all possessions as a reminder that God is giver of all things. Sabbath oriented all of time to God. Giving up one's land in the Jubilee year served as a reminder that land belongs to God. "The land shall not be sold in perpetuity, for the land is mine; with me you are but aliens and tenants" (Lev 25:23). Time, land, and space are God-given things and not one's own. In fact, *all* that one possesses belongs to the Lord (Deut 14:22-29). The festivals of Passover (Unleavened Bread, barley harvest, early spring), Firstfruits (Pentecost, wheat harvest, late spring), and Tabernacles (Ingathering, vintage, fall) were reminders of God's goodness and Israel's response of thankfulness for what God had done. The Feast of Weeks (Pentecost) recognized God as owner, so the firstfruits were to be brought into the house of God (Exod 23:14-17, 19; 34:21-26).

The prophet Amos condemned Israel for its economic injustice (2:6-8). Amos said, "But let justice roll down like waters, and righteousness like an everflowing stream" (5:24). Similarly, Micah denounced Israel's injustices and said, "What does the LORD require of you but to do justice, and to love kindness, and to walk humbly with your God?" (6:8). Malachi 3:8-10 says:

> Will anyone rob God? Yet you are robbing me! But you say, "How are we robbing you?" In your tithes and offerings! You are cursed with a curse, for you are robbing me—the whole nation of you! Bring the full tithe into the storehouse, so that there may be food in my house, and thus put me to the test, says the LORD of Hosts; see if I will not open the windows of heaven for you and pour down for you an overflowing blessing.

Also insightful is Proverbs 30:7-9:

Two things I ask of you;
do not deny them to me before I die;
Remove far from me falsehood and lying;
give me neither poverty nor riches;
feed me with the food that I need,
or I shall be full, and deny you,
and say, "Who is the Lord?"
or I shall be poor, and steal,
and profane the name of my God.

In first-century Palestine about 93 percent of the Jewish people were poor peasants. In the first century, the income of a moderately wealthy person would have been seven hundred times greater than that of a poor person (Bell: 190). Given the economic injustice of the time, it is not surprising that many of Jesus' teachings were directed to rich persons. In Luke's Gospel, Jesus tells the parable of the rich fool (12:16-21) and the story of the rich man and Lazarus (16:19-31). Conversely, he commends Zacchaeus for his willingness to make financial restitution: "Today salvation has come to this house" (19:1-10). Jesus commends the poor widow who gives out of her poverty (21:1-4). Luke calls for economic conversion to enter the kingdom of God.

In the early church, Ananias and Sapphira were disciplined because they were dishonest about money matters (Acts 5:1-11). Peter rebuked Simon the magician, who thought he could purchase religious power with money (8:14-24). Using religion as a means of financial gain was confronted when the Christian message first came to Ephesus (19:23-27) and was condemned again at a later time at Ephesus, according to 1 Timothy 6:5b. Economic sharing was part of the early church's life (Acts 2:45; 4:34-35; 11:29). Barnabas is commended for sharing his wealth with the church (4:36-37).

Paul calls attention to the goodness and graciousness of God, who satisfies our needs and teaches Christian stewardship (2 Cor 8–9). Rich Christians in Ephesus are not to set their hope on the uncertainty of riches (1 Tim 6:17a) but to place their hope in the *God who richly provides* (6:17b). Rich Christians are instructed to respond in four ways to God's grace: (1) to do good, (2) to be rich in good works, (3) to be generous, and (4) to be ready to share. If rich Christians practice stewardship in this way, they will be *storing up for themselves the treasure of a good foundation for the future, so that they may take hold of the life that really is life* (6:19).

THE TEXT IN THE LIFE OF THE CHURCH

Care of Widows

Sixteenth-century Anabaptist believers were committed to the church as Christian community and therefore expected radical economic sharing within that community of faith. In the case of the Anabaptists of Moravia in the 1520s and 1530s, community sharing led to an organized community of goods. All Anabaptists believed that Christian community meant caring for people who were poor, widowed, and orphaned, and generally living as members of one body (Snyder and Hecht: 6).

Article 9 of the Dordrecht Confession of Faith of 1632 says, "And that also honorable aged widows should be chosen and ordained deaconesses, that they with the deacons may visit, comfort, and care for, the poor, feeble, sick, sorrowing, and needy, as also the widows and orphans, and assist in attending to other wants and necessities of the church to the best of their ability. 1 Timothy 5:9-10; Romans 16:1-2; James 1:27" (Wenger: 380). Nearly all of the confessions of faith in Mennonite history assign deacons the responsibility to care for the poor, including widows (Stuckey: 24-33).

Margarethe Prüss, of Strasbourg, France (d. 1542), was widowed two times. Her father began a printing business in Strasbourg, and Margarethe learned much about the printing business before his death in 1510. Knowing that she would not be recognized as an owner of a printing business as a woman, she married a printer who took over her father's business when he died. Nevertheless, she was the business manager and took care of paying the debts, handled the shop purchases, and distributed the salaries to the employees. In 1519 her first husband, Reinhardt Beck, began printing evangelical works, including a treatise written by Martin Luther. In 1522, he died, leaving Margarethe as a widow. Normally a widow could only run the printing business for one or two years, according to the printing guild. So in 1524 she married Johannes Schwann, who had left the monastery in Basel and made his way to Strasbourg, where he also learned the printing business.

Schwann's marriage to Margarethe allowed the printing business to continue. Together Johannes Schwann and Margarethe printed some of Luther's writings and the writings of Andreas Karlstadt. They also became aware of early Anabaptist writings. Johannes Schwann died in 1526, leaving Margarethe a widow for a second time. On May 27, 1527, she married her third husband, Balthasar Beck. He, too, learned the printing trade, and together they continued the business Margarethe had obtained from her father. From their press came the works of Anabaptist leaders. At the time of her death on May 23, 1542, Margarethe and her third husband had printed a large amount of Anabaptist literature. Despite being widowed twice, she was able to keep the printing business going. Each time she married, she and her new husband increased Lutheran and Anabaptist publications. The printers she married were either Anabaptist sympathizers or Anabaptists themselves (Snyder and Hecht: 270). As a printshop owner and a woman, Margarethe overcame the limits of the role assigned to women by sixteenth-century culture and, as a result, made a significant contribution to the early Anabaptist movement far beyond the city of Strasbourg (Snyder and Hecht: 270). Perhaps Margarethe's story of widowhood can be appreciated in the context of 1 Timothy 5:9 as one who should be placed on a special list of widows who have served the church.

Elders in the Church

The term, role, and function of elders have gone through several changes in the history of the church. The Catholic Church has followed a hierarchical model of deacon, priest, bishop, archbishop, cardinal, and pope. Its recent catechism (§1541) notes that the priesthood of Aaron and the service of the Levites, as in the institution of the seventy elders, prefigures the ordained ministry of the new covenant (Ratzinger: 385). The Catechism (§1554) goes on to say:

> Catholic doctrine, expressed in the liturgy, the Magisterium, and the constant practice of the Church, recognizes that there are two degrees of ministerial participation in the priesthood of Christ: the episcopacy and the presbyterate. The diaconate is intended to help and serve them. For this reason the term *sacerdos* in current usage denotes bishops and priests but not deacons. Yet Catholic doctrine teaches that the degrees of priestly participation (episcopate and presbyterate) and the degree of service (diaconate) are all three conferred by a sacramental act called "ordination," that is, by the sacrament of Holy Orders: "Let everyone revere the deacons as Jesus Christ, the bishop as the image of the Father, and the presbyters as the senate of God and the assembly of the apostles. For without them one cannot speak of the Church. (Ratzinger: 388-89)

John Calvin used the terms *bishops, presbyters, pastors*, and *ministers* for those who rule the church, understanding *bishop* and *presbyter* as names for the same office (1060). Presbyterian polity distinguishes between teaching elders and ruling elders. Methodist churches have bishops, who provide oversight for conferences. Methodists also have district superintendents, who give oversight to churches within conferences. Baptist churches follow a congregational polity, with a pastor and a board of deacons. Baptists do not have elders or bishops, though some have deacons. Baptist congregations are autonomous and relate to one another in associations.

Until the middle of the twentieth century, the Church of the Brethren had a denominational and pastoral advisory body of elders, to whom pastors went for counsel. Congregations have deacons and an administrative board. A district executive gives oversight to congregations in a given geographical area.

The Emden Protocol (1579) treats in detail the call and function of elders and ministers among early Mennonites (*ME* 2:178). Ministers preached and elders carried out the full ministry of baptism, serving communion, ordaining others, and exercising discipline (178). In some Mennonite history, the term *elder* (*Ältester*) was interchangeable with *bishop*. Mennonites of North America followed the threefold ministry of bishop, minister, and deacon for three centuries. In the Russian-Canadian Mennonite tradition, the terms *Ältester*, *lay minister*, and *deacon* were used.

In the mid-twentieth century, many Mennonites of Swiss-German heritage began to use the term *elder* in a new way. In these circles, *Ältester*" or *elder* had much earlier been set aside in favor of the term *bishop,* and now laypersons were chosen as elders to assist the pastor. In 1996, *A Mennonite Polity for Ministerial Leadership* was published, which outlines a threefold pattern of ministry. First, an overseer or bishop gives spiritual oversight to churches and has the right to ordain persons. Second, pastoral leadership includes preaching, teaching, and shepherding the congregation. And third, elders, deacons, and lay ministers help with pastoral kinds of ministry without being ordained. The polity says, "*Elders* are chosen in some congregations to do pastoral care with the pastor, creating a ministerial leadership team, providing spiritual oversight of the congregation, and serving as a support group for the pastor" (Thomas: 78-79). They also are to look after the needy (Thomas: 79). Thus in the Mennonite Church the term *elders* presently means those who, as laypersons, nonordained leaders, help the pastor(s) carry out spiritual ministry. It is clearly distinguished from the administrative oversight ministry of bishops or overseers.

Slavery and the Church

From the eighteenth to the twentieth centuries, the Western church, particularly in the United States, divided over the question of slavery. Slaves were brought from Africa to the United States, where they were used for economic gain. Slavery became an institution based on race, education, and economics. Some Christian denominations in North America split over the slavery issue. Sunday morning became the most segregated hour of the week in the Christian church. In South Africa, the white Dutch Reformed Afrikaners separated themselves from black people. Only in the latter part of the twentieth century did the church speak out against racial segregation and start to bring change in the political, social, and economic life of the people in the United States and in South Africa.

On the basis of the Israelite exodus from Egyptian slavery, Martin Luther King Jr., the major civil rights advocate of the twentieth century, argued that God is on the side of the oppressed. He called for social and economic justice and led a civil rights movement that changed the economic and political climate in the United States. His speeches and writings reflect the liberation theology that was developing and growing in Latin America. Liberation theology emphasizes social and economic justice through God's work in liberating the poor and oppressed.

King's famous letter to American pastors from a Birmingham Jail exposed the sin of slavery, with its social, economic, and racial injustice. King wrote:

> Any law that degrades human personality is unjust. All segregation statutes are unjust because segregation distorts the soul and damages the personality. It gives the segregator a false sense of superiority, and the segregated a false sense of inferiority. . . . Segregation, to use the terminology of the Jewish philosopher Martin Buber, substitutes an "I-it" relationship for an "I-thou" relationship, and ends up relegating persons to the status of things. Hence segregation is not only politically, economically, and sociologically unsound, it is [also] morally wrong and sinful. Paul Tillich has said that sin is separation. Is not segregation an existential expression of man's tragic separation, his awful estrangement, his terrible sinfulness? . . . I urge men to disobey . . . segregation ordinances, for they are morally wrong. (Freeman: 356)

In South Africa, the Dutch Reformed Church promoted racial segregation for many years. Black church leaders, such as Bishop Desmond Tutu, called for justice. Blacks in South Africa pointed out the failure of the Afrikaner church's interpretation of the Bible. Social, political, and economic change came late in the twentieth century. Significant in this period of change was the Truth and Reconciliation Commission, which offered white leaders forgiveness if they honestly acknowledged their sinful participation in apartheid, with its heinous deeds against the blacks. As the Christian blacks in the United States sang "We Shall Overcome" in their freedom marches, so also Christian blacks in South Africa sang, "If you believe and I believe and we together pray, / the Holy Spirit must come down and set God's people free" (Zimbabwe traditional text).

Money and the Church

In 1 Timothy 6:17-19, rich persons are challenged to do good with their wealth. Several examples of putting these verses into practice are found in the history of the church. The expansion of the church through missions, growth in Christian educational institutions, and the building of healthcare institutions can often be traced to persons who generously shared their wealth.

A major concern of Moravian Anabaptists in the sixteenth century and their leader Peter Riedemann was economic sharing. They believed that faithful Christians share both spiritually and economically with one another. Peter wrote a major confession of faith, in which he said:

> Community of goods applies to both spiritual and material gifts. All of God's gifts, not only the spiritual but also the temporal, have been given so that they not be kept but be shared with each other. Therefore, the fellowship of believers should be visible not only in spiritual but also in temporal things. (119)

Two twentieth-century examples putting 1 Timothy 6:17-19 into practice show the positive dimensions of sharing wealth. Jacob Shenk owned and operated a successful chicken hatchery in Harrisonburg, Virginia. He was a generous person and supported Eastern Mennonite College and mission work in Kentucky. Income from the hatchery business grew far beyond Jacob's expectations. His mission interests led him to provide leadership and financial support for missions in Kentucky. Unknown to most persons, from his hatchery business Jacob gave large amounts of money for the operation and gradual development of Eastern Mennonite College. He worked out a special arrangement with the U.S. government so that he could give 90 percent of his profits to charity. His life came to an end in an airplane accident while flying to and from the mission field in Kentucky.

J. A. Schowalter was a Mennonite farmer, stockman, and businessman who lived near Newton, Kansas. At the time of his death, Schowalter had extensive holdings in five counties in central and western Kansas and in four counties in Oklahoma. He had holdings in natural gas and oil production in Oklahoma and Kansas as well as investments in stocks and bonds. Believing in Christian stewardship and the importance of doing good with what one has, Schowalter formed a foundation that would manage his wealth and do good by giving to the church. Over a period of fifty years, the Schowalter Foundation has made grants of more than nine million dollars, with significant amounts going for college scholarships for students in Mennonite colleges and seminaries. The Schowalter Foundation also has funded several projects in poor countries and assisted programs for people with disabilities.

1 Timothy 6:11-16, 20-21

Final Instructions for Timothy

PREVIEW

Paul now turns directly to Timothy with final instructions. The importance of Timothy's life and work is stated in 6:11-12, with four imperatives that relate to daily activity, followed by a doxology emphasizing God's sovereignty (6:13-16). Finally, in 6:20-21, Timothy is commanded to guard the deposit of faith.

OUTLINE

Four Commands, 6:11-12
Doxology, 6:13-16
Guard the Trust, 6:20-21

EXPLANATORY NOTES

Four Commands 6:11-12

Paul gives his final instructions in the form of imperative commands. The first imperative, *shun*, is strong: Timothy is to flee from the desire to be rich, with its accompanying evils (1 Tim 6:9-10). Turning from these evils, Timothy is commanded with a second imperative: *Pursue* six virtues. The combination *shun* and *pursue* also occurs in 2 Timothy 2:22 and calls to mind Paul's ethical instructions elsewhere to "put off" and "put on" (Eph 4:22-24; Col 3:8-17). In turning away from the vices of the opponents (1 Tim 6:4-5), Timothy is to pursue three pairs of virtues: *righteousness* and *godliness*, *faith* and *love*, *endurance* and *gentleness* (6:11). These virtues also appear in 2 Timothy 2:22-25; 3:5, 10 (NIV). The first pair, *righteousness* and *godliness*, calls Timothy's attention to right relationship with God and to a life fully consecrated to God. The second pair, *faith* and *love*, calls attention to a trusted and loving relationship with others in the church. *Faith* and *love* appear together several times in the letters to Timothy and Titus (1 Tim 1:5, 14; 2:15; 4:12; 6:11; 2 Tim 1:13; 2:22; 3:10; Titus 2:2). The third pair, *endurance* and *gentleness*, emphasizes *steadfastness* as an enduring quality needed in Timothy's leadership in the midst of opposition (2 Tim 3:10; Titus 2:2).

A third imperative, *fight*, speaks of Timothy's athletic effort to win the race (1 Tim 6:12). Timothy must pursue the good fight of faith with all his effort. He is to keep and protect the Christian faith (6:20) and remain faithful. This imperative emphasizes Paul's call to daily perseverance and ties into the athletic imagery used elsewhere in the letters to Timothy and Titus (1 Tim 4:10; 2 Tim 2:2-4; 4:7).

Finally, the fourth imperative, *Take hold of eternal life*, means to grasp tightly and hang on to eternal life (Mounce: 356). God called Timothy to eternal life. Now Timothy must persevere and hang on to it. Regarding this eternal life, Timothy *made the good confession in the presence of many witnesses* (6:12b). Some NT scholars take *good confession* to refer to Timothy's ordination, when hands were laid on him. Others take *good confession* to refer to Timothy's confession of faith in his baptismal vows. Since the call to eternal life came at the same time as Timothy's good confession, and this confession was made in the presence of many witnesses, I take it to mean his baptism. Christian baptism took place in the presence of the congregation and was accompanied by one's confession of faith in Christ. These four imperatives "exhort Timothy to persevere both in his life in Christ and his ministry (the present) and thereby to secure the awaited prize (the future), by being reminded of his beginnings—God's call and his own response (the past)" (Fee 1988: 150).

Doxology 6:13-16

In addition to a public confession of faith, Timothy lives and carries out his ministry in the presence of God and of Christ Jesus (6:13a). Verses 13-16 are one sentence in Greek. Fee notes a chiastic pattern (Fee 2007: 435):

A The living God
    B The historical Christ who bore witness preceding his crucifixion
    B′ The coming of Christ
A′ The eternal and only God

Timothy is charged to keep the commandment in the presence of God and Christ Jesus and to continue to keep the commandment until the eschatological appearing of Christ Jesus. The text climaxes with a doxology. Timothy is given this command in the presence of Christ Jesus, who made a good confession before Pontius Pilate. Jesus' faithfulness as a specific historical act becomes the basis by which Paul exhorts Timothy to faithfulness, in contrast to the unfaithful teachers. Timothy is charged *to keep the commandment without spot or blame until the manifestation of our Lord Jesus Christ* (6:14). The commandment is the entire work that Paul has commissioned Timothy to do. The command is to remain unblemished, above reproach, never contaminated by deviant teaching or vain speculations. Faithfulness and perseverance are required until the appearing (*epiphaneia*) of our Lord Jesus Christ.

Instead of using the more common term for our Lord's appearing (*parousia*), Paul uses *epiphaneia* or its cognate verb several times in the letters to Timothy and Titus (2 Tim 1:10; 4:1, 8; Titus 2:11,13; 3:4). *Epiphaneia* is the same word that was used for the appearance of the Roman emperor. By applying the term *epiphaneia* to Christ Jesus, Paul makes a direct assault on emperor worship.

Here Paul breaks out in a doxology (1 Tim 6:15-16). The content of the doxology declares God's sovereignty and kingship in opposition to Roman imperial worship *[Names for God and the Imperial Cult, p. 357]*. Seven phrases are stated in the doxology.

The blessed and only Sovereign emphasizes God's sovereignty. God is not one sovereign among many sovereigns; God is the *only* Sovereign.

King of kings and Lord of lords calls attention to two OT ideas: King of kings was first used for the Babylonian and Persian emperors (Ezek 26:7; Dan 2:37; Ezra 7:12). By the time of the Maccabees, it was applied to God (163 BC; 2 Macc 13:4). *Lord of lords* expressed God's exclusive sovereignty over all other deities (Deut 10:17; Ps 136:2-3). Both terms were brought together in late Judaism (*1 Enoch* 9.4) and together designate Christ in Revelation 17:14 and 19:16.

He alone has immortality declares that God alone is eternal, not the mortal emperor. Nor does the human soul naturally possess immortality, as many Greeks taught (I. H. Marshall 1999: 667).

And dwells in unapproachable light. In the OT, God's glory comes in the form of light, cloud, or smoke, which are associated with God (Exod 13:21; 33:17-23; 40:34-38; Ps 104:2; Isa 10:17). In the NT the heavenly city is described as needing no light because God's presence provides light (Rev 22:5). Indeed, "God is light" (1 John 1:5-7).

Whom no one has ever seen or can see shows that the invisibility of God is clearly set forth in both the OT (Exod 33:20) and the NT (John 1:17-18).

To him be honor and eternal dominion indicates that only God is worthy to be honored because of his eternal rule (1 Tim 1:17; Eph 1:19-20; 6:10; 1 Pet 4:11; 3:22; Jude 25; Rev 1:6; 5:13).

Gordon D. Fee aptly describes the significance of this doxology. "Ephesus was not only the haven of Artemis, but an early center of emperor worship as well. This doxology, therefore, is Paul's parting shot that the God with whom the church has to do in the gospel of Christ is none other than the supreme Ruler of the universe, the Lord over all other lords" (Fee 1988: 154).

Guard the Trust 6:20-21

Paul closes the letter with a final warning about the opponents' activities. Two exhortations are found in these final verses: a positive one exhorting Timothy to guard what has been entrusted to him, and a negative one condemning the unhealthy teachers. For the third time in this epistle, Paul addresses Timothy by name (1:2; 18, 6:20), thus personalizing the final command and warning in this direct address.

Timothy is commanded to *guard what has been entrusted to you* (6:20a). The term *deposit* or *what has been entrusted to you* refers to a valuable possession placed in the hands of another person for safekeeping. A person whom another entrusts with a treasured possession was under a sacred and legal duty to keep the deposit safe (Fee 1988: 160). The word *deposit* catches one's attention in light of what Paul said earlier in this chapter about riches. Timothy has been entrusted with the *gospel*, not with money. His task is to resist unhealthy teaching, persevere in the faith, proclaim, and teach the true gospel of Jesus Christ (1 Tim 4:12-14; 6:2b; 2 Tim 1:14). Timothy is to guard this deposit, to protect it like a guard watching over a prisoner. As Paul was entrusted with the good news of Jesus Christ, so Paul now entrusts Timothy with the gospel. Timothy must protect and pass the gospel on to the next generation (2 Tim 2:2).

Negatively, Timothy must avoid the constant chatter of the opponents (1 Tim 6:20b). He must turn away from and avoid their constant evil language and contradictions of the truth, which they falsely claim as knowledge (*gnōsis*). The opponents' emphasis on knowing or having secret insight into truth came to full fruition later in the second century with fully developed Gnosticism. In reality, the opponents do *not* perceive or have insight into the truth of the gospel, since they have turned aside from it. Their false claim is indicated by the phrase *by professing it some have missed the mark as regards the faith* (6:21a). These words call to mind 1:6, where the same verb is used for their error. *Some* implies that some persons within the church have strayed away from the faith. These unhealthy teachers are the underlying reason for this letter. Instead of having faith in Christ, they have gone astray in asceticism, legalism, and denial of the resurrection (1 Tim 4:1-3; 2 Tim 2:18). At the same time, they selfishly used religion as a means of financial gain (6:3-10). Consequently, they have missed the mark regarding the faith. Therefore Timothy is commanded to avoid their speech and arguments *[Unhealthy Teaching, p. 366]*.

Finally, Paul closes the letter with a simple *Grace be with you* (6:21b). This is the shortest final farewell of any NT letter. It is a goodbye message stated in the language of God's goodness and grace, from which the church finds its life and can preserve despite the havoc opponents have brought upon it.

2 Timothy

Introduction to 2 Timothy

Historical Setting

The historical situation of 2 Timothy is different from that of 1 Timothy and Titus. Paul is now in captivity (2 Tim 1:8, 16; 2:9; 4:16). Although the place of captivity is not specifically stated, the fact that Onesiphorus was in Rome and visited him "in chains" indicates that the imprisonment is in Rome (1:16-18; 4:19). Only Luke is with Paul, which may suggest that Luke had a hand in writing the letter (4:11). The book of Acts ends with Paul spending two years in Rome under a soldier's guard, proclaiming the kingdom of God and teaching about Jesus Christ (Acts 28:16-31). He may have been released from the captivity described at the end of Acts. If so, after some mission work, he must have been arrested a second time. Paul refers to his "first defense" in 2 Timothy 4:16, likely referring to a preliminary hearing rather than a formal trial. While waiting for the trial, Paul assumes that death is imminent (4:6). In the meantime, the apostle has written to Timothy, urging him to come to Rome (4:9)—preferably *before winter* (4:21)—and to bring some personal items with him (4:11, 13). Tychicus has carried this letter to Timothy in Ephesus so that Timothy can come to Rome and be with Paul (4:12).

In contrast to 1 Timothy and Titus, which lists only a few names, 2 Timothy gives the personal names of more than twenty people. This large list of names exceeds the number of persons listed in Romans 16 and the long list of names in Colossians 4:7-17. Many of the persons named are Paul's personal acquaintances. Some have helped Paul in missionary work. The many names support Paul as the main author of this letter.

Second Timothy also has many more geographical references than 1 Timothy and Titus. Second Timothy mentions Asia (1:15), Rome (1:17), Ephesus (1:18; 4:12), Antioch, Iconium, Lystra (3:11), Thessalonica, Galatia, Dalmatia (4:10), Troas (4:13), Corinth, and Miletus (4:20). This long list of places recounts areas to which the apostle likely traveled as a missionary.

Personal Tone

In 2 Timothy, one discovers a unique relationship between Paul and Timothy. The tone and focus of the letter are more personal. This personal tone and the biographical elements suggest that Paul is offering advice and encouragement to Timothy as a young evangelist and leader of the church at Ephesus. Not only is Timothy a *child* (1:2; 2:1), there is also movement back and forth between Paul as example (cf. the personal pronouns *me* and *my*) and Timothy (*you*). Timothy's ministry is to follow the pattern of ministry set forth in Paul's own life and work. This short letter of only four chapters does not emphasize church order or household behavior, which clearly distinguishes 2 Timothy from 1 Timothy and Titus.

Paul presents Timothy with four exhortations in this short letter (2 Tim 1:6-14; 2:1-7, 22-26; 3:10-17). In a typical Pauline manner, the author ties the exhortations to theological claims, which adds power and substance (Aageson 1997: 708). Moreover, Paul uses his own suffering (1:12; 2:9; 3:11) to exhort Timothy to accept suffering as a servant of God (1:8; 2:3; 4:5). The sufferings of both Paul and Timothy are related to the suffering of Christ (1:8). Timothy is not to be ashamed of the testimony of our Lord, nor of Paul the prisoner. His participation in suffering does not rest on Paul's personal example alone but also is directly tied to God's activity. The grace of God in Christ Jesus is the foundation upon which Timothy can stand strong in Christian ministry and from which Timothy will entrust others with the message of the gospel (1:9; 2:1-2). The theological reality of what God has done and will do makes Paul's example compelling and authoritative to Timothy (Aageson 1997: 711).

Kind of Literature

Scholars debate the literary genre of 2 Timothy. One view identifies 2 Timothy as an example of the farewell discourse or testament found in ancient literature, such as the farewell speeches of Moses, Jacob, David, and Mattathias (Gen 47:29-49:33; Deut 29-32; 1 Kings 2:1-9; 1 Macc 2:49-70). Collins says:

> In general, works that belong to the testamentary type of literature present a hero from the past who gathers family and close friends around him as he faces his own death. He frequently reminisces about his past, pointing to an occasional failing that he urges his family and friends to avoid after his departure. He urges those left behind to carry on the tradition or the work that he has begun, sometimes giving instructions for how this is to be done and even naming those who are to succeed him in his work. . . . Most features of the testamentary genre are found in 2 Timothy. Were it in the form of a speech rather than the form of a letter, one could almost characterize 2 Timothy as a model of the farewell discourse. (182-83)

A last will and farewell discourse is most clearly seen in 2 Timothy 4:6-7. Parallels between Paul's farewell speech in Acts 20:17-35 and some parts of 2 Timothy may indicate Luke's influence as secretary.

Some elements of paraenetic literature are also found in 2 Timothy. Paraenetic literature is advice given in the form of exhortation that encourages certain actions and discourages other actions. In 2 Timothy, contrasts are made between some teachers and Timothy. Paul characterizes these teachers in third-person language and directs his exhortations to Timothy in second-person language. The memory of the respected teacher Paul, whom Timothy is to model, arises out of the presentation of maxims ("Do this, avoid that"). These maxims are presented in antithetical fashion against the teachers, thus stating what Timothy is to avoid and what he is to follow, with Paul as model.

Hence 2 Timothy is a combination of testamentary and paraenetic literature. In 2 Timothy, exhortations appear in the body of the letter, and Paul concludes with testamentary material (4:6-8).

Authorship

The mode of argumentation in 2 Timothy is similar to the mode of argumentation in Philippians. The connection between 2 Timothy and Philippians is more intimate and subtle. Both share the common theme of suffering. The structural paradigm of 2 Timothy goes like this: I have suffered, I am your example, now follow my example and suffer as I have suffered (Aageson 2008: 77). Other ties between 2 Timothy and Philippians include a retrospective look (2 Tim 1:3-7; Phil 1:3-5), autobiographical material (2 Tim 3:10-11; 4:6-8; Phil 3:4-16), the presence of opponents to the Christian faith (2 Tim 1:15; 2:22-26; 3:1-13; 4:1-16; Phil 3:2-11, 17-19), a sense of partnership (2 Tim 2:1-26; Phil 1:12-30; 3:17-21; 4:10-20), affection (2 Tim 1:3-7; Phil 1:3-11), and suffering and imprisonment (2 Tim 1:8, 12; 2:3, 9; 3:11; 4:5; Phil 1:7, 12-14, 22-23; 2:17; 3:8).

However, some parts of 2 Timothy are more like 1 Timothy and Titus and less like Philippians. When comparing 2 Timothy with

Philippians and with 1 Timothy and Titus, one discovers an interesting dynamic. As James W. Aageson says, "Where 2 Timothy is most like 1 Timothy and Titus it is least like Philippians, and at the points where 2 Timothy is least like them it is most like Philippians" (2008: 78). An important difference appears: 1 Timothy emphasizes divine training, order, and godliness for those within the household of God, which may imply a greater readiness to conform to Roman society. In contrast, 2 Timothy assumes a more countercultural stance toward the Roman Empire and has emphases similar to those in the book of Philippians (e.g., suffering is to be expected and embraced).

Given the farewell discourse (2 Tim 4:6-8), the personal notes (4:9-22), the suffering motif (1:8, 12, 16; 3:11), the I-you terminology (1:3-14; 2:1, 10; 3:1, 10, 14; 4:1, 5-6, 9, 21), and the tie with the suffering theme in Philippians, one can conclude that Paul is the author of 2 Timothy. Luke is likely secretary, since Paul specifically says that *only Luke is with me* (4:11). In this letter, more of the content comes directly from Paul and less additional wording comes from Luke than in 1 Timothy and Titus. The letter was likely written before Paul's death in AD 67 (Witherington 2006: 304, 306).

Content

Second Timothy 1:8 introduces the reader to the themes in this letter. These themes are shame, witnessing, suffering, and power. In Roman culture, the death of Jesus by crucifixion was considered shameful. Witnessing to the gospel, which recalls the suffering of Christ, leads to more suffering on the part of Paul and Timothy. Suffering evokes the possibility of shame, and shame has the power to discourage witnessing to the gospel. Timothy's apparent failure to embrace suffering is shameful in that it expresses a lack of confidence in God's power to save *[Honor and Shame, p. 354]*.

By not being ashamed of the gospel or of Paul, Timothy will rise above the accusation of shame in his culture and be a vessel of honor useful to the owner of the house (2:20-21, 24). Timothy will guard the good treasure entrusted to him with the power of the Holy Spirit (1:14). Thus, Paul reminds Timothy to rekindle the gift of Christian ministry given to him, to lay aside cowardice, and to accept the Holy Spirit's power, love, and self-discipline in carrying out his ministry (1:6-7). Paul calls attention to the promises of God and emphasizes the Christian tradition (1:9-12; 2:8-13; 3:14-17). As Timothy lays hold of this Christian teaching and endures like a good soldier, athlete, and farmer (2:3-7), he will regain confidence and faithfully carry out the Christian ministry.

In addition to calling attention to what God has done, Paul summons Timothy to upright moral character (2:22-26). Character ethics arise out of what God has done in chapters 1 and 2. As a vessel cleansed by God, Timothy is to shun youthful passions and pursue righteousness, faith, love, and peace. In contrast to the generally positive character traits in 2:22-26, a catalog of vices describes evil persons in the last days in 3:1-5 *[Vice Lists, p. 368]*. These vices are followed by an appeal for Timothy to live a wholesome life, based on Paul's own example (3:10-15). Timothy must remain steadfast in pointing out these sins, preaching the word of God regardless of its acceptance. The impending arrival of the kingdom and eschatological judgment gives a sense of urgency to the task (4:1-4).

Eschatology receives significant attention in this epistle (1:9-12, 18; 2:11-13; 3:1-5; 4:1, 6-8). The phrase *last days* points to an eschatological time that is characterized by sinful living and the refusal to respond to the true gospel (3:2-5; 4:3). The epiphany of Christ and the resurrection theme are evident (1:10, 2:8, 11-13, 18; 4:1). The believers' suffering and future glory are tied into the passion and resurrection of Christ in 2:11-13.

Fee calls attention to the rich variety of metaphors around the theme of salvation in Christ in 2 Timothy (1:9-10, 13; 2:1, 8, 22; 4:18). Salvation is a divine activity, initiated and carried out by God the Father. Salvation is effected through the death of Christ, who is Son and Lord. Salvation is made effectual by the gift of the Spirit, as an act of pure grace, and thus a person enters it and sustains it by trusting Christ. Salvation is an eschatological reality both "already" and "not yet." Grace that is revealed in Jesus and in holy history rests upon the faithfulness of God as seen in the faithful saying in 2:11-13 *[Faithful Sayings, p. 344]*. Everything rests upon the faithfulness of God: God's grace and salvation in Jesus Christ, Timothy's calling to ministry, the exhortation to live according to holy virtues, and willingness to suffer with Paul.

Second Timothy links the virtues of truth, faith, and faithfulness (1:5, 11-14, 16-18; 2:2, 11-13, 22, 24; 3:10, 16; 4:2). Faith is both the action of believing in Christ and holding to a body of belief. As a body of belief, faith was taught and passed on to Timothy from his grandmother and mother (1:5). Faith is sound teaching that Timothy is to guard as a deposit of Christian doctrine (1:12-14). And as a body of belief, faith is to be passed on to *faithful people* (2:2). Faith is faithfulness: the action of believing and living. Timothy's faithfulness has an ethical quality as he pursues the Christian virtues (2:22) and is faithful in carrying out his calling to Christian ministry (4:1-5). As Paul has kept the faith, so Timothy is to keep the faith and pass it on to others (4:7).

Timothy's believing is to be matched by right living—by Christian virtues and character ethics. In the Greco-Roman culture, character was learned best by imitation. "Thus for Paul to teach Timothy, he must exemplify the virtues he teaches, and for Timothy to teach virtue as Paul's delegate, he must also live them out. The character of the teacher, and that which is taught, coalesce" (Johnson 2001: 325). As Timothy remembers what he has learned from the Jewish Scriptures (1:5; 3:14-17), from the gospel of Jesus Christ, and from Paul as model, his own teaching and life will be fruitful in Christian ministry.

Finally, the faith of Paul in the face of death begs our attention. Towner says, "We cling to the promise of eternal life hardest when the life in our bodies can no longer be taken for granted" (1994: 153). In addition to the confessional material (1:9-10), the historic material (2:8-10), and the faithful saying (2:11-13), Paul states his own firm conviction in these words.

> But I am not ashamed, for I know the one in whom I have put my trust, and I am sure that he is able to guard until that day what I have entrusted to him. (1:12)

> As for me, I am already being poured out as a libation, and the time of my departure has come. I have fought the good fight, I have finished the race, I have kept the faith. From now on there is reserved for me the crown of righteousness, which the Lord, the righteous judge, will give me on that day, and not only to me but also to all who have longed for his appearing. (4:6-8)

OUTLINE

Salutation, 1:1-2
Thanksgiving, 1:3-5
Paul as a Model for Timothy in Christian Ministry, 1:6-18
Faithfulness and Endurance in Christian Ministry, 2:1-13
Timothy as Teacher in Contrast to Unhealthy Teachers, 2:14–3:9
Ingredients of Timothy's Ministry, 3:10-17
Final Charge to Timothy, 4:1-5
Paul's Final Testimony, 4:6-8
Final Instructions, 4:9-18
Final Greetings, 4:19-22

2 Timothy 1:1-2

Salutation

Three major ingredients commonly found in Hellenistic letters comprise the salutation of 2 Timothy: the name of the sender, the name of the addressee, and a greeting formula.

The Sender

Paul is sender of this letter. He identifies himself as *an apostle of Jesus Christ*, similar to the way he introduces himself in 1 Timothy, Titus, and the other Pauline epistles. Second Timothy differs from the self-designation in 1 Timothy and Titus in the two phrases *by the will of God* and *the promise of life that is in Christ Jesus.* The will of God appears in the salutation in Paul's other epistles and calls attention to the source of his apostleship. Paul's position and authority as an apostle has originated in God and was conferred upon him by God's will. Thus God is the ultimate authority behind what Paul has said and done.

Moreover, Paul's apostleship is identified with the eschatological promise of life in Christ Jesus. Life in Christ Jesus is the purpose and goal of Paul's ministry. This life is both present and future and was promised by God. As promise or guarantee, life in Jesus Christ provides the foundation for Christian hope, even in the midst of suffering (2 Tim 1:10-12; 2:11-13; 4:7-8).

The Addressee

Timothy is the recipient of this letter. Instead of *loyal child*, as in 1 Timothy 1:2, here Paul calls Timothy *my beloved child* (2 Tim 1:2a). *Beloved child* goes beyond personal friendship and identifies Timothy's faithfulness to the gospel and to Paul. As a faithful and beloved child, Timothy serves as an example for believers. Instead of giving primary emphasis to the behavior of various groups within the church, some of which are disloyal, 2 Timothy speaks primarily of Timothy's behavior as a church leader. Paul builds his exhortation for this kind of behavior on a personal relationship with Timothy. He writes as an authoritative apostle and as a father to a beloved child *[Timothy, p. 364].*

Greeting Formula

The greeting in 2 Timothy 1:2b is identical with the greeting in 1 Timothy 1:2b. The typical Hellenistic greeting is "grace," and the typical Semitic greeting is "peace." Paul modifies this typical greeting by adding the word *mercy* and making clear that *grace and peace* come *from God the Father and Christ Jesus our Lord.* This combination unites the Hebraic and Christian emphases, since both grace and peace derive from God the Father and Christ Jesus our Lord.

2 Timothy 1:3-5

Thanksgiving

PREVIEW

Three themes in Paul's thanksgiving and prayer point to a personal relationship between Paul and Timothy. First, terms for "remembering" are repeated three times in these verses. Paul remembers Timothy in his prayers (v. 3b), he remembers Timothy's tears (v. 4), and he remembers Timothy's sincere faith (v. 5a). Second is imitation. Paul sees a relationship between his own life and Timothy's life. He upholds Timothy in his prayers and invites Timothy to imitate the faith passed on by their ancestors (vv. 3, 5). And third is growth in character (v. 5b). Paul expects Timothy to grow in faithfulness, the kind of faithfulness seen in Paul and to some degree in Timothy's mother and grandmother. The thanksgiving moves sequentially from Paul's faith heritage (v. 3a) to his relationship with Timothy (v. 3b-4), to Timothy's faith heritage (v. 5). Second Timothy 1:3-5 is one sentence in Greek. English translations often break up this complicated Greek sentence into three sentences (e.g., NRSV, NIV, and TNIV).

OUTLINE

Paul's Faith Heritage, 1:3a
Paul's Personal Relationship with Timothy, 1:3b-4
Timothy's Faith Heritage, 1:5

EXPLANATORY NOTES

Paul's Faith Heritage 1:3a

Second Timothy begins with a lengthy thanksgiving prayer. Paul's life is God-centered. Normally Paul uses the verb "to give thanks," but here he chooses an idiom meaning *to have gratitude,* which occurs rarely in the NT. In addition to gratefulness, Paul worships God. Obviously, he is referring to Israel's God and the Father of Jesus Christ rather than the gods of the Greco-Roman world. Paul worships God *with a clear conscience.* In contrast to those in Ephesus and Crete whose consciences are seared (1 Tim 4:2) and corrupted (Titus 1:15), Paul speaks of a good conscience (1 Tim 1:5, 19; 3:9). The apostle recalls his own testimony of a pure or clear conscience in 1:3, which he has openly declared before the Jewish council (Acts 23:1) and the governor (24:16). The word *conscience* means moral consciousness, or awareness of moral rightness or wrongness before God (Knight 1992: 367) *[Conscience, p. 338].* This suggests that Paul has served God without hypocrisy, with undivided attention, with sincerity, and with single-mindedness in his devotion to the God of his ancestors (Collins: 191). By linking faith to his ancestors, Paul anchors Christianity in its Hebrew history as a religion with credible antiquity. It is no fly-by-night religion; it is deeply rooted in salvation history. As a good example, Paul establishes a parallel between himself and Timothy's Christian faith, which he also traces back to his forebears.

Paul's Personal Relationship with Timothy 1:3b-4

The relationship between Paul and his beloved child Timothy is seen in Paul's constant prayer for him and his inner longing to see him again. The phrase *when I remember you constantly in my prayers night and day* (v. 3b) does not mean continuous prayer. It means Paul prayed for Timothy consistently and faithfully in morning and evening prayers. In the second missionary journey, Paul and Timothy traveled as missionary companions. Timothy was present at Miletus when Paul met with the Ephesian elders and bade them goodbye. Their farewell concluded with much weeping when they left the Ephesian church leaders and traveled to Jerusalem (Acts 20:4, 17-38). Paul recalls this scene now as he writes this epistle.

The words *I long to see you* indicate that Paul is captive in Rome, writing to Timothy in Ephesus. Lonely and aware of his impending death, Paul invites Timothy to visit him *before winter* (2 Tim 4:21). Nearly everyone else has deserted him (4:11, 16). His deep desire to see Timothy bears witness to the close association they have had with each other as laborers together in the gospel of Christ.

Timothy's Faith Heritage 1:5

Paul turns to Timothy's faith in a third reminder. *I am reminded of your sincere faith* (v. 5a) identifies the quality of faith by which Timothy has lived. This faith is genuine and reflects faithfulness or steadfastness (Fee

1988: 223). Though the teaching of some in Ephesus may have discouraged Timothy, he did not lose faith in God. Onesiphorus has likely carried a report of Timothy's faith to Paul. Now Paul commends Timothy both for his faith and for his faithfulness. In the next section he urges Timothy to not be ashamed of the gospel even in the face of suffering.

Timothy's faith has roots in his mother and grandmother. It is a faith deeply rooted in the OT Scriptures. Paul writes, *But as for you, continue in what you have learned and firmly believed, knowing from whom you learned it, and how from childhood you have known the sacred writings that are able to instruct you for salvation through faith in Christ Jesus* (3:14-15).

Timothy's mother is mentioned in Acts 16:1 as a Jewish believer in Christ. Timothy's father was a Hellenist (a Greek person), and there is no evidence that he became a Christian. Children born to Jewish women normally were considered to be Jews. But if a Jewish woman married a Greek man who did not join the Jewish faith, the surrounding society generally considered their children to be Gentile since women tended to defer to their husbands in religious matters in the Greco-Roman world (Collins: 193). To clear up any possible misunderstanding in the Jewish and Christian communities about Timothy's faith, Paul had Timothy circumcised before taking him along as a missionary co-worker (16:3). Thus the faith that Paul talks about is *Jewish-Christian* faith. Indeed, Timothy's mother, Eunice, was a believer (16:1), as was Timothy's grandmother, Lois (2 Tim 1:5).

Timothy's religious heritage had stability and antiquity. Genuine faith is not limited to one generation; it transcends generations. Thus Paul concludes, *I am sure* [that this faith] *lives in you* (2 Tim 2:5b). Timothy had a vital, personal, contemporary faith in Jesus Christ. Paul's confidence in Timothy's faith becomes the springboard for the appeal that follows (1:6-8). On the basis of that faith, Paul urges Timothy not to be ashamed of the gospel and to carry out his ministry to the full, even amid suffering (4:1-5). Faith in 2 Timothy refers to belief and commitment to the truth of the gospel (2:18; 3:8; 4:7). It also includes faithfulness through endurance and loyalty (1:5, 13; 2:22; 3:10).

It is significant that Paul talks about faith reaching across three generations and that Timothy's faith has come through the teaching of women. In light of questions raised about women teaching men in 1 Timothy 2:12, we observe here in 2 Timothy 1:5 and 3:14-15 that Paul specifically affirms the practice of women teaching the faith to men (i.e., Timothy). The implications of faith growing through women's teaching carries greater weight when one remembers that early Christian churches met in houses. In Lois and Eunice's household church, these women taught at least one man—Timothy—and perhaps more. Johnson says, "If women are indeed capable of transmitting the faith in a truthful and competent fashion within the most important realm of the home through the raising of children, then the burden of proof is on those who would restrict women's role only to that domestic 'sphere'" (Johnson 2001: 343).

2 Timothy 1:6-18

Paul as a Model for Timothy in Christian Ministry

PREVIEW

As outlined in this commentary, 2 Timothy is structured around Paul's three major appeals to Timothy to be loyal and faithful to the gospel despite opposition (1:6–2:13; 2:14–3:9; 3:10-17). Paul serves as a model for Timothy to follow amid suffering for the sake of the gospel.

The first appeal (1:6–2:13) lays the foundation for the other appeals. It consists of two parts (1:6-14 and 2:1-13). The first part of the appeal (1:6-18) lays out Paul's gospel and why he is unashamed of it—even in the midst of suffering. It includes a contrast between specific named persons, of whom some are faithful and some are not. The second part of the appeal, treated in the next section, exhorts Timothy to endurance in Christian ministry (2:1-7) based on Jesus' endurance. It concludes with a faithful saying (2:11-13).

OUTLINE

Paul Models Faithfulness to the Gospel Despite Suffering, 1:6-14
Examples of Ashamed and Unashamed Associates, 1:15-18

EXPLANATORY NOTES

Paul Models Faithfulness to the Gospel Despite Suffering 1:6-14

A literary analysis of 1:6-14 suggests a chiastic arrangement in which the Holy Spirit provides the dynamic for Timothy's ministry, Paul's suffering provides an example for faithfulness in ministry, and God's salvation in Jesus Christ is the focal point of ministry. Timothy is exhorted to follow Paul's example. He is not to be ashamed (v. 8), just as Paul is not ashamed (v. 12). Timothy is to join in suffering as Paul has suffered (v. 12), and he is to preserve what has been entrusted to him (v. 14). The chiastic arrangement is as follows *[Chiasm, p. 334]*:

A The Holy Spirit and Timothy's Ministry, 1:6-7
  B Faithfulness amid Suffering, 1:8
    C God's Salvation in Jesus Christ, 1:9-10
  B′ Faithfulness amid Suffering, 1:11-12
A′ The Holy Spirit and Timothy's Ministry, 1:13-14

Using the words *for this reason,* Paul begins the exhortation by tying into what was said about his faith heritage in verse 5. As Timothy thinks back on that spiritual heritage, he is reminded *to rekindle the gift of God that is within* him (1:6a). The verb *rekindle* occurs twice in the LXX for reviving the human spirit (Gen 45:27; 1 Macc 13:7). The term means to set on flame again. It is a metaphor for rekindling a waning fire. The verb tense suggests continuing action, implying that Timothy is to keep on fanning into flame the gift of God. Timothy's faith is not dying or wavering, though his gift has become weak or timid in the face of opposition.

What is this God-given gift? One view is that it is the gift of prophecy, which came through prophetic utterance (1 Tim 4:14). Another view is that it is the gift of the Holy Spirit. From Paul's instruction in this letter, I suggest that Timothy's gift is the gift of Christian ministry, which includes preaching, teaching, evangelism, modeling Christian living, suffering for the gospel, and relating to opponents with gentleness (2 Tim 1:8; 2:1-2, 15, 22, 24; 3:14-17; 4:2, 5). In calling to mind this God-given gift, Timothy realizes once more that the authority undergirding his ministry comes from God. Paul uses the term *gift* (*charisma*) to distinguish the gift of grace for effective ministry from the ecstatic phenomena called spiritual gifts (*pneumatika*) in 1 Corinthians 12:1-4. This gift of grace makes his ministry effective regardless of the opposition. It is a gift from God for the good of the body of Christ and not just for the individual. Through this gift, God acts through the Holy Spirit in the world (Collins: 196). The gift did not come through the laying on of hands but was already present and publicly affirmed by *the laying on of . . . hands* (1 Tim 4:14; 2 Tim 1:6b) *[Ordination, p. 359].*

Paul draws a sharp contrast (*not . . . but . . .*) in 1:7, showing the radical difference between a negative *spirit of cowardice* and the positive Holy Spirit, which gives Timothy *power, love, and self-discipline.* What Paul wants Timothy to perceive is not fear of failure, but his lack of reliance on the power of God for Christian ministry. The positive side of the contrast makes this clear. God's Holy Spirit provides Timothy with the triad of power, love, and self-discipline (1:7b). The power of the Spirit is inherent within the gospel message itself as it is preached in the face of opposition (Rom 1:16; 1 Cor 2:4-5; 4:20). This power also enables the Christian believer to live a holy life (Rom 8:13; 14:17-18; Gal 5:16-26). The power of the Spirit is not so much the ability to do mighty deeds or miraculous signs. Rather, Spirit power in ministry is the inner presence of God, providing confidence that God is at work here and now in and through the Christian minister *[Holy Spirit, p. 351].*

Instead of retaliating or rejecting opponents, Timothy is to treat opponents with love and gentleness (2 Tim 2:24-26). More sinners come to the Lord through a pastor's love than through words of condemnation. Finally, the Holy Spirit provides self-discipline for Timothy. The word *self-discipline* in Greek moral philosophy means moral right thinking, with nuances such as prudence, temperance, self-control, sobriety, and moderation (Johnson 2001: 346). As used in 1:7, self-discipline means both the ability to control the inner self and a measure of control over one's thinking and actions. It provides Timothy with wise thinking, moderation, and levelheadedness in the midst of deviant teaching.

In 2 Timothy 1:8 we come to the central theme of this epistle. With this verse, Paul begins a seventy-nine-word sentence that extends through verse 11 (GNT). Paul exhorts Timothy in a negative way, *Do not be ashamed*, and then invites Timothy in a positive way, *But join me in suffering for the gospel.* Timothy is not to be ashamed because Paul is not ashamed (v. 12) and because Christ defeated *death and brought life* (v. 10). Honor and shame characterized Greco-Roman culture. Honor was ascribed to noble deeds and shame was ascribed to ignoble behavior or rank. To act in a way that earned the honor of others was an unquestioned good, just as earning the contempt of others was considered evil. Nothing was more shameful in the eyes of the first-century world than the death of Jesus by public execution. Imprisoned persons were shamed in the first century (MaGee: 338-53). Shame also was associated with those who gathered in the name of Jesus and proclaimed him as their Lord. Timothy faces shame by associating with

Jesus the Messiah and by associating with the apostle Paul, who is suffering as a criminal for proclaiming the gospel of Jesus (2:9). Moreover, Timothy faces opposition from opponents (2:16-18; 3:8, 14), is tempted to cowardice (1:7), is allowing his ministry of the gospel to die out (1:6), and may be hesitant to join Paul in suffering (1:8).

Timothy is not to be ashamed in a twofold way: he is not to be ashamed of the witness of Jesus, and he is not to be ashamed of Paul as a prisoner. Paul's own tie to the suffering of Christ in 1:8 propels the apostle to urge Timothy to join that suffering for the sake of the gospel. Paul is *Christ's* prisoner, not Nero's. Paul wants Timothy to perceive that he too is a prisoner and a witness to the crucified Christ. Two imperatives in verse 8—*Do not be ashamed* and *Join with me in suffering*—exhort Timothy to avoid neither the public humiliation of associating with Christ nor the humiliation of associating with Paul the prisoner. These two imperatives beg Timothy to three loyalties: to Christ (and his gospel), to Paul, and to Timothy's own ministry (Fee 1988: 228).

To counteract this shame, Paul reminds Timothy of his faith heritage. Paul also reminds Timothy that Jesus in his death and resurrection *destroyed death and brought life and immortality to light* (1:10 NIV). Seen within the larger view of the Christian gospel, preaching and teaching the good news of Jesus Christ is an honor rather than a shame. The good news of the gospel and the missionary task of the church are too important to withdraw from society and hide in shame. Timothy's life and ministry will find strength by *relying on the power of God*. The answer to Timothy's shame comes in verse 7, the reminder that the Holy Spirit's gift for ministry includes *power*. It is a different kind of power from the power of the demonic or the social and psychological power of shame. It is God's power—power that cuts across the forces of opposition to the gospel and will make Timothy's ministry effective even in the midst of suffering.

Paul now turns to the center of the chiasm in verses 9-10: the gospel itself. Paul uses a confessional formulation to describe this gospel in a manner similar to what we see in Titus 2:11-14 and 3:4-7. But here the confessional statement, particularly in verse 10, counteracts Roman imperial religion: God's purpose and grace were given *before the ages began* (v. 9), in contrast to what was offered by the Roman emperor. The confessional formula may be laid out as follows (see I. H. Marshall 1999: 701):

[God]
who saved us
and called us with a holy calling

not according to our works
but according to his own purpose and grace
which he has given to us
A in Christ Jesus
B before the ages began
but has been revealed
B′ now
A′ through the appearing
of our savior Christ Jesus
who abolished death
and who brought life and immortality to light
through the gospel.

Second Timothy 1:9-10 are the first verses in this letter that speak of salvation (1:9-10; 2:10; 3:15; 4:18). The verb in the past tense means salvation has already taken place. God is Savior in 1:9, and Christ Jesus is Savior in 1:10. Salvation and holy calling are mentioned in the same sentence. But what is a *holy calling*? Is it a call tied to God's purpose and thus similar to election? Or is it a call to the ministerial vocation of Timothy? Or is it a call to a holy life? The plural pronoun indicates that Paul is talking about Christian believers. The Greek construction could be translated *with* a holy calling (NRSV) because it comes from God. Or it could be translated *to* a holy calling (TNIV), resulting in a holy people. The latter option is preferable. The call is holy not only because it proceeds from God; it also is a call to live a holy life. Salvation and Christian discipleship come together here.

This salvation is *not according to our works but according to his own purpose and grace* (1:9b). By using the *not . . . but . . .* construction, Paul turns from the negative to the positive. As in Titus 3:5, persons cannot save themselves by their own works. Salvation comes in a positive way by the grace of God. Paul links together God's purpose and God's grace not only here, but also elsewhere (Rom 8:28; 9:11; Eph 1:11; 3:11; 2 Tim 1:9; Titus 3:10). In Roman 8:28, God's purpose is set forth in the context of God's love (8:35, 39). In Romans 9:11 God's purpose is given in the context of his mercy (9:15-18). And in Ephesians 1:11 and 3:11, God's purpose is carried out in the context of grace (1:6-7; 3:2). By graciously giving of Godself, God makes salvation available to human persons. The personal God of Israel (not an impersonal, mechanistic fate) is intervening with love in the history of God's alienated creatures (Quinn and Wacker: 599).

Specifically, *this grace was given to us in Christ Jesus* (2 Tim 1:9b). Paul repeats what he wrote about grace in Romans: God's grace abounded to many in the one man, Jesus Christ (Rom 5:15). There is an abundance of grace through Jesus Christ (5:17), and God's grace superabounds (5:20). Paul also repeats what he wrote in Ephesians (1:6-7; 2:8; 3:2).

Here Paul joins God's grace and the person and work of Jesus Christ by means of two time frames, *before the ages began* and *now* (2 Tim 1:9-10). God's grace was given to us from all eternity. Grace was in the mind of God before creation and *before the beginning of time* (1:9 TNIV)—literally, *before the ages*. The thought moves from eternity to time. This God-given grace from all eternity *has now been revealed through the appearing of our Savior Christ Jesus* (1:10a). As in Titus 1:2-3, God promised eternal life before the ages of time and then revealed this eternal life at the right time. In Jesus Christ, God's grace is made visible and effectual within time *[Christology, p. 335]*.

Grace is revealed in Jesus, and that grace does something: it changes the world. Significantly, this grace has appeared in Jesus Christ; thus Jesus is Savior. Often God is called Savior in the letters to 1 Timothy and Titus (1 Tim 1:1; 2:3; 4:10; Titus 2:10; 3:4), but here as elsewhere in Paul's epistles, Jesus is Savior (Eph 5:23; Phil 3:20; Titus 1:4). The source of salvation and grace is God, and the instrument is Jesus, who reveals God's work within time. In some Hellenistic religions, the title savior (*sōtēr*) was given to pagan gods and to the Roman emperor. While the Roman world acclaimed Caesar as Savior, early Christianity forthrightly claimed that Jesus Christ was Savior (*sōtēr*) and not the pagan gods or even the imperial Caesar. The term *appearing* (*epiphaneia*) was used in the Roman world for the appearance of the Roman emperor or some other important imperial cult official in a given city. The emperor bestowed gifts of benevolence upon the city, as present-day politicians often do, to win the favor of the people. Paul uses the same term to describe the second coming of Jesus Christ into the world (2 Thess 2:8; 1 Tim 6:14; 2 Tim 4:1, 8; Titus 2:13). Here in 2 Timothy 1:10, the first coming of Christ is the subject of the appearing. And Christ Jesus, not Caesar, is the manifestation of divine benevolence (Collins: 203) *[Names for God and the Imperial Cult, p. 357]*.

Paul took Hellenistic terms normally used with reference to the Roman emperor's coming to a city (*grace* or *favor* or *benevolence*, *savior*, and *appearance*) and applied them to God's historical work of grace and salvation in Jesus Christ. In short, Paul took the historic gospel (1 Cor 15:1-5) and expressed it in language that everyone in the Hellenistic world could understand (Collins: 204). In so doing, Paul was communicating the gospel cross-culturally. Previously Paul demonstrated the ability to communicate the gospel in other cultural settings, such as Lystra (Acts 14:8-18) and Athens (17:22-34). Both at the beginning of ministry and now at the end of ministry,

Paul has communicated the gospel in language that people understood in different cultural settings.

Even as the political leaders brought benevolence to Ephesus, so also Christ Jesus brought a benevolence. However, his far outstrips theirs: he *abolished death and brought life and immortality to light through the gospel* (2 Tim 1:10b). No emperor or modern politician's pork-barrel benevolence compares with the gracious gift of God's salvation in Christ Jesus! With two phrases, one negative and one positive, Paul describes the saving work of Christ. Negatively, Jesus Christ abolished that which people fear most: death. The term abolished (*katargeō*) means "to make completely inoperative, to put out of use" (*TDNT* 1:453). This term is used elsewhere in the NT for the work of Christ in abolishing the law and its commandments (Eph 2:15), for destroying the body of sin (Rom 6:6), for the final destruction of death itself (1 Cor 15:26), and for the destruction of the one who has the power of death—that is, the devil (Heb 2:14).

Positively, Jesus brought life and immortality, which are the opposite of death. *Immortality* is a characteristic of God (1 Tim 1:17). What is brought to light through the gospel is deliverance from spiritual death for Christians—already in this world (Rom 6:3-11; Col 3:1)—and ultimate deliverance from the final power of death in the future resurrection of the body at Christ's return (1 Cor 15:20-28; Phil 3:20-21). In one fell swoop, Paul declares null and void both imperial religion and the teaching promoted by those at Ephesus who said the future resurrection has already taken place (1 Tim 4:3; 2 Tim 2:18).

Paul now returns in the chiasm to the theme of suffering, which was previously named in 2 Timothy 1:8. He writes, *For this gospel I was appointed a herald and an apostle and a teacher, and for this reason I suffer as I do* (1:11-12a). Manuscripts differ at this point. External evidence supports a longer reading, *teacher of the Gentiles*, but the shorter reading is preferred (Metzger 1994: 579). With three nouns, Paul describes his appointment. He was appointed a *herald* of the gospel. Just as the messenger shouted the good news of an emperor's ascension to the throne or the birth of a child in the imperial household (Collins: 210), so Paul announces the good news of the gospel as an evangelist (4:2). In contrast to the heralds at the temple of Artemis in Ephesus, Paul announces the good news of Jesus Christ. He was appointed a *teacher* of the gospel.

Paul taught the gospel in Ephesus for two years (Acts 19:8-10). His appointment as an apostle calls attention to the authority of the gospel message that he proclaims. Just as Paul was appointed to preach and teach the good news, so also Timothy must preach and teach it.

For this reason, Paul suffers. The longer textual reading, *I suffer even these things*, is preferred (J. K. Elliott: 122). The emphasis in 2 Timothy 1:12a is not so much on the chains of imprisonment as it is on the reason for his suffering. Despite the situation in which Paul finds himself, his confidence in God and in the gospel remains firm.

Paul asserts, *But I am not ashamed.* The strong adversative *but* contrasts Paul's outlook with Timothy's apparent hesitancy to embrace suffering in 1:7-8. As in Romans 1:16, Paul is not ashamed of the gospel of Jesus Christ. His current imprisonment causes no personal shame because this imprisonment is for the good news of the gospel of Jesus Christ. Furthermore, Paul is not ashamed: *For I know the one in whom I have put my trust, and I am sure that he is able to guard until that day what I have entrusted to him* (2 Tim 1:12). Three verbs lay out why Paul is not ashamed: he knows, he has trusted, and he is sure. First, Paul knows for certain (in his knowledge and in his experience) the one *in whom* he has trusted. Second, the tense of the verb *trusted* or *believed* means that the act of trusting or believing is a past action or decision with continuing consequences. His belief is not in philosophy or human ideas, but in a person. He knows *in whom* this faith commitment fully rests. The *whom* is obviously God, who saves through Jesus Christ (1:9-10). This is the God who gave grace before the beginning of time. Third, Paul is fully convinced of God's ability to guard the trust or deposit. The tense of the verb *I am sure* indicates that Paul is fully persuaded. Paul is certain that God, in whom he has placed his faith, is able to guard what the apostle has entrusted. The tense of the verb *to guard* means to continue watching over and protecting, as a guard watches over a prisoner.

What is guarded? The term *deposit* (GNT: *parathēkē*) was used for the deposit of money or property that was entrusted to another (BDAG: 764). As used in 2 Timothy 1:12, there are two possible meanings: (1) the *gospel* that God entrusted to Paul is now entrusted to Timothy's guardianship, or (2) the *commitment* that Paul has entrusted to God. The latter is preferred because the personal pronoun *my* (with *deposit*; GNT) indicates that it is Paul's deposit that is entrusted to God's care. Fee says, "Just as the gospel announces a salvation that God in grace initiated and effected, and through which he rendered death ineffective, so also the same God can be trusted to guard, . . . for the End of life that [which] has been entrusted to his care" (Fee 1988: 232). In short, Paul is not ashamed in the midst of suffering because he is fully convinced that God will keep safe his deposit of faith until the very end.

In the chiastic pattern, Paul returns in 1:13-14 to where he began in 1:6 (see chart above): the Holy Spirit and Timothy's ministry. Two imperatives stand out in verses 13-14. Timothy is to keep or hold on to the pattern of sound teaching and to guard the good deposit entrusted to him. The first imperative calls attention to the *standard* (NRSV) or *pattern* (TNIV) of sound teaching. The verb tense indicates that Timothy is to continue keeping the pattern of healthy words. The term *pattern* likely means *standard* (*hypotypōsis*; BDAG: 1042) in the sense of model or pattern, since it comes from what Timothy heard from Paul. The pattern is *sound teaching*, (lit.) *healthy words*, which Paul has passed on to Timothy. The concepts of healthy teaching and speech are familiar language in the letters to Timothy and Titus (1 Tim 1:10; 6:3; 2 Tim 4:3; Titus 1:9; 2:8). Timothy is to pass on to other faithful people these healthy words (or sound doctrine) that he received from Paul (2 Tim 2:2). Paul urges Timothy to keep these healthy words in his own life and also to pass them on to other faithful people. He can keep sound doctrine by unashamedly following sound words in his own life, even amid suffering, faithfully passing healthy doctrine on to others.

How Timothy keeps the pattern of healthy words is important. Paul instructs him to keep these words *in the faith and love that are in Christ Jesus* (1:13b). The term *faith* calls attention to the faith that Timothy learned from his mother and grandmother (1:5)—the faith that Paul kept to the end of his life (4:7). It is Timothy's sincere faith (1:5). Furthermore, Timothy is to keep these healthy words (sound doctrine) in love. In the midst of those bringing pain and suffering to Timothy's ministry, right belief is not enough. Timothy may win back these opponents through love by exercising patience and gentleness while speaking to them (2:24-26). Faith and love come from life in Jesus Christ. They are not merely human qualities.

The second imperative is *Guard the good treasure entrusted to you* (1:14a). The verb *guard* corresponds to the guardianship that God provides for Paul's faith in 1:12. Timothy is to stand guard over the deposit of the gospel message that was placed into his hands. Paul is saying, "Keep safe what I have deposited with you; it is a sacred trust" (Fee 1988: 233). Moreover it is a good deposit (TNIV) or treasure (NRSV), indicating its value and worth. Just as Timothy is to keep the healthy words of the gospel and pass them on to other faithful teachers, he is also to protect the good deposit of faith so that no part of the good news of the gospel is lost or harmed. Guarding the deposit of faith does not mean to hide it away in safekeeping. It means to pass it on faithfully to others in such a way that none of it is lost (2 Tim 2:2).

As Timothy keeps the healthy words of the gospel by the faith and love that are in Christ Jesus, so now he guards the good treasure *with the help of the Holy Spirit living in us* (1:14b). Paul reminds Timothy that the same Holy Spirit that defies cowardice and provides power, love, and self-discipline for Christian ministry in 1:7 also helps to safeguard the message of the gospel. This Holy Spirit dwells not only in Timothy's life, but also in all Christian believers. In contrast to the temple of Artemis, which the people of Ephesus considered holy, the Holy Spirit of God dwells in the house churches in Ephesus as God's temple. This Holy Spirit is God's power at work in Timothy's life, enabling him to preserve the pattern of sound words, the gospel message, and to pass it on to the next generation. In short, the message that saves and the grace of God it announces are worth the suffering, and the Holy Spirit has been given to provide strength to persevere (Towner 1994: 167). Timothy can lay aside cowardice and not be ashamed of the Lord, or of Paul his mentor, because God has acted in grace through Jesus Christ to bring about salvation. The Holy Spirit makes Timothy's ministry effective and helps him preserve sound doctrine as a good treasure. With this assurance, the chiastic exhortation comes to a close. It has moved full circle and ends where it began, stressing the Holy Spirit's presence in Timothy's life and work, removing shame and giving confidence in Christian ministry.

Examples of Ashamed and Unashamed Associates 1:15-18

The phrases *you are aware* (1:15a) and *you know very well* (1:18b) indicate that Timothy personally knows the individuals named in this section and their reputation in the church. Although two persons have previously been disciplined in the church in Ephesus (1 Tim 1:19-20), the defection from Paul has continued. The phrase *all who are in Asia turned away from me* (1:15) refers to the geographical area of the Roman province in western Asia Minor, which included the city of Ephesus as its capital. Paul does not mean every Christian in this province turned away from the Christian faith. He uses hyperbole or exaggeration to point out that many of his Christian friends no longer want to associate with him as a prisoner.

In 2 Timothy 4:10, Paul says that Demas has deserted him. In like manner, *Phygelus and Hermogenes have turned away from* him (1:15). Perhaps these two men were lay leaders in the church. Whether they departed from the faith or simply abandoned Paul is not clear. Clearly they were unwilling to associate with Paul as a prisoner in Rome. The verb *turned away* (NRSV) or *deserted* (TNIV) refers to rejection or disaffection (Johnson 2001: 360). The verb may combine physical abandonment with spiritual disaffection. By abandoning their loyalty to Paul, they have essentially abandoned the gospel, since that is about the only way one could desert the apostle (Fee 1988: 236).

Paul names two of the deserting Asians: *Phygelus and Hermogenes*. They are not the persons named in 2:17, who had left the faith and are promoting the unhealthy view that the resurrection has already taken place. *Phygelus* does not appear elsewhere in early Christian literature, though the name is found in western Asia. *Hermogenes* does not appear elsewhere in the NT, though the *Acts of Paul* mentions a coppersmith by the name of Hermogenes. I. H. Marshall thinks Phygelus and Hermogenes had been in Rome, had turned away from Paul, and had returned to Asia (1999: 717). Their abandonment of Paul indicates they were ashamed of the apostle as a prisoner and therefore ashamed of the gospel of Christ Jesus.

In contrast, *Onesiphorus* is unashamed of Paul. All we know about him is found in these three verses (1:16-18). He is commended for supporting Paul, the prisoner, in three ways. First, Onesiphorus *refreshed* Paul in prison. The term means "to revive" and implies that he offered Paul both financial support (1 Cor 16:18; 2 Cor 7:13; Philem 7, 20) and food (I. H. Marshall 1999: 719). Since Paul was considered a criminal, Onesiphorus has provided this refreshment and risked his Christian reputation by identifying with this criminal. Second, Onesiphorus was *not ashamed of my chain* (2 Tim 1:16b). Here Paul subtly contrasts Onesiphorus with Timothy, who is exhorted not to be ashamed of the testimony of the Lord nor of Paul as prisoner (1:8). As a loyal Christian supporter, Onesiphorus was willing to risk visiting the apostle in prison. Third, not only is Onesiphorus not ashamed; he also searched eagerly for Paul in Rome.

Only in 2 Timothy 1:17 is it clearly stated that Paul's (second) imprisonment is in Rome. He was not under house arrest, as in Acts 28:30. Instead, Paul is on death row, held in a secret location, and it took much effort for Onesiphorus to find him—as the words *eagerly searched* imply. Finding Paul chained indicates that Onesiphorus ministered to Paul in the presence of a Roman guard, which confirms that he was unashamed, since showing kindness to Paul as prisoner could have tainted Onesiphorus with the crime for which Paul had been arrested (Quinn and Wacker: 615). These two examples are clear enough for Timothy. Some are ashamed (1:15), but not Onesiphorus (1:16-17), so be like him!

Paul then states two wishes. First, *May the Lord grant mercy to the household of Onesiphorus* (v. 16); second, *May the Lord grant that he will find mercy from the Lord on that day!* (v. 18). The first wish or prayer is for the entire household of Onesiphorus. Since the household is the object of the wish, one wonders what happened to Onesiphorus. The second wish or prayer is for God's mercy for Onesiphorus on the final day. Taken together, these wishes imply that Onesiphorus has died. The second wish does not necessarily support prayer for the dead. Rather, it calls attention to Paul's own admiration for Onesiphorus and Paul's desire that in Christ's second advent, Onesiphorus will be greeted and accepted by the Lord as a result of God's mercy and grace.

Finally, Onesiphorus is commended for service rendered in Ephesus. Onesiphorus was active in the church at Ephesus and may have been a deacon or minister. Both Paul and Timothy know the good reputation that Onesiphorus had in Ephesus.

THE TEXT IN BIBLICAL CONTEXT

Honor and Shame and Christian Ministry

First-century culture highly valued the social mechanisms of honor and shame. One experienced honor by associating with persons of dignity. Honor was achieved by belonging to a group of honorable persons. In contrast, shame was ascribed to publicans and sinners, lepers, women, and outcasts *[Honor and Shame, p. 354]*. Jesus often associated with outcasts and ascribed dignity to persons shamed in society. His death on the cross was a source of shame (Heb 12:2), since it was associated with a criminal's death (Gal 3:13). In contrast, Paul undermines these mechanisms when he says that the gospel is God's foolishness, God's weakness. "God chose what is foolish in the world to shame the wise; God chose what is weak in the world to shame the strong; God chose what is low and despised in the world, things that are not, to reduce to nothing things that are, so that no one might boast in the presence of God" (1 Cor 1:27-29). In 1 Corinthians 4:13 Paul says, "We have become like the rubbish of the world, the dregs of all things, to this very day." To the unbeliever, the gospel was "a stone that makes them stumble, and a rock that makes them fall" (1 Pet 2:8).

Preaching the gospel was met with opposition. Stephen and James were martyred (Acts 7:58-60; 12:2). Paul often was persecuted for preaching the gospel (2 Cor 11:23-29). Because of the shame of the cross and the shame associated with preaching the gospel, Timothy was in danger of becoming ashamed of the testimony of the Lord and of Paul, who was a prisoner for Christ (2 Tim 1:7-8).

Instead of interpreting the cross as shame, early Christians claimed that through the cross of Christ, God had won the victory over the powers of evil (Col 2:15). In the resurrection, God put his stamp of approval on Christ's death, raised Jesus Christ, and gave him the highest place of honor (Phil 2:9-11).

Despite the accusation of shame and the sufferings that came with that accusation, Paul openly stated, *But I am not ashamed* (2 Tim 1:12). Paul believed that God was at work in changing the world through the gospel message. At the cross, God was in Christ, reconciling the world to Godself (2 Cor 5:19). The apostle was not afraid to face Rome, the center of worldly power, and to preach the gospel in that great city because the gospel was powerful enough to penetrate Roman political power (Rom 1:15-16). As Paul now comes to the end of life and faces death as a prisoner for the Lord, he is unashamed of the gospel (2 Tim 1:12; 4:6-8). So he urges Timothy to reinterpret honor and shame by looking at the world through the eyes of the gospel and by discovering therein the dignity and honor of preaching and teaching God's saving message of Jesus Christ (2 Tim 1:7–2:13). Similarly, the Christian church at Smyrna, suffering under persecution, is told, "Be faithful until death, and I will give you the crown of life" (Rev 2:10).

Suffering for the Gospel

In the Bible, suffering and death are associated with the Christian message. The Servant Songs of Isaiah climax in the suffering servant of Isaiah 52:13–53:12. Jesus picked up this suffering servant theme and tied it to the Son of Man theme (Dan 7:13-14) in Mark 10:45. Parts of the Jewish community emphasized the reign of the Son of Man, but we know of no tie between "Son of Man" and Isaiah's suffering servant before the New Testament. Jesus taught his disciples the way of suffering and death, though they did not easily grasp what he was saying (Mark 8:31-36; 9:30-32; 10:32-34). After the resurrection, Jesus interpreted his suffering and death: "Was it not necessary that the Messiah should suffer these things and then enter into his glory?" (Luke 24:26). On the day of Pentecost, Peter declared, "You crucified [Jesus], . . . but God raised him up" (Acts 2:23b-24a). In Philippians 2:8, Paul cites an ancient Christian hymn: "[Christ] humbled himself and became obedient to the point of death—even death on a cross."

Paul enumerates his own sufferings (2 Cor 4:7-15; 11:23-29), identifies places where he suffered (2 Tim 3:10-13), and tells Timothy that not only will he suffer, but also that all Christians will suffer persecution (3:12). "Suffering produces endurance, and endurance produces character, and character produces hope" (Rom 5:3-5). Suffering is described as discipline from the Lord. It is painful at the time, "but later it yields the peaceful fruit of righteousness to those who have been trained by it" (Heb 12:5-11).

The church continues the suffering of Christ. Paul says that in his own "flesh" he is "completing what is lacking in Christ's afflictions for the sake of his body, that is, the church" (Col 1:24). Also in 1 Peter 3:13-18, the author ties the suffering of the church to the sufferings of Christ. Rather than retaliate in the face of suffering and persecution, Christians follow the example of Christ (1 Pet 2:21). Christians find motivation to endure sufferings because their hope is in the ultimate victory of Christ (Rom 5:3-5; 8:31-39). The crucified and resurrected Lord stands at the end of time as the one who opens the meaning of history and is the ultimate victor over sin, evil, and death. The slain lamb is the victorious lamb (Rev 5:6-14). Christian suffering is swallowed up in hope and victory.

Christ Abolished Death and Brought Life

In 2 Timothy 1:10 Paul says that the saving grace of God has been revealed through the appearing of our Savior Christ Jesus, who abolished death and brought life and immortality to light through the gospel. The theme of death emerges as early as the story of Adam and Eve in the garden of Eden. The sad story is that all persons sin and die. "Therefore, just as sin came into the world through one man, and death came through sin, and so death spread to all because all have sinned" (Rom 5:12). Negatively the Bible depicts sin as death, meaning life without God (Eph 2:5). It also depicts death as physical death. In contrast, God is the God of the living (Luke 20:38; 1 Tim 1:17; 6:16).

Salvation in Christ Jesus is described as destroying death, or rendering it ineffective (Rom 6:6, 14). Salvation renders inoperative the enemies that stand against God's purposes. The death of Jesus Christ has canceled the power of death (Rom 6:6, 10; 14:8-9; 2 Cor 4:10; 1 Thess 5:10; Heb 2:14). Physical death is described as an enemy that will be destroyed. Christians live in the victory of Christ over the power of death that is now in sin. And though Christians die, this physical death does not have ultimate control, for in the final analysis it, too, is destroyed in the resurrection (1 Cor 15:20-26; 1 Thess 4:13-18).

Positively, Christ Jesus brought life and immortality. The word *immortality*, also translated *incorruptibility*, is a Pauline term (Rom 2:7; 1 Cor 15:42, 50, 53-54; Eph 6:24). *Immortality* and *life* are tied together in 2 Timothy 1:10. The resurrection of Christ Jesus has introduced a new order of life in the universe (Rom 5:18-21), an order proclaimed by the earliest Christian preaching (Acts 2:25-36). In Christ's death and resurrection, we see triumph over death. In its place, eternal life shines forth—something that Christians already experience and will experience in its fullness in the future bodily resurrection. So significant was the resurrection in the mind of the early Christians that worship was changed from the Sabbath to the Lord's day as a symbol of the centrality of the resurrection in their lives (Rev 1:10; Acts 20:7; 1 Cor 16:2).

Ezekiel's promise of bones coming alive has been fulfilled (37:7-14), as has the promise that emerged in early Judaism: "Many of those who sleep in the dust of the earth shall awake, some to everlasting life, and some to shame and everlasting contempt" (Dan 12:2). Martha knew her brother Lazarus would be raised "on the last day" (John 11:24). But Jesus already embodied the reality of resurrection: "*I am* the resurrection and the life. Those who believe in me, even though they die, will live, and everyone who lives and believes in me will never die" (John 11:25-26, stress added). Already in Jesus Christ, Christians are given eternal life (1 John 5:11-12). They have been raised up with him (Eph 2:6; Col 3:1). Yet Christians *will* be raised in the final resurrection, at which time their bodies will be transformed for the heavenly world, as Paul wrote:

> Our citizenship is in heaven, and it is from there that we are expecting a Savior, the Lord Jesus Christ. He will *transform* the body of our humiliation that it may be *conformed* to the body of his glory, by the power that also enables him to make all things subject to himself. (Phil 3:20-21, stress added)

Thus Paul concludes, "Death has been swallowed up in victory" (1 Cor 15:54b).

THE TEXT IN THE LIFE OF THE CHURCH

The Suffering Church

Already in the first century, Christians were put to death because of their faith in Jesus Christ (Acts 7:59-60; 12:1-3; Rev 2:13). During the postapostolic period, some Roman emperors unleashed official persecutions against the Christians, which ceased only when church and state became one under Constantine.

Another wave of persecution came upon the Anabaptists in the sixteenth and seventeenth centuries in Europe, beginning with the Swiss Anabaptist Felix Manz in 1527 (*ME* 3:472-74). The last Anabaptist martyr in the Canton of Zurich was Hans Landis in 1614 (*ME* 3:280-81). Persecution to the point of death ended in the Canton of Bern only when Anabaptist Hans Haslibacher was martyred in 1571 (*ME* 2:675-76). Because of widespread persecution, not only in Switzerland but also in Germany, Austria, Moravia, and the Netherlands, the Anabaptists developed a theology of suffering. They believed that suffering was the sign that they belonged to Christ, participated with Christ in life, and walked the path of Christian discipleship. Such suffering was tied to baptism. For the Anabaptists, baptism was a kind of sealing to suffering and death. As a Hutterite hymn declared, "Whosoever will enter into a covenant with God needs three witnesses in heaven—Father, Son, and Holy Ghost—and three witnesses on earth—spirit, water, and blood. The first baptism is the baptism with the Spirit, the second the baptism with water, and the third is the baptism with blood" (Pipkin 1994: 231; cf. 1 John 5:7-8 KJV). For Menno Simons, suffering was a mark of the true church; if it is not suffering, the church is false (*CW*: 751). If Christians do not share in the cross of Christ, they are not true followers of Christ (*CW*: 548).

Anabaptists believed that the cross not only stood upright in history when Christ was crucified in AD 30, it also lies across history as Christians walk the path of discipleship. Following Christ requires an attitude of yieldedness, what the German and Swiss Anabaptists called *Gelassenheit*. Yieldedness to Christ means accepting defenselessness and not going to war as part of Christian obedience to Christ. Anabaptists believed that vengeance is in *God's* hands, not theirs. Consequently, they believed that the righteous would ultimately be victorious and that their persecutors, whether religious or civil, would be defeated.

A disciple is not only on the way to the cross, but through death is also on the way to glory. The Anabaptists wrote hymns about martyrdom. As the church sang these hymns year after year, it became aware that it was surrounded by a host of martyrs as it marched forward in its victory in Christ. Thus martyrdom had eschatological meaning. It was a sign that God's reign was breaking into human history.

The Christian church continues to shed its blood across the pages of human history. More Christians were martyred in the twentieth century than in any other century in the history of the church. In recent years many Christians in Vietnam, the former Soviet Union, Ethiopia, Colombia, China, and Central America have experienced persecution for their commitment to Christ. In some of these countries the church went underground and experienced rapid growth. One sees victory amid suffering even in modern times.

Cowardice and Boldness in Christian Ministry

The contemporary church in North America has experienced a loss of nerve and finds itself wavering with regard to the significance of Jesus Christ (Brunk: 7). In some parts of the world, the church is losing its boldness in preaching the gospel due to relativism, which views the exclusiveness of the gospel of Christ as a stumbling block and scandal to modern humanity. Meanwhile, the rise of other monotheistic world religions has created less interest in proclaiming the truth of the Christian gospel.

Passion is needed in proclaiming the gospel in a postmodern world. However, passion needs to be tempered by sensitivity to persons of other faiths. Christian mission includes living out the gospel with integrity, thereby making Jesus Christ a viable choice. We can see examples of this kind of boldness in Christian ministry in postcommunist Eastern Europe. In Lithuania, people disillusioned with communism are now coming to faith in Jesus Christ. A high percentage of the students enrolled in Lithuania Christian College come from atheistic backgrounds in Eastern European countries. By the end of their four-year experience, a large number of students become Christians. In Indonesia, a high percentage of the people are Muslim. Despite persecution, the Christian church is reaching out in love toward Muslim friends, some of whom are becoming Christians. In Ethiopia, many former communists and Muslims have come to faith in Christ. In each of these examples, the Christian church is unashamed of the gospel of Jesus Christ. The church is reaching out with sensitivity to persons in other religions or with no religion as it presents the gospel of Jesus Christ in word and deed.

Life and Immortality

Christians have always believed in the resurrection. The earliest Christian preaching recorded in Acts places the resurrection of Jesus Christ at the center of its proclamation (2:22-36). In combating false teaching, the Apostolic Fathers affirm teaching on the resurrection of the body (N. T. Wright 2003: 481-94). In contrast to a Greek view of the soul's natural immortality, early Christian creeds affirm the resurrection of the body.

During the Enlightenment, some scholars looked for clear evidence that Jesus was raised from the dead and concluded that the story of the resurrection in the Gospels was a projection of second-century Christians. Some NT scholars applied existential philosophy to their understanding of resurrection, concluding that resurrection refers to one's own existential experience of the Lord, which gives meaning to life now. Such views tended to negate future bodily resurrection.

N. T. Wright's massive study of the resurrection of the Son of God challenges these Enlightenment and existential views. Wright declares that the present body is not a prison from which to escape; what it needs is transformation. The resurrection and ascension of Christ make clear that his body was not abandoned to corruption, but was transformed from the humiliation of death to the glory of resurrection (2003: 231, 233). In like manner, the Christian's body will be transformed, not abandoned.

In the hymns and poetry of the eighteenth and nineteenth centuries, English writers began to interpret physical death as the transfer of one's soul directly to heaven. This interpretation led to a popular belief that when one dies, one goes immediately to heaven. In contrast, the NT teaches that death is followed by a waiting period, after which comes the resurrection of the body (but cf. Luke 23:43; 2 Cor 8–9; Phil 1:22-24; Rev 7:14-15). This view is based on Jesus' death, waiting in the tomb, and then being raised on the third day. While mystery surrounds this waiting period, the intermediate state of the dead, Christians can be sure that the dead in Christ rest from their labors and that their sufferings are over. Like the living, the dead also experience the tension of the "already but not yet" of Christ's victory. They already are in Christ's safekeeping (Rom 8:38-39), yet they await Christ's final cosmic victory, which comes with the future bodily resurrection and the consummation of all things (Finger 1985: 140-41).

Sixteenth-century Anabaptists talked about resurrection in four ways. First, they affirmed that Jesus had been crucified and buried, and that he rose on the third day. Second, they affirmed that there is a future bodily resurrection for Christians, which offers courage and hope in the midst of suffering (*CW*: 53). Third, they talked about resurrection in relation to the new birth and the experience of salvation. In baptism the Christian believer is buried and raised with Christ (Rom 6:4). Baptism is an outward sign of an inward transformation by the "new birth" (1 Pet 1:3; "born from above, . . . of the Spirit"; John 3:3-6). Fourth, they talked about walking in the resurrection of Christ. In the 1527 Schleitheim Confession, the Anabaptists agreed:

> Baptism shall be given to all those who have been taught repentance and the amendment of life and [who] believe truly that their sins are taken away through Christ, and to all those who desire to walk in the resurrection of Jesus Christ and be buried with Him in death, so that they might rise with Him. (art. 1; in Yoder 1973: 36)

Walking in the resurrection of Christ is central to the Anabaptist understanding of discipleship. To walk in the resurrection means to put away the old life of sin, to experience new birth through the Spirit, to put on the new life in Christ, and to live in obedience to Christ by the power of the Holy Spirit (Bender: 96-110).

By emphasizing these four dimensions of the resurrection, the Anabaptists brought together the reality of the work of Christ in abolishing death (2 Tim 1:10) in its dual dimensions of sin and physical death. The first dimension of death is done away with in the new birth, and the second dimension will be done away with by the future resurrection of the body.

2 Timothy 2:1-13

Faithfulness and Endurance in Christian Ministry

PREVIEW

With an emphatic *you then,* Paul turns to the second part of the exhortation to faithfulness and suffering that began in 1:7 and is illustrated by the example of Onesiphorus. The exhortation began with an emphasis on the gift of God that Timothy is to fan into flame. He is no longer to be ashamed of Christ nor of Paul. Paul outlines three duties here in 2:1-7. Timothy is to be strong in the grace that is in Christ Jesus (2:1), to entrust the message of the gospel to faithful people who will be able to teach others (2:2), and to share in suffering for the gospel (2:3a). Sharing in suffering recalls what Paul said in 1:8. Paul now extends the exhortation with three analogies used as standards for moral instruction in the Greco-Roman world: the soldier, the athlete, and the farmer. In each example the person strives under duress.

Then Paul turns to Jesus Christ in 2:8-13. Paul reminds Timothy of the historic gospel of Jesus Christ (2:8-9) and that the apostle desires people to receive salvation in Christ (2:10). Finally, Paul concludes with a faithful saying based on this salvation in Jesus Christ (2:11-13).

OUTLINE

Three Duties Timothy Is to Follow, 2:1-3a
Three Analogies: The Soldier, the Athlete, the Farmer, 2:3b-7

The Historic Gospel of Jesus Christ, 2:8-9
Paul's Motivation for Suffering, 2:10
Faithful Saying, 2:11-13

EXPLANATORY NOTES

Three Duties Timothy Is to Follow 2:1-3a

You then is highly emphatic both in terms of its meaning and its position. Timothy's first duty is to *be strong in the grace that is in Christ Jesus* (2:1). This duty reaches back and summarizes who Timothy is to be and what he is to do. God is the source of Timothy's strength. Strength comes as Timothy continues to walk by means of *the grace that is in Christ Jesus* (2:1). Timothy is strengthened by the Holy Spirit (1:7, 14) and by the eternal grace of God revealed in Jesus Christ (1:9-10).

A second duty is for Timothy to entrust to faithful people what he has heard from Paul and many witnesses. Paul wants Timothy to leave Ephesus and come to visit him in prison as soon as possible (4:9, 21). To make sure that the gospel continues, Timothy is instructed to *entrust to faithful people* what he has heard before leaving Ephesus. The message he heard comes from many witnesses, including his mother and grandmother (1:5) and other traveling companions on Paul's missionary journeys (Acts 15:40; 16:1-5). To entrust means to place this gospel fully into the hands of others. The true teaching is to be preserved and spread by passing it on to responsible people who will preserve it unchanged (I. H. Marshall 1999: 726).

To safeguard this message, Timothy is to pass it on to *faithful people*. To whom one entrusts the gospel is important. *Faithful people* are competent, *reliable* (TNIV), and capable of teaching others. The term *able* refers to competent persons and is used twenty-seven times in Luke-Acts. The emphasis is not on apostolic succession or status, but on the trustworthiness and reliability of people. While the elders at Ephesus may be in Paul's mind (see 1 Tim 3:1-7; 5:17-18), the plural noun *anthrōpoi* (human beings) indicates that the persons to whom Timothy is to entrust the message are not necessarily or exclusively men (2 Tim 2:2). Faithful people are persons *who will be able to teach others as well* (2:2b). Here is the principle of multiplication: each one teaches another. In so doing, Timothy can leave Ephesus and visit Paul in Rome, fully assured that trustworthy persons will communicate the good news of the gospel to others and that the deposit of faith will be preserved as the church continues to expand in the Greco-Roman world.

Third, Timothy is once more commanded to *share in suffering* (2:3a). *Endure hardship* is too weak a translation of this command (KJV, NIV, NEB). The verb means *suffering with*, as in 1:8.

Three Analogies: The Soldier, the Athlete, the Farmer 2:3b-7

Paul illustrates what he means by calling attention to three examples of strenuous life and struggle for self-mastery found in Hellenistic moral teaching: the soldier, the athlete, and the farmer. Paul uses these same metaphors in an earlier letter (1 Cor 3:6-9; 9:7, 24-27). Here in 2 Timothy 2:3-6, the emphasis is on endurance. The soldier is characterized by discipline. A soldier does not become entangled with the affairs of everyday living, nor does he allow other things to distract him from the task at hand. The soldier has a single aim: to give undivided attention to carrying out his superior's orders. In like manner, Timothy is to give wholehearted devotion and perseverance to his master, Jesus Christ.

The athlete illustrates determination and dedication to the task. One must compete according to the rules, both the rules of training and those of the contest. At least ten months of training were required to participate in the Greek races. Any mistake in the contest disqualified one immediately. Timothy prepares by training himself in godliness (1 Tim 4:7) and must faithfully fulfill his charge (2 Tim 4:1-5).

In the third example, the farmer exercises diligence. The farmer reaps no crop without hard work, labor to the point of exhaustion (Johnson 2001: 366). Lack of labor leads to the ruin of the land and lack of crops (Prov 20:4). But the hard worker can expect a share of the crops. As in the case of the athlete, future reward requires endurance. With these three metaphors, Paul exhorts Timothy to endure suffering through discipline, determination, and diligence. An eschatological reward comes with endurance. As C. K. Barrett says, "Beyond warfare is victory, beyond athletic effort a prize, and beyond agricultural labour a crop" (1963: 102).

As Timothy meditates on these three metaphors and their application, God will provide wisdom (2:7) so that Timothy can understand why he should endure and share in suffering with Paul and with Christ.

The Historic Gospel of Jesus Christ 2:8-9

With the command to *remember*, Paul calls attention to the historic gospel of Jesus Christ and ties into the memory motif in this epistle (1:4-6; 3:14-15). The verb *remember* indicates continuing action. Continually Timothy is to *remember Jesus Christ, raised from the dead, a descendant of David* (2:8). This description of Jesus Christ is similar to Romans 1:3-4, which also calls attention to Jesus as the seed of David and the resurrected Lord. However, here the order is reversed, with the resurrection mentioned first. Nothing is said about the meaning of Jesus' death. The focal point is the resurrected Lord. The tense of the verb *to raise* indicates past action with continuing consequences.

Jesus was raised bodily by God from the dead and continues to be the living, resurrected Lord. As such, Jesus is victor over death, and his resurrection points to the future bodily resurrection of Christian believers. For suffering Christians, this is a word of hope and is incorporated into the first two sentences of the faithful saying, in 2:11-12. Further, Jesus is a descendant of David and fulfills the Davidic promise. Paul's gospel is not a new philosophy or a new idea. The good news is the historic act of God in the person of Jesus Christ. Paul's emphasis on the incarnation calls attention to Jesus' humanity, in opposition to the proto-Gnostic opponents. By identifying Jesus as a descendant of David, Paul declares that the gospel is rooted in history.

For which I suffer hardship, even to the point of being chained like a criminal (2:9a). As Jesus Christ suffered and died, so Paul also suffers for this gospel. Being chained like a criminal was humiliating and grossly unfair to Paul, an innocent Roman citizen. The word *criminal* means one who commits gross deeds and serious crimes, and is associated with extreme penalties, such as crucifixion (I. H. Marshall 1999: 736). The same term is used for the persons who were crucified with Jesus in Luke 23:32-33, 39. Jesus died like a criminal. Now, too, Paul is treated as a criminal, even though both Jesus and Paul were innocent. In contrast to the chains that bind him, Paul says, *the word of God is not chained* (2:9b). The contrast between the chained Paul and the unchained Word of God could not be greater. Paul is shackled by chains, but the Word of God is not shackled (cf. Acts 28:31). The two terms (*chained, not chained*) come from the same root. Opponents may stop the messenger, but they cannot stop the message (Fee 1988: 247).

Paul's Motivation for Suffering 2:10

Paul's suffering is not in vain. Paul writes, *I endure everything for the sake of the elect* (2:10a). He suffers for the sake of God's chosen people. Elsewhere Paul wrote, "I have become all things to all people, that I might by all means save some" (1 Cor 9:22b). Paul is motivated, even amid suffering, as one who sees beyond suffering that the living gospel does something in the world. Paul suffers for the sake of the elect, *so that they may also obtain the salvation that is in Christ Jesus, with eternal glory* (2:10b). In contrast to the Roman emperor, who was called savior, Christ Jesus is the true Savior (1:10). This salvation is in Christ Jesus (Acts 4:11-12; Rom 10:10) and has the eschatological reward of eternal glory, since Jesus *abolished death* (1:10). Paul willingly suffers because he knows that suffering is tied into the historic gospel of Jesus Christ (2:8), that the word of God is not chained (2:9b), and that salvation in Christ Jesus is for the people of God now and for their eternal glory.

Paul's sufferings have positive evangelistic significance, and he invites Timothy likewise to suffer and proclaim this gospel unashamedly. The summary and climax to this long first exhortation to Timothy (1:6-2:13) come in the sure saying that follows in 2:11-13.

Faithful Saying 2:11-13

In 2 Timothy 2:11-13 we come to another *sure saying* in the letters to Timothy and Titus (1 Tim 1:15; 3:1; 4:9; Titus 3:8) *[Faithful Sayings, p. 344]*. Scholars debate whether this faithful saying refers back to what comes previously in 2 Timothy 2:8-10, or whether it refers to what follows in 2:11-13. I interpret the formula as referring to what follows in 2:11-13. The rhythmic structure of the four "if" clauses paired with "then" clauses in verses 11-13 clearly sets it off as a poem or hymn that functions much like a confessional statement.

It is not clear whether this poem or hymn is a piece of early Christian tradition that Paul is incorporating or whether it was created by Paul himself. Fee says, "The hymn, in all of its parts, fits the context so well that, whatever its origins or original setting, it now functions to inspire loyalty to Christ" (Fee 1988: 252). The faithful saying is composed of four pairs of clauses; each pair begins with a conditional ("if") clause followed by a result ("then") clause. The first two sentences say what believers *should do* in the present and what God will do. The third sentence calls attention to what believers *should not do* in the future and God's response. The fourth sentence says what believers *should not be*, followed by God's contrasting action, based on a final affirmation that God cannot deny himself.

"If" clause (protasis)	**"Then" clause (apodosis)**
Positive	
If we have died with him,	we will also live with him;
If we endure,	we will also reign with him;
Negative	
If we deny him,	he will also deny us;
If we are faithless,	he remains faithful—
	for he cannot deny himself.

The content of this poem or hymn is thoroughly Pauline. Line 1 emphasizes Christian conversion as dying and rising with Christ, in language similar to Romans 6. It has both present and eschatological dimensions. Line 2 stresses perseverance amid present suffering and encourages

Timothy to keep in mind that such endurance results in reigning together with Christ in the future. Line 3 turns to the future and emphasizes that lack of endurance in Christian faith, denying Christ, results in God's judgment in the future. Line 4 emphasizes God's faithfulness, even if some believers are unfaithful. The poem or hymn sets forth the believers' participation in present suffering and contrasts it with the promise of participation in the resurrection (Elias 2006: 492).

If we have died with him, we will also live with him (2:11a). Here *died with* and *will live with* are compound verbs. Paul similarly uses the phrase *died with* and the compound verb *live with* in Romans 6:8, where Christian conversion is described in the language of death to the old self and new life in Jesus Christ. It is likely, however, that the statement goes beyond the present experience with Christ. Here in 2 Timothy 2:11 the use of the past tense (*died with*) and the future tense (*will live with*) implies an eschatological dimension. In the context of 2 Timothy, the sentence points beyond Christian conversion to Christian martyrdom and has an explicit hortatory force for the reader (I. H. Marshall 1999: 739). We die to self in Christian conversion and experience new life in Christ. But suffering for the gospel's sake to the point of death is not the end. As Jesus' death was followed by resurrection, so too the Christian martyrs will live with him. We participate with Christ in death and resurrection.

If we endure, we will also reign with him (2:12a). *Endurance* is a Christian virtue in the letters to Timothy and Titus (1 Tim 6:11; 2 Tim 2:10; 3:11; Titus 2:2). *To endure* means to remain faithful amid trouble, affliction, or persecution, just as Paul endures while in chains (2:9-10). The verb appears in the present tense: *continue* to endure. Endurance results in an eschatological promise of reigning with Christ, as it did for Timothy and Paul. The sentence fits well in the overall appeal for Timothy to remain loyal and be willing to suffer (1:6–2:13). The word *also* points to the future kingdom. Participation in the reign of Christ is both present and future (cf., e.g., 1 Pet 2:9; Rev 1:6; 5:10). Endurance to the point of death is possible because there is something beyond death. Expecting to participate in Christ's reign in the future gives the Christian believer hope (cf. 1 Tim 1:1; Titus 1:2).

The third line in the poem or hymn moves from the preceding positive action to a negative action. *If we deny him, he will also deny us* (2:12b). The verb *deny* is translated *disown* in the TNIV. The verb tense in the "then" clause is future: If we deny him, Christ also will deny us. As Paul writes these words, he may be thinking about Timothy's temptation to shame and possible unwillingness to suffer for the cause of the gospel. There is also a change in the apodosis from the plural pronoun *we* to an emphatic *he* (*that one*). A similar saying of Jesus is found in Matthew 10:33. In lines 1 and 2 an eschatological promise is given, but in line 3 an eschatological warning appears. If it is not possible to disown faith in Christ, there is no need for these words. The possibility of Timothy and others disowning the faith is real. Some already have disowned the faith (2 Tim 2:18, 25). There are dire consequences to such action, and Timothy is warned that if he disowns the faith, Christ will also disown him.

If we are faithless, he remains faithful (2:13a). The verb *to be faithless* is in the present tense and means continuing resistance to God's word. Luke uses this verb to describe the apostles' unbelieving response to the women's report of the resurrection and appearance of Jesus (Luke 24:11, 41). The verb expresses acts of unfaithfulness, possibly even apostasy; as addressed to the readers and hearers of this epistle, it warns of the temptation to which they are exposed (I. H. Marshall 1999: 741). In sharp contrast to the apodosis in the previous three statements, here *he* [GNT: *that one*] *remains faithful.*

Here in the fourth statement the action differs from that of the first part of the statement (faith*less* . . . [but] faith*ful*). The faithfulness of God and of Christ is not deterred by human unfaithfulness. Faithfulness does not mean that God overlooks human unfaithfulness with his grace. When some Christian believers prove faithless, God continues to be faithful in character. In other words, the unfaithfulness of some Christians is no reason for other Christians to assume that God will respond likewise to all Christians by turning away from them.

Fidelity is an essential characteristic of God. God is loyal to the covenant with his people. The phrase, "his steadfast love [faithfulness] endures forever" often occurs in the OT (e.g., Pss 119; 136). Similarly, Jesus Christ continues to be faithful. Regardless of the circumstances in which Paul, Timothy, the Ephesian believers, and countless other Christians find themselves, Jesus Christ remains faithful to them. If there is any break in the relationship between a Christian believer and Christ, it is not a result of or lack of faithfulness on Christ's part. Despite the unfaithfulness of some (2:17-18), Christ remains faithful to his church because he cannot be untrue to his own nature (I. H. Marshall 1999: 742). Timothy can count on the faithfulness of Christ despite the fact that some believers in Ephesus have left the faith.

Why is it the case that *he cannot deny himself* (2:13b)? Literally, the text reads, *For that one is not able to deny himself* (GNT). Christ cannot be untrue to himself (Knight 1992: 407). The statement indicates that fidelity is an essential quality of Jesus. To be unfaithful would be to deny or repudiate his very being (Johnson 2001: 377). As in Romans 3:3-4, the faithlessness of some does not nullify the faithfulness of God. To be God is to be faithful. If

God is not faithful, then God cannot be trusted (Aageson 2008: 43). To deny himself would mean that God and Christ cease to be. Hence, eschatological salvation as outlined in this poem or hymn is rooted in the character of God (Fee 1988: 251). This final comment assures Timothy and other Christian believers who suffer hardship that the Lord whom they serve is and will be faithful to them (2 Tim 1:12).

With the lines of this poem or hymn, Paul brings the first exhortation to Timothy in its two parts to a close. Timothy is exhorted not to be ashamed of the gospel or of Paul, despite suffering. With the presence of the Holy Spirit (1:7, 14), the historic gospel of Jesus Christ (2:8), and the faithfulness of God (2:13b), Timothy is urged to move forward in Christian ministry, knowing that God's Word is not chained and that the eschatological promise of salvation is sure. This assurance rests on the character of God and of Christ.

THE TEXT IN BIBLICAL CONTEXT

The Centrality of the Gospel

In 2 Timothy 2:8 the apostle calls attention to the person of Jesus Christ and affirms, "That is my gospel." Throughout Paul's epistles, the gospel centers on the person, life, death, and resurrection of Jesus Christ. Here in 2 Timothy 2:8, Jesus Christ is identified as a descendant of David. Likewise in Romans 1:3, Jesus Christ is called a descendant of David. Then Paul adds, "And [he] was declared to be Son of God with power according to the spirit of holiness by resurrection from the dead." In writing to the church in Galatia, Paul says, "May I never boast of anything except the cross of our Lord Jesus Christ" (Gal 6:14a). Writing to the Corinthian church, Paul says, "For no one can lay any foundation other than the one that has been laid; that foundation is Jesus Christ" (1 Cor 3:11).

The centrality of the historic gospel of Jesus Christ is more than an objective article of belief in Paul's theology. It also has a subjective dimension in that Paul wants to participate personally in the sufferings and glory of Christ. Dying and rising with Christ is set forth in Romans 6. In Philippians the apostle says, "I want to know Christ and the power of his resurrection and the sharing of his sufferings by becoming like him in his death, if somehow I may attain the resurrection from the dead" (Phil 3:10-11). For Paul, participation with Christ leads to dying with Christ. And dying with Christ leads to ongoing life with Christ (2 Tim 2:11-13).

The Faithfulness of God/Christ

God is faithful. God's faithfulness is implied in the name for God in Exodus 3:13-15, which speaks of God's self-existence and unchangeableness. In the Psalms, God is faithful to his covenant promises (40:10); his faithfulness reaches to the clouds (36:5) and extends to all generations (100:5). The psalmist talks about God's steadfast love in language similar to Paul in 2 Timothy:

> As for mortals, their days are like grass;
> they flourish like a flower of the field;
> for the wind passes over it, and it is gone,
> and its place knows it no more.
> But the steadfast love of the Lord is from everlasting to everlasting
> on those who fear him,
> and his righteousness to children's children,
> to those who keep his covenant
> and remember to do his commandments. (Ps 103:15-18)

In the NT, the adjective *faithful* describes God's fidelity to the covenant promises. Covenant faithfulness is grounded in God, who cannot lie (Titus 1:2) and cannot deny himself (2 Tim 2:13). Christians hold fast to their confession of hope because God is faithful to God's promise (Heb 10:23), including the promise to forgive our sins (1 John 1:9). God and Christ keep covenant promises even when Christians face difficulties. Faithfulness is a matter of the divine nature.

Christ, who is God in human flesh, possesses God's character of faithfulness. Despite the apostasy and faithlessness of some Christians, Christ remains faithful to his cause and to his church. He cannot be untrue to his own nature. When Christians suffer hardship, they can be assured that the Lord is faithful to the gospel. The faithfulness of God and of Christ does not necessarily mean that persons who continually turn away from God and reject Christ are included in God's promise to show covenant faithfulness. A distinction can be made between lapses into unfaithfulness on one hand and continuing, persistent unbelief and unfaithfulness on the other hand. Perhaps a temporary lapse is the case in the "if" clause of 2 Timothy 2:13. If this is what the writer had in mind, then the faithfulness of Christ in the "then" clause means that Christ *remains faithful* and *we* can return to him.

The faithfulness of Christ all the way to the cross may be what Paul has in mind when he talks about the "faith of Christ" (*pistos Christou*). Grammatically, the phrase can be translated either "the faith *of* Jesus" (subjective genitive: Jesus having faith) or "faith *in* Jesus" (objective genitive: our having faith in Jesus). If it is a subjective genitive, it speaks of the subject of the action. If it is an objective genitive, it speaks about the object of the action.

A growing number of NT scholars interpret the phrase "faith of Christ," which appears several times in Paul's letters (e.g., Rom 3:22, 26; Gal 2:16; 3:22; Phil 3:9), as a subjective genitive, which indicates the active faith of Christ, or the faithfulness of Christ. Jesus was faithful to God, and that faithfulness extended all the way to his willing self-sacrifice at the cross (Hays 2002: 249-97; N. T. Wright 2005: 119-20). In this interpretation, the faith of Christ is closely associated with the declaration "He humbled himself and became obedient to the point of death—even death on a cross" (Phil 2:8).

This way of interpreting the faithfulness of Christ places less emphasis on the human response of faith, though it too is important, and places more emphasis on what God has done in Christ for us because of his faithfulness to God (Toews: 108-10). This interpretation gives Christian believers a greater awareness of the assurance of salvation. They know that Christ and God are faithful to the covenant promise in Christ's atoning death for our forgiveness (1 John 1:9). As Jesus was faithful to God all the way to the cross, so Jesus is faithful to the believers in Ephesus, even though some have lapsed into unfaithfulness. Unfaithful persons cannot blame God or Jesus when they turn away from him.

THE TEXT IN THE LIFE OF THE CHURCH

The Faithfulness of God/Christ

Extreme forms of divine election based on philosophical determinism have permeated the church. One extreme form leaves some persons believing that they are Christians even though they do not actively practice the faith, since they are considered one of God's elect. Another extreme places so strong an emphasis on obedience to Christ that if a person falls into sin, the person feels completely defeated and gives up the faith. Christian perfectionists who fail and then give up the faith, and Christian libertarians who assume they are saved regardless of how they live—both kinds of people are interpreting the NT incorrectly (1 John 1:10-2:2). Christian believers are assured of God's faithfulness in times of temptation (1 Cor 10:13) and in times of persecution. God's faithful action coupled with our faithful human response to what God has done leads to assurance of salvation. Neither God's action alone nor our human response alone gives assurance. Both are needed.

One hymn greatly appreciated and sung by Christians speaks of faithfulness in God's being, in creation, and in redemption.

Great is thy faithfulness, O God my Father.
There is no shadow of turning with thee.
Thou changest not, thy compassions they fail not.
As thou has been thou forever will be.

Summer and winter, and springtime and harvest,
Sun, moon, and stars in their courses above,
Join with all nature in manifold witness
To thy great faithfulness, mercy, and love.

Pardon for sin and a peace that endureth,
Thine own dear presence to cheer and to guide,
Strength for today and bright hope for tomorrow;
Blessings all mine, with ten thousand beside!

The refrain follows each verse:

Great is thy faithfulness! Great is thy faithfulness!
Morning by morning new mercies I see.
All I have needed thy hand hath provided.
Great is thy faithfulness, Lord, unto me!
—Thomas O. Chisholm

2 Timothy 2:14–3:9

Timothy as Teacher in Contrast to Unhealthy Teachers

PREVIEW

Having completed the first major exhortation with his own suffering as a model for Timothy, Paul moves into the second major section of this letter and explains to Timothy how to respond as a teacher to those who are skewing Christian faith. Paul's opponents wrangle over words (2:14), use profane chatter (2:16), have departed from the truth (2:18), and are guilty of stupid and senseless controversies (2:23). In contrast, Timothy is to explain the word of truth rightly (2:15), pursue righteousness (2:22), and correct those in error with gentleness (2:24-26). And when the opponents practice evil in the last days, Timothy and other church leaders are to avoid them (3:1-9).

The section begins with a contrast between Timothy's teaching and the others' teaching (2:14-19). Timothy is to remind the Christians of the danger of unhealthy teaching (v. 14), handle the word of truth rightly (v. 15), avoid the error of deviant teaching (v. 16-18), and rest assured of *God's firm foundation* (vv. 19-20). Second, a metaphor of household utensils illustrates the need for cleansing by God to be useful in God's house (2:20-21). This cleansing makes Timothy useful in God's house and may also suggest that the opponents can likewise become useful in God's house if they experience God's cleansing. Third, the kind of utensils useful in God's house is applied to Timothy's ministry (2:22-

26). Timothy is also to flee youthful passions (v. 22a), pursue godliness (v. 22b), reject unhealthy teaching (v. 23), exercise patience while teaching (v. 24), correct the opponents *with gentleness* (v. 25a), and hope that some *will repent* and *escape* damnation (v. 25b-26). Fourth, the nature of ungodliness is summarized with a long list of sins that characterize the *last days* (3:1-9). In response to these sins, Paul gives Timothy a two-word command: *Avoid them!* (3:5b).

Structurally, the section consists of a series of negative commands followed by contrasting positive commands. Imperatives (2:14-16a, 22-23) are followed by supporting information (2:16b-21, 24-26). In this second exhortation of the book, Paul shifts from the memory-and-imitation model of the first major exhortation of the book and uses a more direct form of moral instruction through maxims (Johnson 2001: 389). These maxims, a form of paraenesis, are short and direct commands, occasionally expanded with explanation or illustration. By using second-person singular imperatives, Paul focuses on Timothy's character, life, and ministry amid opponents at Ephesus.

OUTLINE

Unhealthy Teaching in Contrast to True Teaching, 2:14-19
Useful Utensils in the House of God, 2:20-21
How the Lord's Servant Ministers to Opponents, 2:22-26
Behavior in the Last Days, 3:1-9

EXPLANATORY NOTES

Unhealthy Teaching in Contrast to True Teaching 2:14-19

Paul says, *Remind them of this* [GNT: *these things*] (2:14). The tense of the verb *remind* indicates continuing action: Timothy is to *keep* reminding them of these things. This is the only occurrence of *these things* with an imperative in 2 Timothy, and it refers back to the things Paul has talked about in 2:11-13. Timothy must also warn them before God. The warning goes on at the same time as the reminding, which indicates the seriousness of wrangling over words. This warning is in the presence of God. The phrase *before God* is the preferred reading by most textual critics (e.g., Metzger 1994: 579).

Warnings *to avoid wrangling over words* are common in the letters to Timothy and Titus (1 Tim 2:8; 6:4-5; Titus 3:9). Some church leaders have spent much time debating about words, even fighting over them. Battling over words was a common charge in philosophical disputes (Bassler 1996: 150). Wrangling over word definitions in philosophical discussion undermines the faith of those listening. Engaging in polemics with Paul's opponents is useless and should therefore be avoided.

If the discussion were about serious Christian doctrine, Timothy would engage in serious conversation with them.

Paul commands Timothy, *Do your best to present yourself to God as one approved by him, a worker who has no need to be ashamed, rightly explaining the word of truth* (2:15). The words, *do your best,* imply a sense of urgency in Timothy's work of rightly proclaiming the gospel. If proved to be worthy, Timothy has no need to be ashamed, for he is following in the unashamed path of Christ (1:8), Paul (1:12), and Onesiphorus (1:16).

As an approved worker in God's sight and unashamed of the gospel, Timothy is to rightly explain the word of truth. *Word of truth* as used here and elsewhere in Paul means the gospel, the Christian message as a whole (Eph 1:13; Col 1:5). The term *rightly explain* (*orthotomeō*) means literally "to cut a straight path" or "to cut a path in the right direction" by clearing difficult land to make a road (I. H. Marshall 1999: 748). In OT wisdom literature, the term appears in Proverbs 3:6; 11:5 (LXX) and suggests going the right way, in a moral direction. Cutting a straight path for Timothy means to declare the word of truth in contrast to wrangling over words. Timothy is to teach the gospel correctly. He is to guide the word of truth along a straight path, without being turned aside by wordy debates (I. H. Marshall 1999: 749). In the first century, as in the present one, some people immerse themselves in philosophical debate over semantics and miss the centrality of Christ's person and the good news of Christ's gospel as the word of truth.

In a second negative command, Paul urges Timothy to *avoid profane chatter* (2:16). The verb means that Timothy is to keep avoiding such talk. Profane chatter is unholy chatter: meaningless talk (1 Tim 1:6), profane myths (1 Tim 4:7), and disputes about words (1 Tim 6:4). Profane chatter has a subtle way of leading people further away from God rather than toward God. It takes one step-by-step into moral degradation. In 2 Timothy 3:5, Paul describes this sin as holding to an outward form of godliness while denying its power. This impious talk has a way of spreading unhealthy teaching like gangrene. Not only is ungodly speech dangerous to the individual; it is also injurious to others. Using a medical term, Paul says that this sin is a spreading disease that consumes and destroys (Johnson: 2001: 385). It spreads and eats away like a disease that cannot be stopped. In contrast to healthy teaching, this sin is not only unhealthy; it also leads to death.

Paul illustrates the point by calling attention to two persons who hold unhealthy views. Hymenaeus was already mentioned in 1 Timothy 1:20, along with Alexander. Both were disciplined for making shipwreck of their faith. Apparently Hymenaeus is still in Ephesus, wreaking havoc upon the church. We know nothing more about Philetus. These two men *have swerved from the truth* (2:18a). The danger is more than possible; it is real and spreading. Unlike Timothy, who cuts a straight path to the word of truth, these men have missed the mark of the truth.

What is their unhealthy teaching? They have swerved from the truth *by claiming that the resurrection has already taken place* (2:18b). In denying the future bodily resurrection, they proclaim the resurrection has *already* taken place. And since there is no marriage or eating in heaven, the opponents have said that sex and certain foods should be denied. Paul rejects this teaching and says that both sex and food were created by God and are to be received with thanksgiving and prayer (1 Tim 4:3-5).

Which resurrection is Paul talking about in 2 Timothy 2:18? In other passages (Rom 6:3-11; Eph 2:6; Col 2:20; 3:1), Paul talks about Christian conversion, baptism, and new birth while using the language of being raised with Christ. If that is what Paul is referring to here, the problem is an over-realized eschatology, counting believers' present spiritual resurrection as complete fulfillment of any promise of resurrection. The presence or absence of the article (*the*) before the word *resurrection* is crucial in understanding what Paul is saying. If the article is *not* present, as in the manuscripts known as Sinaiticus (א), F, G, and a few other Greek witnesses, Paul would be speaking about *a* resurrection. If, however, the article is present, as it is in the manuscripts known as Alexandrinus, Ephraemi Rescriptus, Bezae, and in the Koine tradition, then Paul is speaking about *the* resurrection. The evidence is fairly well-balanced, and deciding between the two readings is difficult (Metzger 1994: 579-80). Both the NA text and the UBS*GNT* include the article within brackets. If the article (*the*) is original, Paul is talking about the future bodily resurrection.

Gnostics denied a future bodily resurrection because they thought that the body—indeed, matter itself—was evil. Many Greeks believed in the immortality of the soul, but not in the resurrection of the body (cf. Acts 17:32). Paul counters both of these views by calling attention to the fact that Jesus Christ was raised from the dead (1 Cor 15:3-5, 20-23; 2 Tim 1:10; 2:8). To deny the resurrection of Christ and the future bodily resurrection at Christ's return is to deny the Christian faith (1 Cor 15:17)! No wonder these teachers were upsetting the faith of some Christians in Ephesus! For Paul, to deny the future bodily resurrection is to deny the faith itself because it denies the past resurrection of Christ; our present life in Christ, the living Lord; and our future eschatological existence (Fee 1988: 257) *[Eschatology, p. 342]*.

With the strong adversative *nevertheless* (NIV), Paul affirms that despite this unhealthy teaching, *God's firm foundation stands* (2 Tim 2:19a). He supports this affirmation with two quotations. By *foundation*, Paul points to what he has said elsewhere about the church (1 Tim 3:15), the apostles (Eph 2:20), and Christ himself as the foundation (1 Cor 3:11). Paul also points forward to what he will say about the vessels in a large house in 2 Timothy 2:20-21. The foundation of the church is none other than Jesus Christ. Metaphorically, Paul is saying that the church stands on a firm foundation.

Many Christians in Ephesus were not swayed by unhealthy teaching. These faithful Christians bore an *inscription* or *seal* (NJB). They had the mark of ownership that an architect or owner inscribes on a foundation stone (Fee 1988: 257). Written on this seal are two inscriptions: *The Lord knows those who are his* (2:19b), and *Let everyone who calls on the name of the Lord turn away from wickedness* (2:19c). The first inscription is a quote from Numbers 16:5 via the LXX, which speaks of Korah, Dathan, and 250 leaders who rebelled against Moses. Moses claimed that God knows those who are his. Ultimately Korah and his followers were removed. In like manner, God knows those who are his in the church at Ephesus. Those who are not faithful (cf. v. 18) will eventually repent or leave the church.

The second inscription recalls the words of Paul in Romans 10:13 and a quotation from Joel 2:32 (3:5 LXX) in Peter's sermon at Pentecost (Acts 2:21). Persons who call on the name of the Lord for salvation will turn away from wickedness. Those who claim to belong to God verify that faith claim by their conduct (Towner 1994: 185). While the first inscription on the seal may refer to God's election, the second inscription clarifies the need for a human response of repentance and faithfulness. The teachers at Ephesus may yet repent and come to know the truth (2 Tim 2:25). If they do not repent, God will cut them off from the church like Korah and his followers in the OT. Only by turning away from wickedness and committing themselves to the truth of the gospel can they become authentic followers of Christ.

Useful Utensils in the House of God 2:20-21

Building on the need for faithfulness in the church as God's house, Paul uses an analogy of the great house in verses 20-21. Verse 20 offers the analogy, and verse 21 applies the analogy to the church. Paul turns the readers' attention from the foundation in verse 19 to the building itself. Elsewhere the apostle speaks of the church as the house of God (1 Cor 3:11-15; Eph 2:19-22; 1 Tim 3:15). His analogy begins with the normal understanding of utensils used in the household, but by emphasizing cleansing and dedication to God as owner of the house, Paul portrays the idea of temple instead of the normal Greek household.

In the normal house are two kinds of utensils. Gold and silver vessels are the richest and most valuable kind. Wood and baked clay are the more common and cheapest vessels. A vivid contrast is made between these two kinds of utensils by the terms *not only . . . but also*. The contrast is not only in the *costs* of the utensils but also in the *uses* of the utensils. Important guests are served with the gold and silver vessels: the finest and most costly china on the table. Then there are the cheap, mundane, everyday dishes, made of wood and clay, utensils for ordinary use. At Ephesus, people with views and teachings that Paul considers to be deviant are still in the church. The contrast is not so much between good and bad people in the church as it is on how people can cleanse themselves and become useful, special utensils in God's house. Timothy himself will be a useful servant in God's ministry if he shuns passions and pursues righteousness and godliness (2 Tim 2:22), if he avoids useless controversies (2:23), and if he is kind and gentle in dealing with the misguided group (2:24).

All who cleanse themselves of the things mentioned will become special utensils, dedicated and useful to the owner of the house, ready for every good work (2:21). As the vessels in the temple were sanctified and dedicated for use in God's house, so the believers in the church at Ephesus should cleanse themselves of the unhealthy teachings and become useful utensils in God's house. Anyone who is cleansed from these will be useful in God's house. A believer is to personally separate oneself from the unhealthy teachings. In so doing, one actually becomes cleansed by God, sanctified and dedicated to God for special use. With this language, Paul turns the idea of cleansing or separation from bad teaching into the direction of ritual language used in Jewish temple worship and usefulness in God's house (Johnson 2001: 388).

Only as a human vessel is cleansed does it become useful to the owner of the house. As Timothy sets himself apart from the unhealthy teachings, he will be cleansed, dedicated, and useful in God's service. Likewise, as other persons at Ephesus separate themselves (2:25-26), they too will change and become vessels of honor to the master of the house. These changed persons will know the truth of the gospel and express readiness for good work by upright, moral behavior.

How the Lord's Servant Ministers to Opponents 2:22-26

In these verses, Paul builds on the theme of cleansing and dedication to the owner of God's house and tells Timothy how to be the Lord's servant in the midst of opposition. The argument moves back and forth between negative and positive kinds of responses.

First, Timothy is to pay attention to his own spiritual life. With two imperatives, Paul commands Timothy to *shun youthful passions* and *pur-*

sue Christian virtues. To shun means (lit.) to *flee* (NIV), to escape from an immediate danger. *Passions* is often used in the NT for sexual urges and desires, but nothing in the context here favors this interpretation. Rather, the term *youthful* suggests headstrong enthusiasm that leads to impatience, immature conduct, and eagerness for dispute (I. H. Marshall 1999: 764).

As a young leader in the church, Timothy may be tempted to get into a heated argument with the opponents. Instead, he is to flee that kind of response. Next Paul turns from the negative to the positive and commands Timothy to pursue four virtues: *righteousness, faith, love, and peace*. The first three virtues also appear in 1 Timothy 6:11. The fourth virtue, *peace*, is added to the list. When faced with the opponents' assaults, the Lord's servant responds with uprightness of character (*righteousness*), a genuine *faith* in God, and an expression of *love* to others. In addition, the Lord's servant works to resolve conflicts and make peace even amid difficult times. In so doing, Timothy will identify himself with the people of God and respond with an authentic life similar to Paul's clear conscience in 2 Timothy 1:3.

Second, Timothy is to respond negatively to the opponents: *Have nothing to do with stupid and senseless controversies; you know that they breed quarrels* (2:23). Nothing will be gained by entering into stupid, foolish activity promoted by foolish people (Johnson 2001: 401). Senseless controversies are ill-informed arguments that show lack of instruction. These arguments come from persons who do not know what they are talking about. As in 1 Timothy 1:7, the opponents are without understanding regarding their assertions. Long-winded controversy ends only in quarrels (2:14, 23). Timothy is to have nothing to do with such conversation.

Third, as the Lord's servant, Timothy's life and ministry is characterized by one negative and three positive traits. *And the Lord's servant must not be quarrelsome but kindly to everyone, an apt teacher, patient, correcting opponents with gentleness* (2:24-25a). In contrast to those whose arguments breed quarrels, the Lord's servant is not quarrelsome. Instead, the Lord's servant is kind to everyone. Kindness goes further in turning someone to the Lord than arguments and quarrels. Timothy must be an apt teacher. By teaching the truth of God's word, Timothy will disarm the others. Having the ability to teach with patience goes further in winning others to the Lord than does an approach that depends on unequal power, such as a prophetic or kingly method of response. Teaching God's word with patience suggests a process by which someone is gently led to the truth. Thus the final positive trait is correcting others with gentleness. Instead of debate and argument, Timothy is to educate and guide them. The word *correcting* can mean discipline or corporal punishment. Here it takes on the meaning of instruction and education. As Timothy educates the others with a gentle attitude, some may yet return to the Lord and to the knowledge of truth.

Finally, the Lord's servant relies on God and others' response to the truth of the gospel. *God may perhaps grant that they will repent and come to know the truth, and that they may escape from the snare of the devil, having been held captive by him to do his will* (2:25b-26). Hopefully, gentle teaching will bring positive results. The word *perhaps* suggests hope for repentance, but not certainty of repentance. Above all else, the Lord's servant desires that those opposing the gospel will repent and turn back to God. Yet the Lord's servant realizes that one can only teach with patience and entrust that teaching to the listener and to God. It is not clear whether God grants the repentance or grants the opportunity for repentance. Paul hopes that the opponents will come to their senses and change their minds. Here the word *repent* refers to a changing of one's mind, and this is its only use in the letters to Timothy and Titus. As used in verse 25, it has both a negative and a positive meaning. Negatively, Paul's opponents will change their mind and reject unhealthy teachings. Positively, they will turn their minds in the direction of the full knowledge of the truth of the gospel.

By repenting, Paul's opponents *may escape from the snare of the devil, having been held captive by him to do his will* (2:26). Is the devil snatching them alive and holding them in a snare while they do the devil's will? Or is the devil snatching them and holding them captive? If they respond to the Lord's servant and repent, may they yet do God's will? The latter view is preferred, given the context of the passage. The emphasis throughout verses 22-26 is on the work of the Lord's servant in relating to others in such a way as not only to refute error, but also to exercise patience while teaching the truth. The hope is that those who have been entrapped by the devil will repent and turn away from unhealthy teaching. Such is the goal and desire of the Lord's servant in ministering to people who have become entangled in deviant teaching.

Behavior in the Last Days 3:1-9

With this paragraph, Paul focuses Timothy's attention on the context of Christian ministry. In 3:2-5 a catalog of eighteen vices describes behavior in the last days. In 3:6-9 the behavior condemned includes subverting women and is compared with that of the magicians who opposed Moses in Egypt. Paul concludes, *So these people, of corrupt mind and counterfeit faith, also oppose the truth* (3:8). Two imperatives are given to Timothy: *You must understand this* (3:1) and *Avoid them!* (3:5b). Paul uses the future tense but makes it clear that the danger is already present and creating a threat to the church. With the exception of 3:13 and 4:3, this is the final word in 2 Timothy regarding the unhealthy teachers *[Unhealthy Teaching, p. 366]*.

Building on the apocalyptic idea of the last days, Paul uses the future tense to describe his opponents' sinful behavior. He is not speaking of behavior that appears just before the Lord's second coming. Paul is talking about the period of time between the first and second comings of Christ and especially the present time, as implied in 3:6. *In the last days*, evil will abound. Indeed, Paul understands that those last days have now arrived.

In 3:2-5, Paul lays out an extensive vice list like what we see in Hellenistic moral discourse, which typically contained both vices and virtues. With the exception of Romans 1:29-31, it is the longest vice list in the NT. These lists contain eighteen vices. Six occur here in 2 Timothy 3:3-5, four of which also occur in Romans 1:29-31, and five are found also in Luke-Acts. Only five of these vices appear elsewhere in the letters to Timothy and Titus. In Romans 1:29-31, the list applies to pagan society in general. In 1 Timothy 1:9-10, the list is tied to the Ten Commandments. Here in 2 Timothy 3:2-5, the list speaks of practices prevalent in Ephesus. The list is unusual both for its length and for the internal rhymes and rhythms created by the combinations of sounds when read aloud (GNT). The list begins with *lovers of themselves* (3:2) and ends with *lovers of pleasure rather than lovers of God* (3:4b), indicating a strong antithesis between a selfish egoist and a person whose life is characterized by love for God (Collins: 245) *[Vice Lists, p. 368]*.

Lovers of themselves and *lovers of money* (3:2a) point to the sin of selfishness. Paul taught that love of money is the root of all kinds of evil (1 Tim 6:10). *Boasters* and *arrogant* (3:2b) indicate that both in word and in thought, the teachers are haughty and assume that their status is superior to others' (1 Tim 1:7; 6:4). *Abusive* and *disobedient to parents* (3:2c) refers to malicious talk and destructive behavior that shows lack of respect and tears down other persons. Defying the OT command to honor parents (Exod 20:12; Deut 21:18-21), the deviant teachers set themselves in opposition to others.

A series of negative terms comes next (2 Tim 3:2d, 3a). *Ungrateful, unholy, unloving* (TNIV: *without love*), *unforgiving* (TNIV). These teachers lack gratefulness to parents and to God (1 Tim 4:4). They are unholy and therefore wicked and profane. They lack the ability to love and to experience natural affection. This has led to antisocial behavior toward other persons (I. H. Marshall 1999: 774). They have an attitude of enmity toward others. The list continues with two more negative terms (3:3b): *slanderous* and *without self-control* (TNIV; NRSV: *profligates*). *Slanderous* indicates a destructive use of the tongue to spread false rumors and lies about others (Towner 1994: 192). Slander is condemned in 1 Timothy 3:11 and Titus 2:3. *Without self-control* means these teachers are undisciplined persons, in contrast to the self-discipline required of leaders and others in the church (1 Tim 3:2; Titus 1:8; 2:2, 5-6). Then come two more negative terms: *brutal, not lovers of the good* (TNIV). A brutal person lacks gentleness and is even savage (Johnson 2001: 405), quite in contrast to the desired character of church leaders (1 Tim 3:3; Titus 1:7). One who does not love the good actually loves evil, in contrast to the kind of life expected of elders in Titus 1:8.

Four more terms end the list of vices (3:4 TNIV): *treacherous, rash, conceited,* and *lovers of pleasure more than lovers of God.* All four indicate misguided and faulty behavior. The treacherous person is a traitor, one who betrays others; the term is associated with murder. A rash person is reckless and thoughtless. The term is used for people who talk without thinking, who are impulsive and may act violently (I. H. Marshall 1999: 774). Conceited persons have a mistaken view of themselves. They are puffed up and deluded. They make self-gratification through pleasure a driving force in their lives. They become slaves to their own desires and serve self rather than God.

Finally, the list is summarized with the words *holding to the outward form of godliness but denying its power* (3:5). What a tragedy! Like the Cretans, they profess to know God but deny him by their actions (Titus 1:16). These teachers have an outward form or appearance of godliness, but inside are spiritually hollow. They have the right words and expressions of Christianity . . . on the surface. They have a Christian face but no Christian heart. Paul may be referring to an appearance of godliness through ascetic practices (1 Tim 4:3) or their distorted view of Christian faith (2 Tim 2:18). Knowing things about God, without experiencing the reality of God's power in one's life, is useless and deceptive (Titus 1:16).

With this verse the writer touches a foundational concern in the letters to Timothy and Titus: knowledge and behavior belong together in the Christian life. Saying and doing, belief and discipleship, cannot be separated. These teachers stand condemned in their own vices because their form of godliness displays a kind of irreligion or ungodliness that characterizes the pagan world (Fee 1988: 271). Paul concludes with an imperative directed to Timothy in 3:5b: *Avoid them!* As TNIV translates, *Have nothing to do with such people.*

Having summarized the teachers' sad condition in 3:2-5, Paul equates them with the magicians who opposed Moses in Egypt (3:6-9). Among the teachers *are those who make their way into households and captivate silly women, overwhelmed by their sins and swayed by all kinds of desires, who are always being instructed and can never arrive at a knowledge of the truth* (3:6-7). Unlearned women (and men!) are susceptible to unhealthy teaching and thus are easy targets. These women are called *silly*, a pejorative term meaning weak-willed or easy prey (TNIV: *gullible women*). The women are overwhelmed by sins as they follow these teachings. The concluding phrase indicates that they are seeking instruction here and there but are never able to arrive at the truth of the gospel.

As Jannes and Jambres opposed Moses, *so these people, of corrupt mind and counterfeit faith, also oppose the truth* (3:8). These two persons are not named in the OT but are mentioned in non-Jewish and Jewish sources from the Second Temple period. According to rabbinic tradition, Jannes and Jambres were Egyptian magicians who vied with Moses and Aaron in the contest of the plagues before the exodus (Collins: 251-52). Just as Jannes and Jambres opposed the truth of God's messenger, Moses, in a decisive moment of Israel's redemption from Egypt (Exod 7:11–8:19), so the teachers in Ephesus are opposing the truth of the gospel. Both groups oppose the message of God, and both experience failure due to folly and deception. Their opposition to the gospel is an indication of corrupt minds and counterfeit faith. Quinn and Wacker call them "numbskulled counterfeiters of the faith" (711). Like the godless world of Romans 1:18, 28 and the pagan Cretans (Titus 1:15), their minds are depraved and their consciences are corrupt. In contrast to Timothy, who is approved by God (2 Tim 2:15), Paul declares that the deviant teachers are rejected by God.

How effective will these teachers be? Paul tells Timothy not to be overly threatened by them. *They will not make much progress* (3:9) because their folly will become plain to everyone, as it was with Jannes and Jambres. Deception always loses in the long term. The opponents' present success actually is regression in the long run because people will perceive their folly. The triumph of Moses over the magicians through God's presence and power assures both Paul and Timothy that the promoters of unhealthy teaching in Ephesus, though serious, will not win in the long run. The truth of the gospel will prevail. The portrait of these opponents is relentlessly negative. They reveal in their character and actions all the negative traits that Timothy is to avoid (Johnson 2001: 410).

THE TEXT IN BIBLICAL CONTEXT

Rightly Explaining the Word of Truth

In 2 Timothy 2:15, Paul exhorts Timothy to explain rightly the word of truth. The metaphorical term (*orthotomeō*) is translated as *correctly handle* (TNIV), *rightly explaining* (NRSV), *keep strictly to* (REB), and *rightly dividing* (KJV). In short, Paul instructs Timothy to interpret the word of truth aright.

Biblical interpretation occurs within the Bible itself. In the OT, Israel understood God's revelation differently from that of the pagan gods. Israel's God, Yahweh, revealed himself as a living God, who works in and through Israel's history (Deut 26:5-9; Josh 24:1-28; Ps 136; Neh 8:6-18; Acts 7:2-53). The prophets interpreted the meaning of the law and applied it to the life of the people, calling them back to the covenant agreement at Mount Sinai and the need to repent of social and economic sins of injustice. Later, the Jewish rabbis studied the law and sought to explain its meaning.

In the NT, Jesus interpreted the law in the Sermon on the Mount (Matt 5–7). He contrasted his teaching with others' interpretation of the law by using the formula, "You have heard that it was said, . . . but I say to you . . ." Jesus also interpreted the OT by showing that it pointed to him (John 5:39). The NT writers interpreted the OT in light of God's revelation in the person and work of Christ. In so doing, they emphasized some spiritualizations of OT themes already present within the OT (e.g., Matt 1:23; Rom 2:29; Gal 5:6; cf. Deut 10:16; Jer 4:4; 9:26; Ezek 44:9). At the Jerusalem conference, the early Christians interpreted the word of truth by turning aside from what was written in the OT and did not require circumcision of new Gentile Christians (Acts 15:1-29). In Paul's theology, the OT is to be interpreted in light of the truth in Jesus Christ. Paul based his ethical views on the person, life, teachings, death, and resurrection of Christ.

For Timothy and Titus, rightly explaining the word of truth means to follow the apostolic understanding of the gospel of Jesus Christ, in contrast to the distortion of the gospel by unhealthy teachers.

The Lord's Servant

In 2 Timothy 2:24, Paul speaks of the Christian minister and Timothy as the Lord's servant. Throughout the Bible, leaders of God's people are identified as servants. Moses was called "the servant of the LORD" (Deut 34:5). After Moses' death, his successor, Joshua, is repeatedly reminded to follow the way of Moses, the servant of the Lord. As God's servant, Moses called the people beyond himself to the revealed will of God.

Several Servant Songs are found in Isaiah (42:1-4; 49:1-6; 50:4-9; 52:13–53:12). First, Israel is a servant, then faithful Israel is a servant, and finally the coming Messiah is the servant of the Lord, who gives his life for the people (52:13–53:12). Israel's role in the world was not so much to rule over the other nations as to serve them. Jesus came in the likeness of Isaiah's servant of the Lord. Using language from Isaiah

53:10-11, Jesus said, "For the Son of Man came not to be served but to serve, and to give his life a ransom for many" (Mark 10:45). Jesus warned the disciples against lording it over others (Luke 22:24-26).

An early Christian hymn describes Jesus as the servant of the Lord par excellence (Phil 2:5-11). Jesus took the form of a slave and became obedient to the point of death—even death on a cross (2:7-8). Paul used the term *servant* to describe himself and often introduced himself to the churches as a servant of God and/or Jesus Christ (Rom 1:1; Gal 1:10; Phil 1:1; Titus 1:1). At times Paul addressed his co-workers as servants (Col 4:12; cf. 2 Cor 4:5; Phil 1:1).

Timothy is to confront the opponents in Ephesus while also exercising patience with them. Whereas in 1 Timothy and Titus opponents are to be addressed directly, in 2 Timothy the Lord's servant is to be an agent of kindness, to have the ability to teach, and to exercise patience (2:24). By exercising this kind of attitude, Timothy will be able to correct the opponents with gentleness, in the hope that some may repent and come to the truth.

Set Apart for God's Service

At different points in Scripture, persons are set apart for service in the Lord's house. In the OT, even the furniture of the tabernacle was set apart and consecrated to the Lord (Exod 30:22-29; Lev 16:16-17). Aaron and his sons were set apart and consecrated for service to the Lord (Exod 28:3; 29:29-30), as were the Levites (Deut 18:1-2).

Christians in Corinth are told to depart from wickedness and consecrate themselves to the Lord (2 Cor 6:17-18). To be the temple of the Lord, the assembly of believers at Corinth needed to be separated from sin and cleansed of sin (1 Cor 3:16-17; 5:7). Barnabas and Saul were set apart for missionary service by the church at Antioch (Acts 13:1-3). Paul goes so far as to say that he was set apart for God's service before he was born (Gal 1:15).

Timothy is to turn away from all evil and pursue righteousness (1 Tim 6:11-12; 2 Tim 2:22). In doing so, Timothy will be able to explain rightly the word of truth (2 Tim 2:15) and be ready to do every good work (3:17). Peter says, "Instead, as he who called you is holy, be holy yourselves in all your conduct; for it is written, 'You shall be holy, for I am holy'" (1 Pet 1:15-16). John writes, "If we walk in the light as he is in the light, we have fellowship with one another, and the blood of Jesus his Son cleanses us from all sin" (1 John 1:7).

As these verses indicate, all of God's people are to turn away from sin, be cleansed, and be set apart as God's holy people, thereby becoming the temple of the Lord. In addition, some Christians are called by God, set apart, and consecrated by the church for the Lord's service in ministry.

THE TEXT IN THE LIFE OF THE CHURCH

Biblical Interpretation

The phrase "rightly explaining the word of truth" (2 Tim 2:15) is used widely in the Christian church. Luther and other sixteenth-century Reformers freed biblical interpretation from the allegorical interpretation popular in the early church and Middle Ages. Biblical interpretation then focused on the plain sense of Scripture: its literary and historical meaning. In the nineteenth century, F. C. Baur and others influenced by the Enlightenment engaged in higher criticism and questioned the traditional answers with regard to many issues, including the authorship of the NT books.

In the early twentieth century, many Bible scholars engaged in form criticism, asking what was taking place behind the writing of Scripture. Studies in form criticism eventually were replaced with redaction criticism, which examined how the Bible writers worked with the material found in their sources to create particular theological emphases in their writing. In the last part of the twentieth century, some scholars moved away from what may have been taking place behind the writing of Scripture to how the Bible functions as Scripture in its present form. This movement, called canonical criticism, emphasized how the canon was formed. In the twenty-first century, Bible scholars are focusing on narrative, reexamining story and how the various books of the Bible can be interpreted in a narrative way.

Biblical scholars in believers churches have also interacted with the various methods of interpretation. Believers churches look carefully at the literary and historical nature of the biblical text as they interpret Scripture, looking at the three worlds of the text (Swartley 1983: 224-28). First is the world *behind* the text, the historical and cultural context in which the text originated. Second is the world *of* the text, a careful reading of the text itself, noting its literary and theological nuances. And third is the world *in front of* the text—the readers' world, where we see how the texts speak to readers today in different contexts and call them to new life, thought, and action.

Believers churches in the Anabaptist tradition attend to several theological principles in their biblical interpretation. First, believers churches interpret the biblical text from the fullness of divine revelation in Jesus Christ. The person, life, teachings, death, and resurrection of Christ become the focal point of God's revelation. This Christocentric method is foundational in interpreting Scripture. It takes the whole

Christ into consideration and is distinguished from a narrower christological focus on the cross of Christ as a method of interpretation (Murray: 70-96).

Second, believers churches interpret the OT from a NT point of view. Since Jesus is God in human flesh, one discovers a completed revelation in Jesus Christ and the NT. This is not a denial of the OT. Rather, it means interpreting the OT from a NT perspective.

Third, believers churches interpret Scripture within the context of the believing community, the church. In the gathered Christian community, the Holy Spirit is at work, testing the various interpretations (Matt 18:18; 1 Cor 12:10; 14:29; 1 Thess 5:20-22; 1 John 4:1). In short, "God's will is revealed in Scripture, interpreted by all believers through the power of the Holy Spirit, discerned in community, and tested by the measure of Christ" (Snyder 1999: 14).

Fourth, believers churches interpret Scripture by holding Word and Spirit together. The Holy Spirit illuminates the written word (the Bible) in the interpreting process. By holding Word and Spirit together, the interpreter finds protection from the extremes of spirit without the written word and also from the literalism of word without the Holy Spirit. The same Holy Spirit who guided the process of writing the Scriptures guides the interpreting process so that one interprets according to the norm of truth revealed in Jesus Christ.

Finally, believers churches interpret Scripture with a predisposition to obedience. Christians interpret Scripture in order to live more fully the way of Christ laid out in the NT. The Bible is to be read, studied, and obeyed. We read the Scripture not only for information, but also for transformation. We read the Bible, but the Bible also reads us and calls us to repentance, faith in Christ, and a life of obedience to Christ.

The Church Leader's Response to Opponents

The greatest test of a pastor's character comes in one's response to criticism in the congregation. The pastor's work includes pointing out sin—especially unhealthy teaching—when it arises. Here Paul lays that responsibility on Timothy's shoulders. Paul also tells Timothy to be kind, patient, and not quarrelsome. The letters to Timothy and Titus emphasize the Christian virtues and character traits for church leaders. A person with a quick temper is ruled out, and gentleness rates high on the list of desired qualities (1 Tim 3:3; 2 Tim 2:25; Titus 1:7). Insecure pastors easily lash out at their critics.

Gentleness and self-control are gifts of the Holy Spirit that pastoral leaders are to exercise in the midst of criticism. Pastoral search committees do well to observe a pastoral candidate's gifts in preaching, teaching, administration, and evangelism. In addition, search committees look at the candidate's personality and consider the person's relational skills, their sense of personal worth, and their ability to handle criticism and work through conflict. Spiritual and pastoral formation seminars in pastoral education institutions aid growth in these expressions of the Holy Spirit's presence in the pastoral candidate's life. A pastor's failure in a congregation is seldom due to questions of theological orthodoxy. More often, a pastor's failure is due to lack of self-perception and inability to understand who the pastor is as a person amid the dynamics of congregational life. Pastors who find themselves in difficult situations in congregations can find help in clinical pastoral education experiences and spiritual formation classes, which build awareness of the pastor as person and how their personality characteristics bear upon the pastoral ministry.

Consecrated to the Lord

Revival movements in the nineteenth and twentieth centuries often included a consecration service where Christians were invited to give themselves fully for the Lord's service. In these consecration services, the life vocations of young men and women were changed as many went off to college and seminary to prepare for missionary or pastoral service.

One person who experienced this kind of consecration is Ralph Lebold. As a young man, Lebold attended a tent revival meeting. In a consecration service, he publicly dedicated his life to the Lord for whatever God had for him for the future. In his memoirs Lebold wrote:

> In 1953 the Steinman congregation and area Mennonite churches sponsored a series of meetings for about two weeks, where many people made commitments under the preaching of Ohio evangelist Howard Hammer. These meetings had a profound and positive impact on area churches; many people made serious commitments and some older people rededicated their lives to Christ. . . . On two occasions Hammer gave a second invitation for people to make a commitment to "full-time Christian service." I, along with roughly thirty others, walked "the sawdust trail" (actually, wood shavings in the aisles) to make this public declaration. I sensed an inner voice calling me to respond. This would prove to be a truly life-altering experience for me.

In a footnote Lebold indicates that about one-quarter of these responding to the invitation went into missionary service. Most of the others ended up serving as pastors in congregations (Lebold: 16, 21).

Lebold's own journey took him to college and seminary. Following seminary he pastored a congregation. After more graduate study, Lebold began to train pastors in supervised pastoral education. He served as moderator of the Mennonite Church and as president of Conrad Grebel College in Waterloo, Ontario. In his later years, Lebold developed training programs for pastors across the denomination. In retirement, Lebold looked back over his life of service and said:

> My path to Christian ministry began because I experienced a very clear call to service in the church. The public commitment I made on that Sunday afternoon evangelistic service so many years ago became a benchmark for my spiritual and vocational journey. That decision set me in the direction of becoming a minister of the gospel and serving in the Mennonite church for four decades. (Lebold: 145)

2 Timothy 3:10-17

Ingredients of Timothy's Ministry

PREVIEW

In 2 Timothy 3:10-17, only one imperative is used (3:14), commanding Timothy to continue in what he has been taught. In this paragraph, Paul addresses Timothy directly and unites the concerns of the first two sections of the letter. Timothy is to be loyal to Paul and to the gospel, even amid suffering (3:10-11), as in the first section of the letter (1:6–2:13). In recalling Paul's example (3:10-11), Timothy is to reject deviant teachings and to teach the truth of the gospel (3:10-13) in an attempt to win back the unhealthy teachers, as in the previous section of the letter (2:14–3:9). Therefore, Timothy needs to give heed to the Scriptures, which point to Christ and are useful for the ministry tasks he is called to carry out (3:14-17).

OUTLINE

Paul's Example of Suffering, 3:10-12
The Opposite Way of the Unhealthy Teachers, 3:13
The Scriptural Foundation of Timothy's Ministry, 3:14-17

EXPLANATORY NOTES

Paul's Example of Suffering 3:10-12

Paul turns Timothy's attention to himself with the observation *Now you have observed my teaching, my conduct, my aim in life, my faith, my patience, my love, my steadfastness* (3:10). He addresses Timothy directly with the words *now you*. The verb translated *observed my teaching* means to follow with the mind as the person one is following presents an argument for a certain point of view (Johnson 2001: 416).

The letters to Timothy and Titus make a distinction between *teaching* in the singular, as used here, and *teachings* in the plural, which refers to the unhealthy teachings of the opposition. Timothy is exhorted not only to follow the path of the apostle Paul, but also to lay hold of the reasons Paul walked that path. He is to reflect on Paul's *teaching* as apostolic doctrine, on Paul's *conduct* (TNIV: *my way of life*), and on Paul's purpose or resolve (*my aim in life*). Moreover, these traits of Paul's life are supported by four virtues: faith, patience, love, and steadfastness. *Faith* refers not only to Paul's faith or trust in Christ, but also to his faithfulness to Christ. *Patience* suggests forbearance: the ability to control one's anger in the midst of opposition. *Love* is the chief Christian virtue (1 Cor 13:13), produced by the presence of the Holy Spirit in one's life (Rom 5:5; Gal 5:22). *Steadfastness* goes beyond patience. It includes the inner ability to cope with difficulties, as the athlete who puts up with pain and opposition (Collins: 256). It is the ability to face suffering with courage.

To increase Timothy's awareness of these virtues, Paul calls attention to the persecutions and sufferings he endured in three cities: *Antioch, Iconium, and Lystra*. These sufferings underscore the steadfastness of the apostle and the power of the gospel. Paul could also have talked about the persecution he faced in Philippi and in his present imprisonment. Instead, he calls attention to the persecutions and sufferings during the first missionary journey, before Timothy joined the missionary team. Timothy may have been told about these persecutions during the second missionary journey. The three cities mentioned in 3:11 were located in the Roman province where Timothy grew up. Luke reports the persecutions Paul endured in Antioch of Pisidia (Acts 13:50), in Iconium (14:1), and at Lystra (14:19). At Lystra, Timothy's hometown, Paul was stoned and dragged outside the city since his persecutors thought they had killed him. Surely Timothy has heard about this event.

Despite these persecutions, Paul declares, *Yet the Lord rescued me from all of them* (3:11b). Here Paul quotes Psalm 34:19: God rescues from all afflictions. Paul does not mean that he has been set free from persecution, since he is writing while in prison. He means that the Lord has rescued by giving him power to endure and carry on in spite of the pressures of persecutions and sufferings (Towner 1994: 199). As God has rescued Paul in each situation, so God will rescue Timothy amid opposition in Ephesus. Later in 2 Timothy, Paul says that he was rescued from the lion's mouth (4:17) and is fully confident that the Lord will rescue him from every evil attack and save him for his heavenly kingdom (4:18).

Indeed, all who want to live a godly life in Christ Jesus will be persecuted (3:12). With assurance that God keeps the believer even amid persecution, Paul wants Timothy and hearers of this epistle to be aware of opposition to the gospel. Jesus made it clear that his followers would suffer persecution and that they would be blessed for it (Matt 5:10-12). Paul talks about his own sufferings elsewhere in his letters (2 Cor 11:23-29; Phil 1:12-14). The evidence of persecution in the book of Acts and in Paul's epistles is now stated as the Christian's lot in this world (2 Tim 3:12).

The Opposite Way of the Unhealthy Teachers 3:13

Once more Paul discredits the deviant teachers. *But wicked people and impostors will go from bad to worse, deceiving others and being deceived* (3:13). These persons are not only evil; they are also *impostors,* (lit.) magicians. Like Jannes and Jambres, these evil people dabble in the magical arts (cf. Acts 19:13-19). They are swindlers, magicians, or jugglers who dupe people (Collins: 260). Their magical teaching and practices will get worse. Eventually, other people will discover their falsehood (3:9). These teachers actually deceive themselves. Elsewhere in this letter the apostle declares that these teachers have corrupt minds (3:8) and that their disputes are stupid and senseless (2:23). As with the Cretan opponents, their minds and consciences are corrupt (Titus 1:15b) *[Unhealthy Teaching, p. 366]*. As Paul has remained steadfast in faith despite sufferings and persecutions, so Timothy is to remain steadfast in the presence of these teachers in Ephesus, who deceive others and themselves.

The Scriptural Foundation of Timothy's Ministry 3:14-17

But as for you, continue in what you have learned and firmly believed (2 Tim 3:14). The words *but you* appear a second time in direct address to Timothy. The command *continue* picks up the underlying theme of 3:11-17: Timothy is to continue steadfast in the Christian faith. Two reasons are given for this exhortation. First, Timothy is to recall the past teaching he learned from his mother and grandmother and from Paul. Second, Timothy is to give heed to the Holy Scriptures, which lead one to Christ and supply what is needed for the task of ministry.

Timothy was taught the Holy Scriptures from infancy (3:15). The term *childhood* or *infancy* (TNIV) is used six times in Luke-Acts. Since his mother and grandmother were Jews, Timothy's training followed the Jewish practice. A rabbinic teaching said that "at five years old [one is fit] for the Scripture, at ten years for the Mishnah, at thirteen for [the fulfilling of] the commandments, at fifteen for the Talmud" (Mishnah *'Abot* 5.21; Danby: 458). Timothy was taught at an early age by his mother and grandmother, later by Paul, and perhaps by others. The plural *from whom* is the preferred reading of the text, based on a better and wider range of witnesses and being the harder reading (Collins: 254).

Sacred writings or *Holy Scriptures* (TNIV) is terminology used widely among Greek-speaking Jews to designate the Jewish Scriptures. These OT Scriptures are capable of instructing Timothy. They make Timothy wise with regard to the *salvation* that is *in Christ Jesus*. The OT Scriptures are dynamic. They point beyond themselves to the Messiah. Jesus said, "You search the scriptures because you think that in them you have eternal life; and it is they that testify on my behalf" (John 5:39). These OT Scriptures provide learning and spiritual formation. They point one to salvation in Jesus Christ.

In contrast to the powerlessness of the unhealthy teachers, the OT Scriptures have instructional power. As Psalm 19:7-8 says, "The law of the LORD is perfect, reviving the soul; the decrees of the LORD are sure, making wise the simple; the precepts of the LORD are right, rejoicing the heart; the commandment of the LORD is clear; enlightening the eyes." The OT as Holy Scripture is able to instruct *for salvation through faith in Christ Jesus* (3:15b). Here, as in Romans 1:16-17 and 10:1-4, salvation and faith are linked. Clearly, salvation is in Christ Jesus.

Does Paul mean that salvation comes through an individual person's faith, or does it come through the faithfulness of Christ? Salvation is provided through the faithfulness of Christ and is appropriated by an individual person's faith commitment to Christ. Properly understood, the OT points to Jesus Christ and instructs in the way of salvation through him. Without knowledge of Christ and faith in him, the OT is not properly understood. In contrast to the teaching that Timothy learned from childhood, which leads to Christ, the unhealthy teacher's message leads nowhere other than to deception.

All scripture is inspired by God and is useful for teaching, for reproof, for correction, and for training in righteousness, so that everyone who belongs to God may be proficient, equipped for every good work (2 Tim 3:16-17). Having stated the importance of the Holy Scripture in leading one to salvation by faith in Jesus Christ, Paul assures Timothy that the message of the gospel based on Holy Scripture has adequate authority and usefulness in Christian ministry to meet the needs of the Ephesian people. The term *Holy Scriptures* (TNIV) in 3:15 means the whole OT.

Several issues confront us in this text. Does the word *all* (*pasa*) mean "every" or "all"? Is the writer saying that each and every part of Scripture is inspired of God, or is the writer saying that the Scripture as a whole, in its entirety, is inspired of God? The Greek can be translated either way. If it means *every* Scripture that is inspired, one might conclude that *some* Scriptures are not inspired of God. The rabbinic tradition held that every part of Scripture is important, no matter how small (Collins: 263). The Greek can be translated "every God-inspired Scripture is useful," or it can be translated "every [or all] Scripture is God-inspired and is useful." The verb *is* does not occur in Greek and needs to be supplied in the English translation. The words *inspired by God* can be either attributive or predicative. If attributive, the text says, *All* [or: *every*] *Scripture inspired of God is also useful*, suggesting that only the inspired ones are useful. If predicative, a larger affirmation is in view: *All* [or: *every*] *Scripture is inspired and therefore useful*. Given the context in which the deviant teachers interpreted some parts of Scripture as myths (1 Tim 1:4) and the similar grammatical construction in 1 Timothy 4:4, Paul likely intends to emphasize that Scripture in its entirely is inspired of God.

The term *inspired of God* (*theopneustos*) calls attention to the origin of Scripture. It is breathed out by God (cf. TNIV: *God-breathed*). Just as the life-giving power of God's breath brought humanity into being at creation (Gen 2:7), so Scripture comes from the breath of God. Its authority lies not so much in a theory of inspiration as in its origin. Scripture comes from God through human writers. Peter adds, "Prophets, though human, spoke from God as they were carried along by the Holy Spirit" (2 Pet 1:21 TNIV). God made himself and his will known to humankind. Human writers recorded the activity of God as guided by the Holy Spirit. Thus the Holy Scriptures come to us from God through human instrumentality. As the record of God's revelation, the Bible has both a divine and a human side. More important than inspiration is the usefulness of Scripture. Collins writes, "The many citations of 2 Timothy 3:16 in the patristic period—more than one hundred in all!—emphasize the usefulness of Scripture far more than they do their inspiration" (264). The term *useful* means something that transforms life and practice (1 Tim 4:8; Titus 3:8) and is contrasted with the deviant teachers, whose words are only myths and merely tickle the ears (2 Tim 4:3-4). The usefulness of Scripture and its dynamic is tied to the Spirit's breath that produced it.

The usefulness of Scripture is expressed in four words which can be arranged in a chiastic order with the first and fourth words emphasizing the pedagogical function of Scripture and the second and third terms emphasizing Scripture's ability to point out sin and change one's life.

A teaching
  B reproof
  B′ correction
A′ education

The first word, *teaching*, is obvious. Many times Timothy is told to engage in sound or healthy teaching (1 Tim 4:6, 13, 16; 6:3). Teaching based on the Scriptures leads people to salvation and faith in Christ (2 Tim 3:15). Scripture is useful for *reproof* in that it brings conviction of sin and makes a sinner aware of the wrong one has done (Num 5:18-22). Scripture is useful for *correction* as it speaks to improper behavior and calls for change and improvement, or setting things right. Finally, Scripture is useful for instruction or education. It disciplines or trains a person in the direction of righteousness. The emphasis here is on *righteousness*—right relationship with God and with others (Collins: 265).

Paul concludes with a result clause: *so that everyone who belongs to God may be proficient, equipped for every good work* (3:17). By immersing himself in Scripture, Timothy will be thoroughly equipped for every good work. He will be able to meet the demands of the Christian ministry in Ephesus. Scripture is a useful instrument to build up Timothy's spiritual life, to keep his thoughts and teaching centered on the truth in Christ, and to meet the demands of the ministry, which involve responding to the unhealthy teachers in Ephesus.

Thus the call for Timothy to rekindle the gift of ministry in 2 Timothy 1:6 is brought to a conclusion. As Fee says, "Paul urges loyalty—to his [Timothy's] own calling, to himself [Paul], to Christ and the gospel, and to his ministry, including the teaching of Scripture—and to continue in loyalty despite suffering and in the face of opposition" (Fee 1988: 280). Paul is now ready to give Timothy a final charge in 4:1-5.

THE TEXT IN BIBLICAL CONTEXT

In 2 Timothy 2:9b Paul asserts, *But the word of God is not chained.* And in 2 Timothy 3:15 Paul reminds Timothy, *From childhood you have known the sacred writings that are able to instruct you for salvation through faith in Christ Jesus.* Paul speaks not only about the origin of Scripture and its inspiration, but also goes on to point out its pedagogical usefulness to expose sin and point one to Christ.

Throughout the Bible, the word of God is given special attention. In the OT the *word of God* came to God's spokespersons. This word of God came to Abram in a vision (Gen 15:1). The Pentateuch speaks of God's commands and statutes given at Mount Sinai when the covenant was established between God and God's people. The Torah was a revelation of the will of God. Torah called for obedience because it was the word of the Lord. The importance of obeying God's word is emphasized in the book of Deuteronomy. These words of God are "for our lasting good, so as to keep us alive" (6:24). Near the end of his life, Moses said to the people,

> Take to heart all the words that I am giving in witness against you today; give them as a command to your children, so that they may diligently observe all the words of this law. *This is no trifling matter for you, but rather your very life;* through it you may live long in the land that you are crossing over the Jordan to possess. (Deut 32:46-47, stress added)

Later, when the kingdom of Judah declined spiritually, the book of the law was discovered while repairing the temple. Josiah commanded that this book of the law be read in the hearing of the elders of Judah. It brought spiritual renewal among the people and commitment to the covenant by both King Josiah and the people (2 Kings 23:1-3).

The Psalms speak of the importance of the word of God (19:7-10; 119:97-104). Many times "the word of the Lord came to" the OT prophets. Sometimes the prophets said that the word of the Lord came by way of a vision or in an audible way. The prophet Isaiah said, "Hear the word of the LORD" (Isa 1:10). And then the prophet cries out, "The grass withers, the flower fades; but the word of our God will stand forever" (Isa 40:8). After returning from exile, the children of Israel heard Ezra, their leader, read audibly from "the law of Moses." This return to the law in the days of Ezra and Nehemiah began the scribal tradition (Neh 8), with its emphasis on copying the Law and the emergence of rabbis who studied and taught the law.

In the Sermon on the Mount Jesus said, "Do not think that I have come to abolish the law or the prophets; I have come not to abolish but to fulfill. For truly I tell you, until heaven and earth pass away, not one letter, nor one stroke of a letter, will pass from the law until all is accomplished" (Matt 5:17-18).

Because Jesus is God in human form, he is the Word of God become flesh, and he reveals God's grace and truth (John 1:14, 17). Jesus said, "Whoever has seen me has seen the Father" (14:9). Paul says, "For in him all the fullness of God was pleased to dwell" (Col 1:19), and "in him [Jesus] the whole fullness of deity dwells bodily" (Col 2:9). Paul also said that the "truth is in Jesus" (Eph 4:21). The author of Hebrews sums up this truth: "In the past God spoke to our ancestors through the prophets at many times and in various ways, but in these last days he has spoken to us by his Son. . . . The Son is the radiance of God's glory and the exact representation of his being, sustaining all things by his powerful word" (Heb 1:1-3a TNIV).

Jesus is the full and complete revelation of the will of God. As such, Jesus is the key to understanding the revelation of God that preceded him in the OT. Jesus affirmed the OT (Matt 5:17-18; John 10:35) but went beyond Moses in declaring God's will by who he was, what he said, and how he lived. In the Sermon on the Mount, Jesus said, "You have heard that it was said. . . , but I say to you. . . ." (e.g., Matt 5:21-26). As two disciples walked on the road to Emmaus, Luke reports, "Beginning with Moses and all the prophets, he [Jesus] interpreted to them the things concerning himself in all the scriptures" (Luke 24:27).

The OT and NT Scriptures are understood as God's Word written. The Holy Scriptures are not merely human in origin and development. They also originated with God and were breathed out, as Paul says in 2 Timothy 3:16. The combination of the human and the divine (2 Pet 1:20-21) gives the Scripture authority for faith and life. The authority of Scripture lies in its ability to lead one to Christ. When read honestly for its intended purposes as a book of salvation, it will not lead us astray.

THE TEXT IN THE LIFE OF THE CHURCH

Although the Christian church has always accepted the authority of Scripture, it has not always agreed on the boundaries of what is Scripture (the biblical canon), on how to understand that authority, or on how best to express its belief in the inspiration of Scripture. And it has differed greatly on how to *interpret* Scripture.

The early church fathers accepted the writings of Paul and the Gospels as authoritative Scripture. In time these books were included in the NT canon by virtue of the church's consensus regarding the authority and faithful content of these writings over against other writings that did not measure up and thus were not recognized as inspired Scripture. The Bible was read in the monasteries and cathedrals during the medieval period, though the masses of people largely did not have access to it personally.

The Renaissance and the sixteenth-century Protestant Reformation brought about a return to the Scriptures. With the invention of printing and translations of the Bible into vernacular languages, such as Martin Luther's German version, the Word of God became available to the people. Ulrich Zwingli preached directly from the book of Matthew by exegeting the Greek text, thereby bringing reform to Switzerland. Some Swiss Brethren were taught by Zwingli and drawn into a study of God's Word. When Zwingli was slow to introduce reform in Zurich, allowing the town council to make the difficult decisions, the Swiss Brethren felt obligated to follow the authority of Scripture. Thus the Anabaptist movement was born. In the court records of Anabaptists who were tried and persecuted for their faith, one discovers the following:

- a profound knowledge of the Bible.
- a desire to obey the Scriptures by following Christ in a path of discipleship.

- an interpretation of the Bible through the full revelation of God in Jesus Christ.
- a desire to enter into consultations and dialogue with other Christians regarding the meaning of God's Word.

The Anabaptists saw God's will for humankind in the Bible as the Word of God written and in Jesus Christ as the living Word of God. They sought to live according to the NT commands of Christ. They were Christ centered, guided by the Holy Spirit, and ecumenical (Murray: 70-96, 125-56, 220-63). For the Anabaptists, the Bible was the Word of God and their guide for life. They sought to live by it and used the Bible as an instrument to teach and guide them in the truth rather than a book to be defended.

In response to the authority of the church in Catholicism, seventeenth-century Protestant orthodoxy tried to establish the authority of Scripture. In the thirteenth century, Thomas Aquinas (d. 1274), a scholastic theologian, had sought to unite the philosophy of Aristotle with Christian theology and placed reason before faith. In the seventeenth century, the Reformed theologian Francis Turretin (d. 1687) borrowed this Aristotelian-Thomistic method and established the authority of Scripture as the sole principle of theology. By reasoning out the existence and truth of God, Turretin logically moved to the idea of a perfect revelation of God and thus coined the phrase "the inerrancy of Scripture." B. B. Warfield's book *Revelation and Inspiration* (Oxford University Press, 1927) and its reprint, *The Inspiration and Authority of the Bible* (Presbyterian & Reformed, 1948) became the classic text by which many conservative Christians defended the inerrancy of Scripture over against more liberal views of the Bible that emerged out of the Enlightenment period in Europe.

In their response to the modernist movement with its liberal view of Scripture, believers churches in North America were attracted to a conservative emphasis on the inspiration and authority of Scripture. Nevertheless, some believers churches were uncomfortable with the term *inerrancy.* It was a negative term (what Scripture is not), and those familiar with the Bible noticed that although the Bible affirms its own witness to God's trustworthiness, it never itself claims to be without error. Affirming instead the method of inductive Bible study, believers churches generally moved away from using the term *inerrancy* by the mid-twentieth century. Most churches affirm both the human and divine side of Scripture. The Mennonite Church in the United States and Canada says in its current confession of faith:

> We believe that all Scripture is inspired by God through the Holy Spirit for instruction in salvation and training in righteousness. We accept the Scriptures as the Word of God and as the fully reliable and trustworthy

> standard for Christian faith and life. We seek to understand and interpret Scripture in harmony with Jesus Christ as we are led by the Holy Spirit in the church. (Mennonite: 21)

Building on insights from the Anabaptists, believers churches

- accept the Bible as the Word of God.
- interpret the Bible through the full revelation of God in Jesus Christ.
- interpret under the guidance of the Holy Spirit within the context of the believing community, the church.
- read the Bible with a desire to obey its truth in life.
- see the Bible as what guides us to salvation in Christ and what equips us for teaching and right living.
- are willing to enter into ecumenical dialogue on the meaning of Scripture for Christian living.

2 Timothy 4:1-5

Final Charge to Timothy

PREVIEW

Second Timothy 4:1-5 is a direct exhortation to Timothy. It contains several commands. The exhortation is divided into three parts. The first part is a solemn charge to be faithful in Christian ministry. It contains five imperative commands for Timothy to carry out in verse 2. The second part recapitulates the growing apostasy and its effect upon the people, due to the influence of the deviant teachers (4:3-4). With four imperatives, the third part returns to Paul's commands for Timothy's personal life and ministry. These three parts pave the way for Paul's final testimony, in 4:6-8.

Second Timothy 4:1-5 has the literary characteristics of a last will and testament (I. H. Marshall 1999: 797). The repeated second-person imperative (9 times) and the emphatic *but you* in 4:5 (TNIV) set forth Paul's personal address to Timothy in comparison with Paul's final testimony in 4:6. In this last will and testament, Paul passes the baton of Christian ministry to Timothy. Like a dying person, Paul is giving the final word to his heir apparent (Fee 1988: 283). Verses 2 and 5 may be viewed as an ordination charge, and today it is often used in ordination ceremonies.

OUTLINE

A Solemn Charge, 4:1-2
A Warning That Some Reject the Truth, 4:3-4
A Full Ministry, 4:5

EXPLANATORY NOTES

A Solemn Charge 4:1-2

The farewell charge begins with a formula that is like a solemn oath used in the Hellenistic world in legal acts of succession (Collins: 266). It has parallels in 1 Timothy 5:21 and 6:13-14. *In the presence of God and of Christ Jesus, . . . I solemnly urge you* (2 Tim 4:1). The phrase *in the presence of God* recalls the OT expression "before the Lord," implying a solemn occasion (1 Sam 7:6; Pss 56:13; 68:3). Already in 2 Timothy 2:14, Paul urges Timothy to warn the people *before God.* And as in 1 Timothy 5:21, Paul solemnly urges Timothy *in the presence of God and of Christ Jesus.* To call God and Christ as witnesses to this solemn charge heightens the seriousness of Paul's exhortation in 2 Timothy 4:1-2.

Eschatological comments strengthen the charge. Christ Jesus will return and *judge the living and the dead.* Elsewhere Paul speaks of Christ's participation in the final judgment (Rom 2:15; 2 Cor 5:10). Peter also talks about Jesus as the one who judges the living and the dead (Acts 10:42; 1 Pet 4:5). Later the church included these words in the Apostles' Creed. Next, Paul charges Timothy in view of Christ's appearing (*epiphaneia*, 2 Tim 4:1). As noted earlier, the term *appearing* was used when Roman government officials, including the emperor, visited cities of the empire. Here Christ Jesus takes their place and supersedes the government officials. Christ's appearance marks the eschatological end of time. Finally, the charge is given in view of Christ's kingdom, promised to the righteous after the judgment (4:8, 18).

The charge itself contains five imperatives. *Preach the word* (4:2 TNIV). Timothy is commanded to *proclaim the message* of the gospel. He is to herald the good news. This word is not bound (2:9), it is faithful (2:11), and Timothy is to delineate this word rightly (2:15). The charge to preach the word is similar to the charge to *guard the good deposit* (1 Tim 6:20; 2 Tim 1:14 TNIV). *Be persistent whether the time is favorable or unfavorable.* This word *time* means the moment of opportunity, the acceptable time (2 Cor 6:2). As teacher, Timothy will seize the opportunities that offer themselves. The double adverbs regarding time, *favorable or unfavorable* can be interpreted as referring to either the subject (Timothy) or the object (Timothy's hearers; 2 Tim 4:2). If it is subjective, it means that Timothy is to preach the word whether the time is convenient for him or not. If it is objective, Timothy is to preach the word whether the time is convenient for the hearers or not. In light of what is said about the unhealthy teachers in the following two verses, the objective use is preferred. Timothy is to preach the gospel persistently, whether the teachers and their followers are open to hearing it or not. To be always on the alert to preach the gospel is "to bring home the stringency of the situation and the need to act before things become so bad that appeal to the hearers will be in vain" (I. H. Marshall 1999: 801).

The last three imperatives in 4:2 appeal to the reason, the conscience, and the will (Kelly: 206). *Convince* suggests logical engagement with the listeners in leading them to an awareness of their sin. Timothy is to preach and teach the true Word of God with a reasoned argument, to persuade the followers of the unhealthy teachers both morally and intellectually. *Rebuke* means to censure, to warn those who do not give heed to Timothy's preaching and teaching. This rebuke may include public address to the erring ones as well as private conversation with individuals. Finally, *encourage* means to exhort the people to repent and to persevere in the faith. The manner in which Timothy is to carry out these three imperative commands is *with the utmost patience in teaching.* How Timothy teaches is important. He is to teach with patience or long-suffering. The content of teaching will be healthy doctrine, the gospel of Jesus Christ. The method employed in teaching will lend itself to persuasion and encouragement.

A Warning That Some Reject the Truth 4:3-4

For a final time Timothy is reminded of the growing apostasy (4:3-4), described in four clauses. The first and third clauses express the apostates' negative attitude toward the truth, and the second and fourth clauses express a positive attitude toward error (I. H. Marshall 1999: 801). With an explanatory *for,* Paul indicates that *the time is coming when people will not put up with sound doctrine* (4:3). This negative clause declares that some people will turn away from healthy teaching. They turn away because their ears are tuned to other voices. Instead of following the objective truth that Timothy teaches, these persons are guided by subjective desires. The words *itching ears* literally means being itchy with respect to hearing (Johnson 2001: 429). They are filled with curiosity and look for interesting and spicy bits of information. Their ears tickle (BDAG: 36) with the unhealthy teaching to which they are listening. They do not listen to the sound doctrine that Timothy is teaching (1 Tim 1:9-10; Titus 1:13; 2:1-2). Instead, they give heed to teachings from unhealthy teachers. The third clause shows their negative attitude toward the truth. They *turn away from listening to the truth* and toward *myths* or fables (2 Tim 4:4). In the letters to Timothy and Titus, *truth* means the truth of the gospel of Jesus Christ. Turning to myths, the fourth clause, means that the opponents turn to half-truths or fables (1 Tim 1:4; 4:7; Titus 1:14). The final word about the unhealthy teaching in 2 Timothy 4:3-4 is much like the first word in 1 Timothy

1:3-7. Because this deviant teaching dupes those who turn to it and deceives those who follow it, the followers of these teachers have turned from truth to a lie *[Unhealthy Teaching, p. 366]*.

A Full Ministry 4:5

Paul returns to Timothy with a direct address in 2 Timothy 4:5: *but you* (TNIV). Four commands are given. *Always be sober*, or *Keep your head in all situations* (TNIV). Timothy's life must be characterized by self-control. Sobriety literally means "not intoxicated." Positively it means to control the self, to be well-balanced, to be in control of one's life and what one is saying. *Endure suffering* picks up an underlying theme of 2 Timothy (1:8; 2:3; 3:12). In addition to physical suffering, Timothy is commanded to endure the emotional and psychological suffering that comes when he is faced with opposition. *Do the work of an evangelist* is a command to proclaim fearlessly the good news of the gospel. It means to preach the word (4:2). Like Philip (Acts 21:8), Timothy is to exercise his gift of evangelizing by teaching and preaching the gospel. Obstacles stand in the way of preaching, including opponents of the gospel, problems with cross-cultural communication of the gospel, and lack of respect in an honor-and-shame society. Despite these obstacles, Timothy must pursue the missionary task of spreading the good news of Jesus Christ. *Carry out your ministry fully* summarizes Timothy's task to bring his ministry to fullness. In this short letter, Paul begins by urging Timothy not to be ashamed (2 Tim 1:7-8). He ends with the command to meet the obligation in full as a minister of the gospel. As Timothy exercises Christian ministry in its fullness, he, like Paul (4:6-8), will come to the end of life with assurance that he has completed the work that God called him to do and is ready to receive the crown.

THE TEXT IN BIBLICAL CONTEXT

Second Timothy 4:2 sets forth the solemn charge *Preach the word* (TNIV). This command sums up Timothy's task and includes teaching and evangelizing (2:2b, 5). It calls attention to the prophetic side of Christian ministry.

In the OT, God called both men and women prophets to announce God's will to the people. One term for prophet is *nabi*, one who speaks forth God's message. Prophets spoke for God at God's initiative. As spokespersons for God, they declared God's message to God's people in light of their situation. Often they addressed the social and economic sins of the people and God's resulting judgment. The prophet's message called for repentance by inviting the people to turn back to the covenant behavior outlined at Mount Sinai (Exod 19–24) and repeated in the book of Deuteronomy. Sometimes a prophet was called a "sentinel" (Ezek 33:1-20; Hos 9:8), one who watches for God's message and warns the people of the impending danger of evil. At other times the prophet was called a "seer" (1 Sam 9:9-19; Amos 7:12), since the prophet had insight and the ability to perceive the spiritual condition of the people and to bring God's message to bear upon the situation. Sometimes the prophet's message included a word of hope when the people saw only despair in the midst of judgment. That word of hope included the promise of a new covenant, a messiah, and a servant who would usher in the new kingdom of God.

Jesus began his ministry in the synagogue at Nazareth by quoting Isaiah 61:1-2:

> The Spirit of the Lord is on me
> because he has anointed me
> to proclaim good news to the poor.
> He has sent me to proclaim freedom for the prisoners
> and recovery of sight for the blind,
> to release the oppressed,
> to proclaim the year of the Lord's favor. (Luke 4:18-19 TNIV)

Following the temptation of Jesus in the wilderness, Matthew reports, "From that time on Jesus began to preach, 'Repent, for the kingdom of heaven has come near'" (Matt 4:17 TNIV). Mark characterizes the ministry of Jesus as one of preaching (1:14) and mentions preaching nine times in his gospel. Matthew (9 times) and Luke (7 times) each describe Jesus as engaged in preaching. Jesus preached the good news of the gospel.

In Acts, the early apostles preached in Jerusalem (10:42), in Samaria (8:5), and to the ends of the earth. Paul preached in his missionary work (9:20; 19:13; 20:25; 28:31). Luke concludes the book of Acts by reporting that Paul was in Rome preaching the kingdom (28:31). Paul's preaching centered on Jesus Christ. To the Corinthian church, Paul wrote, "For we do not proclaim ourselves; we proclaim Jesus Christ as Lord and ourselves as slaves for Jesus' sake" (2 Cor 4:5). In Romans, Paul explains the importance of preaching: "How are they to call on one in whom they have not believed? And how are they to believe in one of whom they have never heard? And how are they to hear without someone to proclaim him? And how are they to proclaim him unless they are sent? As it is written, 'How beautiful are the feet of those who bring good news!'" (10:14-15).

In 2 Timothy 4:2, Paul solemnly urges Timothy to *preach the word* (TNIV, GNT). The term *word* refers to the Christian message in preaching. The Christian message is called *the word of God* (1 Tim 4:5; 2 Tim 2:9;

Titus 1:3; 2:5), *the word of truth* (2 Tim 2:15), and *words of faith* (1 Tim 4:6). In the letters to Timothy and Titus, preaching is related to the trustworthy, or faithful, sayings. Paul believed that preaching was essential to the life of the Christian community.

THE TEXT IN THE LIFE OF THE CHURCH

Most Christian groups believe that the central task of the Christian minister is to preach the word of God. They often include 2 Timothy 4:2 in their ordination charge. In the history of the Christian church, many outstanding preachers can be identified: John Chrysostom among the early church fathers; Ulrich Zwingli in Zurich, Switzerland, in the early 1520s; John Wesley and George Whitefield in England and the American colonies; Alexander MacLaren; and twentieth-century preachers such as Gardner Taylor in Brooklyn, New York; Billy Graham; Catholic priest Fulton Sheen; and Englishman John R. W. Stott.

Roman Catholicism upholds the homily as God's people are gathered to worship God, although the sacraments overshadow the homily in the service. Eastern orthodoxy places higher value on orthodoxy of worship than on preaching. Protestantism tends to view preaching as the central sacrament of the church. For Luther, the church exists where the Word of God is preached and the sacraments are observed. Preaching is even more central in the Reformed movement.

The Anabaptists understood the congregation as a hermeneutical community. Balthasar Hubmaier, a trained Anabaptist theologian and preacher at Nikolsburg in Moravia, preached regularly to a large congregation. The voice of the preacher of God's word was essential in Anabaptist life, but it was not the only voice that was heard. Divine authority was based on Scripture and Holy Spirit together, rather than on the Scripture alone, as was typical of Protestantism (Greiser and King: 78). The Holy Spirit and Scripture both point to Jesus Christ. The Holy Spirit takes the words of Scripture and does something in the hearts and lives of the people as they hear the Word of God preached.

The Anabaptists emphasized Scripture and the Spirit as discerned in the community of Christian believers. Community discernment was not an alternative to preaching for Anabaptists. The voice of the Bible scholar and preacher was given much attention as the church community discerned the meaning of Scripture. However, the word of the preacher was tested and discerned in the community of believers. Historically, this discernment found expression in the *Zeugnis* (testimony), bearing witness to the sermon through a verbal response to the sermon by some other person—often the deacon—in the congregation (Greiser and King: 20-22).

Believers churches continue to emphasize preaching. The preaching, teaching, and equipping task is so important in the life of the church that persons with this gift are called out and set aside for this work of passing on normative Christian beliefs and practices. Preaching in the believers church includes the following:

- preaching the good news of salvation in Jesus Christ.
- preaching God's action through the covenants, especially in the cross and resurrection of Jesus.
- preaching OT themes as they are interpreted through God's full revelation in Jesus Christ.
- proclaiming reconciliation in Jesus Christ both between the individual and God and between brothers and sisters in the church.
- preaching that brings Word and Spirit together.
- proclaiming the way of the kingdom of God and the ethical teaching of Jesus.
- preaching as shepherding and pastoral care.
- preaching that applies the Scriptures and God's will to the larger social and economic setting as seen in the OT prophets.
- preaching on the meaning of being church, the Christian community, God's people in the world today.
- preaching that proclaims the promises of God, including divine hope.
- preaching that applies Christianity to life so that congregational members, as disciples of Jesus, walk in the obedience of faith.

Preaching in believers churches tends to privilege biblical exposition. Many ministers have preached expository sermons as they worked their way through books of the Bible. Today, a growing number of believers churches follow the Common Lectionary and use a narrative method of preaching. In the postmodern period, many pastors of believers churches, like many other Protestant pastors, find storytelling and narrative preaching an effective method of communication, especially when followed by a sermon discussion group in the congregation.

2 Timothy 4:6-8

Paul's Final Testimony

PREVIEW

In 2 Timothy 4:6-8, Paul turns to himself in what can be called his last will and testament. In contrast to *as for you* (Timothy) in 4:5, attention is now drawn to *as for me* in 4:6. Paul calls attention to his imminent death (4:6). Two metaphors in verse 6 support this way of reading the text. Paul's life is being poured out like a drink offering, and the time of his departure has come.

A testimony of Paul's faithful life as a follower of Jesus Christ is stated in verse 7. With three perfect-tense verbs utilizing athletic imagery, Paul says that his life and work stand completed. No more needs to be added. Verse 8 follows with anticipation of receiving a final reward when he meets the Lord. Because Paul has been faithful in the past, his work stands completed in the present, and he anticipates receiving a reward in the future. Interpreted within the larger context of 2 Timothy, Paul is not emphasizing his personal accomplishments in 4:6-8 as much as encouraging Timothy to take up the work as successor and remain faithful in the calling to Christian ministry.

OUTLINE

Death Is Imminent, 4:6
Testimony of a Faithful Life, 4:7
The Anticipated Reward, 4:8

EXPLANATORY NOTES

Death Is Imminent 4:6

With two metaphors, Paul writes of his impending death. First, *I am already being poured out as a libation* (2 Tim 4:6a). In the Hellenistic world, a libation of wine was often added to a sacrifice and was poured out to the gods before drinking or after a meal (Collins: 273). In the Hebrew world, a drink offering was offered as a sacrifice to God (Num 15:5, 7, 10). The verb *poured out* means literally to be poured out as a drink offering. In Philippians 2:17, Paul uses this verb to speak about his death. He repeats that idea here along with the adverb *already*, which suggests that his imprisonment will soon end in death. Death is imminent, and the whole present ordeal that will culminate in death is a pouring out of his life as a drink offering to the Lord (Fee 1988: 289).

A second metaphor is added, *and the time of my departure has come* (2 Tim 4:6b). The term *departure* echoes Philippians 1:23, where Paul talks about his death. The term *departure* was used for soldiers breaking camp or sailors loosing a ship from its moorings (Mounce: 578). As the last drops of Paul's life are poured out as an offering to God, the time for leaving this world in death is imminent.

Testimony of a Faithful Life 4:7

Changing to athletic metaphors, Paul sums up his life with three statements. In each case he uses the perfect tense, which indicates that the action stands complete: his ministry has come to an end. *I have fought the good fight* (4:7a). Paul has been in the race of life. He has run in the noblest *good fight* of all races: the ministry of the gospel (Fee 1988: 289). Just as Paul has commanded Timothy to fight the good fight (1 Tim 6:12), so now Paul testifies that he himself has successfully fought in the contest to the very end.

I have finished the race (4:7b). The word *race* is used for a course or racetrack where horse or foot races were held. Here in verse 7 the term means that Paul's life has come to the finish line. He has completed the course. For Paul, running the Christian race has been brought to completion. It is not that the Christian race is done; it is that Paul has completed his part, and Timothy must now do his part. The Christian race is like a relay race (Heb 12:1-2), in which several runners complete their portion of the race.

In Acts 20:24 Paul states his desire to finish his course and the ministry given to him by God. Here Paul says, *I have kept the faith* (2 Tim 4:7c). Paul has preserved the faith; he has kept sound or healthy doctrine. Just as Timothy is to keep the deposit entrusted to him, so also Paul comes to the end of life and honestly says that he has kept the faith (1:14). He has been loyal to the divine mandate given to him in his apostolic calling throughout life. Paul's testimony to Timothy at the end of life also encourages every minister of the gospel to carry out one's faith and ministry in its fullness.

The Anticipated Reward 4:8

Paul turns to the future and anticipates receiving a reward for winning the race. Using an athletic metaphor, Paul talks about the *crown*, a laurel wreath given to the winner (1 Cor 9:25). Here it is *the crown of righteousness* (2 Tim 4:8). Does Paul mean a prize awarded for a righteous life, or a crown consisting of righteousness? Since he speaks of the righteous judge awarding that crown, Paul is speaking of the crown that righteous ones receive. He has achieved that righteousness through God's work, which makes it possible to enter into right relationship with God and others. Thus the crown given by the righteous judge ties into the life that Paul has lived by God's power at work in his life.

This crown of righteousness is not only for Paul but also for all who have longed for his appearing (4:8b). In 2 Timothy 4:1 Paul solemnly urges Timothy to carry out the Christian ministry in light of the future return of Christ. What awaits Paul also awaits Timothy and everyone else who longs for Christ's return. Thus Paul ends his testimony on an eschatological note, encouraging Timothy in the Christian ministry.

THE TEXT IN BIBLICAL CONTEXT

Paul came to the end of life with complete confidence in God (2 Tim 4:6-8). Many saints of God come to the end of life with a similar faith. Abraham's story ends with these words: "This is the length of Abraham's life, one hundred and seventy-five years. Abraham breathed his last and died in a good old age, an old man and full of years, and was gathered to his people" (Gen 25:7-8).

Abraham's faith did not weaken. Paul says, "No distrust made him waver concerning the promise of God, but he grew strong in his faith as he gave glory to God, being fully convinced that God was able to do what he had promised. Therefore his faith was reckoned to him as righteousness" (Rom 4:20-22). The writer of Hebrews describes Abraham's faith: "For he looked forward to the city that has foundations, whose architect and builder is God" (11:10).

Moses, the great leader of the children of Israel, was 120 years old when he died. The book of Deuteronomy reports Moses' death and says, "His sight was unimpaired and his vigor had not abated. . . . Never since has there arisen a prophet in Israel like Moses, whom the Lord knew face to face" (34:7, 10). Reflecting on the faith of Moses, the writer of Hebrews said, "He considered abuse suffered for the Christ to be greater wealth than the treasures of Egypt, for he was looking ahead to the reward. By faith he left Egypt, unafraid of the king's anger; for he persevered as though he saw him who is invisible" (11:26-27).

Stephen, an early Christian martyr, came to the end of life with a firm faith in Jesus Christ. Luke records Stephen's death with these words:

> Filled with the Holy Spirit, he gazed into heaven and saw the glory of God and Jesus standing at the right hand of God. "Look," he said, "I see the heavens opened and the Son of Man standing at the right hand of God!" . . . While they were stoning Stephen, he prayed, "Lord Jesus, receive my spirit." Then he knelt down and cried out in a loud voice, "Lord, do not hold this sin against them." When he had said this, he died. (Acts 7:55-56, 59-60)

The apostle Paul made Christ the center of his life. He said, "We walk by faith, not by sight. Yes, we do have confidence, and we would rather be away from the body and at home with the Lord. So whether we are at home or away, we make it our aim to please him" (2 Cor 5:7-9). After talking about the resurrection of Jesus Christ, Paul said, "Thanks be to God, who gives us the victory through our Lord Jesus Christ. Therefore, my beloved, be steadfast, immovable, always excelling in the work of the Lord, because you know that in the Lord your labor is not in vain" (1 Cor 15:57-58). With great faith and confidence in God, Paul told Timothy, "I am not ashamed, for I know the one in whom I have put my trust, and I am sure that he is able to guard until that day what I have entrusted to him" (2 Tim 1:12). Indeed, Paul came to the end of life with great awareness of God's presence in the midst of Christian ministry and assurance of God's final reward for him: *I have fought the good fight, I have finished the race, I have kept the faith. From now on there is reserved for me the crown of righteousness, which the Lord, the righteous judge, will give me on that day* (2 Tim 4:7-8).

THE TEXT IN THE LIFE OF THE CHURCH

Like the apostle Paul in 2 Timothy 4:7-8, Christian ministers can come to the end of ministry with deep satisfaction in their life calling, confident in Christ and in their future. Pastoral ministry consists of several stages.

Pastoring begins with a trial/exploratory stage in the first five years of ministry. During this stage the new pastor experiences ups and downs and seeks stability. The assumed glory of the pastorate and the idealism of training for ministry declines as reality sets in. Some pastors do not make it beyond this stage.

Next, pastoring reaches an advancement stage between six and twelve years in the ministry. In this stage, pastors are more realistic. They build on a relationship of trust established with the congregation and grow in their personal life and knowledge of Christian ministry. The advancement stage is one of the best in the pastoral calling.

In the midcareer stage, the pastor can become stagnant unless one makes an effort to grow in the pastoral ministry. Successful pastors continue reading and take enrichment courses and seminars. During this stage, pastors work at developing the gifts of others and encourage young adults to hear and accept the call of God to Christian ministry.

Pastors who reach the preretirement stage give more time to reflection, evaluation, and focusing their ministry. In the preretirement stage, they work harder at raising up leaders in the congregation and gradually transferring responsibility to them. As Paul worked with Timothy and Titus, the pastor prepares others to carry on the good work of preaching the gospel and shepherding the people, knowing that their own life span is limited. It is important that the pastor finish well during this stage.

A pastor who reaches the retirement stage passes the mantle of leadership to the successor. In the early years of retirement, pastors work diligently to make the transition to their successors go well. In this stage, pastors relinquish the accumulated power and authority gained over the years and pass that authority on to their successors. A pastor who has done well will retain a significant amount of accumulated personal authority and must be careful not to take away the right of the successor to lead. During this time, the aging pastor will work carefully to mentor without dominating and to give counsel without getting in the way. During this stage the pastor moves from leader to supporter and encourager of the successor. This is one of the more important stages of pastoral ministry. The early years of retirement are the most crucial in the adjustment from pastoring to supporting one's successor.

Finally come the later years of retirement. Like the apostle Paul, pastors will remain firm in faith. They will look across the years of pastoral ministry with a sense of satisfaction in what God has done in and through their ministry. Personal faith in Christ will continue to grow as they draw closer to death. A deep sense of gratefulness to God will well up within the retired pastors as they rejoice in Jesus Christ and the church. Finally *all* believers will breathe a last breath in anticipation of the resurrection body and a heavenly reward.

2 Timothy 4:9-18

Final Instructions

PREVIEW

Paul closes 2 Timothy with personal instructions about himself, Timothy, and several colleagues. The section has two units. In the first unit (4:9-15), Paul requests Timothy to come and visit him soon. Three colleagues have left Paul, and he is alone. Timothy is to bring Mark with him. Then Paul comments on three other matters. Tychicus and his mission are mentioned, and Timothy is instructed to bring important items with him to Paul. Alexander has done evil deeds, and Timothy should be aware of him. The first-person pronoun appears in every verse.

With all the names and details given in 4:9-18, it is difficult to reject Paul's authorship of this section. Whether it is a Pauline fragment included by the writer or evidence that the whole epistle is Pauline does not need to be decided here. In verses 9-15, Paul mentions eight names: Demas, Crescens, Titus, Luke, Mark, Tychicus, Carpus, and Alexander. Three of these persons (Luke, Demas, and Mark) are named in Philemon 24 and Colossians 4:10, 14. Paul also mentions the geographical sphere of these associates: Thessalonica, Galatia, Dalmatia, Ephesus, Troas, Corinth, and Miletus (2 Tim 4:10, 12-13, 20). These many names and places show the extent of Paul's ministry in the Roman provinces of Macedonia, Galatia, Illyricum, Asia, and Achaia.

In the second unit (4:16-18), Paul comments on the lack of human support at his trial. Yet the Lord has stood by him, and Paul is confident that the Lord will save him for his heavenly kingdom. With that said, Paul breaks out into a short doxology (4:18b).

OUTLINE

Instruction to Associates, 4:9-15
Lack of Human Support, 4:16-18a
Doxology, 4:18b

EXPLANATORY NOTES

Instruction to Associates 4:9-15

Paul begins by urging Timothy to come to Rome and visit him soon. The word *soon* means without delay. In 4:21 Paul repeats the request and asks Timothy to *come before winter*. With the first part of the trial over and winter coming on, Paul wants companionship and clothing for the days ahead before his death. Paul states why Timothy should come quickly. All of his close friends, except Luke, have left him. Demas, a co-worker during Paul's first imprisonment, has deserted him (Col 4:14; Philem 24). This desertion was painful for the apostle. Instead of focusing attention on love for Christ's appearing (2 Tim 4:8), Demas loved the present world. Demas may have feared that if he stayed close to Paul, who was facing death at the hands of the Roman court, he too could be martyred. Perhaps Demas returned to his hometown, Thessalonica.

Crescens went to Galatia. We know nothing more about Crescens. Some manuscripts read *Gallia*, meaning Gaul, now called France. It is more likely that Paul is speaking of Galatia, the Roman province in Asia.

Titus went to Dalmatia. In Titus 3:12, Paul refers to having sent Artemas and Tychicus to Crete. One of them likely stayed at Crete to guide the church so that Titus could meet Paul at Nicopolis, which was not far from Dalmatia. If 2 Timothy was written after Titus, it would be logical that Titus was now at Dalmatia. Dalmatia was the name of the Roman province in the southern part of Illyricum, which was separated from the rest of Illyricum after the Illyrian/Pannonian revolt in AD 6-9.

Luke is the only person who remains with Paul. "The beloved physician" (Col 4:14) and traveling companion of Paul stood by the exhausted apostle. Because of Luke's continuing association with the apostle, Luke as Paul's secretary may have had a hand in writing one or more of the letters to Timothy and Titus.

Get Mark and bring him with you, for he is useful in my ministry (2 Tim 4:11). Young John Mark accompanied Barnabas and Paul on their first missionary journey as their "assistant" (Acts 13:5 NJB). In Pamphylia, Mark left the missionary team and returned to Jerusalem. After the Jerusalem conference, Barnabas wanted to take Mark along again on a second missionary journey. Paul would not allow Mark to go, and the sharp difference between Barnabas and Paul regarding Mark resulted in separation, with Barnabas going to Cyprus. Paul, Silas, and Timothy comprised the missionary team for the second missionary journey (15:36-41). By the time Paul wrote Colossians, he had accepted Mark back as a trusted co-worker (Col 4:10). Now Paul wants to see Mark once more because Mark is useful in Paul's ministry. The term *ministry*, or *service* (*diakonia*), suggests that Mark is needed to help care for Paul's personal needs. Mark is needed because Paul has sent Tychicus to Ephesus to carry a copy of the present letter to Timothy (2 Tim 4:12). Likely Tychicus stayed in Ephesus and carried on the ministry there while Timothy came to be with Paul in Rome.

Next, Paul tells Timothy what to bring. *When you come, bring the cloak that I left with Carpus at Troas, also the books, and above all the parchments* (4:13). Paul asks for his *cloak*, a heavy circular garment formed of a round piece of material with a hole for the head, much like a modern poncho or an old-fashioned cycling cape (I. H. Marshall 1999: 818). The cloak is made of heavy material and thus able to shed water as well as protect one from the cold. Ceslaus Spicq thinks that Paul may have made this garment himself (Spicq: 400). With winter arriving soon (4:21), Paul needs this heavy garment to keep him warm in an unheated prison. Apparently Paul left the cloak with Carpus when he passed through Troas. Paul also asked Timothy to bring his books. The term *books* refers to any kind of literary works. In Judaism, the term was used for the scrolls of the Torah (Johnson 2001: 440). Paul may be asking for scrolls or codices of the Scriptures. In addition, he asks for the *parchments*, which were used as writing materials. Parchments were skins of sheep and goats that could be written on, scraped, and used again. Although parchment was stronger and more durable than papyrus, it was also more expensive. It is likely that *books* refers to some of the OT Scriptures and that the parchments were personal documents (I. H. Marshall 1999: 821).

One final time Paul mentions someone who has opposed him. *Alexander the coppersmith* (TNIV: *metalworker*) *did* him *great harm* (4:14). This person may be the same Alexander who, with Hymenaeus, was removed from the church by Paul in 1 Timothy 1:19-20. Or he may be a Jew by the name of Alexander who tried to quiet the crowd at the time of the riot in Ephesus in Acts 19:33-34. Or he could be a man by the name of Alexander from Troas, since there was a guild of metalworkers in Troas. More likely he was the person from Ephesus mentioned in Acts 19:33-34 or 1 Timothy 1:19-20. At any rate, a certain Alexander did much harm to Paul and stands under the Lord's judgment. Paul warns Timothy to be aware of him because this Alexander has greatly opposed Paul's message.

Lack of Human Support 4:16-18a

Paul describes his feeling of isolation. No one assisted him in his first defense. *All deserted me* (2 Tim 4:16) may be an indication that Luke and Tychicus were not present at his first defense and that Paul felt deserted without their presence and help. The term *first defense* (*apologia*) is legal terminology for a judicial hearing that is followed by a second hearing or trial, which would then lead to the apostle's anticipated death (Collins: 285). Often this hearing took place before the emperor or a magistrate (Fee 1988: 296). When imprisoned the first time, Paul apparently waited two years after the preliminary hearing before being released (Acts 28:16, 30). Now during a second imprisonment, Paul summons Timothy to come to him because his impending death may not take place immediately.

Despite the absence of support by fellow workers, Paul has experienced the presence of the living Lord. Amid dire circumstances, the Lord has done two things for Paul. First, *the Lord stood by* him and *gave* him *strength* (2 Tim 4:17a). The Lord's strength made it possible to use imprisonment at Rome in such a way that through Paul *the message might be fully proclaimed and all the Gentiles might hear it* (4:17b). The missionary task of the church does not end with imprisonment. Despite persecution and imprisonment, God has worked through Paul to bring the good news of salvation to the Gentiles. Second, the Lord *rescued me from the lion's mouth* (4:17c). Speaking metaphorically and quoting from Psalm 22:21, Paul says the Lord has rescued him. Paul was saved from extreme danger, just as Daniel was rescued from the "lions' mouths" (Dan 6:22). With that awareness, Paul expresses full confidence that God *will rescue* him *from every evil attack* in the future and *save* him *for his heavenly kingdom* (2 Tim 4:18). Echoing the Lord's Prayer (Matt 6:13), Paul believes God will deliver him from evil. Moreover, the Lord will save Paul in the future for his coming heavenly kingdom. The salvation that Paul has already experienced will also be his in the future.

Doxology 4:18b

With eschatological certainty, Paul believes that what Christ has accomplished in him will extend through the final consummation. With that note of victory, Paul breaks out into a doxology. *To him be the glory forever and ever. Amen* (2 Tim 4:18b). This doxology is much like the one in Philippians 4:20. Such a doxology is typically Pauline. The classic choral response, "Amen," confirms its liturgical use (Collins: 288). With this note of eschatological victory, despite impending circumstances, Paul brings his encouraging words to Timothy to a close.

2 Timothy 4:19-22

Final Greetings

PREVIEW

Paul's final letter is brought to a close with five parts: greetings to certain people (4:19), personal news of friends (v. 20), an important request (v. 21a), greetings from several people (v. 21b), and a final benediction consisting of two parts (v. 22).

OUTLINE

Greetings to Certain People, 4:19
Personal News of Friends, 4:20
An Important Request, 4:21a
Greetings from People, 4:21b
Final Benediction, 4:22

EXPLANATORY NOTES

Greetings to Certain People 4:19

Greet Prisca and Aquila, and the household of Onesiphorus (4:19). Here Paul asks Timothy to pass on greetings to well-known associates. Prisca (= Priscilla) and Aquila were a husband-wife team in Christian ministry (Acts 18:2, 18-19, 24-26; Rom 16:3; 1 Cor 16:19). Aquila was a Jew from Pontus, and likely his wife Prisca was also a Jew.

Paul first met them in Corinth after they were expelled from Rome by the edict of Claudius (likely in AD 49; Acts 18:1-3). They went to Ephesus with Paul, where they helped in ministry for some time (18:18-26). Later they appear in Rome, where they had a house church (Rom 16:3-4). Now they are back in Ephesus. In four of the six times they are mentioned in the NT, Prisca is mentioned first, which is highly unusual in antiquity. It is likely that she had a stronger Christian personality and was more active in Christian ministry (Fee 1988: 300). Onesiphorus is commended in 2 Timothy 1:16-17 for visiting Paul in Rome while the apostle was chained. Now Paul asks Timothy to greet the household of Onesiphorus. Calling attention to his family rather than addressing Onesiphorus directly may indicate that he has died and Paul sends greetings to the household.

Personal News of Friends 4:20

Next Paul gives personal news of friends: *Erastus* and *Trophimus* (4:20). The name *Erastus* is mentioned also in Acts 19:22 and Romans 16:23, where he is called the treasurer of the city of Corinth. An inscription found in Corinth reads, "Erastus, commissioner of public works, bore the expense of this pavement" (via Mounce: 600). A person by the name of Erastus was sent with Timothy to Macedonia some years previously (Acts 19:22). We do not know to which of these two persons Paul is now sending greetings—or whether they were the same—but we do know this Erastus is living in Corinth (2 Tim 4:20). Trophimus, an "Ephesian," was a traveling companion of Paul (Acts 20:4; 21:29). He was present when Paul gave his farewell address to the elders of the Ephesian church at Miletus, a suburb of Ephesus (20:15, 17). And Trophimus traveled with Paul to Jerusalem, where his presence in the temple area stirred up a riot (21:29). Did Paul later get as close to Ephesus as Miletus? What we know is that Paul left Trophimus, who was ill, in Miletus, and now he is sending special greetings to him. This greeting gives the reader insight into the warmth and graciousness of the apostle.

An Important Request 4:21a

Then Paul makes a request to Timothy. *Do your best to come before winter* (4:21). This short command points to the difficulties of sea travel in the Mediterranean world from November to March. Ship owners were paid bonuses if they risked their property to deliver goods under such conditions (Johnson 2001: 444). Paul needs his cloak for the cold winter months, hence the urgency for Timothy to come soon. These winter-weather conditions suggest that Paul may have written this second letter to Timothy sometime between spring and late summer so that Timothy could get on his way and arrive before winter.

Greetings from People 4:21b

Paul passes on greetings to Timothy from four persons known by name. Three are Latin names and may therefore be local believers in Rome and perhaps leaders in the church. *Eubulus* was a common name in the

Hellenistic world. *Pudens* is likely a son of a Roman senator. *Claudia* is a woman, perhaps a slave from a royal household (Collins: 291-92). According to Irenaeus, *Linus* was the first overseer of the church in Rome after Peter, although Tertullian disputes this (I. H. Marshall 1999: 830; Collins: 291). To make sure that no one is missed, Paul sends general greetings to *all the brothers and sisters.*

Final Benediction 4:22

Second Timothy closes with a benediction in two parts. First, Paul says to Timothy, *The Lord be with your spirit* (4:22a). Most often Paul uses a grace formula at the end of his letters. The phrase *the Lord be with your spirit* is an expanded form of "the Lord be with you." Paul may have written it this way to assure Timothy that the Lord will strengthen Timothy's charisma for ministry (I. H. Marshall 1999: 831). Second, Paul gives a final benediction for the church: *Grace be with you all* (TNIV). The plural form of *you* is Paul's direct address to the Ephesian community, which lies in the background in this letter. "It is altogether fitting that the very last words from Paul should be a benediction, a desire for God's grace to be with all his people" (Fee 1988: 302).

Titus

Introduction to Titus

Crete

Crete is a small island off the southern coast of Greece, in the Mediterranean Sea. The island is 156 miles long and ranges up to 30 miles wide. Citizens of Crete believed that their race emerged from the earth, which made them the original Greeks (Diodorus 5.64.1). Cretans also believed that their island was the birthplace of the majority of the gods, including Zeus, who was buried in Crete (5.77.3). Moreover, Cretans believed that the gods were men and women from Crete who were elevated to deity (5.64:2). A Christian church began in the midst of this pagan Cretan culture. Paul wrote a letter addressed to Titus with instructions on how to lead this young church in its cultural setting.

Titus, a Loyal Child

In Titus 1:4, Paul addresses Titus as his *loyal child in the faith.* Like Timothy, Titus is likely one of Paul's Greek converts to the Christian faith. Though his name does not appear in the book of Acts, we learn about Titus and his relationship to Paul from Paul's other letters. Titus went to the Jerusalem Conference with Paul to bear witness to the missionary expansion of the church among the Gentiles and was not compelled to be circumcised (Gal 2:1, 3).

Recognizing Titus's potential as a church leader, Paul sent him to Corinth with a harsh letter for the Corinthian church. He apparently handled the situation skillfully since the church community responded with new loyalty and obedience (2 Cor 2:12-13; 7:5-7). After reporting back to Paul in Macedonia, Titus was sent back to Corinth with another letter to complete the financial collection there (2 Cor 7:6-16; 8:6; 12:17-18). Though Titus did not have as close a relationship with Paul as did Timothy, his service started earlier and covered a longer period of time *[Titus, p. 365]*.

The Church in Crete

The letter to Titus comes from Paul while en route to Macedonia and Nicopolis in northwest Greece (western Macedonia; Titus 3:12). Crete is the letter's destination. The letter assumes a previous mission to Crete that resulted in the church's beginning on this island. Paul passed this island as a prisoner journeying on ship from Jerusalem to Rome in AD 61 (Acts 27:7-21). Paul advised the ship's captain to stay there, but his advice was rejected. Aside from the question of safety, one wonders if Paul wanted to begin mission work in Crete at this juncture of his life.

Paul may have traveled to Crete after a first release from Roman imprisonment and did missionary work on this island in the mid-60s, before his second imprisonment and death. Or there may have been an earlier visit to Crete in Paul's missionary travels that is not recorded in the book of Acts. As a travel companion and trusted leader, Titus is left behind in Crete as Paul likely returned to Macedonia.

The long introduction in 1:1-4 may indicate that Titus was written before 1 Timothy and that it introduces the pattern of thought that came later in 1 Timothy. Paul instructs Titus to put in order what remains to be done (Titus 1:5), which includes selecting leaders for the churches on this island. Christian congregations have emerged in many towns on the island (1:5). Some small house churches are predominately Jewish in origin and are susceptible to anti-Pauline teachers *of the circumcision* (1:10), who promote controversy about the Mosaic law (3:9). Other house churches are a combination of Hellenistic Jews and non-Jewish Hellenists and are susceptible to Cretan pagan culture.

All of these young congregations have been left in the care of Titus and need leadership. Though Timothy is to bring about reform in an established church in Ephesus, Titus is to appoint elders and thus set in order what has not yet been accomplished. Though Timothy must deal with unhealthy teaching that comes from outside and inside the church, Titus must deal with opposition that is largely influenced by persons who have fallen prey to dishonesty and those who promote endless controversies (1:9-11; 3:9-11).

Kind of Literature

Titus, along with 1 Timothy, represents deliberative, paraenetic rhetoric. The deliberative rhetorical style of Titus is a call to action. Though its tone is less urgent than 1 Timothy, in content Titus is closer to 1 Timothy than to 2 Timothy. In Titus, Paul gives ethical exhortation to bring about change in the lives of the Cretan church members. Leaders are to live exemplary lives (Titus 1:5-9). On one hand, all members are to live in such a way that persons outside the church cannot accuse these early Christian communities of being a subversive movement within the Roman Empire. On the other hand, Cretan Christians are to live in such a way that pagan Cretans are won to the Lord by the church's evangelistic witness (2:5-11; 3:1, 8).

Content

A theology of God, Christ, salvation, and hope of eternal life underlies the ethical and practical teaching in Titus. God made promises about eternal life before the ages began. These promises are based on a God who never lies, in contrast to Cretans, who have a reputation for lying (1:12). In good Pauline fashion, salvation and grace come through Jesus Christ, who gave himself for us that he might redeem us from all iniquity and purify for himself a people of his own (2:14). This salvation comes not by any works of righteousness that we have done (3:4-7), but by God's grace, which teaches us to live godly lives (2:12; 3:8).

Except for the opening (1:1-4), the final greeting (3:12-15), and two confessional passages (2:11-14; 3:4-7), the epistle of Titus has content similar to 1 Timothy. Titus must rebuke the opponents and put elders and an overseer in place (Titus 1:5-9), who will teach sound doctrine (1:9) and show Christian integrity (1:6-8). The charge to choose qualified leaders is similar to the one in 1 Timothy 3:2-7. In Titus, elders are chosen for the first time, indicating an early development of church life in Crete.

In both 1 Timothy and Titus, Paul focuses on household behavior that supports a stable social order within the context of commitment to Christ (Titus 2:3-10; 3:1-2; 1 Tim 2:8-15; 5:1-16; 6:1-2). *Household of God* and the role of leaders in the household receive greater attention in 1 Timothy than in Titus (1 Tim 1:4; 3:15; 5:17-22; Titus 1:5-9). Both Titus and 1 Timothy list vices and virtues. In Titus, virtues are tied to Christian teaching and truth. Truth and hope of eternal life are based on God, *who never lies* (1:2). Because God is truthful, the word of God taught by Titus and the appointed elders is trustworthy (1:9). The term *sound* literally means healthy and occurs several times in Titus (*sound doctrine*, 1:9; 2:1; *sound in faith*, 1:13; 2:2; *sound speech*, 2:8). In Titus, healthy doctrine and practice are contrasted with the unhealthy teaching and practice of the opponents.

However, there are also some differences between 1 Timothy and Titus. The tone of Titus is less urgent. Second-person imperatives rarely appear in Titus. Unlike 1 Timothy, Titus is not urged to *fight the good fight* (1 Tim 1:18), nor to *guard what has been entrusted to you* (6:20), nor to give heed to his ministry (4:11-16). There is no mention of endurance for Titus, no direct address or appeal, and only once is Titus told to *teach these things* (Titus 2:15, cf. NIV). "It is not that no urgency lies behind Titus; rather, the urgency is of a different kind, with different emphasis" (Fee 1988: 11). In Titus, more emphasis is placed on the church and its mission in the world, as seen in the use of the term *good works* (1:8, 16; 2:7, 14; 3:1, 8, 14) and concern that persons outside the church do not turn against Christianity (2:5-11; 3:1, 8). In Titus, household behavior becomes a means by which the church carries out its mission in the midst of first-century Greco-Roman culture. Again and again, Christian household behavior is prescribed in such a way *so that* the mission of the church moves forward (1:9; 2:5, 8, 10).

Titus begins with a comprehensive salutation (1:1-4). This salutation is followed by instruction on appointing elders and a bishop for the churches in Crete (1:5-9). Next come teachings against the opponents, whose teachings and manner of life are corrupt (1:10-16). In 2:1-10 we have instructions for family members on behavior within the household of faith, and in 3:1-2 instructions on how to relate to government and persons in the Cretan society. Two important confessional statements appear in 2:11-14 and 3:4-7. These confessional statements are Pauline in character but worded to fit the Cretan context. Again, there are instructions on how to respond to evildoers in 3:8b-11. After giving personal comments in 3:12-14, Paul closes the letter with final greetings in 3:15.

The letters to Timothy and Titus are arranged in the canon by descending length, making Titus last, with only forty-six verses. An alternative canonical order is found in the Muratorian Fragment and in a fourth-century commentary on the Pauline epistles by Ambrosiaster, which places Titus before 1 and 2 Timothy (Quinn 1990: 3). Some commentaries (e.g., Quinn [1990], I. H. Marshall [1999], and Witherington [2006]) treat Titus first among the three letters. Other commentaries (e.g., Mounce [2000], Collins [2002], and Towner [2006]) follow the canonical order, as does the present commentary.

Authorship

In addition to Paul, Luke's influence is found in Titus (Quinn 1990: 19). Approximately thirty-four words appear in the letters to Timothy and Titus that are found nowhere else in the New Testament except in Luke-Acts. As the Holy Spirit was poured out at Pentecost on the Jewish believers and on Cornelius, a Gentile believer (Acts 2:1-4; 10:45-48), so in Titus the Holy Spirit is *poured out on us richly through Jesus Christ our Savior* (Titus 3:6). The catalog of five vices to be avoided in Titus 1:7 corresponds with the traits of the untrustworthy servant in Luke 12:43-47. The teaching on uprightness for the church leader looks backward to the teaching of Jesus rather than some bourgeois Greco-Roman ethic now taken on by the church (Witherington 2006: 113).

Familiarity with the Roman world and its imperial religion is reflected in the words *God our Savior* (1:3). The emperor's promises are only a sham in comparison with the reality of God's salvation and rule. The medical terminology used metaphorically—*sound doctrine* (1:9; 2:1), *sound in faith* (1:13; 2:2) and *sound speech* (2:8)—may have come from Luke's purported medical profession. Religious terminology in the word group *godliness* is at home in the Greco-Roman world of Luke. The word group *self-control* (*sōphrōn*) appears in Titus 1:8; 2:2, 4-6, 12. This word group represents one of the cardinal virtues of Greek civilization. Its use in Titus indicates that the writer engages with the Hellenistic culture.

I suggest that both Paul and Luke wrote the letter to Titus. Many of the main ideas likely came from Paul and were put into writing at a later time by Luke. In doing so, Luke adapted Paul's thought to fit the immediate post-Pauline period of the church in the Hellenized world while retaining Paul's name (Titus 1:1). If so, the date of actual writing can be anywhere from the later years of Paul's life (AD 64-67) to the later years of Luke's life.

OUTLINE

Salutation, 1:1-4
Appointment of Church Leaders, 1:5-9
Opponents, 1:10-16
Family Relationships in the Church, 2:1-10, 3:1-2
Confessional Statement on God's Grace, 2:11-14
God's Transforming Work in Christ and in the Holy Spirit, 3:3-8
Final Exhortations and Warnings, 3:9-11
Personal Instructions, 3:12-14
Final Greetings, 3:15

Titus 1:1-4

Salutation

PREVIEW

The salutation to Titus—one long, sixty-five-word sentence—is the longest of the letters to Timothy and Titus. Only the salutation of Paul's epistle to Romans is longer (1:1-7). The difference in length lies primarily in Paul's emphasis on God's salvation history, which centers in Jesus Christ (Titus 1:4). Paul's own role and purpose as an apostle who is proclaiming salvation also receives major attention.

As with the standard form of secular letter writing in the ancient world, the salutation contains the sender's name, the name of the person addressed, and a greeting. Paul expands all three parts to set forth his authority as the main author of this epistle, to identify the Christian character of the recipients, and to emphasize the Christian nature of the greeting.

OUTLINE

The Sender, 1:1-3
The Addressee, 1:4a
The Greeting, 1:4b

EXPLANATORY NOTES

The Sender 1:1-3

Paul describes himself as *slave of God and an apostle of Jesus Christ* (NRSV footnote). Of the 124 times the word *slave* (*doulos*) is used in the NT, 30 are in the Pauline epistles, including Titus 2:9; 1 Timothy 6:1; and 2 Timothy 2:24. A slave in the Hellenistic world was mere property belonging totally to the owner, without rights, family, or home ownership. As Moses was God's slave (Deut 34:5; Josh 1:1-2), so also Jesus took upon himself the form of a slave (Phil 2:7). Similarly, Paul is totally committed to God. He is neither a human's slave (Gal 1:1) nor Nero's slave (2 Tim 1:8), but a *slave of God*. Paul does not view his role as lack of freedom so much as carrying out God's work, which is in line with other great leaders in Israel's history. Paul is totally committed to God, and his energy is exerted in carrying out God's mission and purpose in the world.

As a slave, Paul has a task to fulfill: he is an apostle of Jesus Christ. Paul repeatedly uses the term *apostle* to define himself and his work. The term *apostle* indicates the calling given to him by the risen Jesus Christ (Gal 1:12). Paul is an authoritative witness of the resurrected Lord. As such, the apostle Paul is an agent of divine revelation, and his message carries divine authority among the congregations emerging out of his missionary work. As *apostle*, Paul comes on the scene like a herald dispatched by a victorious king, announcing a triumphal appearance (Quinn 1990: 62). This king is none other than the resurrected Lord Jesus Christ.

Instead of defending his apostolic claim at length, as in Galatians 1:1-12, Paul immediately describes the purpose of his ministry. He is an apostle *for the sake of the faith of God's elect* (Titus 1:1). Jewish Christians in Crete easily recognize the significance of *God's elect*. The OT often speaks of the elect, meaning God's people. Here in Titus 1:1, *the faith of God's elect* means the Jewish people who live by faith or who come to a faith commitment to Jesus Christ and thereby are the true continuation of the people of God. This interpretation is substantiated by the definition *and the knowledge of the truth that is in accordance with godliness* (1:1b). Faith and knowledge are brought together, indicating that the faith Paul is talking about is tied to knowledge of the truth. *Truth* in the letters to Timothy and Titus refers to the gospel.

The connection between faith and knowledge in Titus 1:1 suggests a knowledge that is not only correct intellectual understanding, but also a matter of life commitment (Collins: 304). It is more than embracing God's revelation. It also implies a commitment to God's revelation and salvation in Jesus Christ that rejects all competing messages. This faith and knowledge of the truth is further defined as *in accordance with godliness*. *Godliness*, a term for authentic Christianity, is directly related to truth. Godliness is visible Christianity. It is right faith. It is the faith of persons who believe in Jesus Christ and live in faithfulness to him [*Godliness, p. 346*]. It is what Paul calls sound (healthy) doctrine in 1:9 and 2:1. With these additional definitions, we conclude that *the faith of God's elect* really refers to those who commit their lives to Jesus Christ and who live in obedience to him.

A second purpose is given for Paul's apostolic ministry. He is an apostle *in the hope of eternal life* (Titus 1:2a). One goal of faith and knowledge is the hope of eternal life. Hope has its foundation in the promises of God revealed in salvation history. Certainty of eternal life rests on two qualities of God's character: God *promised* it *before the ages began*. And God *never lies*. God's truthfulness and absence of deceit are well-attested in the Scriptures. Therefore, God's promise of eternal life before the ages began is sure and reliable.

Paul strengthens the foundation for eternal life by saying that God promised it *before* time began. Two words for time in Titus 1:2b and 3a strengthen the argument. The first word, *chronos*, means ongoing time. The words *before the ages*, or *before the beginning of time* (TNIV), mean the promise of eternal life came prior to creation, before time began, or literally, before all ages (see 2 Tim 1:9). The second word, *kairos*, means an opportune moment in time. Here *kairos* is translated *in due time*. At this opportune time *he [God] revealed his word through the proclamation* (Titus 1:3a). At this especially suitable time for the coming of the good news, the apostles now proclaim salvation in Jesus Christ. God's timeless promise of eternal life has now come to the people of Crete through Paul's preaching.

To assure persons in Crete that this gospel is for them, Paul adds *with which I have been entrusted by the command of God our Savior* (1:3b). With these words Paul returns to the beginning of the sentence in verse 1: his apostleship. Paul's preaching arises out of God's *command,* indicating that he is under royal orders. Hence, Paul's preaching and apostleship arise out of a sacred trust (see 1 Cor 9:17; Gal 2:7; 1 Tim 1:11; 2 Tim 1:11). He is on a legitimate mission in that his apostolic call has arisen from God's command and ties Paul the person-as-apostle with the Christ event and salvation rather than any human authority (I. H. Marshall 1999: 131).

This apostolic command has come to Paul from *God our Savior*, the One who promised eternal life before time began and has now revealed the good news of salvation in Jesus Christ. In contrast, the Greco-Roman world used the term *Savior* for pagan gods, including the supreme god Zeus and his daughter Artemis. The term *Savior* was also used for various helpers, such as Asclepius, the god of healing, and especially for the Roman emperors. Paul boldly declares that the Savior is not one of the political emperors or civic benefactors, but is the God of the Hebrew tradition, who promised eternal life before the ages began and is now making it known through Paul's preaching *[Names for God and the Imperial Cult, p. 357]*.

The Addressee 1:4a

Finally, after one long sentence comprising verses 1 to 3, Paul identifies the person addressed in the letter: *Titus*. Titus is Paul's *loyal child in the faith*. Coming from pagan background with a Roman name, Titus likely became a Christian at Antioch, perhaps under Paul's preaching and teaching. Along with Barnabas, Titus traveled with Paul to the Jerusalem conference (Gal 2:1, 3). Paul described Titus as his brother, partner, and fellow worker when he sent him to the Corinthian congregation to settle their disputes (2 Cor 2:13; 8:23). As with Timothy (1 Tim 1:2), Titus's relationship with Paul is likened to a father-son relationship. As a loyal child from near the beginning of Paul's ministry until its very end (2 Tim 4:10), Titus is well qualified to give leadership to the churches in Crete *[Titus, p. 365]*.

The Greeting 1:4b

The salutation concludes with Paul's standard Greek and Hebrew greeting, *grace and peace* from God the Father and Christ Jesus. Whereas this standard greeting normally comes from Christ Jesus our Lord, or Jesus Christ our Lord, here it is *Christ Jesus our Savior* (Titus 1:4b). In describing Jesus as Savior, Paul reverses the order in verse 1, where Paul is an apostle of Jesus Christ and salvation comes from God. Now Jesus is also Savior. This reversed order agrees with Titus 2:13, where Jesus is identified both as *God and Savior*, and with Titus 3:6, where Paul talks about *Jesus Christ our Savior*. Paul does not use the title *Lord* for Jesus in this letter. In Titus, *Savior* refers to both God and Jesus, in contrast to the Greco-Roman practice of calling political leaders "savior."

Titus 1:5-9

Appointment of Church Leaders

PREVIEW

Paul immediately states the purpose for writing to Titus. Unlike the other Pauline epistles (except for Galatians), there is no thanksgiving at the beginning of this epistle. Instead, Paul states the reason Titus was left behind in Crete: to finish the missionary task of organizing these new congregations by appointing church leaders in every town. Titus must appoint elders so that those are not teaching healthy doctrine cannot gain a foothold in these new congregations (1:10-16). Titus's task is not so much rooting out error as it is putting leaders in place whose teaching will prevent error from creeping into the church.

Elders are to be appointed in every town, indicating that small communities of Christian believers had emerged in many towns on this island in the Mediterranean Sea. Persons qualified to be chosen as elders must be blameless. Then Paul changes the language from elders to bishop (singular) and notes several vices that disqualify a person for this leadership role. Titus must look for personal virtues in appointing someone as bishop in the church. These virtues culminate in a firm grasp of the apostolic understanding of Christian faith so that the bishop's preaching and teaching will lead these new Christian communities to maturity and thereby refute those opposed to sound Christian doctrine.

OUTLINE

Charge to Titus, 1:5
Appointment of Elders, 1:6
Appointment of a Bishop, 1:7-9

EXPLANATORY NOTES

Charge to Titus 1:5

Cretan civilization goes back at least to the Late Bronze Age and from the second century BC onward, a large Jewish population lived on the island (Collins: 320). Although historians are unable to say when the church first began in Crete, 1:5-9 indicates that these Christian communities are young. When Paul says *I left you behind in Crete* (Titus 1:5), he means he also had been on this island and had then gone elsewhere. Now Titus is given the charge to finish the work and to appoint elders as Paul's normal way of arranging leadership for new mission churches (Acts 14:21-23). There are no comments in this letter about removing bad elders. Instead, Titus is to appoint elders where previously there were none. No mention is made of deacons or anyone other than Titus until the final greetings in Titus 3:12-13. Nothing is said about choosing a newly converted person as elder, as we find in 1 Timothy 3:6. Instead, Titus is to choose elders whose children are Christian believers (1:6). Taken together, these comments may suggest a Christian community not more than ten years old. In short, here is a new church without an administrative structure facing pressure from opponents.

Titus's commission is presented in a twofold way. He is to *put in order what remained to be done* and *to appoint elders in every town* (Titus 1:5). The first part of the commission indicates that more work was needed to establish these churches. A special part of the remaining work was to appoint elders in every town. The verb *appoint* also means "to put in charge" (BDAG: 492). Though some translate the term *ordain*, none of the other occurrences of this word in the NT supports this translation (Luke 12:14; Acts 7:10, 27, 35; Heb 5:1; 7:28; 8:3). The phrase *as I directed you* (Titus 1:5b) is strong language and indicates that just as Paul is under the command of God to proclaim the gospel as an apostle (Titus 1:3b), so too is Titus under authoritative command to exercise leadership over the churches in Crete.

Appointment of Elders 1:6

Building on the Jewish synagogue model, elders became the earliest form of congregational leadership in the NT church (Acts 11:30; 14:23; 15:2, 4, 6, 22-23; 16:4; 20:17; 21:18). *Elders* is a collective term for a small group of leaders—often older—who provide leadership for a congregation. Historically, elders were wise men in the Jewish community. They had authority over the people—not because of their age, but because of who they were as respected persons.

A general qualification heads the list. Titus is to appoint *someone who is blameless*. As in 1 Timothy 3:2, where the leader is to be *above reproach*, so here the elder is to be blameless, without a basis for criticism. The same is said for the bishop in Titus 1:7. *Blameless* is a comprehensive virtue. The accompanying virtues in verse 6 lay out the areas of life in which the elder is to be blameless. Why such a high standard of behavior? The church's leaders, as Towner says, must exhibit "the highest moral standard in all aspects of life; to expect less is to place the church's reputation and ministry in jeopardy" (Towner 1994: 224). Paul wants the leaders of the congregation to live up to the basic standards of Christianity so that the church's witness is not hindered. The integrity of the church's leaders or lack thereof has a direct tie to the integrity of the church's message.

From this comprehensive virtue come two other major virtues centered in family life. A blameless elder is one who is *married only once* and *whose children are believers* (Titus 1:6). *Married only once* may be interpreted several ways (see also the comments on 1 Tim 3:2):

1. It could mean married at least once. Thus, one never married is disqualified. This interpretation is supported by Jewish tradition. The first words spoken by God to human beings were "Be fruitful and multiply" (Gen 1:28). The Jewish rabbinic tradition interpreted God's words in Genesis 1:28 as one of the 247 mandatory commands in the Torah. The rabbis said, "You should perpetuate the human race by marrying according to the Law" (via Collins: 321). However, this rabbinic interpretation, if applied to Titus 1:6a, would disqualify the apostle Paul himself, unless 1 Corinthians 9:5 means that he once had a wife.
2. It could mean that a polygynous man (having more than one wife) is disqualified. Polygamy was practiced in some places in the ancient world (cf. Gen 29–30; Judg 8:30; 1 Sam 1:2; 2 Sam 5:13; 1 Kings 11:3) and was banned at Qumran, indicating that some male Jews were polygynous. Polyandry (having more than one husband) is forbidden for women given special duties in the church (1 Tim 5:9). Yet polyandry and polygyny are not symmetrical in the same culture (Quinn 1990: 85).

3. It could mean that a man who is divorced from his first wife is disqualified if he marries a second time.
4. It could even mean that a man whose first wife dies is disqualified if he marries a second time.
5. It could simply be a requirement for marital fidelity.

This last interpretation seems most likely, given that the letters to Timothy and Titus emphasize honesty, integrity, and sexual holiness.

Domestic life is taken a step further in that the person qualified to be appointed as an elder is one *whose children are believers, not accused of debauchery and not rebellious* (Titus 1:6b). Having believing children may mean children who willingly accept the Christian faith, which characterizes their father. Or it can mean they conduct themselves in the manner of faithful Christians. Both interpretations suggest that the elder's children are not to be stubborn or headstrong. The word *debauchery* has a wide range of meaning, such as drunkenness (Eph 5:18), excessive behavior with regard to money (Luke 15:13), and gluttony (Prov 28:7). Here in Titus 1:6b the word points to a wild, uncontrolled lifestyle, as seen in the wayward prodigal son's life described in Luke 15:11-19. *Rebellious* means headstrong, disobedient, and insubordinate. The word is used in the LXX to describe the behavior of Eli's sons in 1 Samuel 2:12 (Symmachus, trans.; cf. 10:27). Persons chosen as elders in the churches in Crete were converts to Christianity who were householders and heads of families. Their integrity in marriage and their ability to raise God-fearing children said much about their ability to exercise leadership in the church.

Appointment of a Bishop 1:7-9

In Titus 1:7, Paul moves from the qualifications of an elder to the qualifications for a bishop. Again, *blameless* is given as a general requirement, followed by several vices and virtues. Many commentaries suggest that the word *bishop* (*episkopos*) is the Greek equivalent of the Jewish term for elder (*presbyteros*), implying that the word *elder* indicates the man's status and *bishop* implies his overseer function (Collins: 322). Exegetically, this way of interpreting takes the word *bishop* in verse 7 as a generic singular for a group of elders in verse 6. However, we can see a major difference between elder and bishop in the difference between the plural form for elders and the singular form for bishop. In Titus 1:7, the bishop is identified as *God's steward,* which is not said of elders. As God's steward, the bishop is in charge of God's house (1 Tim 3:5; 15; 2 Tim 2:20-21) and is accountable to God to discharge the duties of oversight and teaching in the church. Moreover a major qualification for a bishop is the ability to teach (Titus 1:9; 1 Tim 3:2b). Though a distinction can be made between teaching elders and ruling elders in 1 Timothy 5:17, the weight of evidence seems to point in the direction of calling out one person from among the elders who is especially gifted in management and teaching as the bishop of the congregation.

Although Paul emphasizes the domestic relationships of the elder in verse 6, he turns to personal vices and virtues for the bishop in verses 7-9. These personal vices and virtues are likely illustrative rather than exhaustive. He lists several vices, each marked by the negative word *not* in verse 7. The first two deal with personal character deficiencies. First, the bishop *must not be arrogant*. This term is not used in 1 Timothy 3 and may suggest a common vice in Crete (I. H. Marshall 1999: 161). The term ranges from the narrower sense of being self-willed and stubborn to the wider sense of being arrogant. It is a trait of opposing teachers (Prov 21:24; 2 Pet 2:10). Second, the bishop is not to be *quick-tempered*. This personal trait means inclined to the kind of anger that leads to explosive action—a vice that threatens human relationships. Third, the bishop is not to be *addicted to wine* (see also 1 Tim 3:3). Literally, the term means to be drunk or known as a drunkard. It implies rowdy behavior and lack of self-control, which are characteristics of drunkards. Fourth, the bishop is not to be *violent*, whether through physical violence or verbal abuse. And fifth, as in 1 Timothy 3:3, the bishop is not to be *greedy for gain*. Using religion as a means for financial gain is a trait of the unhealthy teachers (Titus 1:11). A dishonest person in business practices cannot be chosen as bishop, nor can one whose motivation is to achieve financial gain out of Christian service. Because the bishop is in charge of the church as God's house and handles the finances of the congregation, he must be fiscally trustworthy.

A number of contrasting virtues, introduced by the strong adversative *but*, follow in the text (1:8-9). First, the bishop *must be hospitable*. He is to love the stranger. Hospitality characterized the first-century Mediterranean culture much more than modern Western culture. The Christian household received fellow Christian refugees into their homes from other areas of the Roman Empire. As overseer of the house of God, the bishop welcomes visitors, provides lodging for travelers, and welcomes fellow Christians to the Eucharist.

Second, the bishop must be *a lover of goodness*. In contrast to unbelievers who love themselves (2 Tim 3:2), the bishop loves what is good and upright and is able to discern the difference between good and evil. Third, the bishop is *prudent*: he is able to control himself (Titus 2:2, 5;

1 Tim 3:2). Self-discipline is one of the cardinal virtues that marks a person of true character (Towner 2006: 689). Fourth, the bishop is *upright*, holy in conduct, and treats other people with justice (Titus 2:12; 1 Tim 1:9; 2 Tim 2:22). Fifth, the bishop is *devout*; his inward piety finds outward expression in worship of God. He is pure and holy in his devoutness so that his outward expression of piety is an honest expression of the inward self. Sixth, the bishop is *self-controlled [Self-Control, p. 363]*. A bishop must maintain control of self to be effective in leading the church. Self-control is a fruit of the Spirit (Gal 5:23).

Finally comes the seventh and last virtue required of a bishop. *He must have a firm grasp of the Word that is trustworthy in accordance with the teaching, so that he may be able both to preach with sound doctrine and to refute those who contradict it* (Titus 1:9). A bishop is a student of God's Word, a Bible teaching scholar-in-residence who is able to teach and preach sound doctrine. In addition to administration, the one major task of the bishop in the letters to Timothy and Titus is the ability to teach (1 Tim 3:2; 2 Tim 2:24; Titus 1:9). A bishop must have a firm grasp of the Word. He must hold fast to a clearly defined word and not just cling to any word. He is to hold fast to the word that is in accordance with *the teaching* of the apostles. The call to teach includes not only the activity and skill of teaching but also the right content of teaching. What is taught must be in agreement with the apostolic teaching that is handed down from Paul to Titus. Teaching includes the apostolic way of interpreting the OT in light of the coming of Jesus Christ and in keeping with faith and life in Christ. This kind of teaching will exhort the faithful and correct the opponents (Titus 1:9b). It is a trustworthy word in contrast to the unhealthy teachings of the Cretans, about which we learn in Titus 1:10-16.

The importance of having a firm grasp on this trustworthy word finds expression in two purpose clauses translated *so that he may be able both to exhort . . . and . . . to refute . . .* (GNT). The first purpose clause calls for the ability to exhort. The word *exhort* (*parakaleō*), translated *preaching* in the NRSV, is frequently used in the letters to Timothy and Titus to give commands by church leaders. It means to encourage, but in this context carries the idea of urging Christian believers to *sound doctrine*. *Sound teaching* is both doctrinal and ethical and occurs often in Timothy and in Titus. The word *sound* is a medical term meaning "healthy or life-giving." Luke uses this term for physical health (Luke 5:31; 7:10; 15:27). By teaching in accordance with what has been handed down by the apostles, Titus will develop spiritually healthy minds in the Christian believers. This is the opposite of the sick, unhealthy teaching of the opponents seen in Titus 1:10-11.

A second purpose clause arises immediately: *and to refute those who contradict it. Refute* suggests a strong rebuttal, as indicated by the charge to *rebuke them* [*the Cretans*] *strongly* in Titus 1:13, where the same Greek word is used. The word translated *refute* and *rebuke* is the antithesis of exhorting the believers. The best way of preventing error is to teach sound doctrine. Both the negative purpose of rebuking those who contradict the trustworthy word of the apostles and the positive purpose of exhorting the believers with healthy doctrine can be achieved when a bishop has a firm grasp of God's Word. There is no better way for church leaders to provide a healthy diet of teaching and to refute those opposed to Christian truth than immersing oneself in the living Word of God. Surely the bishop will be skilled both in management and ability to teach.

THE TEXT IN BIBLICAL CONTEXT

The Teacher in Biblical Perspective

Teaching God's Word has a long tradition in the Bible. In early Israel, parents were commanded to teach their children:

> Hear, O Israel: The LORD is our God, the LORD alone. You shall love the LORD your God with all your heart, and with all your soul, and with all your might. Keep these words that I am commanding you today in your heart. Recite them to your children and talk about them when you are at home and when you are away, when you lie down and when you rise. Bind them as a sign on your hand, fix them as an emblem on your forehead, and write them on the doorposts of your house and on your gates. (Deut 6:4-9)

The children of Israel received God's statutes for their good and as a basis for their life (Deut 6:24).

Jeremiah wrote, "For instruction shall not perish from the priest, nor counsel from the wise, nor the word from the prophet" (18:18). While the prophets gave oracles and the wise gave counsel, priests were specifically responsible for instruction. The occasional word of the prophet was not always true, since false prophets also existed in Jeremiah's day (28:1-17). Thus the role of instructor became increasing important as priests such as Ezra read the Torah before the people in late Judaism (Neh 8:1-12). By putting the Torah and God at the center, the Jewish community survived through the centuries even when it had no temple, king, or national boundaries.

In the intertestamental period, three groups of people gave special attention to the Torah. Scribes took responsibility for the theoretical development of the law, rabbis taught the law, and lawyers administered the law. Professional rabbis taught by expositing the law and then carefully summarizing its teaching in a few sentences, which their ten to twelve followers learned by memory. Disciples paid careful attention to their rabbi so they could "receive" the word and then faithfully "deliver" that word to the next generation. Paul used similar terminology when he said that he delivered to the Corinthian believers what he received concerning Jesus from the early church leaders in Jerusalem (1 Cor 11:23; 15:3). In one piece of rabbinic literature, this process of receiving and delivering the law is described as follows (Barrett 1987: 177-80):

> Moses received the Law from Sinai and committed it to Joshua, and Joshua to the elders, and the elders to the Prophets; and the Prophets committed it to the men of the Great Synagogue. (Mishnah *'Aboth* 1.1; Danby: 446)
>
> Hillel and Shammai received the Law from them. (1.12; Danby: 447)
>
> Rabban Johanan b. Zakkai received [the Law] from Hillel and from Shammai. . . . Eliezer b. Hyrcanus is a plastered cistern which loses not a drop. (2.8; Danby: 448)

In rabbinic circles, to teach meant to expound the law as the sum of the revealed will of God for ordering the relationship between the individual and God as well as the individual and the neighbor. Of the ninety-five occurrences of the verb *teach* in the NT, two-thirds are in the Gospels and the first part of Acts. Teaching played a central role in Jesus' public ministry. As a Jewish rabbi, Jesus taught by expounding the Law's meaning about how one relates to God and to a neighbor (Matt 22:37-39). However, Jesus' teaching differed from that of the rabbis so much that the crowds were astonished at his teaching, "for he taught them as one having authority, and not as their scribes" (7:29).

The kingdom of God was the central theme of Jesus' teaching. Jesus constantly appealed to the will of humankind, calling for a decision to follow the will of God or to reject it. Moreover, Jesus fulfilled the law in his own person. By his word, by his person as Son of God, and by his life of faithfulness to God, Jesus surpassed the OT law as the revealed will of God and thereby brought the law to its fullness and completion (Matt 5:17; Rom 10:4). In the Sermon on the Mount we see the phrase, "You have heard that it was said, . . . but I say to you. . . " (Matt 5:21-22, 27-28, 31-32, 33-34, 38-39, 43-44).

Early Christian preaching and teaching presented Jesus as Lord and Messiah (Acts 2:36). From the OT Scriptures, the early Christians taught accurately the things concerning Jesus (18:25). The will of God is seen in Jesus. The summons to live according to the way of Jesus in moral conduct became the teaching content of the apostles. In Paul's letters, the content of preaching and teaching is Jesus Christ as Savior and Lord (Rom 10:9; 2 Cor 4:5; Col 1:15-20; Phil 2:5-11). Jesus revealed God fully (Col 1:19; 2:9). Therefore, the "truth is in Jesus" (Eph 4:21), and Jesus is the model for ethical behavior (Rom 8:29; 2 Cor 3:18; Phil 2:5; Col 3:1-3).

Paul cites *apostle, prophet,* and *teacher* as gifts (1 Cor 12:28-30; Eph 4:11). Apostles were given apostolic authority because they were witnesses of the resurrected Lord, and divine revelation was granted to them. Paul regarded teachers as office gifts and an integral part of the church (Rom 12:7; 1 Cor 12:28-30; Gal 6:6; Eph 4:11). Teaching was the first gift to take on a more professional role in the church (Gal 6:6). Authority rested largely upon the content of teaching, which needed to conform to apostolic tradition. Paul lists the gifts of prophecy and teaching side by side, indicating that the teaching function in the church is an indispensable complement to prophecy (Dunn: 583). Teaching preserves continuity, while prophecy gives a sense of immediacy and life. In the letters to Timothy and Titus, there is less emphasis on prophecy (1 Tim 4:14) and more emphasis on teaching (1 Tim 2:7; 3:2; 4:11; 6:1-2; 2 Tim 1:11; 2:2, 24; 4:2; Titus 1:9, 11).

In the letters to Timothy and Titus, Paul uses paraenetic forms of teaching in topics of moral concern, vice and virtue lists, and codes of household behavior. Thus, one chosen as bishop in the churches of Ephesus and Crete *must have a firm grasp of the word that is trustworthy in accordance with the teaching, so that he may be able both to preach with sound doctrine and to refute those who contradict it* (Titus 1:9). Having a firm grasp of the word means understanding the whole Bible interpreted through God's fullness of revelation in Jesus Christ, as set forth by apostolic teaching. This firm grasp of the Word is necessary so that the bishop can be *an apt teacher* (1 Tim 3:2; 2 Tim 2:24; Titus 1:9) who preaches and teaches sound doctrine and refutes those who contradict it.

THE TEXT IN THE LIFE OF THE CHURCH

Teachers of God's Word

In the sixteenth century Dirk Philips, an Anabaptist leader in Holland, wrote:

> Out of this it follows forcefully that the ministers of Christ, the teachers and bishops in his congregations, must have the Holy Spirit through whom they first and before all things must be well instructed in God's Word. The common people will err and walk in darkness if the teachers themselves are unwise.... Therefore, I say again, that the teachers themselves must before

> all things be well-instructed and taught in God's Word. As it is written, "For the lips of a priest should guard knowledge, that one may seek the law from his mouth, for he is the messenger of the LORD of hosts," Mal. 2:7. And Paul says that "a bishop must hold firm to the sure Word, so that he may be able to give instruction in saving doctrine and to admonish those who contradict it," Titus 1:9. (Dyck, Keeney, and Beachy: 203-4)

In Titus 1:9 the bishop *must have a firm grasp of the word.* The office of oversight goes beyond administration of the congregation to minding the faith, keeping congregations focused on core values, and assisting congregations in spiritual discernment on theological issues. A bishop's task is to make sure the content of the church's teaching is trustworthy, in accordance with apostolic teaching.

Along with the question of *being* (what kind of person is qualified to lead the church?) and *doing* (what skills are needed for congregational leaders?) is the question of *knowing.* What must the congregational leader *know* in order to lead God's people? And what must an overseer or bishop *know* to be an effective leader? The bishop must know the good news of Jesus Christ, which has come through apostolic teaching.

In the history of the church, special schools for training pastors arose precisely for this purpose. In North America, Presbyterians established Princeton Theological Seminary in 1812. Methodists, Baptists, and other denominations likewise established seminaries. Believers churches established seminaries later than Catholic and mainline Protestant denominations. Mennonites in Holland started a theological seminary in Amsterdam in 1735. The Church of the Brethren started a seminary in 1905. North American Mennonites relied on informal training for several years, then started Bible schools and Bible institutes. North American Mennonites also started seminaries, the first in 1868.

As with other Christian traditions, believers churches desire congregational leaders who have a firm grasp of the Word of God. While Anabaptist churches emphasize community discernment, they also make room in the congregation for the teacher trained in the Word of God. Pastors and overseers shape the spiritual community more than anyone else. While all members of a given congregation enter into the biblical interpretation process, trained pastors have a privileged position at the hermeneutical table. When they fail to lay hold of this responsibility, congregational leaders contribute to an interpretive Babel and forfeit their nurturing role (Sawatzky: 81). Overseers who mind the faith and guide congregations, conferences, and denominations in the true gospel carry an important and necessary role in the life of the church. As believers churches grow through mission in other parts of the world, institutions for pastoral education also arise.

Titus 1:10-16

Opponents

PREVIEW

Having laid out the task of the bishop as one who refutes opposing teaching by preaching and teaching sound doctrine (1:9), Paul exposes the Cretan opponents in Titus 1:10-16. Their teaching has a local flavor in that the Hellenistic Jews, *those of the circumcision*, are opposing the truth. By reminding them of a self-deprecating comment from one of their own prophets (1:12), Paul encourages Titus to deal with their unhealthy thought and life directly. Fearing that the young church in Crete may be severely damaged by the opponents, Paul instructs Titus to rebuke them so that they and the church may become healthy in Christian faith (1:13). This rebuke is necessary because of the extent and influence of the error.

Paul describes the hypocrisy of their ritualism in verse 14 and gives a summary of their situation in verse 15a. Moving beyond their outward life to the inward self, from which behavior comes (v. 15b), Paul declares that their thinking and moral discernment are corrupt. Though outwardly they have professed to know God, their actions actually indicate that they deny God and are unfit for any good work (v. 16). The opponents think they can separate belief from practice, but their practice actually indicates wrong belief. On the one hand, Titus must rebuke these opponents sharply (1:13). On the other hand, he must appoint leaders (elders and bishop) who will live and teach the truth of the gospel so that a healthy church can emerge in Crete (1:5-9, 13b). A full description of the opponents' teaching is not given. But Paul indicates they are *of the circumcision* (v. 10b), they are *paying attention to Jewish myths* (v. 14a), and they *reject the truth* (v. 14b). These descriptive phrases suggest that the opponents are turning away from the apostolic teaching of the gospel.

OUTLINE

Why Opponents Need to Be Rebuked, 1:10-11
Appeal to a Cretan Prophet, 1:12-13
Response to the Teaching of the Opponents, 1:13-16

EXPLANATORY NOTES

Why Opponents Need to Be Rebuked 1:10-11

Titus 1:10 and 11 comprise one sentence in Greek, in which Paul gives three reasons for the need to rebuke these opponents. First, their teaching grows out of their rebellion, and it is idle talk and deceptive (10a). Second, they are upsetting whole households (v. 11a). And third, they are teaching for sordid gain (v. 11b).

Paul refers to *many rebellious people* (10a), indicating that the number of opponents is large. These persons are defiant and refuse to submit to apostolic authority and the gospel. They also are guilty of empty words, speech without meaning or substance. And they are deceptive. Their teaching leads others in a false direction. The phrase *especially those of the circumcision* (v. 10b) identifies a major part of the opponent group. Paul uses the phrase *of the circumcision* elsewhere of Jews (Rom 4:12) and of Jewish Christians (Gal 2:7, 12; Col 4:11; cf. Acts 10:45; 11:2). There were many Hellenistic Jews in Crete, and some of them likely have become Christians. Thus it is reasonable to assume that some of Paul's opponents are Hellenistic Jews.

With direct, blunt language, Paul tells Titus that these opponents *must be silenced* to prevent their teaching from spreading (Titus 1:11a). The term *silenced* means to stop the mouth. The verb refers to restricting horses by muzzling their mouths (Collins: 333). In literary Greek, the term is used for silencing opponents in debate (I. H. Marshall 1999: 196 n. 116). The opponents are actually *disrupting whole households* (v. 11 TNIV), not just leading a few persons astray.

While the full contents of these opposing views are not specified, the underlying motive of the opponents is clear. They teach *for the sake of dishonest gain* (v. 11b TNIV). Greed and dishonest gain are well-known elements in the traditional criticism of Cretan behavior (I. H. Marshall 1999: 198). From the larger Cretan culture, the opponents have absorbed a sinful motive. Greedy for shameful gain, the opponents use unhealthy teaching to fill their pockets with money, as do the Ephesian teachers (1 Tim 6:5-10). Their teaching is counterfeit, their underlying motive is greed, and their work is disrupting Christian households. In contrast, the true leader of God's people must not be greedy for gain (1 Tim 3:3, 8; Titus 1:7).

Appeal to a Cretan Prophet 1:12-13a

Paul buttresses accusations against the opponents by turning to a self-deprecating proverbial saying from one of the Cretans' own prophets. *Cretans are always liars, evil brutes, lazy gluttons* (Titus 1:12 TNIV). Many scholars identify this threefold accusation with Epimenides, a sixth-century BC poet. By quoting this self-deprecating saying from one of their own prophets, Paul does not necessarily say that he agrees with the statement. Ironically, if this statement is true, and if the one who said this was a Cretan, then not *all* Cretans *always* lie, because this one once said the truth, . . . which makes the proverb a lie! But it is probably a mistake to insist on tight logic here. Surely not everyone has always lied. The statement simply affirms in a general way that some Cretans have deprecated their culture with this derogatory quote. Cretans lied in claiming to have the tomb of Zeus. Callimachus, a Cretan poet of the third century BC, wrote, "Cretans are always liars. For a tomb, O Lord, Cretans built for you; but you did not die, for you are forever" (via Mounce: 399).

What does this threefold accusation include? First, they are *always liars. Always* is a general way of saying that the Cretans deride their own culture as lacking honesty. Second, *evil brutes* means the Cretans are known for wild behavior, much like animals. The term *evil* combined with the term *brutes* suggests beasts of prey and was applied to rude, course people in Greek literature (I. H. Marshall 1999: 201). And third, they are *lazy gluttons*. The self-deprecating Cretans, according to their prophet, do not want to work, but they do want to fill their stomachs. Their sensuality expressed in gluttony indicates their desire for self-gratification.

Paul responds to the Cretan culture by informing Titus, *For this reason rebuke them sharply* (1:13a). The force of the adverb *sharply* with the imperative verb is extremely strong. Titus must declare a strong "No!" to the Cretan opponents so that they and their followers can hear God's great "Yes!" in the gospel of Jesus Christ. The command *Rebuke them sharply* is followed by a purpose clause, *so that they may become sound in the faith* (1:13b). Titus dare not compromise. Urgent action is needed to correct the situation, with the goal of leading the opponents and their followers to spiritual health. Paul believes the Cretan opponents may repent and turn back to the true faith. The phrase *sound in the faith* means to be healthy in the faith. By affirming the truth of the gospel of Jesus Christ, in contrast to the opponents' denial of it, Titus will promote a healthy faith (1 Tim 1:10-11).

Response to the Teaching of the Opponents 1:13b-16

To become sound in faith, they must lay aside the evil thoughts and practices described in verses 14-16. They must *pay no attention to Jewish myths or to the merely human commands of those who reject the truth* (Titus 1:14 TNIV). The twofold accusation charges them with following Jewish myths and human commands. Myths are condemned elsewhere in the NT (1 Tim 1:4; 4:7; 2 Tim 4:4; 2 Pet 1:16) and refer to legends that are contrary to the truth (Knight 1992: 300). Here in Titus 1:14 they are identified as *Jewish* myths. It is not entirely clear what the author means by *Jewish myths*, but the author understands them as human commandments that are opposed to God. These human commandments go against the truth.

Paul employs the language of ritual purity to summarize the opponents' situation. *To the pure all things are pure, but to the corrupt and unbelieving nothing is pure* (1:15). The term *pure* occurs three times in this summary, but nowhere else in Titus. Jesus taught against traditional understandings of ritual purity in Mark 7:1-9 and stated, "It is not what goes into the mouth that defiles a person, but it is what comes out of the mouth that defiles" (Matt 15:11). In Romans 14:20, Paul said, "Everything is indeed clean." In contrast to biblical ritual laws, Peter learned through a vision and in contact with a Gentile named Cornelius that some rejected food was clean. Peter exclaimed, "God has shown me that I should not call anyone profane or unclean" (Acts 10:28). In the first part of the summary statement, *to the pure all things are pure* (Titus 1:15), Paul indicates that one's outward purity arises out of inward moral purity, what Jesus called purity of heart (Matt 5:8). Purity of heart is similar to the virtue of devoutness that qualifies a person to be bishop (Titus 1:8).

Antithetical parallelism exists between *all things* in the first part of the summary and *nothing* in the second part of the summary. *But to the corrupt and unbelieving, nothing is pure* means that unless the inward person is made pure by the gospel of Jesus Christ, outward ritual purity amounts to nothing. Those who do not believe are inwardly defiled, and their outward life, including religious piety, is not pure at all. The real problem is not ceremonial, but moral. Those living in a state of moral defilement are not true Christian believers.

Why is this? Paul answers, *In fact, both their minds and consciences are corrupted* (Titus 1:15b TNIV). "By saying that the defilement is in their mind and conscience, Paul signifies that it is internal and thus intrinsically moral and religious" (Knight 1992: 303). The problem is not external, such as marriage and defilement through food (1 Tim 4:3), but internal: corrupt minds and consciences. With these words, Paul uses the language of Hellenistic anthropology to say that the defiled are totally corrupt (Collins: 336). The term *mind* refers to one's thinking ability or way of thinking. As elsewhere in Paul, when the mind is controlled by sin, one's way of thinking goes off track (Rom 1:28; Eph 4:17; 1 Tim 6:5; 2 Tim 3:8). The term *conscience* signifies the human faculty for making moral evaluation of one's actions. The opponents lack the ability to make good moral evaluations. In short, both the opponents' way of thinking and their ability to make moral evaluations are corrupt. The use of *both . . . and* together in the text indicates that the mind and conscience are tied together; both are corrupt and neither can discern the truth.

A corrupt mind and conscience are condemned in Titus 1:16. In reality, *they profess to know God, but deny him by their actions* (1:16a). Because of their immoral actions, the opponents fail to pass the test of knowing God. Sadly, they have not discerned their lack of fellowship with God. They think they know God and that their ritual actions are pure when in reality both their thinking about God and their actions deny the true God. They have separated actions (ethics) from belief (theology). The tie between behavior and belief in God is an underlying theme in Titus, as seen in the two confessional statements that unite obedience and salvation (Titus 2:11-14; 3:4-7). As Hellenistic Jews, the opponents think that they know God and the pagan Gentiles do not. But their actions expose the reality that they do not know God at all and are self-condemned, as Paul states elsewhere several times (Rom 2:1-24; Gal 4:8; 1 Thess 4:5; 2 Thess 1:8). "Not only do they not know the truth about God as revealed in the gospel, but their behavior in particular also demonstrates their lack of knowledge" (Fee 1988: 182).

With an interpretive triad, Paul comes to an exaggerated conclusion that the opponents are *detestable, disobedient, unfit for any good work* (Titus 1:16b). First, they are abominable because they pervert moral distinctions. They do not make good moral decisions and thus are guilty of defilement. Second, they are disobedient in that they do not yield to the gospel as taught by the apostles. In reality, they are like pagan unbelievers. And third, they disqualify themselves from any good work in that they fail to stand the test of Christian character. Their lack of true faith produces only illegitimate fruit. Hence, the opponents are worthless and unqualified for any good work. These three "*d*" words—detestable, disobedient, and disqualified—sadly describe in a derogatory way the condition of the Cretans who have corrupted their minds and consciences by turning away from the true word of God, the gospel of Jesus Christ.

THE TEXT IN BIBLICAL CONTEXT

The Mind and Conscience

Speaking of sinful opponents, Paul says that *their very minds and consciences are corrupted. They profess to know God, but they deny him by their actions* (Titus 1:15b-16a). The effects of sin on the human mind and conscience are mentioned elsewhere in Paul's writings. In Ephesians, Paul writes, "You must no longer live as the Gentiles live, in the futility of their minds. They are darkened in their understanding, alienated from the life of God because of their ignorance and hardness of heart. They have lost all sensitivity and have abandoned themselves to licentiousness, greedy to practice every kind of impurity" (Eph 4:17-19). And in Romans, Paul says, "Though they knew God, they did not honor him as God or give thanks to him, but they became futile in their thinking, and their senseless minds were darkened. Claiming to be wise, they became fools" (Rom 1:21-22). Paul adds, "Since they did not see fit to acknowledge God, God gave them up to a debased mind and to things that should not be done" (1:28).

Religious syncretism led the children of Israel to idolatry and finally into exile. Israel forgot God's word to Moses, "I am the LORD your God, who brought you out of the land of Egypt, out of the house of slavery; you shall have no other gods before me" (Exod 20:2-3). In the midst of Baal religion, Elijah asked the people, "How long will you go limping with two different opinions? If the LORD is God, follow him; but if Baal, then follow him" (1 Kings 18:21). At the end of the exile, Isaiah called the children of Israel back to God by lifting up his voice with strength and shouting, "Here is your God!" (40:9).

When mind and conscience no longer perceive the good, all else fails. Theology and moral character are intertwined. Jesus said that the one "who resolves to do the will of God" will perceive that Jesus' teaching comes from God (John 7:17). Willingness to obey Christ leads to perception of truth. Paul accused the Gentiles of failure to worship God, who has been known since the time of creation. In failing to worship God, human beings "suppress the truth" (Rom 1:18). Ignorance is the consequence of human rebellion rather than its cause (Hays 1996: 385). The human problem is not so much not *knowing* what is right; it is not *doing* what one knows is right. The human mind has a crucial role in shaping conduct (Rom 12:2). A mind functions correctly when it depends on the light of God's revelation of truth. In a similar way, Paul condemns the Ephesian Gentiles' hardness of heart, which has resulted in a darkened understanding. Consequently, the Gentiles have lost all sensitivity and abandoned themselves to all kinds of sin (Eph 4:18-19). In contrast, Paul tells the Christian believers in Ephesus, "That is not the way you learned Christ!" (4:20).

In a similar way, the human conscience becomes dysfunctional. Conscience is that part of human consciousness that speaks an inner voice about moral behavior. By the term *conscience*, Paul means the human aspect that functions in controlling, assessing, and bringing to consciousness one's own conduct according to given norms. It is not the voice of God; it is an inner voice conditioned by the social, religious, and cultural norms within the society in which one lives. In contrast to the more neutral function of conscience in the undisputed Paulines, in the letters to Timothy and Titus, conscience is viewed from a theological perspective. The opponents' consciences are defiled (Titus 1:15) and seared (1 Tim 4:3) because they have rejected the apostolic faith. Those living in accordance with the sound teaching of the apostolic faith have a good conscience (1:5, 19) or a clear conscience (1 Tim 3:9; 2 Tim 1:3). As the conscience is educated theologically, it bears affirmative witness to moral conduct based on the norm and truth of Christian faith and life. When educated according to the truth of God, the conscience gives human guidance in matters of moral behavior. If taught by the mores of society, as was the case among the Cretans, the conscience no longer is sensitive to godly morality and becomes corrupt. One may claim to know God, but in reality one denies God by one's actions (Titus 1:15-16) *[Conscience, p. 338].*

THE TEXT IN THE LIFE OF THE CHURCH

How does one attain knowledge of God? Thomas Aquinas (d. 1274), a major scholastic theologian, brought Aristotelian philosophy and Christian theology together by elucidating proofs for the existence of God. Thomas sought first to understand in order that he might believe. In contrast, Anselm (d. 1109) held to an approach of "faith seeking understanding." Anselm wrote, "For I do not seek to understand that I may believe, but I believe in order to understand. For this also I believe, —that unless I believed, I should not understand" (7). Anselm did not rule out the place of reason in Christian faith, but he countered unbelief by stating an ontological proof for the existence of God.

> That the non-existence of God is inconceivable. This proposition is indeed so true that its negation is inconceivable. For it is quite conceivable that there is something whose non-existence is inconceivable, and this must be greater than that whose non-existence is conceivable. Wherefore, if that thing than which no greater thing is conceivable can be conceived as non-existent; then, that very thing than which a greater is inconceivable is not that than which a greater is conceivable; which is a contradiction.

> So true is it that there exists something than which a greater is inconceivable, that its non-existence is inconceivable: and this thing art Thou, O Lord our God! So truly therefore dost Thou exist, O Lord my God, that Thy non-existence is inconceivable; and with good reason; for if a man's mind could conceive aught better than Thou, the creature would rise above the Creator and judge Him; which is utterly absurd. And in truth whatever else there be beside Thee, may be conceived as non-existent. Thou alone, therefore, most truly of all, and therefore most of all, hast existence: because whatever else there is, is not so truly existent, and therefore has less the prerogative of existence. (Bettenson: 191-92)

Theologians who follow scholastic theology argue that unbelief is illogical and therefore reflects a depraved mind. In the Enlightenment and the modern periods, unbelief and skepticism grew. With the coming of postmodernism, people are turning away from the so-called proofs of God's existence to a narrative approach to truth. On the one hand, postmodern ways of thinking run the danger of pluralism and relativism, which make truth subjective and personal and tend to deny universal truth: each can have their truth claim without persuading others. On the other hand, postmodernism provides opportunity for personal faith in God and its application in life's experience.

A different way to talk about epistemology—how we know truth—is found in Jesus' teaching on discipleship. "If you continue in my word, you are truly my disciples; and you will know the truth, and the truth will make you free" (John 8:31-32). Following Christ in the midst of life is a way of knowing truth. An epistemology of obedience characterized Anabaptists in the sixteenth century. For example, Hans Denck wrote, "But the means is Christ, whom no one can truly know without following him in life. And no one can follow Christ without first knowing him" (45, alt.).

Titus 2:1-10; 3:1-2

Family Relationships in the Church

PREVIEW

After listing qualifications for church leaders (1:5-9) and contrasting these character traits with the opponents (1:10-16), Paul now prescribes the behavior of various groups within the church (2:1-10). The text gives more attention to relationships between age groups than to gender distinctions. To these first four groups the author adds slaves in verses 9-10. The four age groups mentioned in Titus 2:1-8 can be arranged in chiastic order.

A Older Men
  B Older Women
  B´ Younger Women
A´ Younger Men

All of these groups, plus slaves, resided in the typical Greco-Roman household in the first century. Paul is responding to the traditional house code and adjusting it on the basis of Christian principles. Elaborating on household behavior, Paul talks about the church as an alternative community and deals with its relationship to government and to persons outside the church in the Cretan culture in 3:1-2.

Paul attends to three major themes. First is the importance of self-control, which Paul applies to older men (v. 2), older women (v. 4), younger women (v. 5), and to younger men (v. 6). Second, Paul emphasizes the need for spiritual health. Titus is to teach *healthy doctrine* (v. 1 NJB), older men are to be healthy in faith (v. 2), and Titus is to make use of healthy speech that cannot be condemned by any opponent (v. 8). Third, several purpose or result clauses appear (introduced by the Greek conjunction *hina*), indicating the mission effect of upright living upon the pagan Cretans.

OUTLINE

Older Men, 2:1-2
Older Women, 2:3
Younger Women, 2:4-5
Younger Men, 2:6-8
Slaves, 2:9-10
Church as Alternative Community, 3:1-2

EXPLANATORY NOTES

Paul commands Titus to *teach what is consistent with sound doctrine* (2:1). The words *but you* (GNT) turn attention away from what is said about the opponents' teaching and lives (1:10-16). Attention is now turned to Titus, who is commanded to proclaim, teach, and instruct with healthy doctrine. *Sound* or *healthy doctrine* (NJB) occurs several times in the letters to Timothy and Titus (1 Tim 1:10; 6:3; 2 Tim 1:13; 4:3; Titus 1:9, 13; 2:1-2). Sound teaching is consistent with the teaching of the apostles (see notes on Titus 1:9). The kind of teaching described in 2:1-10 emphasizes the behavioral side of the gospel; sound or healthy doctrine includes ethical principles. These ethical principles affect the everyday life of the Christian household and have a direct bearing on relationships between various groups and on the moral character of individuals within each age group. As Titus teaches (lit., *speaks*, GNT) healthy doctrine, people in the Christian churches will grow in Christian faith and life.

Older Men 2:1-2

Older men are mentioned first because deference was given to older people in ancient societies. Leviticus 27:7 suggests that persons over sixty years are old (1 Tim 5:9). The Jewish philosopher Philo (d. ca. AD 50), following Hippocrates, divided human life into seven ages of seven or more years each: 0-7, 8-14, 15-21, 22-28, 29-49, 50-56, and 57 and above (I. H. Marshall 1999: 239; Philo, *On the Creation of the World* 36; Hippocrates, *On Sevens* 5). According to this formula, older men were fifty years old and above. They have several characteristics. The first three—*temperate, serious, prudent*—form a triad of social virtues that are also desirable qualities for church leaders (1 Tim 3:2; Titus 1:7). The fourth characteristic, *sound*, or *healthy* (NJB), is expanded into a classical triad of Christian virtues: *faith, love, endurance.*

Temperate means sober or modest in the use of wine. Metaphorically, it has the meaning of clearheadedness, sober in judgment, and self-controlled. *Serious* (TNIV: *worthy of respect*) means dignified and is a quality that elicits respect from other people (I. H. Marshall 1999: 240). *Prudent*, better translated *self-control* (TNIV), is the ability to control oneself by exercising proper restraint in all things. In addition to these three social virtues come soundness of faith, love, and endurance. *Faith, love, and endurance* present a distinctly Christian emphasis to the virtues desired of older men. The same triad appears in 1 Timothy 6:11 and 2 Timothy 3:10 (NIV). Early in Paul's writings, this triad appears as "faith, hope, and love" (1 Cor 13:13; 1 Thess 1:3). Here in Titus 2:2, the term *endurance* instead of "hope" suggests that patience results in endurance and is a quality of hope. Endurance or steadfastness has within it the quality of constancy and perseverance, which enables older persons to live out their faith and love in the senior years of life (I. H. Marshall 1999: 241).

Older Women 2:3

Women's behavior is described by four qualities (2:3). These four qualities are arranged in a positive-negative/negative-positive order, with the fourth expanded into a purpose clause.

A reverent behavior (positive)
    B not slanderers (negative)
    B′ not slaves to drink (negative)
A′ teach the good (positive)

In employing the term *likewise*, the writer continues the emphasis on sound doctrine in 2:2 and gives a series of commands as virtues for older women. Again, these women are fifty years old or more. Titus is commanded to teach them in a positive direction, *to be reverent in behavior* (2:3). Their demeanor indicates what is befitting an older person; these older women are to conduct their lives in the manner of a priestess in the temple (Knight 1992: 306). As with older men, these older women are to conduct themselves in relation to God.

Turning to the negative side, older women are *not to be slanderers* (2:3). The term *slanderers* means malicious gossips (Knight 1992: 306). Furthermore, older women are not to be *slaves to drink* (2:3). Older women, who are surrounded by food and wine in the home, are not to become enslaved by it. Drunkenness was a problem in the early church and is warned against several times in the NT (Rom 14:21; 1 Cor 11:20-34; Eph 5:18; 1 Pet 4:3). Drunkenness was a vice among older women in Hellenistic culture, particularly among rich women (I. H. Marshall 1999: 245). The Talmud has much to say about it, suggesting that it was also a problem among Jewish women (Collins: 341). In every list of character traits for choosing church leaders, alcoholism is a rejected vice (1 Tim 3:3, 8; 5:23; Titus 1:7).

Turning to the positive side, the older women *are to teach what is good* (Titus 2:3b). As Jewish teachers transmitted the Torah and the knowledge of God (Deut 33:10; Hos 4:6; Mal 2:4-7), so older women taught younger women Christian conduct. A major goal of this teaching is to prevent younger married women from flighty, careless living that would attract criticism against Christianity. Older women are to teach younger women upright living *so that* no opponent can find a reason for discrediting *the word of God* (Titus 2:5b).

Younger Women 2:4-5

Married women who are young—perhaps in their twenties—are to be taught what is conducive to wholesome family living. Older women are to teach younger married women several virtues. These virtues may be grouped into three pairs. The first pair of virtues, *to love their husbands* and *to love their children* (2:4b), was common in the Hellenistic world (Collins: 342). These virtues reflect the primary concern of wife and mother in the first-century home. Though the domestic code emphasized husbands loving their wives (Eph 5:25; Col 3:19) and wives living in submission to their husbands (Eph 5:22; Col 3:18), in Titus 2:4-5 the wife is to respond in love also and to submit to her husband. In contrast to the pagan world, which at times rejected children, the Christian wife is to love her children and provide a good home for their nurture and human development. Nothing is said about the husband's duty to his wife and children here in Titus.

The second pair, *to be self-controlled* and *chaste* (2:5a) focuses on the piety desired in young married women. The young woman is to maintain self-discipline and sexual chastity in her marriage. The third pair, *good managers of the household* and *kind* (TNIV: *to be busy at home, to be kind*) speaks of the young married woman's work world and attitude toward others within her sphere of work. The term *oikourgous* (*good managers*) is the preferred reading (J. K. Elliott: 181-82; Metzger 1994: 585); it means that the young married woman is to run the household efficiently. She is to be kind to all the persons she meets in her domestic duties. A young woman was mistress of both male and female slaves in some Christian households (2:9). Therefore, she is to not only to keep the house, but also to manage the household so it runs efficiently. This third pair of words suggests not only the work the wife does herself, but also her supervision of those who work for her (Quinn 1990: 137).

Finally, young married women are *to be submissive to their husbands* (2:5b). Interestingly, Paul uses the word *to submit* (*hypotassomai*) instead of the word "obey." A wife's *submission* does not give the husband a right to abuse her. *Submission* speaks of a voluntary act and appears in other NT household codes (Eph 5:22; Col 3:18). In these household codes, children are to "obey" (*hypakouō*; Eph 6:1; Col 3:20), but wives are to submit to their husbands. Submission becomes acute if the husband is not a Christian and the young married wife is. The reputation of the Christian churches in Crete is at stake if the wife in this kind of marriage becomes insubordinate. Her willingness to suffer shame, if necessary, becomes a means by which the integrity of Christian faith is promoted in a cultural setting where pagans look for ways to bring accusations against the church and blaspheme *the word of God* (Titus 2:5b). The young married wives are to submit to their own husbands, not to men in general. The command is not gender-specific female submission to male. Rather, it is Christian marriage-specific submission each to her *own* husband. There is no directive here that husbands are to demand submission of their wives. Rather, the wife voluntarily submits to her Christian husband.

Paul's instruction for younger women ends by pointing to the missionary purpose in younger women following the teaching of older women. *So that the word of God may not be discredited* (2:5c) indicates why Paul prohibits disregard for Christian virtues in new Christian households in Crete. Disregarding these virtues opens the church to criticism by non-Christians and to the blaspheming of the word of God, especially the gospel. According to the OT, ungodly behavior of God's own people leads other nations to blaspheme God's name (Isa 52:5; Ezek 36:20-36). The credibility of the Christian message is undermined when Christian people do not live godly lives. Respectable behavior bears witness to the power and truth of God and enhances the Christian witness (Towner 1994: 239).

Younger Men 2:6-8

Next, instruction is given for younger men and for Titus (Titus 2:6-8). Paul says, *Urge the younger men to be self-controlled.* This is the fourth use of the term *self-control* in this section. Older men (v. 2), older women (v. 4), younger women (v. 5), and now younger men (v. 6) are to be self-controlled. Younger men are to restrain themselves. Moreover, teaching for young men is expanded by Titus's behavior, which models how young Christian men in Crete are to live (2:7-8). Just as older women teach and model behavior for younger women, so Titus teaches and models behavior for younger men. *Show yourself in all respects a model of good works* (v. 7). Titus is to display good works in his own life. Modeling Christian behavior is a common theme in Paul (Phil 3:17; 1 Thess 1:7; 2 Thess 3:9). Just as Timothy models Christian virtues in speech, conduct, love, faith, and purity (1 Tim 4:12), so also Titus models Christian faithfulness. The term *model* refers to a moral example or pattern of a determinative nature (I. H. Marshall 1999: 254). Both Titus and Timothy are younger men living in a culture that respects older persons, but not necessarily younger ones. Older men will respect their leadership only if they model good behavior.

Paul commands Titus to take his teaching role seriously. Titus's teaching must meet three criteria. First, *integrity* implies transparency and honesty (Titus 2:7). Second, *gravity* speaks of seriousness and dignity. And third is *healthy teaching* (*sound speech*, 2:8). If Titus lives as an ideal example of the believer and teaches in this way, then opponents will have no accusation against Christianity. Teaching with integrity suggests that the authority of the message is related to the manner in which it is taught. The word *integrity* means without decay. Here in verse 7 it means unblemished or healthy teaching (Collins: 344). Second, Titus is to teach with *gravity*. This word is translated as *seriousness* in TNIV. Titus's teaching is serious and reverent, in contrast to the contemptible, laughable, and idle talk of the opponents (1:10). Titus's teaching commands respect. And third, his teaching includes *sound speech that cannot be censured*. It is health-giving teaching that is free from accusation by the opponents. Actually, two ideas come together in this phrase. The *sound* part of teaching is taken from the domain of health. And the *not-censured* part comes from the language of the courtroom, where a person is declared innocent. In short, Titus's teaching is to be healthy and thus above reproach. If young men are guided by Titus's example of personal integrity and if his teaching induces spiritual health, no accusation can be brought against the Christian gospel.

Paul ends Titus's example with a purpose or result statement (2:8b). If interpreted as a purpose statement, it means that the purpose for Titus's life and teaching is to create a situation in which an opponent will have nothing evil to say and will thus be put to shame. If it is a result statement, it means that Titus's life and teaching will be such that no opponent has anything to say in opposition to Christianity. Both the NRSV and TNIV interpret it as a result clause by using *then* or *so that*. Shame will fall to the opponents because their criticism against sound doctrine will prove to be groundless and their reputation and message will be discredited in society (Towner 2006: 734). The opponents will have no legitimate grounds to say anything bad about Christianity and may actually be converted. Paul goes so far as to say that the opponents will be without accusation not only against Timothy, but also against *us*, meaning Paul, Titus, and the Christian believers in the churches of Crete. In short, Titus's character and sound teaching have a missionary effect upon the pagan Cretans.

Slaves 2:9-10

Paul concludes his household instruction with a word about slaves who were part of the Christian church (Titus 2:9-10). In doing so, Paul moves beyond age and sex groupings to another social group in the Greco-Roman household: male and female slaves. Slaves are to submit themselves to their masters. Then Paul presents two positive and two negative commands, arranged chiastically:

A Give satisfaction in every respect (positive)
  B Not talk back (negative)
  B′ Not pilfer (negative)
A′ Show complete and perfect fidelity (positive)

These positive and negative commands expand what is meant by slaves submitting themselves to their masters. Again, a missionary appeal concludes the teaching. We can see some literary similarity between the teachings on young women in verses 4-5 and the teaching on slaves in verses 9-10. Both are to willingly submit to their own husband/master. By upright living, both bear witness to the Christian gospel, as seen in the purpose clauses that follow the instruction given in each case.

As younger men are urged to conduct themselves according to Christian virtues, so Christian slaves are urged to conduct themselves in a Christian way. The desired response is stated in an overall way by the infinitive *to submit oneself*. The term *submission* suggests showing humility, respect, and love toward some superior authority, whatever it may be (*TDNT* 8:45, I. H. Marshall 1999: 259). Nothing stated here tells masters to demand obedience of their slaves. In contrast to the household codes in Colossians 3:18, 22 and Ephesians 5:21-22; 6:5, where the wives are to submit to their husbands and slaves are to obey their masters, in Titus 2:9 slaves are to submit to their masters just as wives are to submit to their husbands (2:5). Moreover, submission is directed toward their own *masters* (plural), indicating that individual slaves may have several male and female masters.

Slaves are *to give satisfaction in every respect* (2:9). As Christians, slaves are more than property; they are human persons with dignity. In seeking to be "pleasing" or "acceptable" to their masters in all aspects of their service, Christian slaves will offer a positive and winsome attitude in addition to passive submission (Knight 1992: 314). This command suggests that a positive view of employee/employer relationships characterizes the Christian's work world.

The positive command is followed by a negative command, *not to talk back* (2:9). The command *not to talk back* refers to contradiction or verbal opposition, talking back to one's masters or slandering them behind their backs (Mounce: 415). The only other use of this term in the letters to Timothy and Titus is opponents' speaking against the gospel (1:9). A second negative command, *not to pilfer*, means not to set aside or to steal (2:10). The only other occurrence of the term in the NT is in the story of Ananias and Sapphira (Acts 5:2-3). Living in the household and occasionally handling household finances presents slaves with a temptation to take some of the household money. The Greek world used this word when talking about robbery, fraud, and embezzlement (Collins: 346). Slave traders were guilty of this sin (1 Tim 1:10). The seriousness of this negative command is seen in the strong adversative *but*, which introduces a positive command: *but to show complete and perfect fidelity* (Titus 2:10b). The verb means to demonstrate visibly their faithfulness and reliability by their quality of character (I. H. Marshall 1999: 260).

Finally, we come to a third purpose clause in this passage (vv. 4, 5, 10): *so that in everything they may be an ornament to the doctrine of God our Savior* (2:10). Again, appropriate behavior is tied to Christian witness (cf. 1 Tim 6:1). Christian slaves who follow the commands given in Titus 2:9-10 validate Christianity in the presence of unbelieving onlookers. The verb *to ornament* means to adorn, to put in order. This verb was commonly used for beautifying a person or adding adornments to an edifice (Collins: 346). As Christian slaves live Christlike lives, they attract nonbelievers to the gospel of God our Savior. One's conduct in the midst of life goes a long way in making the gospel attractive to onlookers. Quinn says, "It is striking that slaves, the last and least in the social order of the ancient world, are the only ones in this *Haustafel* [household code] who are described as positively ornamenting the apostolic teaching and eliciting esteem for it" (150). Slaves, who represent the bottom of the human hierarchy, honor God and increase the attractiveness of the gospel in the hearts of the pagans. The phrase *the doctrine of God our Savior* (2:10c) means teaching *about* God our Savior and prepares the reader for what follows in the confessional statement in 2:11-14.

Church as Alternate Community 3:1-2

Paul extends the discussion about household behavior to include the larger issue of the church's relationship with others beyond itself in 3:1-2. Instructions are given first on the church's relationship to government. Second, attention is given to the church's relationship to all people.

Paul instructs on how to relate to government because the Cretan Christians may have assumed that Paul's anti-emperor language in Titus 2:11-14 gives them freedom to ignore civil authorities and to disobey governing laws. Further, Cretans were known for rebellious behavior (Mounce: 444). As elsewhere in the NT, instructions on how citizens relate to governing rulers are part of the household code (Rom 13:1-7; 1 Tim 2:1-2; 1 Pet 2:13-15). So with three infinitives, Paul commands Titus to *remind* the Cretan believers *to be subject to rulers and authorities, to be obedient,* and *to be ready for every good work.*

Using an imperative verb with a plural pronoun object, Paul commands Titus to *remind them*—the Christians in Crete as a group, not the non-Christians—to be subject to rulers and authorities. The terms *rulers* and *authorities* mean government rulers. The conjunction *and* is missing in the best Alexandrian and Western manuscripts (Metzger 1994: 586), suggesting that the two terms here refer only to governing authorities and not angelic rulers. *Rulers* and *authorities* are used only in Titus 3:1 in the letters to Timothy and Titus, although the same higher authorities are implied in 1 Timothy 2:2a. In Titus 3:1, Paul means government officials, whether imperial, national, or local.

In the NT sometimes the state is viewed positively (Rom 13:1-7; 1 Tim 2:1-4; Titus 3:1; 1 Pet 2:13-17), sometimes negatively (Matt 4:8-10; Mark 10:42; 13:9-13; Luke 13:1-3; 1 Cor 2:6-8; Eph 6:11-12; Rev 13), and regularly as under the lordship of Christ (Rom 8:35-39; 1 Cor 15:24-26; Eph 1:19-23; 3:10; Col 2:10, 15; 1 Pet 3:22; Rev 19:16). Jesus Christ won the victory over evil forces in his death and resurrection (Rom 8:38-39; Eph 3:10; Col 2:15). These evil forces and their earthly counterparts no longer carry ultimate authority. Ultimate authority belongs to God alone. To what degree shall Christians obey rulers and authorities if indeed they no longer have ultimate authority? The early Christian leaders said that when authorities clash, "We must obey God rather than human authority" (Acts 5:29).

Paul responds with several admonitions. First, Christians in Crete are *to be subject* to the governing authorities (Titus 3:1). This term *be subject* (*hypotassomai*) is used also in Romans 13:1, 5, and 1 Peter 2:13 for subjection to political powers. The term *be subject* is not the same as obedience. Rather, the term suggests "being subordinate" (*TDNT* 8:44). Submitting might even entail disobeying government while accepting the consequences of that disobedience at the hands of the state. If obedience to the state goes against God's will, Christians defy the state, even if it means death (see Acts 5:29; Rev 6:9-11; 12:11; 13:1–14:20).

Second, Christians are to accept direction and not be guilty of insurrection against the government. The Greek word is translated *to be obedient* (NRSV, TNIV), but it is not the normal NT word for obedience and it means to accept direction. The term suggests a willingness to listen to the directions of a leader and openness to persuasion to serve the common good according to the leader's guidance (Quinn 1990: 185). Christians are law-abiding citizens when laws do not go against their faith and moral calling in Jesus Christ. But their obedience is conditioned by what follows in the third infinitive: *to be ready for every good work, to speak evil of no one, to avoid quarreling, to be gentle, and to show every courtesy to everyone* (Titus 3:1b-2). *To be ready for every good work*, as used in the letters to Timothy and Titus, means to live according to the fruit of the new life in Christ (I. H. Marshall 1999: 302). It means to go beyond the level of good citizenship, to rise to Christian moral and ethical conduct within a given social and cultural context. This quality of Christian living becomes inviting to governing persons so that they have nothing evil to say about the church and are attracted to the gospel as implied by the behavior of young women (Titus 2:5), young men (2:8), and slaves (2:9).

With the use of the words *no one* and *everyone* in Titus 3:2, Paul moves beyond Christian behavior toward governing officials to Christian behavior toward others. Using four infinitives, Paul describes the kind of behavior desired of these Cretan Christians. First, Cretan Christians are urged not to *speak* maliciously against—literally, not to blaspheme—anyone. In light of the reputation of the Cretans stated in 1:12, Christian speech demonstrates change from the old way of life. Second, Christians are *to avoid quarreling*. The term means to be peaceable and is used in 3:9 in contrast to the sinful trait of quarreling among the Cretans. Third, Christian attitudes toward other persons ought to reflect Christ's way of life. This attitude is spelled out with the phrase *to be gentle and to show every courtesy to everyone* (3:2b). Though the first two commands are given in the negative (what *not* to do), the last two are in the positive. Christians are not aggressive in speech and do not attack their opponents. Christians take initiative in doing good in general. Christ demonstrated the grace of gentleness

(2 Cor 10:1). Gentleness is one of the Christian virtues (Eph 4:2; Col 3:12, "meekness")—a fruit of the Spirit (Gal 5:23)—and this Christian virtue is made visible to non-Christians (1 Pet 3:15).

THE TEXT IN BIBLICAL CONTEXT

Household Behavior Codes

Titus 2:1–3:1 is one of several NT passages on household behavior (Rom 13:1-7; Eph 5:21–6:9; Col 3:18–4:1; 1 Tim 2:8-15; 5:1-2; 6:1-2; 1 Pet 2:13–3:7). Luther called these passages *Haustafeln*, household codes. Edward G. Selwyn calls them Code of Subordination (423). Leonhard Goppelt calls them Station Codes (162-79). The following chart of household codes in the NT shows similarities and differences among the texts.

Household Behavior in the New Testament

Romans	Colossians	Ephesians
Love one another (13:10).	Clothe yourselves with compassion, kindness, humility (3:12).	Be subject to one another (5:21).
Submit to the state (13:1-7).	*Wives*, be subject to your husbands (3:18; as is fitting in the *Lord*).	*Wives*, be subject to your husbands (5:22; as you are to the *Lord*).
	Husbands, love your wives (3:19; never treat them harshly).	*Husbands*, love your wives (5:25; just as *Christ* loved the church).
	Children, obey your parents (3:20; acceptable duty in the *Lord*)	*Children*, obey your parents in the *Lord* (6:1).
	Fathers, do not provoke your children (3:21).	*Fathers*, do not provoke your children to anger (6:4; bring them up in the nurture of the *Lord*).
	Slaves, obey your masters (3:22; fearing the *Lord*).	*Slaves*, obey your masters (6:5; as you obey *Christ*).
	Masters, treat slaves justly (4:1; you have a *master in heaven*).	*Masters*, do the same to them (6:9; you have the same *master in heaven*).

1 Peter	1 Timothy	Titus
Honor civil rulers (2:13-17).	Pray for rulers (2:2).	Be subject to rulers (3:1).
Slaves, accept authority of *masters* (2:18).	*Slaves*, regard *masters* as worthy of all honor (6:1; so that the name of God and teaching may not be blasphemed).	*Slaves*, be submissive to *masters* (2:9; so that in everything they may be an ornament to the doctrine of God our Savior).
Wives, accept the authority of husbands (3:1; so that they may be won over by wives' conduct).	*Women*, learn in submission (2:11).	Young *women*, be submissive to husbands (2:5; so that the word of God may not be discredited).
		Older *women*, be reverent in behavior, teach what is good (2:3; so that they may encourage young women to love their husbands and children).
Younger, accept the authority of the elders (5:5).		Younger *men*, be self-controlled (2:6; then any opponent will be put to shame, having nothing evil to say of us).
Husbands, show consideration to your wives, pay honor to the woman (3:7; so that nothing hinders your prayers).	*Men* should pray without anger (2:8).	Older *men*, be temperate, serious, prudent, sound in faith, love, and endurance (2:2).

A closer look at these household-behavior texts in the above chart reveals the following: All of the texts modify the Greco-Roman household practice *[Household Behavior, p. 355]*. The subordinate persons in each of the couplets (women, children, and slaves) are addressed first, indicating that they are given moral dignity in Christ. Husbands, fathers, and masters are all asked to follow Christ in their relationships with others in the household. Abuse by Christian husbands, fathers, and masters is not permitted. The lordship of Christ, the cross of Christ, and the relationship between Christ and the church provide theological undergirding for Christian household behavior. Wives and slaves are asked to *be subject* rather than *to obey* their husband and/or master. "Subjection" suggests voluntary behavior by a person willing to suffer temporarily for the larger opportunity for transformation. It is a positive virtue that does not put up with injustice, but undergirds right order (Yoder Neufeld: 280).

All household members are to be subject to one another (Eph 5:21; Col 3:12-15; 1 Pet 3:8). For the husband and master to carry out one's duties in mutual submission with members of their household requires a radical departure from the traditional practice of household behavior in Paul's day. As this new kind of behavior takes place in the household, the rights of master over slave are greatly altered. Both master and slave are reminded that they are subject to Christ their heavenly master. Slaves—along with women, children, and men—are addressed as members of the church and not merely as members of a Roman household (Balch 1988: 33).

In Titus 2:1-10 masters and children are not addressed, and where the social classes are paired, the attention of one social group is not always directed toward the paired other. Social superiors have no duty assigned to them. Instead, the instructions are grouped according to age and sex, suggesting that this is not a complete household code.

Some change is seen between freedom in Christ in Paul's early writings (cf. Gal 3:28) and a desire for the church as the household of God to live godly in the midst of the Greco-Roman world. In the letters to Timothy and Titus, the household behavior texts emphasize a mission motive. Slaves serve their masters with honor *so that the name of God and the teaching may not be blasphemed* (1 Tim 6:1). Younger women love and submit to their husbands *so that the word of God may not be discredited* (Titus 2:5). Younger men are self-controlled and follow the model of good works seen in Titus with the result that *any opponent will be put to shame, having nothing evil to say of us* (2:8). And slaves are submissive to their masters *so that in everything they may be an ornament to the doctrine of God our Savior* (2:10). This strong emphasis on mission as a behavioral motivating factor may suggest that the Christians in Crete are under attack by opponents outside the church because they do not follow the household-behavior practice of the Greco-Roman world. Instructions are given in such a way that the opponents of the Christian faith can no longer bring any charges against the Christian men, women, and slaves in the new household of God (Padgett 1987b: 50). Through quality of Christian character, the Cretan Christians will stop the opponents' criticism, win them to Christ, and move forward toward equality and justice for all.

As influential persons within the house, Christian women play a significant role in the missionary expansion of the church. Missionary expansion through women bears witness that the household behavior codes in the NT lead in the direction of freedom rather than in the direction of severe restrictions. As Frances Young says:

> The Pastorals bear witness to the perennial strains occasioned by the fact that the gospel challenges human assumptions about status and power. What is remarkable in these texts is the extent to which social norms were modified rather than the degree to which they were accepted without challenge. In significant ways, the Christianizing of the household table did not leave it the same as before. (157)

When members of the Roman household became Christians, revolutionary change took place. No longer did Christians serve the pagan gods of the head of the house. No longer did female slaves give in to the sexual advances of their male masters. No longer did the head of the house rule over the inferior ones. Surely there were conflicts along the way when one or two of the household members became Christian and not the head of the house (Osiek, MacDonald, and Tulloch: 117). In a society of honor and shame, such a drastic change in household behavior likely brought scorn upon the church. Titus 2:1-10 calls for a balanced approach between new freedom in Christ and a desire that the church not be thought of as a threat to the Roman state and culture. By briefly adjusting freedom in Christ to contextualize mission efforts, the church was able to grow and move in the direction of equality and justice.

An Alternative Community

In the OT the Israelites were a people of God without a human king. Moses was a servant and God was the king. This theocracy extended from the time of the exodus from Egypt and the covenant formation at Mount Sinai until the next generation entered the Promised Land. Then the Israelites wanted to become like the other Near Eastern nations surrounding them and have their own king. In making this change, they departed from God's desire and, on the basis of the Davidic covenant, began to regard the people of God as equal to the political nation under David and Solomon's rule.

Jesus came as Son of David and preached the kingdom of God. God's rule was not Roman or Judean politics. Instead, it was the politics of Jesus in God's reign, beginning in the covenant community. This kingdom of God was an alternative community, with kingdom behavior set forth in the Sermon on the Mount. With Jesus as

Lord, and the people of God as an alternative community living out God's rule, the NT gives a variety of views regarding the relationship of the people of God to the state.

Though Christians *submit* to the state, they need not always *obey* the state. Though Christians pray for state rulers (1 Tim 2:1-4) and submit to them (Titus 3:1), they also recognize that sometimes the state is evil (Rev 13). As an alternative community, the characteristic of the church is *to be ready for every good work, to speak evil of no one, to avoid quarreling, to be gentle, and to show perfect courtesy to everyone* (Titus 3:1b-2).

THE TEXT IN THE LIFE OF THE CHURCH

Change in Household Behavior

Each generation must discern how best to apply the household-behavior texts within its life context. The church in North America finds itself in a vastly different cultural setting from the first-century cultural setting in which the NT household behavior texts arose *[Hermeneutical Issues, p. 347]*. The church has rightly discerned that slavery and the abuse of women and children are not acceptable Christian behavior and are not supported by these NT household-behavior texts (on slavery, see TLC after notes on 1 Tim 6:1-2). As the gospel breaks into new cultures, household behavior begins to change in the direction of more loving and just treatment of household members in the likeness of Christ. Here are a few examples of the change that takes place.

In Ethiopia, the Ethiopian Orthodox Church was established as early as the fourth century. This East African country eventually became an island of Christianity in a sea of Islam. Men were given a privileged place. Women came to church but could not go inside the church building during their menstrual periods because they were considered unclean. Islam in Ethiopia also greatly restricted women. Islamic women could not assert rights, could not go to the cemetery to attend a burial, and at weddings women and men were separated. As evangelical Christianity came, women were treated differently. The Meserete Kristos Church, started by missionaries in the late 1940s, began slowly and struggled through a communist period from 1974 to 1991. During that period, church members gathered secretly in small groups of six to eight persons for worship and nurture. In many small groups, no males were present. Women became leaders and regularly served communion. When the communist period ended and the church came out from underground, the people suddenly realized that God had blessed their efforts and great growth had taken place.

Shortly thereafter, men began to exercise leadership and control again. Women now carried a supportive role rather than a leadership role. Twenty-five years later, as the church studied the Bible more carefully, it received more light on the subject and decided to change its constitution and give room for women to be chosen as leaders in some congregations and to accept female leaders. In small but meaningful ways, the Meserete Kristos Church is moving from the household behavior texts in their first-century context to living out these same texts in the East Africa context of the twenty-first century. They made the change in such a way that the mission of the church moved forward.

Among the Maasai people in Kenya, Christian mission changed the culture. Women in Maasai culture were considered of less value than cattle. Women were important for giving birth to children, but not to love. As Christianity came into the culture, the missionaries taught husbands to love their wives as Christ loved the church. This teaching had a profound effect on new believers among the Maasai people. In the second generation, Maasai Christians rejected polygyny (having more than one wife). Women are given new recognition in Christ and new status in the family relationship. So radical did the change become that after a few decades, the Christian church among the Maasai people agreed to ordain women as well as men to the Christian ministry.

In Latin cultures, machismo prevails. As persons become Christians in these Latin cultures, the church seeks to find the way between equality in Christ and the prevailing cultural practice. The gospel is contextualized in such a way that there is movement away from machismo and toward equality between men and women in Christ. Machismo is not an accepted practice in Christ despite its presence in the culture.

Not all Christians in new cultures change this fast; some change little. But as the new Christians in Crete were learning how to apply the gospel in their cultural setting, so Christian churches today work at contextualizing the gospel with the goal in mind of achieving equality in Christ.

The Church as Alternative Community

Like the church in the first century (Titus 3:1-2), believers churches struggle with the question of how much to accommodate themselves to the surrounding culture for the sake of mission and how much to be an alternative community within the larger culture. The sixteenth-century Anabaptists talked about two kingdoms, which they found in the teachings of Jesus and the rest of the NT. Since in European society church and state were one and Anabaptists saw the church as fallen, they tended to equate the state with evil. Thus they spoke of the state as "outside the perfection of Christ" in the Schleitheim Confession (art. 6; in Yoder 1977: 14). They believed that Christ calls the people of God to reject the sword.

Members of believers churches have a variety of views concerning the Christian relation to the state. Some members vote while other members do not. A few persons from believers churches run for political office. Nevertheless, many members refuse to obey the state when it demands that they take part in the armed forces. Some even refuse to pay the percentage of taxes that are used for supporting the military.

Members of believers churches also relate to culture in different ways. Some take flight from the surrounding culture by migration or withdrawal from society into a subculture. For example, some have carried Germanic traditions with them for centuries, including use of the German language. Other members of believers churches accommodate themselves to culture to the extent that they compromise the gospel. This struggle between withdrawal and accommodation is similar to the struggle that the Christian communities in Ephesus and Crete were experiencing. The church must continually work at discerning between good and evil. Even as the church moves out into the culture in mission, it must at the same time be the faithful people of God as members of Christ's kingdom. This struggle and discernment are an ongoing task of the church.

Titus 2:11-15

Confessional Statement on God's Grace

PREVIEW

With the explanatory term *for,* Paul begins a confessional statement that explains the reason for the ethical instructions in Titus 2:1-10. This confessional statement is a major doctrinal statement in Titus. A few scholars suggest that it may have been used in a baptismal service (Towner 1994: 243). Building on "God our Savior" (2:10b), the doctrinal statement calls attention to God's grace, which becomes the foundation for salvation and for ethical behavior. Salvation and discipleship are tied together through God's grace. Not only does salvation come as a result of God's grace (2:11), but grace also trains and disciplines the Christian believer in upright moral behavior. This educative work of grace is described in 2:12 and picked up again at the end of the doctrinal statement in 2:14b. Thus the author uses a circular argument that begins with ethical behavior in 2:1-10, states the foundation for that behavior in the grace of God, which centers in the person and work of Jesus Christ (2:11, 13b, 14a), and culminates in the Christian's desire to be zealous for good deeds while living in grace (2:14b). New Christian believers in Crete were in danger of claiming salvation without a change in moral behavior. Paul writes this short letter to correct this problem. The relationship of behavior to theology also is found in 3:4-7.

Using language from the Greco-Roman world to describe the appearance of a divinized emperor, Paul says that Christians live between the two appearances (*epiphaneia*) of Christ. Jesus Christ manifested God's grace (favor or benefit) in a first appearance by bringing salvation into the world for all people (2:11). In a second appearance (Christ's second coming), Jesus Christ will manifest God's glory. During the interval between the first and second appearances, Christians live in grace. God's grace saves, instructs, and enables God's people for good deeds. Interestingly, this confessional statement is one sentence in Greek.

OUTLINE

Grace Appeared, 2:11
Grace Trains Us, 2:12
The Blessed Hope, 2:13
What the Savior Did, 2:14

EXPLANATORY NOTES

Grace Appeared 2:11

Using a verb tense to indicate action in the past, Paul says, *The grace of God has appeared, bringing salvation to all* (Titus 2:11). The grammar indicates that the word *salvation* is the predicate of the sentence. The sentence should not be translated "the saving grace of God has appeared to all people" (cf. KJV) because *salvation* functions adverbially as a predicate nominative in the sentence and thus describes the *effects* of the appearing (Mounce: 422). God's grace has appeared, and in that appearance, grace has made salvation possible for all humans. As in 1 Timothy 2:4-6, salvation is for all. Luke's account of Saul's conversion in Acts 22:14-15 includes the call to be a witness to all human beings and may indicate some tie between Luke-Acts and this passage in Titus 2:11.

The verb *to appear* (*epiphainō*) suggests the sudden and surprising appearance of light, its appearance for the first time, and/or its effect in illuminating the darkness (I. H. Marshall 1999: 267). The term was used in the Hellenistic world to describe the appearance of a god, such as the healing gods Asclepius or Serapis, or a divinized emperor that came to a city in the Roman Empire. Collins says, "The religious language that was appropriate to the gods was also used with regard to the emperors who effected a god's beneficence on behalf of their subjects" (349). When the divinized emperor visited cities in the empire, he graced them or brought favors for them. This kind of political favor or beneficence finds expression today in the so-called "pork" added to certain bills in the U.S. Congress, by which politicians bring favors or benefits to their constituency—hoping, of course, for a favorable vote by the people in the next election [*Names for God and the Imperial Cult, p. 357*].

In contrast to the god of the imperial cult, Paul says that *Jesus Christ* came into the world as the expression of God's grace or favor.

God's grace finds expression through the whole of Christ's life, from incarnation through resurrection and ascension. Grace brought salvation to all of humanity (not just to men).

In contrast to Jewish exclusiveness and proto-Gnostic restrictions on who can be saved, Paul indicates that none of the groups of persons mentioned in Titus 2:1-10, including women and slaves, is outside of God's abundant grace in Jesus Christ. Moreover, God's grace can reach members of the Roman imperial cult (1 Tim 2:1-6). Thus, Titus 2:11 agrees with Titus 3:4-5 and 1 Timothy 2:1-6; 3:16; 4:10 that God's grace brought salvation in Jesus Christ for all people. The provision of salvation is universal: God is Savior, not the Roman imperial cult.

Grace Trains Us 2:12

God's grace does more than redeem us in Christ. The tense of the verb indicates that grace continually teaches us how to live the Christian life. The verb *training* means instruction (Acts 7:22), correction (1 Tim 1:20; 2 Tim 2:25), and discipline (1 Cor 11:32; 2 Cor 6:9; Heb 12:7). Though the verb sometimes implies punishment (Luke 23:16), here in Titus 2:12 it means discipline through education. It is the kind of discipline used in rearing a child. Grace has an ongoing educative or disciplinary dimension (Kelly: 245). It keeps on instructing and enabling us during the interval between the two appearances or manifestations of Christ. It trains us to say no to some things and to say yes to other things.

Negatively, grace teaches us to *renounce* two vices: *impiety and worldly passions* (Titus 2:12a). The word *renounce* indicates a decisive break with the past and may have been used as part of the baptismal vow (I. H. Marshall 1999: 270). Grace trains the Christian believer to say a decisive no to the past life of sin, indicated by the word *impiety. Renouncing impiety* means to reject idolatry and conduct associated with disbelief in God. It means to reject the Roman imperial cult and the ungodly immoral practices and vices commonly associated with evil in the world (cf. 3:3). Grace also teaches us to say no to worldly passions. *Worldly* indicates that which is opposed to God. By *passions*, Paul means fleshly desires (cf. Gal 5:16, 24) and various lusts among Gentiles, including sexual lust (1 Cor 5:1; 1 Thess 4:5). In the letters to Timothy and Titus, the term *passions* always means evil passions (cf. 1 Tim 6:9).

Positively, grace teaches us to say yes to three virtues: . . . *and in the present age to live lives that are self-controlled, upright, and godly* (Titus 2:12b). Paul uses Hellenistic terms but pours Christian content into their meaning, since grace is the teacher instead of Hellenistic philosophy (Mounce: 425). The three virtues express relationships with self, neighbor, and God. Self-control occurs several times in Titus (1:8; 2:2, 5-6). Self-controlled persons experience God's grace to the degree that they are in control of themselves. *Upright* means to live according to the standards of justice and fairness (I. H. Marshall 1999: 271), to be righteous or just in relationships with other people. Christians disciplined by God's grace live in right relationship with other people. *Godly* means to live in right relationship with God by believing in Jesus and living a life of discipleship.

Grace enables us to live godly, holy lives in the present age, in which we experience "already but not yet" the reign of God in its fullness. Despite the struggles and temptations to sin that Christians face in the present, evil age, God's grace is sufficient to train us and enable us to live godly lives.

The Blessed Hope 2:13

In contrast to Hellenistic thought, which emphasized the immortality of the soul, Christianity taught the resurrection of the body. Our faith is in *the living God* (1 Tim 4:10). Jesus Christ is *our hope* (1:1). And our hope of eternal life centers in God, who promised it before creation (Titus 1:2; 3:7). Paul says that we anticipate and wait for that blessed hope. The term *wait* occurs mainly in Luke, where it is used for welcoming a person (12:36), including sinners (15:2), and also for welcoming the consolation of Israel (2:25), the redemption of Jerusalem (2:38), and the kingdom of God (Acts 24:15). *Blessed* is an attribute of God (1 Tim 1:11). *Hope* is not an inward, subjective emotion. *Hope* is objective since it focuses on what or who is manifested: the returning Lord.

Since only one article governs two nouns in Titus 2:13, *the hope* and *appearing* (TNIV) of Jesus Christ are one event. The word *and* used in the first part of the verse means that Christian believers live in constant expectation of the blessed hope, which is their *great God and Savior, Jesus Christ*. The object and content of hope are centered firmly on the appearing of our great God and Savior. While persons in the Roman Empire looked forward to the manifestation of the divinized emperor, and people in Ephesus shouted, "Great is Artemis of the Ephesians!" (Acts 19:34), Christians in Crete look forward with certainty *to the manifestation of the glory of our great God and Savior, Jesus Christ*. This is our hope.

In Hellenism, the term *great* was applied to gods and goddesses. In Judaism, the term was applied to Yahweh. In the NT, the adjective *great* is not used for God, except here and in Luke 9:43. *Great* in Titus 2:13b counteracts the prevailing practice of ascribing greatness to the pagan gods and the imperial cult of the Greco-Roman world (Dibelius and Conzelmann: 143-46; Acts 19:28; Rev 18:2). In contrast, Paul says that *God* is great. As the first appearance (*epiphaneia*) of Jesus benefited or graced the people, so the second appearance (*epiphaneia*) will declare the fullness of God's glory. In talking about the return of Christ with the terms *appearance* and *great God,* Paul confronts the claims of other religions in the Roman Empire (Mounce: 426).

A major question arises in Titus 2:13b regarding the meaning of the words *God and Savior, Jesus Christ*. Is Paul talking about one or two persons of the Godhead? Is the author talking about a great God or about a great Savior, Jesus Christ, or both together? Is Paul suggesting that Jesus is God, thereby affirming the deity of Christ? In favor of understanding this as a reference to two persons—God and Christ—are the following arguments:

1. It is quite unusual (cf. Rom 9:5) for Paul to refer to Christ as God.
2. In the epiphany passages in the letters to Timothy and Titus, a distinction is normally made between God and Christ (1 Tim 6:13-14; 2 Tim 1:9-10).
3. Paul emphasizes Christ's dependence on God in the letters to Timothy and Titus, and it is unlikely that he would talk about Christ as God here.
4. God our Savior is used for God six times in the letters to Timothy and Titus.
5. The expression "great God" is a late Jewish expression, and it would be exceptional if applied to Jesus.

In favor of understanding this as a reference to one person, emphasizing the deity of Christ, are the following arguments:

1. Only one definite article is used to govern the two nouns *God* and *Savior*.
2. *God* and *Savior* were current in first-century writings, usually meaning one deity.
3. Epiphany language in the NT refers to one person, Christ, and not to two persons. In the letters to Timothy and Titus, epiphany language is used for each appearance of Christ (1 Tim 6:14; 2 Tim 1:10; 4:8).
4. Elsewhere in the NT, hope is centered in Christ and his return.
5. The verse that follows (v. 14) describes the redemptive work of one person.

6. Outside the letters to Timothy and Titus, Paul calls Jesus *Savior* in Ephesians 5:23 and Philippians 3:20. In content, Philippians 3:20 is much like Titus 2:13. And although God is called *Savior* in the letters to Timothy and Titus, in Titus, Jesus is also called Savior in nearby verses (1:3-4; 2:10, 13; 3:4, 6).

Therefore, one can conclude Paul is using the name *Jesus Christ* in apposition to *our great God and Savior*, meaning, according to Murray J. Harris, that Jesus Christ is called *our great God and Savior* (Harris: 271). Understood this way, the text means *our great God and Savior—namely, Jesus Christ.* Thus, Titus 2:13b is one of the rare NT texts, along with Romans 9:5, in which Jesus is designated as *God*, indicating the divinity of Christ (cf. Rom 9:5; John 1:1, 18; 20:28; Col 1:15, 19; 2:9; Phil 2:6; Heb 1:8-13; 2 Pet 1:1). English translations that interpret the text as referring to the deity of Christ include the NIV, RSV, NRSV, NJB, and TNIV.

Yet another way to interpret the text is to place the emphasis on the glory of God that is revealed in Jesus Christ. For example, Towner thinks that a more precise interpretation based on the grammatical, syntactical, and lexical evidence equates Jesus Christ not with God but with *the glory* of the great God and Savior. Thus the blessed hope depicted here is the personal appearance of Jesus Christ, who is the embodiment and expression of God's glory (Towner 2006: 758). Fee argues at length for an emphasis on the glory of God rather than the divinity of Christ (Fee 2007: 440-46). Though Towner and Fee make strong arguments for the coming of Christ as the full and final manifestation of God's glory, I am inclined to follow the majority, who interpret the combination *our great God and Savior, Jesus Christ* as an appositional construction, which thus affirms the deity of Christ. I agree with Witherington: "Here it is likely, since only one manifestation and hope is referred to, that we have an example of Jesus being called both God and Savior" (2006: 144).

What the Savior Did 2:14

The literary style of verse 14 suggests that the writer may be inserting a hymnlike structure within a confessional statement. By introducing the statement with the word *who* (*hos*), followed by three verbal clauses, the author reflects the Semitic style of synthetic parallelism (Collins: 353):

who (*hos*) gave himself for us (14a)
  that (*hina*) he might redeem us from all iniquity (14b)
    and purify for himself a people of his own (14c)

By introducing the statement this way, parallels are evident with the way other christological hymns are introduced in the NT—all with "who" (NTG: Col 1:15-20; Phil 2:6-11; 1 Tim 3:16; Titus 2:14). Perhaps these hymnlike materials were preexisting oral or written traditional units about Jesus Christ, since each of them presents an interpretation of the death of Jesus Christ in the form of a hymn (Collins: 353).

Who gave himself for us is similar to the phrase *who gave himself a ransom for all* (1 Tim 2:6). Similar language is used in Galatians 1:4 and Mark 10:45. In these passages, four elements are repeated in the structure: (1) a verb "to give/hand over"; (2) "himself/his soul"; (3) a preposition "on behalf of/instead of"; and (4) "me/us/many/all" (I. H. Marshall 1999: 282). Jesus said, "The Son of Man came not to be served but to serve, and to give his life a ransom for many" (Mark 10:45). In Titus 2:14a, however, the tense of the verb *gave* indicates that in the past Jesus offered his life for our redemption. The reflexive pronoun *himself* is used instead of "give his life" in Mark 10:45. And the preposition *for* us (*hyper hēmōn*) is used instead of "for many" (*anti pollōn*). Jesus gave himself in a voluntary death at the cross. This voluntary death was a sacrifice "for us," which expresses the substitutionary nature of that death. In presenting Jesus' death in this way, Paul uses language similar to what we find in other NT passages that describe the death of Christ as "for us" (Rom 5:6, 8; 14:15; 1 Cor 15:3; 2 Cor 5:14-15; 1 Thess 5:10). While other NT verses speak of Jesus' death as victory over the powers of Satan and evil (Rom 6:6, 14; Col 2:15), Titus 2:14 states the death of Jesus in the language of sacrifice for sin. Jesus died for us.

Two clauses state the purpose of Jesus' death. The clause *that he might redeem us from all iniquity* is negative. It reflects Titus 2:12, where believers renounce ungodliness and worldly passions. *Iniquity* means lawlessness. To the Hellenistic Jews on the island of Crete, a message of release from the guilt of not keeping the OT law was indeed good news (Quinn 1990: 173). The verb *redeem* means to set free, as a slave is set free. This verb expresses God's action in freeing us from enslavement to sin. In a similar way, God redeemed or liberated the children of Israel from enslavement in Egypt (Exod 6:6; Deut 7:8; 2 Sam 7:23). In Jesus Christ, that which holds one in the slavery of sin is dismissed, eliminated.

The second clause is positive: *to purify for himself a people of his own.* This clause uses language from Exodus 19:5-6 and Ezekiel 37:23. Exodus 19:5-6 indicates that the people God redeemed from Egypt are now God's own possession and are to be holy. Christians are not only set free from sin through the death of Jesus; they are also set apart as God's own possession. Ezekiel 37:23b says, "I will save them from all the apostasies into which they have fallen, and will cleanse them.

Then they shall be my people, and I will be their GOD." The verb *to purify* means to cleanse from sin. Redemption in Titus 2:14 means that persons are released from the control of sin and made holy to the degree that they are claimed as God's own treasure.

Finally, the author comes back to where he began in verses 11-12, with a concluding emphasis on moral behavior. The redeemed and cleansed people of God are *zealous for good deeds* (Titus 2:14c). The author's concern for good deeds is seen also in 1:8, 16; 2:7, 14; 3:1, 8, 14. In using the phrase *zealous for good deeds,* Paul has come full circle with the theme of grace. The grace of God appeared in the incarnation of Jesus Christ (2:11), trains us to live a godly life in the present time (v. 12), transforms us through the death and resurrection of Jesus Christ (v. 14), and enables us to walk in discipleship now (v. 14). Redemption and discipleship go hand in hand. One without the other is incomplete. In contrast to the non-Christian Cretans, who are unfit for any good deed (1:16), the author elaborates on the grace of God, which trains us to say yes to self-control, upright, and godly living (2:12b), and urges us to give ourselves energetically to virtuous living (2:14c). Christians are eager to live out the good deeds of Titus 2:1-10 made possible by participating in God's enabling grace. Christians who are zealous for good deeds are not trying to achieve salvation. Instead, they are living out the saved life made possible by God's enabling grace as the Holy Spirit gives them victory over sin (Rom 8:12-13; Gal 5:16-26).

Paul has clarified the Christian message over against Hellenistic Judaism, imperial religion, and Greco-Roman gods by using imagery and language from contemporary culture. In so doing, the apostle openly declares that God saves us in Jesus Christ and not in Roman imperial religion, with its gods and goddesses, or in pre-Christian Judaism.

A transitional verse (2:15) moves the reader from the confessional statement to a new paragraph that draws attention to the way Christians live and relate to the larger world around them. With a threefold command, Paul tells Titus to carry out his leadership in the church in Crete. *Declare these things; exhort and reprove with all authority. Let no one look down on you.* Titus is commanded to promote *these things* with three verbs: *speak*, *exhort*, and *reprove*. Like Timothy, with full authority from the apostle Paul, Titus must lead the church and not allow anyone to look down on him (1 Tim 4:12). In the first century, aged men were regarded as authoritative and full of wisdom. Neither Timothy nor Titus had yet reached the customary age of having such authority in that society. Nevertheless, they are commanded to speak God's message with authority, since their message comes from the authoritative apostolic tradition and from God.

THE TEXT IN BIBLICAL CONTEXT

The Grace of God

The word *grace* (*charis*) appears 155 times in the NT and 100 times in the Pauline letters. *Grace* occurs 13 times in the letters to Timothy and Titus (1 Tim 1:2, 12, 14; 6:21; 2 Tim 1:2-3, 9; 2:1; 4:22; Titus 1:4; 2:11; 3:7, 15). The root word for *grace* means well-being. In the LXX, it translates two Hebrew words—one meaning favor and the other meaning the action of a stronger person who voluntarily chooses to come to the aid of a weaker person. Often this stronger one is God, who acts to supply grace to weak or needy persons (Gen 39:21; Exod 3:21; 11:3; 12:36).

In the NT, *grace* is often used in greetings at the beginning and end of Paul's letters. Used this way, the term suggests well-being and is associated with peace. Sometimes the term is translated *thanks.* And sometimes it is used for the free gifts (*charismata*) that God supplies for the ministry of the church. More often it is associated with salvation that comes to humanity through God's goodness and love in Jesus Christ.

Paul says in Titus 2:11, *For the grace of God has appeared, bringing salvation to all.* And in 3:7 the writer employs the phrase *justified by his grace*. Why does Paul say *justified by grace* instead of "justified by faith"? Apparently Paul calls attention to what God has done for us in providing salvation rather than on our response of faith in laying hold of that salvation. God is the supplier of grace. He is "the God of all grace" (1 Pet 5:10).

God's graciousness and kindness toward sinful humanity are seen in John's way of interpreting the incarnation of Jesus Christ. "The Word became flesh and lived among us, and we have seen his glory, the glory as of a father's only son, full of grace and truth" (John 1:14). Revelation in Jesus Christ is an epiphany of God's grace similar to that which is described in Titus 2:11. Favor bestowed on others by the superior also is used in Luke-Acts to describe God's bestowal of salvation on the early church. "With great power the apostles gave their testimony to the resurrection of the Lord Jesus, and great grace was upon them all" (Acts 4:33). In Iconium, Paul and Barnabas "testified to the word of his [God's] grace" (14:3). And in a final meeting with the Ephesian elders at Miletus, Paul states, "If only I may finish my course and the ministry that I received from the Lord Jesus, to testify to the good news of God's grace" (20:24). Then Paul says, "And now I commend you to God and to the message of his grace" (20:32).

Paul also uses the phrase "justified by grace" in Romans. He writes, "They are now justified by his grace as a gift, through the redemption that is in Christ Jesus" (3:24). Similarly, Romans 5:9 says that we are justified by Christ's blood. In both 3:24 and 5:9, grace is the Jesus Christ *event* of redemption through his death on the cross. As one experiences this event of grace, one enters into the *state* of grace wherein we have peace or well-being with God (5:1-2).

Paul describes the abundance and power of grace in Romans 5:20-21: "Where sin increased, grace abounded all the more." A more literal translation is "Grace super-abounded." Grace is not only equal to the depth and power of sin; it also surpasses it. Paul concludes, "Just as sin exercised dominion in death, so grace might also exercise dominion through justification." The power of grace renders the power of sin unable to hold humanity in slavery (6:6). "For sin will have no dominion over you, since you are not under law but under grace" (6:14). Therefore, Christians do not continue in sin because God's grace is transformative. It brings change and delivers one from the ruling power of sin (6:1-2, 15). Likewise in Titus, the grace of God brings change in moral behavior by "training us to renounce impiety and worldly passions" and making us "zealous for good deeds" (2:12, 14). This abundance and power of grace leads Paul to use the phrase "justified by his grace" in Titus 3:7 rather than the forensic term "justification by faith."

In Ephesians, Paul talks about the richness of God's mercy and love in making us alive in Jesus Christ. He then adds parenthetically, "By grace you have been saved" (2:5), and summarizes, "For by grace you have been saved through faith, and this is not your own doing; it is the gift of God" (2:8). The antecedent of *gift* is *grace*, the unmerited graciousness and gifting of God for our good, provided in salvation in Jesus Christ. God abundantly poured out the riches of his grace upon the Ephesians through the blood of Christ in redemption (1:7-8). This salvation in Jesus Christ is *according to his [God's] own purpose and grace, . . . given to us in Christ Jesus before the ages began, but has now been revealed through the appearing of our Savior Christ Jesus*" (2 Tim 1:9-10). The grace that brings salvation is a free gift of God and is not based on human righteousness (Rom 11:6; Titus 3:5). In response, Paul became a servant of God's grace (Eph 3:2, 7). The Ephesian church lives "to the praise of his glorious grace" (Eph 1:6). Likewise, the Colossian believers are bearing fruit because they have not only heard of God's grace, but have also "truly comprehended the grace of God" (Col 1:6).

Instead of juxtaposing faith and works, Paul juxtaposes grace and sin. Grace is God's action in Jesus Christ, which sets one free from the ruling power of sin. The greater quality and quantity of God's graciousness given to us in Jesus Christ leads Paul to talk about "justification by grace" rather than only our human response expressed in the phrase "justification by faith" (Rom 3:26; Titus 3:7). Our human response accepts God's grace and lives in that grace by doing good deeds (Titus 2:14; 3:8).

He Gave Himself for Us

In Titus 2:14, Paul says, *He it is who gave himself for us,* and in Titus 3:5, *He saved us.* Salvation through Jesus is a central theme in the letters to Timothy and Titus (1 Tim 1:15; 2:5-6; 4:10; 6:13; 2 Tim 1:9-10; 2:10; 3:15; Titus 2:11-14; 3:4-7).

Several OT motifs point to Jesus' suffering and death, such as slain lamb (John 1:29; 1 Pet 1:19; Rev 5:6-14), blood sacrifice (Rom 3:25; 5:9; Eph 1:7; Heb 9:11-15), and suffering servant (Mark 10:45; Phil 2:5-11). Some NT passages ascribe the death of Christ to the forces of evil. Mark indicates that the religious leaders sought to kill Jesus out of their own fear and jealousy (Mark 3:6; 12:12-13; 14:1-2, 10-11; 15:10). Luke shows a tie between the temple leaders and "the power of darkness" (Luke 22:53). John openly states that Satan entered into the heart of Judas in betraying Jesus (13:2, 27) and that the hatred against Jesus came from the evil ruler (14:30). Speeches in Acts indicate that Jesus was betrayed, rejected, condemned, murdered, and crucified, despite his innocent life (2:23, 36; 3:13-15; 4:10, 26-28; 7:51-52; 13:27-29). Paul also blames the evil rulers of this age and the role of the principalities and powers for putting Jesus to death (1 Cor 2:8). Hebrews speaks of Jesus facing hostility from sinners (12:2-3), and 1 Peter indicates that Jesus' death came through rejection by human beings (2:4, 7). John indicates that Jesus came to destroy the works of the devil (1 John 3:8). And Revelation makes clear that the powers of evil make war on the Lamb (17:4).

Other NT passages present the death of Christ as an act of God's love (John 3:16; Rom 5:8; 1 John 3:16; 4:19). Jesus was aware of his impending death and often spoke about it (Mark 8:31-34; 9:9, 30-32; 10:32-34; 10:45; Luke 9:51-52). Jesus described his coming death in the language of the suffering servant of Isaiah 52:13–53:12, who gives his life as a ransom for many (Mark 10:45), and as the bridegroom who is taken away (2:19-20). The Gospel writers also interpret Jesus' death as the fulfillment of Scripture (Luke 18:31), including Jesus' own interpretation of his death after the resurrection (24:44-47).

In John's Gospel, the death of Christ is voluntary. John speaks of God sending and giving his Son to save the world (John 3:16-17). Jesus is the Good Shepherd who voluntarily gives his life for the sheep (10:11, 15, 18). No one takes his life from him because he has power to lay it down and take it up again (10:14-18). Jesus did not reject the cross. Instead, Jesus saw the cross as the way to glorify the Father

(12:27-28). In John's Gospel, glory is directly related to the cross. Moreover, the death of Christ removes the defilement of our sins (1 John 1:9). In so doing, it changes the sinner rather than changing God.

On Pentecost, Peter openly preached that the religious leaders of the time had killed Jesus, who was "handed over to you according to the definite plan and foreknowledge of God" (Acts 2:23). Paul declared "that Christ died for our sins in accordance with the scriptures, and that he was buried, and that he was raised on the third day in accordance with the scriptures" (1 Cor 15:3-4). Paul also spoke of God's "sending his own son" into the world to "deal with sin" and "redeem those who were under the law" (Rom 8:3; Gal 4:4-5). God put Jesus forward as a sacrifice of atonement (Rom 3:25). Jesus died for us (Rom 5:6, 8; 8:32; 1 Cor 15:3; 2 Cor 1:5; 5:14; Gal 3:13; Eph 5:2; 1 Thess 5:10). However, in describing the death of Jesus in this way, Paul does not make a separation between Jesus and God at the cross. God was present in Christ's death on the cross, reconciling the world to himself (2 Cor 5:19). In the death of Christ, God was not punishing Jesus for our sin. Instead, God absorbed the punishment and wrath of human sin against God in Christ's death on the cross. Through the cross, God demonstrated love and grace in Christ and offered forgiveness to the world. N. T. Wright says, "He would defeat evil by letting it do its worst to him" (1996: 565).

Absorbing punishment for sin points to the cost of forgiveness. Cost is implied in the terms *redeem* in Titus 2:14, *ransom* in 1 Timothy 2:6, and "redemption" in Ephesians 1:7. Peter describes the cost as the "precious blood of Christ" (1 Pet 1:19). Paul says, "You are not your own. . . . You were bought with a price" (1 Cor 6:19-20). He has this same idea in mind when he says that Christ *gave himself for us that he might redeem us from all iniquity and purify for himself a people of his own* (Titus 2:14). It was costly for God to forgive and make us a people of his own.

Reconciliation is at the center of Christ's work at the cross (Rom 5:6-11; 2 Cor 5:18-19). Reconciliation takes place if an innocent one in a broken relationship is willing to absorb the pain and hurt of sin that has disrupted the relationship. In the cross, God and Christ expressed love for enemies. The suffering, pain, agony, and death on the cross point to the ultimate cost of redemption. Jesus, the sinless one, took upon himself the full consequences of sin's power over humanity, which found expression in the violence that killed him. At the cross, sin did its worst by putting Jesus to death. But God raised Jesus and defeated death. The death and resurrection of Christ brought victory over the powers of evil and defeated the power of sin (Rom 5:21; 6:6, 14; 1 Cor 15:20-28; Col 1:13; 2:15). Together the cross and the resurrection became the good news of the gospel. Through them, God poured out divine love in the person, life, teachings, and death of his Son. God raised him from the dead, thereby defeating evil and making it possible for humankind to be set free from sin and the power of the demonic.

THE TEXT IN THE LIFE OF THE CHURCH

Grace in Anabaptist Perspective

All Christian groups value God's grace, but they differ on how grace is effective in Christian conversion and Christian living. Eastern Orthodox and Roman Catholic Christians see the sacraments as the means by which they experience grace. The Protestant Reformers understood grace as God's acceptance and forgiveness, granted by justification.

Justification takes place before sanctification can begin. Understood this way, grace is not primarily a transforming power. Protestant Reformers understood justification in a forensic sense: God *declares* the sinner forgiven through the death of Christ. The death of Christ frees one from the guilt of sin. God pronounces one righteous even though one continues as a sinner. In short, justification by faith is a legal declaration of God's acceptance of the sinner. In justification, one experiences forgiveness, but not necessarily a change within the self. Justification comes at the beginning of the sanctification process rather than at its end. In this view, grace and salvation are largely synonymous with forgiveness. In this view, justification is separated from sanctification.

On the other hand, Anabaptists understood grace as a transforming power. Justification and sanctification take place simultaneously and are not separated. One who becomes a Christian experiences regeneration and new birth by the Holy Spirit. The believer thus puts on Christ and begins to walk in Christian discipleship. Anabaptists talked about "the *obedience* of faith" (cf. Rom 1:5; 16:26) more than *justification* by faith. In emphasizing grace and faith, Anabaptists disagreed with Luther's emphasis on one's legal status before God (forensic justification) at the expense of real personal reformation. Anabaptists said that saving faith transforms believers in the here and now (Snyder 1995: 44). Grace works both objectively and subjectively. Grace brings an ontological change within the new Christian believer (Beachy 1977: 72). In addition to forgiveness, one is changed by the working of God's grace within the human personality.

Moreover grace finds expression through the presence and work of the Holy Spirit, who enables one to walk in obedience to Christ. Repentance characterized the beginning of the saving process, and good works continued this saving work through the transforming and enabling grace of God. Thus justification and sanctification belong together.

Anabaptist writers agreed that salvation comes by the life, person, and work of Jesus Christ on the cross. God's grace in Christ is seen, for example, in the writings of Menno Simons:

> For all the truly regenerated and spiritually minded conform in all things to the Word and ordinances of the Lord. Not because they think to merit the atonement of their sins and eternal life. By no means! In this matter they depend upon nothing except the true promise of the merciful Father, given in grace to all believers through the blood and merits of Christ, which blood is and ever will be the only and eternal medium of our reconciliation; and not works, baptism, or the Lord's Supper, as said above repeatedly. For if our reconciliation depended on works and ceremonies, then grace would be a thing of the past, and the merits and fruits of the blood of Christ would end. Oh, no, it is grace, and will be grace to all eternity; all that the merciful Father does for us miserable sinners through His beloved Son and Holy Spirit is grace. (*CW*: 396-97)

In summary, Anabaptists gave "effective" grace a larger emphasis than Catholic or Protestant Reformers. Grace comes from God and expresses itself in the incarnation, death, and resurrection of Christ. The Christian believer experiences grace not only as forgiveness but also as a change of life as the Holy Spirit's presence enables one to walk in obedience to Christ. The Anabaptists saw in Romans 5:20-21; 6:6, 14 that the forces of sin and evil are defeated by God's grace in Christ and that one can walk in the joy of obedience. This is discipleship in grace.

Views of the Atonement

No one theory of the atonement is sufficient to explain God's work of redemption. In the history of Christian doctrine, three major theories of the atonement have come to us. From the time of the early church fathers until Anselm, the Christus Victor model of the atonement dominated. According to this model, sinful persons are captive to Satan. How then did Christ free persons from the power of the demonic? In the life of Jesus a struggle took place between Jesus and Satan. Jesus was victor by his faithfulness to God. This faithfulness resulted in his death at the cross. At the cross, Jesus paid the price of redemption in order to rescue persons from Satan's hold on them. But the cross alone did not defeat the devil. The resurrection was an integral part of the Christus Victor model: in the resurrection, God triumphed over Satan. "If in killing Christ, Satan overstepped his legal bounds, then this verdict was not rendered until God raised Christ, thereby declaring his innocence" (Finger 1985: 321). Thus the Christus Victor model includes the life, death, and resurrection of Christ. It finds biblical support in NT passages that describe the work of Christ in the language of victory over evil powers (Rom 5:21; 6:6, 14; Gal 4:3-9; Eph 1:19-22; 2:14-16; 3:7-13; 6:12; Phil 2:9-11; Col 1:13-14; 2:8-15; 1 Pet 3:18-22).

During the eleventh century, Anselm of Canterbury (d. 1109) developed what came to be known as the Substitutionary model in *Cur Deus homo*. This model is sometimes called the Satisfactory Theory of the Atonement. It became the predominant view in Western Christianity, especially in Lutheran and Reformed Orthodox Protestantism. It maintains a central place in modern evangelical thought. Anselm's view focuses primarily on the objective side of the cross, on what took place between God and Christ and between God and humankind. It says little about what happens subjectively to the Christian believer in redemption. In Anselm's view, sin consists in not rendering to God what is his due—not being subject to the will of God. Disobedience places one under the wrath of God, since God is holy and cannot tolerate sin. Human failure to honor God makes one guilty. One must therefore pay for this debt of sin. But humankind is unable to pay the debt to God that they owe. For the sake of justice, the satisfaction desired must be equal to the sin committed against God.

No sinner can make this satisfaction, so the penalty must be paid by another person. Only God can make this satisfaction. And since humanity was originally given the task of obeying God and overcoming Satan, none but a human person ought to do this. Consequently, no one but a God-man can carry out this task (Finger 1985: 307). As the sinless human/divine person, Jesus must die to satisfy God's holiness. At the cross, God poured out his punishment upon sin in Jesus' death. Jesus paid the penalty for our sin. Moreover, the obedient life of Christ earned the reward of eternal life, but since the Son of God does not need this reward, it is bestowed on those for whom he died. Jesus, by dying in our place as a substitution for us, paid our deserved penalty of eternal death and thus merited the reward of eternal life for us. Anselm's view was based on logic and a Roman view of law, guilt, and justice.

Reformed theologian Charles Hodge (d. 1878), following the thought of John Calvin, emphasized the penal dimension of the cross in this satisfaction. In the penal view of satisfaction, Jesus bore the wrath of God. "He made him [Jesus] to be sin who knew no sin" (2 Cor 5:21), and thus Jesus became the object upon whom God poured out wrath on sin. Therefore, Christ is punished in death at the cross, a death in place of the individual, and Christ's righteousness is imputed to that individual. In satisfying God's justice, Jesus Christ became the individual's substitute. Justification by faith is an objective transaction between God and Jesus. In the lawcourt of God, the individual is pronounced forgiven, justified by one's faith in Jesus, even though the believer is and continues to be a sinner. In this view, nothing subjectively happens; the individual is not changed.

The traditional Western understanding of the Satisfaction View leaves one with two unanswered questions. First, how can one interpret the cross as God punishing Jesus, thereby separating God from Jesus, when God was present in Christ and thereby reconciling the world to himself (2 Cor 5:18-19)? And second, is there not a subjective element in salvation? Does not the individual believer experience a new birth and release from the power of sin?

A short time after Anselm, a third view of atonement arose in the writings of Peter Abelard (d. 1142), called the Moral Influence view, which had a more subjective dimension. Abelard said that the cross is not so much a propitiation or appeasement of God's *wrath* as it is a demonstration of God's *love*. The moral influence view points to the words of Paul, "God proves his love for us in that while we still were sinners Christ died for us" (Rom 5:8). The Moral Influence view also emphasized the words of Peter:

> For to this you have been called, because Christ also suffered for you, leaving you an example, so that you should follow in his steps.
> "He committed no sin,
> and no deceit was found in his mouth."
> When he was abused, he did not return abuse; when he suffered, he did not threaten; but he entrusted himself to the one who judges justly. He himself bore our sins in his body on the cross, so that, free from sins, we might live for righteousness; by his wounds you have been healed. (1 Pet 2:21-24)

By emphasizing the love and ethical righteousness of God, Abelard believed that God's love awakens a response from the sinner that results in justification. For Abelard, God's justice does not stand in opposition to grace. In his life and death, Christ has been the representative of God's love toward us, and now the risen Lord is our representative before God (Driver: 46).

Nevertheless, the Moral Influence view also raises some questions. Does not the NT emphasize sacrifice and forgiveness in the death of Christ? How does the resurrection apply to our salvation and redemption? Can human sinners change and become more God-conscious if there is not an inner change of life through redemption in Christ?

Believers churches have been influenced by all three of these major views. Believers churches see a tie between the Moral Influence view and Jesus' call to radical discipleship. They see a tie between the Christus Victor view and the Anabaptist emphasis on internal change through the new birth and the joy of walking in victory over sin in the resurrected Lord, through the power of the Holy Spirit. And they connect the Satisfaction view with release from sin in justification through the substitutionary blood of Christ. In reaction to Anselm's Satisfaction theory and Calvin's Penal theory, some scholars are promoting an alternative view of a nonviolent atonement (Weaver: 2001). When first presented, this nonviolent view was criticized for its failure to include all of the NT Scriptures dealing with atonement (C. D. Marshall). Nevertheless, atonement discussion continues in the church at large, and in believers churches some elements of a nonviolent atonement continue to receive attention (Green and Baker; Baker). Believers churches have gone beyond the three major views of atonement in the following ways.

First, believers churches combine justification and reconciliation through the cross of Christ. Reconciliation is at the heart of the atonement. God reaches out to sinners in love and grace and enters into a personal relationship with them through the person, life, death, and resurrection of Christ. The subjective dimension of salvation comes in the new birth and in one's relationship with the risen Lord. Reconciliation gives substance to justification in that it goes beyond legal or forensic justification to an actual experience of entering into right relationship with God. Salvation brings about a change in the individual's life as one experiences sanctification in the new birth. By placing reconciliation at the center of the atonement (at-one-ment), justification and grace are brought together in a dynamic relationship (Augsburger: 23, 39). Instead of being primarily a matter of jurisprudence, justification is a right-wising, or restoration, of right relations. The cross is not God's *punishing* Jesus, but *God's involvement with Jesus in love*, absorbing the punishment of human sin within himself so that sinful persons can be forgiven.

Second, believers churches emphasize a modified narrative Christus Victor view that involves the whole person, life, teachings, death, and resurrection of Christ (Finger 2004: 351-65). Instead of developing rational theories about the atonement, we can look at Christ's life, death, resurrection, and other metaphors describing salvation as metanarrative (McClendon: 229-37). In this narrative view, Jesus lived in faithfulness to God to the point of death at the cross. In his life, death, and resurrection, Jesus defeated Satan and the demonic powers of evil, thereby setting the Christian believer free from the ruling power of sin and Satan. As Christopher D. Marshall says:

> The power of sin was broken, then, not by some violent act of substitutionary punishment but through Jesus' own definitive refusal to perpetuate the cycle of violence and revenge. In his passion, Jesus adopted the position of supreme victim of human evil and depredation. Yet he refused to respond to his victimization by victimizing those who victimized him. Instead he absorbed the sin of human violence in his own bodily experience without retaliation. . . . It was God's will to make "the one who knew no sin to be sin for our sake, so that we might become the righteousness of God in him." This highly compressed, shorthand summary of what happened at the cross does not mean God made Christ into a sinner in order to punish him retributively for our sins. It means that God made the sinless one bear the full consequences of sin's dominion over humanity, displayed most graphically in the inescapable logic of violence. In Christ, sin did its very worst and Christ died. But God raised him from the dead and in so doing triumphed over the power of sin and death. (91-92)

Christian believers walk in the victory of Christ. Now evil expressed through ungodly evil powers, including the power of the state, stand under the lordship and judgment of Christ. Christian believers belong to the kingdom of God and follow the kingdom teachings of Jesus, experiencing victory over the power of sin through the presence of the Holy Spirit as they walk in the resurrection of Christ. Walking with the living Christ in life, including his way of peace, gives Christians freedom as citizens in God's kingdom not to yield to sin and not to give in to the power of the state when it calls for ungodly behavior. It provides accountability in the church as each Christian helps the other in Christian obedience and mutual care.

Third, believers churches emphasize the grace of God in its larger dimension as an expression of God's love and mercy at the cross, by which the cost of forgiveness is paid through the suffering and death of Christ. In this grace the Christian believer is not only forgiven of the sins of the past; one is also changed inwardly and relationally by the grace of God so that one lives in relationship with Jesus Christ and in fellowship with other Christian believers in the body of Christ, the visible church, through the presence of the living God in the Holy Spirit.

Titus 3:3-8

God's Transforming Work in Christ and in the Holy Spirit

PREVIEW

Christian believers in Crete once behaved like non-Christians (Titus 3:3), but now God has changed their lives (3:4-7). Paul contrasts *then* and *now*, as seen in the words *we were once* (3:3a) and *but when* (3:4a). This contrast calls attention to the transforming work of God in their lives by the gospel of Jesus Christ and the work of the Holy Spirit.

Titus 3:4-7 is one sentence in the Greek NT. Scholars debate whether these verses are an early Christian hymn or whether they are a confessional statement. Its nonrhythmic style and lack of poetic elements (Fee 1994: 778-79) suggest that it may be a confessional statement expressing Pauline thought in a form amenable to Hellenistic Judaism (Fee 1988: 203). This confessional statement is not speaking about Christian baptism, as some interpret it. Rather, it declares God's great work of salvation in bringing about a change in one's life before water baptism. The unit of thought closes in 3:8a by identifying the confession as one of the faithful sayings.

OUTLINE

Once We Ourselves Were, 3:3
Second Confessional Statement, 3:4-8

EXPLANATORY NOTES

Once We Ourselves Were 3:3

To further elucidate the difference between Christian and non-Christian behavior in Crete, Paul describes the former manner of life before becoming Christian. The words *we ourselves* refer to Paul, Titus, and the Cretan Christians. Recalling this former way of life prepares for the confessional statement that follows in Titus 3:4-7. The phrases *we ourselves were once* and *but when* make a major contrast between their former manner of life and what they have become now through the gospel. In 1 Timothy 1:15 Paul confesses that he was *the foremost* of sinners. If God can save Paul, God can save anyone. Thus the gospel is for all people (2:3-6). By contrasting the former life of the Cretan Christians with what they have experienced in the gospel, Paul shows the moral change that the gospel makes in their lives as well.

Many vices characterized their pre-Christian life *[Vice Lists, p. 368]*. The first three vices in Titus 3:3 describe a people ignorant of God, disobedient, and deluded (I. H. Marshall 1999: 309). *Foolish* means unintelligent, without spiritual understanding, and insensible to spiritual values. *Disobedience* is behavior in opposition to God and his will for humanity. *Led astray* or *deluded* means people who wander about and are lost. It also refers to those who are deceived doctrinally and ethically to such a degree that they produce a spirituality marked by pagan characteristics (I. H. Marshall 1999: 310). These three vices characterize the deviant teachers in the letters to Timothy and Titus (Titus 1:16; 2 Tim 3:13). The fourth vice is enslavement to *passions and pleasures*. In the letters to Timothy and Titus, *passions* means sinful longings or cravings and refers to sinful pleasures (1 Tim 6:9; 2 Tim 2:22; 4:3; Titus 2:12). The term *pleasures* (*hēdonē*; cf. "hedonism") appears as a vice (pleasures of life) in the parable of the sower in Luke 8:14. Enslavement to passions and pleasures indicates bondage to a lifestyle of addiction. Towner says, "Once one is on this merry-go-round, it is difficult to get off" (1994: 254).

The remaining four vices represent antisocial behavior. *Spending life in malice and envy* implies a useless life. *Malice* means ill will and is used in other NT lists of vices (Rom 1:29; Eph 4:31; Col 3:8; 1 Pet 2:1). *Envy* also appears in NT vice lists and means the kind of attitude that leads to hatred of persons who have what we desire (Rom 1:29; Gal 5:21; 1 Tim 6:4; 1 Pet 2:1). I. H. Marshall concludes, "Malicious and envious people are odious; they cause other people to react with hatred, and they respond in kind. Community and society collapse" (1999: 311).

The last two vices, *despicable* and *hating one another*, mean being the subject of hate and hating one another. *Despicable* in classical literature carried the sense of being hated or abominable, which is the opposite of Christians loving one another (Collins: 359). The term can be used actively of someone who hates God or passively of someone hated by people. Combined with the term *one another* here in Titus 3:3, the term carries both a passive and active sense: being detested *and* hating one another (Mounce: 446). In short, Paul confesses that he himself, Titus, and the Christian believers in Crete formerly were much like the sinful Cretans. How has their change come about? The answer is found in the confessional statement that follows.

Second Confessional Statement 3:4-8

But when contrasts characteristics of God with characteristics of sinful life stated in Titus 3:3. By way of contrast, Paul sets forth a confessional statement about God's work of salvation. The statement includes God (v. 4), Jesus Christ (v. 6b), and the Holy Spirit (v. 5b). Though some NT scholars view Titus 3:4-7 as a pre-Pauline hymn that Paul modifies, it is more likely a confessional statement, for it lacks the literary quality of a hymn (Fee 1994: 778-79). Quinn writes, "There is no introductory formula, no word of praise or thanks for the God who is explicitly named, no regular pattern of syllables or accents per stich, a soft parallelism between the stichs, and no obvious chiasmic features, 'ring composition,' or the like" (Quinn 1990: 211).

This confessional statement is about salvation and is Pauline in thought and language. It describes what happened when God's revelation of kindness and love appeared in contrast to the vices of Titus 3:3. Fee summarizes the statement as follows:

> *What* God did "when" his "kindness and love" for mankind appeared, was to save us. This is the main subject and verb of the whole sentence. The rest of the sentence gives the *basis* (his mercy), the *what* (rebirth, renewal, justified), the *means* (by the Holy Spirit, "by his [Christ's] grace"), and the *goal* (the hope of eternal life) of salvation. (Fee 1988: 203)

But when the goodness and loving kindness of God our Savior appeared calls attention to God's action in the past. The Roman emperor *appeared* to a given city in the vast empire and gave beneficence (gifts) to the people as savior. In direct contrast, Paul refers to *God* as Savior rather than the Roman emperor. And the goodness and loving-kindness of God our Savior *appeared* in the coming of Jesus Christ into the world. The tense of the verb indicates that the incarnation took place in the past, as an act of God our Savior (Quinn 1990: 212). *Goodness* refers to God's kindness. *Loving kindness* (*philanthrōpia*, "benevolence, goodwill") is used of kings who claim that their kindness extends to all

(LXX: Esther 8:12[l] [Rest of Esther 16:11 NRSV]; 2 Macc 14:9; 3 Macc 3:15, 18). In Greek literature from Aristophanes to Plutarch, the term was used to claim that the Greek deities were philanthropic (Quinn 1990: 214). By using well-known terms in the Greco-Roman world, Paul informs the Jewish and Gentile Christians in Crete that the living God of history, rather than the Roman emperor, is the Savior who offers goodness and loving-kindness. God's goodness and philanthropy have appeared in the coming of Christ into the world. Titus 3:4 is like Titus 2:11 and 2 Timothy 1:9-10, which say that Christ manifests God's grace by his incarnate appearance. The gospel of Jesus Christ is the good news about God's goodness and philanthropy.

Basis

He saved us, not because of any works or righteousness that we have done, but according to his mercy (Titus 3:5a). With these words Paul states the *basis* of salvation. The time indicators *once* and *then* (vv. 3-4) show that salvation has already taken place for the Cretan Christians. Their salvation experience has delivered them from their former sinful lifestyle. The main verb, *He saved us*, is preceded by two phrases, one negative and the other positive. Negatively, Paul says that our salvation is *not because of any works of righteousness that we have done.* Positively, our salvation comes *according to his mercy.* Another contrast is made between what we have done and what God did through his mercy.

In the negative phrase, Paul states that no human effort is good enough to save us, as he writes elsewhere in the NT (Rom 3:27-28; 4:2-6; 9:11; Gal 2:16; Eph 2:9; 2 Tim 1:9). Instead, with a positive phrase, Paul says that our salvation comes *because of* God's *mercy* (Titus 3:5 TNIV). The term *mercy* was used in the LXX to translate the Hebrew word for God's covenant love in the OT (*ḥesed*). That same divine mercy undergirds God's motive in initiating a new covenant relationship in Jesus Christ. Mercy is tied to God's goodness and love as motivating factors for saving action. Elsewhere in the letters to Timothy and Titus, salvation is due to God's mercy (1 Tim 1:12, 16), God's grace (1 Tim 1:14; 2 Tim 1:9; Titus 2:11; 3:7), and God's purpose (2 Tim 1:9). Jesus came into the world "to seek out and to save the lost" (Luke 19:10; 1 Tim 1:15). Quinn rightly comments, "In the salvation of human beings, God is wholly subject, men and women are wholly objects" (1990: 217).

Means

Through the water of rebirth and renewal of the Holy Spirit (Titus 3:5b) describes the *means* by which salvation comes. God is the one who saves. Attention is focused on the means by which that salvation is subjectively experienced. Scholars debate whether the author is talking about *two* separate experiences (infant baptism and confirmation in some Christian traditions, or salvation and baptism of the Holy Spirit in other Christian traditions), or *one* Christian experience with two dimensions. Interpreting the text as referring to two separate experiences creates a danger in some Christian traditions of making infant baptism an outward ceremony without an inner transformation of the heart. Interpreting the text as referring to two separate experiences creates the problem of separating salvation from sanctification. By separating the salvation experience from a subsequent experience of baptism with the Holy Spirit, one runs the risk of reducing salvation to forgiveness without a change of life.

It is more likely that the author is describing one event from two different angles (I. H. Marshall 1999: 321). These twin angles (*rebirth and renewal*) of inner transformation are seen in Ezekiel 36:26-27; John 3:5-8; and 1 Corinthians 6:11. Taken this way, the word *and* links two aspects of the one event of Christian conversion (Mounce: 449). Also, only one preposition is used. Ordinarily, if two separate activities are meant, the preposition would be repeated to ensure that the distinction is made by the reader. If two separate events were in the author's mind in Titus 3:5b, he would have used the preposition *through* two times in the phrase.

Paul says that the *Holy Spirit* is the agent at work, *washing* (3:5 TNIV; used metaphorically for conversion; not infant baptism) the person who turns to Christ. This washing is further defined by two metaphors used as synonyms: *rebirthing* and *renewing* the person who responds in faith to God's salvation. The words *rebirth* and *renewing* are twin metaphors for the same spiritual reality (Fee 1988: 205). This washing is characterized by new life and renewal (Fee 1994: 782). The entire phrase is soteriological, modifying the main verb in 3:5a: *He saved us.* Paul is emphasizing the work of the Holy Spirit in cleansing one from former sins (3:3) and creating a new people, who, by the outpouring of the Holy Spirit, are equipped for good deeds (3:8b; Fee 1994: 783).

The term *washing* (TNIV) or *water* (NRSV) signifies a bath, an act of washing. It is used in Ephesians 5:26 for Christ's washing of the church. The term was used for ceremonial washings in late Judaism, and perhaps as a rite of initiation into the Eleusinian mystery religion (Collins: 364). In the Christian context, washing consists of *rebirth*, a term meaning a new beginning or a regeneration (I. H. Marshall 1999: 319-20). It is similar to Jesus' teaching on the new birth (NRSV: birth "from above") in John 3:3-8. Talk of rebirth is found in Hellenistic Judaism and in the mystery cults. In Titus 3:5 the term *rebirth* is like Paul's metaphor of death, burial, and new life in Romans 6:4-14. Moreover, the washing includes *renewal.* This term is used in Romans 12:2 in reference to the renewal of the mind. In 2 Corinthians 5:17, Christians enter into a new created order of existence. In Ephesians 4:24, Christians put on the new person created in God's likeness.

Renewal can be an event or a process, but the context of Titus 3:5 indicates that it is a once-for-all renewal because salvation is seen as an accomplished fact (Mounce: 449). Thus the work of the Holy Spirit in Christian conversion consists of cleansing one from the defilement of sin and renewing or re-creating the inner person. These two aspects take place simultaneously in the one event of normal Christian conversion. The thought is similar to Colossians 3:5-10, which speaks of putting off the old self and putting on the new. Through the work of the Holy Spirit in rebirth and renewal, the Christian believer comes to a new awareness of the self as belonging to God. Christian conversion is change from self-centeredness to God-centeredness as the Holy Spirit cleanses from sin and renews one's life. Experiencing Christian conversion in this way cannot take place through infant baptism, but rather is an existential experience with God.

This Spirit he poured out on us richly through Jesus Christ our Savior (Titus 3:6). The means of salvation includes Jesus Christ and the outpouring of the Holy Spirit. The Holy Spirit, who is instrumental in rebirthing and renewing in Christian conversion, is intimately tied to God and to Jesus Christ. The subject of the sentence is God. God has given the Spirit through Jesus Christ. The verb *poured out* is the same word that describes the outpouring of the Holy Spirit at Pentecost (Acts 2:17-18) and the outpouring of the Holy Spirit upon the Gentile believers (10:45). It is used several times in the NT of the Holy Spirit (Acts 2:17-18, 33; 10:45; Rom 5:5). Additionally, the Holy Spirit is poured out *richly* or profusely, indicating the abundance and lavishness of God's gift of the Spirit (Collins: 366). The word picture suggests a cloudburst of water on a parched land, implying that the Holy Spirit is poured out lavishly *upon us* *[Holy Spirit, p. 351]*.

This lavish supply of the Holy Spirit is available to all who trust God for their salvation. Christian believers who are the recipients of God's loving-kindness and mercy (vv. 4-5) are now also recipients of the Holy Spirit given through Jesus Christ our Savior. As promised in John 14:16, 26, the Holy Spirit is sent by the Father in the name of Jesus. Since the whole Godhead is at work in our salvation, Paul concludes by naming a third person of the Trinity: *Jesus Christ our Savior*. The Holy Spirit is not poured out apart from Jesus. In salvation, God, Jesus

Christ, and the Holy Spirit are at work. In Luke-Acts, the Father is Savior in a hymnic context (Luke 1:47) and Jesus is Savior in kerygmatic contexts (Acts 5:31; 13:23). The outpouring of the Holy Spirit brings about an inner change of life through the washing, regenerating, and renewing work that transpires in Christian conversion. In this confessional statement, the author is not talking about a second, subsequent work of baptism with the Holy Spirit.

Goal

So that, having been justified by his grace, we might become heirs according to the hope of eternal life (Titus 3:7). This verse states the purpose, result, or *goal* of salvation. These words express the purpose of the main verb (*saved*, v. 5a) in the confessional statement. Paul concludes that we have been justified by his grace. Again, attention is drawn to what God has done for us rather than to our response of faith. We are made heirs of eternal life through the Holy Spirit's transformation and God's justifying grace. As elsewhere in the letters to Timothy and Titus, salvation will be fully realized eschatologically, in the future (Titus 2:11-14; 1 Tim 1:16; 4:8-10; 6:12-14). Christian believers have *the hope of eternal life* (Titus 1:2; 1 Tim 1:16; 4:10; 6:12). The ultimate work of the Godhead is that believers become heirs of eternal life. The content of our hope is nothing short of eternal life.

Finally, the author concludes, *The saying is sure* (Titus 3:8a). This is the last of the faithful sayings in the letters to Timothy and Titus *[Faithful Sayings, p. 344]*. Here in verse 8, the faithful saying points backward to the preceding verses in Titus 3:4-7. With this formula, the author affirms and puts in writing what has been passed on by oral communication. The NRSV indicates a break in the thought pattern by separating *The saying is sure* from the remainder of verse 8. However, the TNIV interprets the word *and* to suggest that the author is continuing the thought pattern by adding behavior to the doctrine laid out in 3:4-7.

The confessional statement is followed by the author's command that Titus declare these words to the Cretan Christians. So also Titus is to insist on these things (3:8b). *These things* and the *good works* that describe the Christian believers near the end of verse 8 suggest that Paul unites right theology and right practice. Both right doctrine and right behavior are underlying themes in the letters to Timothy and Titus. Accentuating the positive, Titus 2:14 and 3:8b emphasize *doing what is good* (TNIV).

Recipients of Titus's insistent teaching are *those who have come to believe in God.* The verb tense implies that these Cretan Christians are now being called upon to live out their belief through their behavior. The purpose for insisting on these things is to stimulate the believers in devoting themselves to good works. The positive teaching Titus insists on is *excellent and profitable to everyone*. Titus 3:8 thus serves as a transitional verse to the contrasting behavior that follows in verses 9-11.

THE TEXT IN BIBLICAL CONTEXT

The Holy Spirit and Salvation

In the OT, the Spirit came upon certain individuals at certain times for special tasks. All four Gospels record the coming of the Holy Spirit upon Jesus at his baptism (Matt 3:16-17; Mark 1:9-11; Luke 3:21-22; John 1:29-34, though John does not actually mention Jesus' baptism). A voice from heaven, in fulfillment of Psalm 2:7 and Isaiah 42:1, declared Jesus as the royal Son of God, and the Holy Spirit came upon Jesus "in bodily form" (Luke 3:22). From this point forward, the Holy Spirit was no longer a force or power that came and went, but now abided permanently on Jesus. Abiding in bodily form on Jesus points forward to the coming of the Holy Spirit upon the church as the body of Christ (1 Cor 12:13). Jesus carried out his ministry with the presence and power of the Holy Spirit (Luke 4:1, 14, 18).

The NT presents the Holy Spirit's work in three broad ways. At the time of conversion is regeneration by the Holy Spirit, commonly called the new birth, resulting in new life. Simultaneously, one is baptized with the Holy Spirit, which initiates one into the body of Christ. Second, various metaphors describe the work of the Holy Spirit, which have both a present effect in the Christian's life and a future expression. These metaphors include sealing with the Spirit, down payment of the Spirit, and the firstfruits of the Spirit. And third, many works of the Holy Spirit continue throughout the Christian's sojourn in this world. These works include being filled with the Spirit, being sanctified by the Spirit, and being transformed by the Spirit as one walks in the Spirit, is led by the Spirit, bears the fruit of the Spirit, and shares the gifts of the Spirit.

John the Baptist's work of water baptism was accompanied by the promise that Jesus would baptize with the Holy Spirit (Mark 1:8; Matt 3:11; Luke 3:16; John 1:33). Jesus himself taught the disciples that the Holy Spirit would be a perpetual presence (note the prepositions used to describe the Spirit's presence in John 14:16-17). The Holy Spirit will teach and bring to the disciples' minds what Jesus taught them (14:26), and the Holy Spirit will guide them into the truth as revealed in Jesus (16:13). Thus the Holy Spirit focuses attention not on the selfsame Spirit, but on glorifying Jesus Christ (16:14).

Following the resurrection, Jesus appeared to the disciples and commanded them, "Receive the Holy Spirit" (20:22). A short time later, Jesus commanded them to wait for the promise of the Father in the baptism with the Holy Spirit (Acts 1:4-5). Ten days later this promise was fulfilled in the coming of the Holy Spirit upon them on the day of Pentecost (2:1-4). This coming of the Holy Spirit is described as a pouring out of the Spirit in fulfillment of Joel 2:28 (Acts 2:4, 17).

Following Pentecost, water baptism and receiving the gift of the Holy Spirit are not separated or set in juxtaposition. This close connection between conversion, the gift of the Spirit, and water baptism is illustrated with other conversion stories in Acts, such as conversions of the Samaritans (8:12-17), of Cornelius (10:44-48), and of certain Ephesians (19:1-7). Thus the coming of the Spirit in these subsequent conversion stories in Acts may be described as Samaritan and Gentile mini-Pentecosts, similar to the Jewish Pentecost in Jerusalem.

Mention of baptism with the Spirit occurs four times in the Gospels (see above), twice in Acts (1:5; 11:16), and once in Paul. It is used for the birth of the church or for initiation into the church. It does not indicate a postconversion experience. In its only use by Paul, the phrase means initiation into the body of Christ. "In the one Spirit we were all baptized into one body—Jews or Greeks, slaves or free—and we were all made to drink of one Spirit" (1 Cor 12:13). All the Corinthian believers, without exception, have been baptized by the same Spirit into the one body of Christ.

In Christian conversion the tie between water baptism and Holy Spirit baptism is identified in the words of John: "There are three that testify: the Spirit and the water and the blood, and these three agree" (1 John 5:7-8). In the normal Christian conversion, one experiences the inner new birth by the Holy Spirit, and one bears outward testimony to this inward birth by water baptism as one is initiated into the body of Christ. In some cases there may be a baptism of blood through martyrdom. In Romans 8:9, Paul clarifies that one cannot separate taking Christ as Savior from having the Holy Spirit.

However, the book of Acts narrates subsequent fillings with the Holy Spirit beyond conversion. The disciples who were baptized with the Spirit at Pentecost were filled with the Holy Spirit (Acts 4:31). And Paul commands, "Be filled with the Spirit" (Eph 5:18). In short, baptism with the Holy Spirit in the NT is associated with water baptism, is related to but not the same as regeneration by the Holy Spirit, and initiates a believer into the body of Christ. Paul ties the work of the Holy Spirit to Joel's prophecy: *This Spirit he poured out on us richly through Jesus Christ our Savior* (Titus 3:6).

Paul uses several metaphors for the Spirit's work (Fee 1994: 806-8). "Down payment" calls attention to what we have now and what is yet to be (2 Cor 1:21-22; 5:5; Eph 1:14). It assures us that we have received the promise of the Spirit and that we are guaranteed the full inheritance in the future. In our present existence, the Holy Spirit is both evidence and guarantee that the future is now and yet to be (Fee 1994: 807). We have already received the firstfruits of the Spirit while we wait for the final redemption of our bodies (Rom 8:23). We are sealed with the Holy Spirit, meaning that we are identified as God's own people (2 Cor 1:21-22; Eph 1:13; 4:30).

Paul talks about the Holy Spirit's transforming work in believers as ongoing change into the likeness of Christ (2 Cor 3:18). We are set apart from sin and are constantly being changed as we grow in holiness of life (Rom 15:16; 1 Pet 1:2). The Spirit is the sanctifying agent, and the goal is conformity to the image of Christ (Rom 8:29). The Holy Spirit enables Christian believers to say no to sinful desires and to live holy lives (Rom 8:12-13). Just as there is freedom from the law in Christ, so there is freedom from living according to the flesh by the presence of the Holy Spirit (Gal 5:16-18). Christians who have put on Christ express a Christlike personality through the fruit of the Spirit (Gal 5:22-23). All Christians are given some gift of the Spirit within the body of Christ, to enable the church in mission and nurture so that the corporate body of Christ experiences unity as it grows into the likeness of Christ (Eph 4:11, 16).

As the Holy Spirit initiates one into the body of Christ through the baptism of the Spirit, so also the Spirit brings about spiritual formation within the corporate body of Christ, the Christian community. In Christian community, the unity of the Spirit is maintained in the bond of peace (Eph 4:3). And the Christian community expresses the fruit of the Spirit and the gifts of the Spirit.

THE TEXT IN THE LIFE OF THE CHURCH

Ways of Interpreting the Work of the Holy Spirit

The Christian church does not have a uniform understanding of the work of the Holy Spirit. At least three views are common. A one-stage view claims one major experience of the Holy Spirit. This experience includes regeneration, initial sanctification by the Holy Spirit, and a continuing walk with the Spirit, which produces growth into the likeness of Christ throughout the Christian life.

A two-stage view claims two major experiences in a twofold view of salvation. One kind of two-stage view is found in Christian traditions that practice infant baptism. The first stage is infant baptism, and a later stage is called confirmation. In Puritanism, the first stage is conversion, followed by a second stage, after conversion, in which one experiences confirmation, leading to sonship and assurance. In Wesleyanism, the two stages are defined as justification, in which one experiences forgiveness of sin and partial sanctification at conversion. At a later time, in a second stage, one experiences entire sanctification or Christian perfection. Wesleyan thought makes a distinction between salvation and sanctification, as seen in the words of the song *Rock of Ages.* "Be of sin the double cure: Save from wrath and make me pure" (A. M. Toplady). In the Holiness tradition, the two-stage view consists of conversion as deliverance from the *penalty* of sin, and a later experience of sanctification as deliverance from the *power* of sin. In the Keswick tradition, this second experience is called the "second blessing."

Historically, this second experience came to be associated with the baptism of the Spirit in various groups that have some tie to the Wesleyan movement. Some Methodists interpret the baptism of the Spirit as resulting in entire sanctification. R. A. Torrey (d. 1928) interpreted the baptism of the Spirit as empowerment for prayer and service, rather than sanctification. Others in the Holiness tradition, such as A. J. Gordon and A. B. Simpson, associated the baptism of the Spirit with the gifts of the Spirit, particularly divine healing. The Brethren in Christ, drawing on this Wesleyan heritage, emphasize a two-stage view of salvation, with partial sanctification initially, followed by an experience of whole sanctification.

A three-stage view arose in twentieth-century Pentecostalism, which grew out of the Holiness tradition. First is justification and forgiveness of sin. Second is sanctification by the Holy Spirit. And third is baptism with the Spirit, in which one receives the gifts of the Spirit, with the gift of tongues serving as evidence that one has received the baptism of the Spirit. This third-stage experience, manifested in the gift of tongues, separates the Pentecostal movement from other groups in the Holiness tradition.

The charismatic movement resulted in a new experience of grace and the Holy Spirit within many Christian denominations, including those practicing infant baptism and confirmation. The charismatic movement brought major renewal in the lives of millions of Christian believers. It, too, emphasized baptism with the Holy Spirit, but it did not always insist on the gift of tongues, as in Pentecostalism.

Sixteenth-century Anabaptism strongly emphasized the work of the Holy Spirit in Christian conversion. In Anabaptist thought, the inner work of the Holy Spirit first brings about regeneration. Regeneration or birth by the Holy Spirit is expressed outwardly in water baptism.

Anabaptists talked about three baptisms: of the Spirit, of water, and of blood (martyrdom). Water baptism, or believers baptism, which followed inner Spirit baptism, was for them an outer mark of an inner change. The baptized church was the visible gathering of the inwardly regenerated (Snyder 1995: 91).

Moreover, the Anabaptists tied the work of the Spirit to the Holy Scriptures and talked about the relationship between Word and Spirit. For them, divine authority was based on Scripture and Spirit together, rather than on Scripture alone (Snyder 1995: 88). Word and Spirit interacted dynamically in bringing salvation (Finger 2004: 425). And the work of the Holy Spirit, which brought about an inward change, also brought about the obedience of faith in Christian discipleship. Christian faith was not merely an inward assent to the Spirit, but an outward commitment to a new life in Christ in Christian community, the visible church. Anabaptists believed that the inner and outer realities must be joined together in true Christian experience (Snyder 1995: 92). Holding Word and Spirit together protects one from the stifling literalism of the written word on one hand, and from the subjective spiritualism that lacks obedience to Christ on the other hand. "Once justification by faith becomes real, the Holy Spirit comes to dwell within the believer, and this 'inner' Spirit transforms and allows an 'outer' life which corresponds to Christ's teaching. . . . Discipleship is impossible without a spiritual grounding. Spirituality, life in the Holy Spirit, becomes the only source for ethics" (Blough: 139, 144; cf. also Ewert 1983).

Like many other Christian denominations, Mennonites have experienced the effects of the charismatic movement. But Mennonites are not Pentecostals. Mennonites have a different understanding of the work of the Holy Spirit. As Mennonites enter into dialogue on the Holy Spirit with Pentecostals and charismatics, they emphasize the following:

- The work of the Holy Spirit goes beyond justification and forgiveness in Christian conversion; the Spirit effects the new birth, regeneration, sanctification, and new life in Christ.
- The Holy Spirit and the Word of God are closely related. The inner witness of the Spirit and the outer witness of God's written Word are joined together in understanding God's revealed will.
- Christ and the Holy Spirit work together. The Holy Spirit points to Christ (John 14:26; 16:14), who is the full revelation of God. Jesus Christ is the norm by which one discerns the true work of the Holy Spirit.

- The inner experience of the Holy Spirit coheres with the outer life of Christian discipleship. The reality of the Spirit's presence is also demonstrated in character, not only in charisma. The fruit of the Spirit is the evidence of the Spirit's presence. Christian discipleship expresses itself in holy living in a life of peace. Without the living power of God in one's life through the presence of the Holy Spirit, no one can be a faithful disciple of Christ.
- The individual believer's experience of the Spirit serves the corporate body of believers as the temple of the living God. Individualism yields to the unity of the Spirit in the one body of Christ.
- The Holy Spirit spurs continued growth into the likeness of Christ through spiritual formation.

Titus 3:9-11

Final Exhortations and Warnings

PREVIEW

With the adversative *but* in verse 9, Paul changes from upright Christian living to instruction for Titus on how to respond to opponents. Titus is to avoid one group (v. 9) and to disengage from a second group of opponents who insist on continuing in sin (vv. 10-11). Similar teaching is found in 2 Timothy 2:23-26.

OUTLINE

Things to Avoid, 3:9
Disengagement from Divisive Persons, 3:10-11

EXPLANATORY NOTES

Things to Avoid 3:9

Titus must avoid certain controversies and quarrels. The term *avoid* means literally go around so as to avoid (Knight 1992: 353). Titus is to avoid certain discussions because they are unprofitable and useless. Entering into dialogue with the opponents in these four areas is only a waste of time.

What is Titus to avoid? First, *stupid controversies* (3:9a). These controversies are foolish or stupid, rather than merely half-witted. They are pointless because they are inane and do not contribute to godliness (I. H. Marshall 1999: 334). Speculative, foolish controversies indicate a lack of substantive teaching by the opponents. Therefore, it is not necessary to enter into serious discussion on these matters.

Second, *genealogies* (3:9a). Hellenistic Jews in Crete debated genealogical details. Genealogies were important in OT history to determine the qualifications for priesthood. Plato and other Greek writers linked genealogies and myths (I. H. Marshall 1999: 335). The Cretan problem was similar to that of the opponents in Ephesus, who occupied themselves with myths and endless genealogies that promoted speculations rather than divine training that is known by faith (1 Tim 1:4).

Third and fourth: *dissensions and quarrels about the law* (3:9b). The term *dissensions* (NRSV) or *arguments* (TNIV) means strife, discord, contention. The term *quarrels* means verbal disputes, fighting, and personal quarrels. These are sins of speech and attitude. Quarrels are taking place around the law. The atmosphere of such bickering is unhealthy. What does one gain even by winning such a debate? These four controversies are unprofitable and worthless.

Disengagement from Divisive Persons 3:10-11

Next, Paul instructs Titus on how to engage persons who are divisive in the church. Following the pattern Jesus taught in Matthew 18:15-18, Paul outlines steps that Titus can take. The first two steps are face-to-face confrontation and *admonition*. Titus is to confront the one causing divisions twice (Titus 3:10). If after two attempts there is no change of behavior, he is to take a drastic third step: to *have nothing more to do with* that person. This third step is stated differently in Matthew 18:15-18, where the church is informed of the wrongdoing, warns the offender, and, if the person remains unrepentant, acts to dismiss the member.

In 2 Timothy 2:25, Paul expresses the hope that God will grant repentance to gently corrected opponents and help them come to know the truth. Here in Titus 3:10-11, Paul does not assume that the person will repent, though he does not rule out that possibility. Repentance is less likely because the one who does not give up evil ways after two admonitions *is perverted and sinful, being self-condemned* (3:11). The verb tense of the term *perverted* suggests a continuing, permanent state of perversion. Moreover, such a person remains *sinful*, deliberately and continually missing the mark. A person who does not respond to warning about one's own conduct is without excuse in that they condemn themselves. This calls for discipline. The kind of evil behavior Paul describes already brings condemnation upon such persons. The severity of action called for in 3:9-11 raises the question of whether Paul is exaggerating here.

THE TEXT IN BIBLICAL CONTEXT

Church Discipline

Several passages in the letters to Timothy and Titus speak about the need for church discipline (1 Tim 1:19-20; 5:19-20; 2 Tim 2:24-26; Titus 1:13; 3:9-11). No less than five persons are named who, among others, have left the faith: Hymenaeus (1 Tim 1:20; 2 Tim 2:17), Alexander (1 Tim 1:20; *perhaps* the same Alexander of 2 Tim 4:14), Phygelus and Hermogenes (2 Tim 1:15), and Philetus (2 Tim 2:17). Some may have quietly left the faith and the church. Others may be living in sin but have not yet left the church. In such cases, discipline is required. In the classic passage on church discipline, Jesus said:

> If another member of the church sins against you, go and point out the fault when the two of you are alone. If the member listens to you, you have regained that one. But if you are not listened to, take one or two others along with you, so that every word may be confirmed by the evidence of two or three witnesses. If the member refuses to listen to them, tell it to the church; and if the offender refuses to listen even to the church, let such a one be to you as a Gentile and a tax collector. Truly I tell you, whatever you bind on earth will be bound in heaven, and whatever you loose on earth will be loosed in heaven. (Matt 18:15-18)

Jesus taught similarly in John's Gospel: "If you forgive the sins of any, they are forgiven them; if you retain the sins of any, they are retained" (John 20:23). The desired goal of discipline is clearly stated in Jesus' teaching: that the erring one be corrected and restored to the Christian community. The terms *bind* and *loose* suggest moral discernment in the midst of the process. These terms were used by Jewish rabbis. To bind means to retain or obligate the person to a given command. To loose means to set one free from the obligation, or forgive them. Thus the activity that Jesus prescribes has two dimensions: moral discernment and reconciliation (Yoder 1992: 2). Jesus called for due process in working with the erring brother or sister. According to the Mosaic law, two witnesses are needed before any serious discipline can be exercised (Num 35:30; Deut 17:6; 19:15; John 8:17). Thus, Paul requires two or three witnesses before disciplining an elder (1 Tim 5:19-20). Jesus outlined three steps in an attempt to achieve reconciliation before accepting the fact that the offender must leave the fellowship of the church. The initiative is personal in that the one who addresses the offender is the one who knows about the offense. The intention is restorative, not punitive. Any offense is forgivable. And the goal is not to protect the church's reputation, but to serve the offender's well-being by restoring that person to the community

(Yoder: 1992: 2-3). When done in this way and with this prescribed purpose, believing men and women act in God's name. According to Paul, one works at restoring a fallen brother or sister with a spirit of gentleness (Gal 6:1-2; 2 Tim 2:25). Thus, church discipline is a ministry analogous to evangelism and mission.

> As evangelism and mission bring unbelievers into the way of Christ (discipleship), church discipline seeks to keep in the way of discipleship, or to restore to it, those believers who are in danger of abandoning the faith, whether through transgression, doctrinal error, coldness of heart, or any other cause. (Jeschke, *ME* 5:240)

In Acts 5:1-11, the lack of honesty by Ananias and Sapphira is met with severe punishment by the Holy Spirit. When the gospel reached into Samaria, Simon the magician believed and was baptized, but his commitment lacked honesty and sincerity. Peter confronted him directly, pointed out his sin, and asked him to repent (8:13, 18-24). Paul rebuked the Corinthian church not so much because a man was guilty of incest, but because the church had done nothing about this sin (1 Cor 5:1-2). Paul demanded that the Corinthian church rise to the challenge and discipline this erring brother.

At times NT church discipline is quick and severe (Acts 5:1-11; 1 Tim 1:20). Most often it is an ongoing task of helping a brother or sister who has strayed from the faith. Such is the case, for example, with Paul's confrontation of Peter at Antioch (Gal 2:11-14). If, however, there is no positive response on the part of the erring one when confronted at least twice, Paul tells Titus, *Have nothing more to do with anyone who causes divisions, since you know that such a person is perverted and sinful, being self-condemned* (Titus 3:10-11). Hopefully such hardness of heart is rarely found.

THE TEXT IN THE LIFE OF THE CHURCH

The Disciplined Church

From the time of Constantine until the sixteenth century, discipline was left to the state, which used the power of the sword. Sixteenth-century Anabaptists restored discipline to the life of the Christian community. Similarly, John Wesley called for loving dialogue as a form of discipline among the classes and bands that he organized.

Many times believers churches disciplined members too hastily. Not enough time was given to care lovingly for the person who had sinned, and sometimes persons were disciplined over cultural differences rather than real sin. Such was the case among some sixteenth-century Anabaptists, especially in Holland, and among some North

American Mennonites. Though discipline can be too harsh at one end of the spectrum, it can be too lenient or nonexistent on the other end of the spectrum. A church that has no discipline does not take sin seriously. We do well to find a way between these two extremes by following the advice of Paul: "My friends, if anyone is detected in a transgression, you who have received the Spirit should restore such a one in a spirit of gentleness. Take care that you yourselves are not tempted" (Gal 6:1).

Some believers churches prefer to use the term *discipling* rather than *discipline. Discipling* implies walking alongside another person and gently pointing them to the way of Jesus. *Discipling* is seen in the great commission, where Jesus commanded his followers to "make disciples of all nations, . . . teaching them to obey everything I have commanded you" (Matt 28:19-20). This kind of discipling ties into Titus 2:12, where grace functions pedagogically, *training us to renounce impiety and worldly passions, and in the present age to live lives that are self-controlled, upright, and godly.*

To be part of the church as a covenant community means to be in the sphere where members care for each other. Christians care enough to help a brother or sister who has fallen in sin. Such caring done in a spirit of humility and gentleness often brings about the erring person's repentance and growth. On the positive side, membership in a covenant community of brothers and sisters in the Lord gives each Christian confidence that if we stray from the Lord, our brothers and sisters will care enough for us that they will gently and graciously help us to turn back to the Lord. This kind of caring Christian community is what believers churches seek to become.

Titus 3:12-14

Personal Instructions

PREVIEW

Paul brings this short letter to a close with a few personal instructions. These instructions provide insight into Paul's life as well as the lives and travels of five other influential persons in the church: Titus, Artemas, Tychicus, Zenas, and Apollos. Paul invites Titus to meet him at Nicopolis, which gives some insight into Paul's travels. One final time, Paul encourages the Christians in Crete to devote themselves to good works.

OUTLINE

Instructions for Fellow Workers, 3:12-13
Devotion to Good Works, 3:14

EXPLANATORY NOTES

Instructions for Fellow Workers 3:12-13

The casual way Paul begins these personal instructions, *When I send,* indicates a lack of urgency in this letter in comparison with 1 Timothy. Like 1 Timothy and unlike 2 Timothy, Paul is still ministering in the East—perhaps in Macedonia—when he writes this letter. After spending the winter in Nicopolis, Paul likely plans to travel to Spain so that he can preach the gospel west of Rome (Rom 15:19, 24, 28). Whether he actually traveled to Spain is unknown.

When I send Artemas to you, or Tychicus, do your best to come to me at Nicopolis, for I have decided to spend the winter there (Titus 3:12). Paul plans to send one of the two persons to Crete to relieve Titus so that Titus could travel to Nicopolis and be with Paul again. Based on what we learn from 2 Timothy, Paul apparently decided to send Artemas to Crete, since Tychicus is sent to Ephesus (2 Tim 4:12) and departs from Dalmatia, which is up the coast from Nicopolis (2 Tim 4:10). Nothing is known of Artemas. Apparently he was a Christian capable of leading the churches in Crete after Titus left. His name indicates that he grew up in a Greek family and may have been named after the Greek goddess Artemis, the patron goddess of Ephesus (Acts 19:24, 27-28, 34-35). However, it would be speculative to assume Artemas came from Ephesus (Mounce, 457). Tychicus was Asian (Acts 20:4) and became a well-known traveling companion of Paul. He carried Paul's letters to Ephesus and Colossae (Eph 6:21; Col 4:7) and was later sent to Ephesus (2 Tim 4:12), perhaps to relieve Timothy, although this is not stated. Paul affirms Tychicus as "a beloved brother, a faithful minister, and a fellow servant in the Lord" (Col 4:7).

Paul earnestly desires that Titus meet him in Nicopolis, since Paul plans to spend the winter there. However, at the time of writing this epistle, he is not yet there. This may suggest that Paul wrote the letter to Titus in the late summer or early fall. Sea travel was extremely difficult in the winter, and ships stayed in port until spring (Acts 27:12, 21; 28:11). Like most seafarers, Paul stayed in a seacoast town, where he met people and spread the gospel until sea travel could begin again. The Nicopolis mentioned in Titus 3:12 is Actia Nicopolis, a major city in Epirus founded in 31 BC by Octavian (later called Augustus; I. H. Marshall 1999: 341). This city was a natural site for sea transportation between Achaia and Italy. As the terminating point of an overland trade route, Nicopolis became a commercial city and the site of athletic games. It is also where Epictetus, the Stoic philosopher, was exiled (Collins: 372).

Make every effort to send Zenas the lawyer and Apollos on their way, and see that they lack nothing (Titus 3:13). Apparently Zenas and Apollos are members of Paul's missionary group who carry Paul's letter to Titus in Crete. Titus is to provide hospitality for them so they have no lack of food and clothing and can get on their way quickly to their next destination after Crete. The urgency for them to keep moving is seen in the play on the words *Do your best* in the previous verse and *Make every effort* in verse 13.

Zenas is identified by his profession. He is a lawyer, but it is not stated whether he is versed in Greek, Roman, or Jewish law. It is unlikely that his learning is in Jewish law since he has a pagan, Greek name.

Apollos is also a Greek name. He is a familiar Hellenistic Jewish Christian from Alexandria, Egypt. Apollos is known for insightfully interpreting the OT, and he was given further instruction in the ways of the Lord by Aquila and Priscilla at Ephesus (Acts 18:24–19:1). Apollos was well-known in Achaia and is frequently mentioned in the Corinthian letters (1 Cor 1:12; 3:4-6, 22; 4:6; 16:12). Perhaps Zenas and Apollos are on their way to Alexandria, Egypt, which became an important center of early Christianity.

Devotion to Good Works 3:14

And let people learn to devote themselves to good works in order to meet urgent needs, so that they may not be unproductive (Titus 3:14). In contrast to the opponents, who are *unfit for any good work* (1:16b), Christians in Crete are urged to devote themselves to good works. *Good works* occurs several times in Titus (1:16; 2:7, 14; 3:1, 8b, 14). People are to learn by doing (cf. 1 Tim 5:4). As these Christians *who love us in the faith* (Titus 3:15b) devote themselves to good works, they will be fruitful and productive in life. A faith that does not work itself out in good deeds is not Christian faith. An unproductive life is an empty life. An empty and unproductive life characterizes the non-Christians in Crete (1:16), in contrast to the Christians, who devote themselves to good works.

The urgent needs mentioned in verse 15 could refer to the practical needs that everyone has, or it could refer to the specific needs that Zenas and Apollos will have when they come to Crete. More likely it means the pressing needs of others, as suggested by the use of the words *useless, unproductive* elsewhere in the NT. Quinn says, "The tree itself has no use for its fruit; the latter is meant to support the life of others. So the fraternal charity of the Cretan Christians helps sustain the life and missionary work of others for Christ and his church" (1990: 268).

Titus 3:15

Final Greetings

The letter to Titus closes in the normal way ancient writers gave greetings to those receiving correspondence. In 3:15, Paul and his traveling companions send greetings to Titus. However, the greetings extend beyond Titus to all the Christians in Crete. The qualification *those who love us in the faith* indicates that Paul's greetings extend to those *in the faith*, meaning Christians. This qualification does not mean that some within the church body are excluded from the greeting, but it does exclude those who because of their sin have left the church body. With final words, *Grace be with all of you*, Paul ends the letter. As in each of the letters to Timothy and Titus, the final greeting is given in the plural, suggesting that Paul wants his greetings to be passed on to the church; it is not intended only for its leaders (1 Tim 6:21; 2 Tim 4:22; Titus 3:15).

Outline of 1 Timothy

Managing the Church as the Household of God	**5:1–6:10, 17-19**
Older Men in the Church	5:1-2
Widows in the Church	5:3-16
Elders in the Church	5:17-25
Slaves in the Church	6:1-2a
Money and the Church	6:2b-10; 17-19
Final Instructions for Timothy	**6:11-16; 20-21**
Four Commands	6:11-12
Doxology	6:13-16
Guard the Trust	6:20-21

Outline of 2 Timothy

Salutation	**1:1-2**
Thanksgiving	**1:3-5**
Paul's Faith Heritage	1:3a
Paul's Personal Relationship with Timothy	1:3b-4
Timothy's Faith Heritage	1:5
Paul as a Model for Timothy in Christian Ministry	**1:6-18**
Paul Models Faithfulness to the Gospel Despite Suffering	1:6-14
Examples of Ashamed and Unashamed Associates	1:15-18
Faithfulness and Endurance in Christian Ministry	**2:1-13**
Three Duties Timothy Is to Follow	2:1-3a
Three Analogies: The Soldier, the Athlete, the Farmer	2:3b-7
The Historic Gospel of Jesus Christ	2:8-9
Paul's Motivation for Suffering	2:10
Faithful Saying	2:11-13
Timothy as Teacher in Contrast to Unhealthy Teachers	**2:14–3:9**
Unhealthy Teaching in Contrast to True Teaching	2:14-19
Useful Utensils in the House of God	2:20-21
How the Lord's Servant Ministers to Opponents	2:22-26
Behavior in the Last Days	3:1-9
Ingredients of Timothy's Ministry	**3:10-17**
Paul's Example of Suffering	3:10-12

Outline of Titus

Salutation	**1:1-4**
The Sender	1:1-3
The Addressee	1:4a
The Greeting	1:4b
Appointment of Church Leaders	**1:5-9**
Charge to Titus	1:5
Appointment of Elders	1:6
Appointment of a Bishop	1:7-9
Opponents	**1:10-16**
Why Opponents Need to Be Rebuked	1:10-11
Appeal to a Cretan Prophet	1:12-13a
Response to the Teaching of the Opponents	1:13b-16
Family Relationships in the Church	**2:1-10; 3:1-2**
Older Men	2:1-2
Older Women	2:3
Younger Women	2:4-5
Younger Men	2:6-8
Slaves	2:9-10
Church as Alternative Community	3:1-2
Confessional Statement on God's Grace	**2:11-15**
Grace Appeared	2:11
Grace Trains Us	2:12

The Blessed Hope 2:13
What the Savior Did 2:14

God's Transforming Work in Christ and in the Holy Spirit 3:3-8
Once We Ourselves Were 3:3
Second Confessional Statement 3:4-8

Final Exhortations and Warnings 3:9-11
Things to Avoid 3:9
Disengagement from Divisive Persons 3:10-11

Personal Instructions 3:12-14
Instructions for Fellow Workers 3:12-13
Devotion to Good Works 3:14

Final Greetings 3:15

Essays

AUTHORSHIP Who wrote the letters to Timothy and Titus? This question is not easily answered. Before the nineteenth century, scholars tended to assume Pauline authorship. In the nineteenth and twentieth centuries, most scholars held that someone else had written these letters in Paul's name (that they are pseudonymous), though some scholars continued to hold that Paul had written them.

Pseudonymity, the act of writing in someone else's name, was practiced widely in the ancient world. Almost every Jewish apocalypse was written under the name of a famous person from long ago, some hero of the faith who would give the writing authority. Pseudonymity is not the same as forgery, fictitious writing. Forgery was not accepted in the church's consideration of what books should be treated as theologically authoritative. Pseudonymity might be acceptable if the content of the writing was in keeping with Christian truth. But as Richard Bauckham points out, it would have been difficult to pass off a pseudonymous letter that was situation specific. Not only does the *I* in a pseudonymous letter not refer to the named author; but also the *you* does not likely refer to the individual or the named audience (Bauckham: 475, 488). The identity of the author was not necessary for the church's acceptance of the authority of the writing, as seen with the book of Hebrews. In the past 25 years the authorship question has been reexamined, with mixed results.

THE GREEK TEXT The oldest extant text containing part of the letters to Timothy and Titus is a single page of a papyrus codex ($\mathfrak{p}^{32}$) typically dated about AD 200, from the Oxyrhynchus finds in Egypt. It contains Titus 1:11-15 and 2:3-8. The letters to Timothy and Titus are not included in $\mathfrak{p}^{46}$, which is dated about AD 200 and is often thought to contain a collection of Paul's letters. But $\mathfrak{p}^{46}$ does not contain 2 Thessalonians or Philemon either. Measurements suggest that there was not enough space to include these omitted works in the last seven leaves of this codex, which have been lost. Some have suggested that $\mathfrak{p}^{46}$ is missing these letters because it was intended to contain only the Pauline letters written to churches, not those written to individuals. A late papyrus manuscript, $\mathfrak{p}^{61}$, dated about AD 700, does contains Titus 3:1-5, 8-11, 14-15.

The letters to Timothy and Titus are found in the great fourth-century uncial manuscript Codex Sinaiticus (א) and in the fifth-century Codex Alexandrinus (A). The fifth-century Codex Ephraemi Rescriptus (C) includes 1 Timothy 1:1–3:9; 5:20–6:20; 2 Timothy 1:1-2; Titus 1:1-2. The entire text of 1 and 2 Timothy is found in the fifth-century Codex Bezae Cantabrigiensis (D), but 1 & 2 Timothy and Titus are not in the very important fourth-century Codex Vaticanus (B). Nevertheless, there is good early textual evidence for them in the other manuscripts. In addition to these manuscripts, approximately 20 other uncials contain some or all of the letters to Timothy and Titus.

These manuscripts exhibit a variety of readings. This commentary does not go into detail on variant readings. It follows the text of Nestle-Aland, 27th ed. (= UBS, 4th ed.). Persons who want to pursue text-critical problems should see J. K. Elliott (1968) and B. M. Metzger (1994).

EXTERNAL EVIDENCE Early church fathers felt free to quote the letters to Timothy and Titus. Tertullian cited them freely from the Old Latin in the last decade of the second century, indicating an acceptance of these three letters as Pauline close to the middle of the second century. Irenaeus (ca. 180) quoted from them freely in his *Against Heresies* 2.14.7; 3.3.3. Athenagoras and Theophilus cite 1 Timothy 2:1-2 and allude to other passages about AD 180. Clement of Alexandria (d. ca. 215) cites 1 & 2 Timothy, Titus. Although Marcion did not include them in his canon (ca. 150), Tertullian says Marcion rejected them because of his personal views, as he did most of the NT. As early as about AD 117, Polycarp of Smyrna quoted from 1 and 2 Timothy in his letter *To the Philippians.* Whether Ignatius (ca. 117) and Clement (ca. 96) alluded to the letters to Timothy and Titus is debated, but seems more likely now than it did a generation ago. If Polycarp knew and used these epistles and considered them Pauline, their composition had to precede Polycarp's own writing. The pastorals therefore could not have been written later than AD 120.

Evidence suggests that 1 & 2 Timothy and Titus were included early in the developing NT collection. The *Shepherd of Hermas* refers to these three letters. Most date this writing to the mid-second century, though some prefer a date as early as the time of Clement of Rome (ca. AD 96). The Muratorian Canon says, "[Paul also wrote] out of affection and love one to Philemon, one to Titus, and two to Timothy, and these are held sacred . . . in the esteem of the Church catholic for the regulation of church discipline" (Metzger 1987: 307). Although the Muratorian Canon was once dated to the late second century by nearly all scholars, it now appears that it may come from the fourth century. Nevertheless, there is ample evidence that the letters to Timothy and Titus were firmly fixed in the Christian canon in all of the Roman Empire by the end of the fourth century. The church firmly placed its stamp of approval on these letters as sacred Scripture over the centuries. Textual evidence confirms that 1 & 2 Timothy and Titus were written no later than AD 120. And if Paul is the author, they could have been written as early as AD 64 to 67.

INTERNAL EVIDENCE The opening verses in each letter clearly identify Paul as author of these epistles (1 Tim 1:1; 2 Tim 1:1; Titus 1:1, 4). Since the nineteenth century, however, Pauline authorship has come under serious question. Arguments against Pauline authorship and counterarguments in favor of Pauline authorship abound. One contemporary scholar says:

> It is virtually impossible to determine the date of composition of the letters to Timothy and Titus. They are post-Pauline; their language is the common language of late first and early second century Hellenistic authors; they reflect an ecclesial situation in which the communities for which they were written were trying to find a niche in the Greco-Roman world; and their eschatology has lost its urgency because the expectation of an imminent Parousia has long since waned. These considerations suggest that the Pastorals were probably composed toward the end of the first century, sometime after 80 C.E. (Collins: 9)

What arguments support a post-Pauline author and what counterarguments favor Pauline authorship? First is the literary argument. The letters to Timothy and Titus lack Paul's use of the diatribe (the posing of real or hypothetical objections to an argument in order to address and refute them) found in Romans and the use of midrash (a common Jewish form of biblical commentary that emphasizes homiletical exegesis) found in Paul's other writings. Diatribe and midrash were modes of teaching in both Hellenistic and Jewish schools. Diatribe was a dialogical style of oral argumentation, and midrash was a way of studying texts. Both modes assumed a social context of teacher and students. Does this suggest a later time of writing, or does the literary character of the letters to Timothy and Titus simply reflect that the social contexts for Paul's correspondence as a whole were complex?

About one-third of the words in the letters to Timothy and Titus do not appear in other Pauline writings. In the NT, 175 words occur only in the letters to Timothy and Titus (thus called hapax legomena), and another 130 words appear in the letters to Timothy and Titus and elsewhere in the NT, but not (elsewhere) in Paul. These words appear in late first-century and early second-century Hellenistic literature, and 93 of them appear in the Apostolic Fathers and in the Apologists. This literary evidence leads many scholars to conclude that 1 & 2 Timothy and Titus were written by someone other than Paul.

Weakening this argument is evidence that many of the hapax legomena appear in the first century before AD 50 (Guthrie 1990b: 224-40). Of the 175 hapax legomena, 80 appear in the LXX (Mounce: ciii). Of the 306 words in the letters to Timothy and Titus not found in other Pauline writings, 165 appear in the writings of Philo, who died in about AD 50. Furthermore, 278 of these 306 words appear in Greek literature before AD 50 (Witherington 2006: 61). Several of these words also appear in Hellenistic writers who lived from the middle of the first century to the first third of the second century, such as Epictetus (130 words), Dio Chrysostom (140 words), and Plutarch (217 words). Since first- and second-century communication was largely oral, one may ask whether these hapax legomena arose in oral conversation before Paul's death and in the writings of Philo before they were used by other Hellenistic writers. Did Paul or Luke borrow words from late first-century Hellenistic writers in composing these letters, or did they use terms from the LXX, Philo, and oral communication before their use by late first-century Hellenistic writers?

Interpreting the statistical significance of the hapax legomena in the letters to Timothy and Titus is difficult, given the small amount of linguistic data. Metzger says, "It seems, therefore, that a discreet reticence should replace the almost unbounded confidence with which many scholars have used this method in attempting to solve the problem of the authorship of the PE" (1958: 94). Spicq agrees and adds that such a conclusion mutilates the rich personality and thinking ability of Paul (198). By itself, vocabulary does not determine authorship, since variety in vocabulary is also found in Paul's other epistles.

Another literary feature is syntax: the way in which words are ordered into sentences with Greek moods and tenses. Here one discovers influences of the LXX and Hellenistic Judaism. The syntax of the letters to Timothy and Titus is smoother than that in the dialogical sections of Romans and Galatians. Sentences are longer, and anarthrous nouns (i.e., nouns unmodified by the article *the*) are more frequent. The author's use of particles, prepositions, and pronouns differs significantly from their use in Romans and Galatians. Of the 214 particles in the other ten Pauline letters, 112 do not occur in the letters to Timothy and Titus. Yet this alone does not overthrow Pauline authorship, since Paul's syntax differs considerably between Galatians, Romans, and 1 Corinthians on the one hand, and 1 Thessalonians and Philippians on the other hand.

Style is also a factor. When the Greek text is read aloud, one hears alliteration and assonance. One also senses a paraenetic style in that the author *urges* his points rather than *argues* them. But again, this observation is inconclusive, since we see differences of style among Paul's other letters. Furthermore, the church fathers never questioned the writing style of the letters to Timothy and Titus in determining their canonicity, though they did question the book of Hebrews precisely on this point.

Second is the theological argument. The debate is not so much that the Pastorals are non-Pauline *theologically*, but rather *in the manner in which the author does theology and ethics*. As Fee says, "How one comes down on the question of authorship is ultimately a matter of whether one stresses their considerable Pauline character despite the acknowledged differences, or whether their Pauline character is pushed aside in favor of the differences" (Fee 2007: 419). Elements of Paul's authentic teaching find expression many times. For example, notice God's mercy in Christ toward sinners (1 Tim 1:12-17; Titus 3:3-7). Salvation depends wholly on God's grace (2 Tim 1:9; Titus 3:7). Christ gave himself as a ransom for sinners (1 Tim 2:6); eternal life is enjoyed now and is the goal to which Christians are called (1 Tim 6:12; 2 Tim 1:1; Titus 1:2; 3:7). Note also Paul's attitude toward second marriages (1 Tim 3:2, 12; 5:9), slaves (1 Tim 6:1; Titus 2:9-10), and the state (1 Tim 2:1-2; Titus 3:1). The phrase *in Christ* occurs seven times in 2 Timothy (1:2, 9, 13; 2:1, 10; 3:12, 15) and twice in 1 Timothy (1:14; 3:13). The pastorals include orthodox teaching that has similarities to Paul's defense of the gospel in Galatians 1:6-9. Moreover, in the pastorals one finds creedlike concepts (1 Tim 6:12-16; 2 Tim 2:8; 4:1), and the church is *the pillar and bulwark of the truth* (1 Tim

3:15). There also are other hymns and confessional statements (1 Tim 2:5-6a; 3:16; 2 Tim 2:11-13).

Timothy is told to safeguard the authorized doctrine that is handed down to him from the apostles (2 Tim 2:2). We have expressions such as *sure saying* (1 Tim 1:15; 3:1; 4:9, 2 Tim 2:11; Titus 3:8), *sound doctrine* (1 Tim 1:10 TNIV; 2 Tim 4:3; Titus 1:9; 2:1), and *Guard what has been entrusted to you* (1 Tim 6:20). Some argue that this kind of language suggests a later period—after Paul—when the church was defending itself. Could this not be late in Paul's life, since he had earlier confronted Jewish teachers (Gal 1:6-9; 2 Cor 11:4-6, 13) but now was facing opposing views in a Hellenistic setting? As noted above, some common Pauline themes do not appear in the letters to Timothy and Titus, such as references to the "cross" (*stauros*), "justification by faith," and "body of Christ." But the word "cross" appears only three times in Galatians; twice in each of 1 Corinthians, Philemon, and Colossians; once in Ephesians; and not at all in Romans, 2 Corinthians, or 1 and 2 Thessalonians. In 1 & 2 Timothy and Titus, the author talks about the church in the language of household of God, which is more familiar in Hellenistic society. And Paul uses the phrase *justified by his grace* (Titus 3:7). Though the language of eschatology has changed from Paul's earlier writings, it need not discredit Pauline authorship, since the author draws attention to the effects of the imperial cult in the Jewish Hellenistic world in these three letters.

The question of church governance emerges in the letters to Timothy and Titus, but it does not loom as large as some claim. It is found in only 27 of the 113 verses in 1 Timothy, in 5 of the 46 verses in Titus, and in only 1 verse in 2 Timothy. This means only 33 verses out of 242 deal specifically with church structure (Mounce: lix). Some scholars argue that the church organization fits the second century better, with the rise of the monarchical bishop and a hierarchy of structure to prevent unhealthy doctrine from destroying the church. But here again the argument is weak, since the letters to Timothy and Titus do not reflect the hierarchical arrangement of clergy one discovers in Ignatius's letters (ca. 115). It comes closer to the synagogue structure of Diaspora Judaism. In fact, the elements of church structure in the letters to Timothy and Titus are closer to the undisputed letters of Paul than they are to Ignatius. The description of church leaders calls attention to their *character* rather than to job descriptions, which are found later, in *1 Clement*, Ignatius, and Polycarp (Aageson 2008: 148-51). After looking carefully at church organization, Johnson concludes, "The issue of church order in the Pastorals turns out to be non-determinative for their authenticity. It does not prove that 1 Timothy and Titus were written by Paul. But it certainly does not demonstrate that they had to have been written after Paul's lifetime. If anything, the evidence suggests an earlier rather than a later time of composition" (Johnson 2001: 76).

Third is the historical argument. The majority view holds that the false (unhealthy) teaching confronted in the letters to Timothy and Titus best reflects second-century Gnosticism. There is some evidence in these letters of early forms of Gnosticism (i.e., proto-Gnosticism, with asceticism and license, denial of Christ's physical resurrection, and speculative use of the OT), which existed in the first century. However, the unhealthy teaching seems to have closer ties to first-century problems in Colossae and Corinth than to the more fully developed systems of Gnosticism in the second century.

Some argue that 1 & 2 Timothy and Titus do not fit into the historical account of Paul's life as outlined in the book of Acts. However, Acts leaves us with large gaps in our understanding of the historical development of the early church. Ancient tradition held that Paul was released from a first Roman captivity and preached in Spain before being imprisoned again and martyred. Furthermore, the letters to Timothy and Titus imply that Paul had gone to Macedonia while Timothy was at Ephesus and Titus was at Crete. Then Paul was imprisoned in Rome, according to 2 Timothy, and faced impending martyrdom. The apostle gave instructions for Titus and Timothy and asked Timothy to come to visit him soon. Though neither Acts nor Paul's other letters give us a full account of his life, the letters to Timothy and Titus may give us additional information about Paul's career and captivity not found in other NT writings. If this is the case, they provide an expanded understanding of Paul's movements and do not create larger biographical problems than what is found in Galatians, Philemon, and Philippians.

God is Savior in 1 Timothy and Titus. In Titus, the author calls both God and Jesus Christ *Savior* (2:10, 13). In 2 Timothy, Christ Jesus is Savior (1:10; 2:10; 3:15). God and Christ as Savior serve as a major theme in the letters to Timothy and Titus, intended to contrast with the saviors in imperial religion in the Roman world. What information can be gleaned from first-century Roman imperial religion that could throw light on the date of the letters to Timothy and Titus? During the reign of Emperor Domitian, the provincial cult of the emperors rose to special prominence in Ephesus. Evidence from inscriptions indicates that Ephesus formally dedicated a new temple to the emperors in AD 89/90 (Friesen: 41-49). If Steven J. Friesen's chronology is correct, a colossal new monument in service to the imperial cult dominated the harbor of Ephesus late in the first century, when John probably wrote the book of Revelation, which counters the imperial cult with the claim that God and the Lamb, Jesus Christ, are the ones who are really ruling and reigning (Kraybill: 29). One could argue that 1 Timothy and Titus were written at that time. However, the letters to Timothy and Titus could also have been written earlier, since as early as 9 BC Caesar Augustus was acclaimed as savior (Friesen: 34; Collins: 203; Kraybill: 60). This evidence suggests that one does not have to limit the date of writing of 1 & 2 Timothy and Titus to the last decade of the first century.

CURRENT DEBATE Until the nineteenth century the church held the traditional view that 1 & 2 Timothy and Titus were written by the apostle Paul. Arguments by F. D. E. Schleiermacher (1807), J. C. Eichhorn (1812), and F. C. Baur (1835) questioned the traditional view and said these three letters were written in the second century. Many scholars in the twentieth century, including Dibelius and Conzelmann (1972), agreed with their conclusion about the letters' pseudonymity. The Pauline authorship of other letters has been challenged as well. Other Pauline letters whose authorship is disputed include Ephesians (cf. Yoder Neufeld: 341-44), Colossians (cf. E. D. Martin: 24-27, 284-85), and 2 Thessalonians (Elias 1995: 25-26, 375-77).

More recently, however, such scholars as Johnson (2001), Towner (2006), and Witherington (2006) have been calling into serious question the *underlying assumptions* of the majority view of pseudonymity—assumptions brought *to* the text rather than emerging from a careful reading of the text itself. Johnson and Towner raise serious questions about the assumption that 1 & 2 Timothy and Titus are "letters to Timothy and Titus" that must be studied together as one unified set of writings. These are individual letters written under different circumstances, each with its own mode of argumentation. The literary differences need not preclude Paul's authorship. Literary differences also exist between Paul's earlier letters. Indeed, one prominent feature of the Pauline corpus is the variety of ways in which Paul addresses various contingencies in diverse—though contextually appropriate—ways (cf. Beker 1980). Theological themes in Paul's other writings can be found in these letters. Although new theological ideas emerge when compared with Paul's other writings, they can be attributed to the new Hellenistic setting with its imperial cult and to the continuing rise of teaching that needed to be challenged in the church. Historically and socially, these epistles fit a first-century setting better than a second-century setting.

OPTIONS TO CONSIDER We cannot prove who wrote 1 & 2 Timothy and Titus. Of the three letters, 2 Timothy is most likely written by Paul. First Timothy is least likely written by Paul; Titus lies in between. Does this mean we have two authors—one for 2 Timothy and another for Titus and 1 Timothy? Or does this mean we have three authors, one for each letter? Or does this mean we have one author, Paul, with a secretary or secretaries who freely adapted Pauline thoughts while contextualizing the gospel in the Hellenistic world?

First, scholars holding to pseudonymous authorship believe the letters to Timothy and Titus were written in the late first or early second century. Quinn suggests 1 & 2 Timothy and Titus are a "third volume" of Luke's writing (Quinn 1978: 70-75). J. Christiaan Beker calls for a dual method of *traditum* (the deposit of the Pauline tradition) and *traditio* (the transmission of the tradition). Beker argues for a post-Pauline period in the early church when Paul's thought was applied to a new situation the church was facing in which it relied on Paul's authority (Beker 1980: 27-43). The post-Pauline church may have relied on Pauline authority for two or three decades after Paul, but that does not necessarily require pseudonymity. Arguments can be raised against this view. First is the early use of 1 & 2 Timothy and Titus by Polycarp and others. If these letters were pseudonymous, church leaders would likely recognize them as such. Second, if they were pseudonymous and written in the latter part of the first century, they were too close to the end of Paul's life to have been accepted as authentic. And third, why should someone write three separate letters pseudonymously, rather than just one letter? In light of these objections, I do not think that pseudonymity (the majority view) is the best option.

Second is the view that 1 & 2 Timothy and Titus contain some Pauline fragments along with additional writing by an unknown writer. A fragment theory would attribute to Paul the hymnic and confessional material, sure sayings, salvation, and some ethical teaching, such as the household behavior codes. To be sure, some of the contents of these letters are definitely

Pauline. A problem with the fragment theory is that scholars do not agree on which fragments are Pauline. Furthermore a fragment theory has difficulty in identifying the external evidence for authorship.

Third is the view that an amanuensis (secretary, or possibly secretar*ies*) helped with the writing. In ancient times, persons dictated their letters, and a secretary did the actual writing. Paul identifies several secretaries that he used in writing his letters: Silvanus and Timothy for 1 and 2 Thessalonians, Tertius for Romans, and perhaps Paul himself wrote Galatians with "large letters" (Gal 6:11). No one knows who wrote Hebrews or whether a secretary helped to write it. In 1 & 2 Timothy and Titus, no secretary is openly stated. Possible names for a presumed secretary are Tychicus (2 Tim 4:12; Titus 3:12), Timothy, or Titus (Bauckham: 492-94). The secretary hypothesis explains how these three Pauline letters could be different from the other letters of Paul and still remain Pauline. However, we are beyond the limits of the evidence; one cannot prove this view or any other view.

Fourth is a modified secretary view, which claims that the letters to Timothy and Titus are a combination of Pauline thought with a Lukan hand in the actual writing. As Witherington points out, what distinguishes authentic writing from pseudonymity is that the material of a genuine letter comes from the mind of a particular person, not whether it fully reflects that person's grammar and syntax and vocabulary (Witherington 2006: 26). Witherington notes that 544 words are common to Luke-Acts and the letters to Timothy and Titus. Of these, 34 words are used only in Luke-Acts and the letters to Timothy and Titus and not elsewhere in the NT. Moreover, 55 words in the letters to Timothy and Titus are found in Paul's other letters but are not used elsewhere in the NT (57-58). This evidence suggests that both Paul and Luke had a hand in producing the letters to Timothy and Titus. After working through Titus and 1 Timothy, Witherington says:

> It seems clear to me that we have reached the stage where we can conclude that it is highly probable that Luke wrote these letters for Paul and felt free to use his own way of putting things in various places. Not surprisingly, Paul would have granted Luke more freedom than he did various of his scribes who simply took dictation. The voice is recognizably the voice of Paul, but in some places, seen more strongly and clearly than others, the hand is the hand of Luke. (290)

VIEW OF THIS COMMENTARY The debate, in the words of Aageson, "makes clear that the letters to Timothy and Titus are close to the balance point between the historical Paul on one hand and the Pauline legacy on the other, and the decision about authorship simply moves the Pastorals from one side of that balance to the other" (2008: 7). Although I do not know if Paul did the actual writing, the view taken in this commentary is that much of the content of these letters came from the mind of Paul through Luke, or one of Paul's close associates, who did the actual writing. I lean in the direction of Luke as the likely secretary/writer, since there is evidence of Lukan influence in the writing style.

Since only 96 words in the letters to Timothy and Titus are not found in the biblical writings elsewhere, including the LXX, one can argue that the author uses these 96 words to communicate the gospel in the Hellenized world and these words were terms that Luke knew. If Luke did the actual writing, the date of writing could be as early as AD 64-67, but it could also be anytime between 65 and 85, since Luke-Acts was written in the late 70s or early 80s. Luke bridges the gap between the historical Paul and the Pauline legacy. Each of the letters appeared sometime during this period. Whether Paul did the actual writing or not, these letters speak from within the trajectory of Paul's apostolic tradition and are not forgeries. So we can chart the likely results of this matter:

Paul as author (AD 64-67)	⟷ to	Luke as writer (AD 80-85)
2 Timothy	Titus, 1 Timothy	(Luke-Acts)

(Cf. Young: 23, 45, 122-44; Davies: 105-13; Friesen: 41-49; Kraybill: 26-75; Harding: 9-27; Elias 2006: 478-79; Quinn 1990: 1-22; Johnson 2001: 353; Towner 2006: 1-89; I. H. Marshall 1999: 83-92; Witherington 2006: 23-75; Aageson, 2008.)

AUTHENTEŌ The verb *authenteō* occurs in the present infinitive (*authentein*) in 1 Timothy 2:12. Until the twentieth century, most scholars translated it "to dominate." BDAG defines the verb as "to assume a stance of independent authority, give orders to, dictate to" (150). Is the first or second definition the more likely one? In recent years the first definition was followed in many English translations ("to exercise authority over"), giving it a hierarchical interpretation.

The word appears as a noun twice in the Septuagint. In Wisdom of Solomon 12:6, the noun is used with reference to people practicing child sacrifice and is translated *murderer*. It also appears in 3 Maccabees 2:28-29 in the noun form, where the writer speaks of the hostile attitude of the Ptolemies against the Alexandrian Jews. The Jews are to register and be branded by the symbol of Dionysus in accordance with their "origin" (*authentia*). These two cases from the Septuagint raise serious questions regarding the translation "to have authority over" (NRSV, TNIV). Paul could have chosen from 12 different Greek words if he had wanted to speak of "exercise authority" and as many as 47 Greek words if he had wanted to speak of "rule" or "govern" (Louw and Nida 1989: domains 37.35-47; 37.48-95). Paul chose none of these words because the idea he wanted to present in 1 Timothy 2:12 did not carry the meaning "rule" or "have authority over." In Hellenism, the noun was used in a negative sense to describe a murderer or mastermind of a crime or act of violence. By the first century, *authentēs* described the perpetrator of a murder.

The verb *authenteō* appears only a few times in Greek literary and nonliterary materials. The word group covers a range of meanings: to rule or reign, to control or dominate; to act independently; to be the originator of something; to murder (Towner 2006: 220). If Paul had a routine exercise of authority in view, he would have put it first, followed by teaching as a specific example. Instead, he starts with teaching, followed by *authenteō*. Given this word order, *authentein* as "to dominate" or "gain the upper hand" provides the best fit in the context (Pierce and Groothuis: 216-17).

Köstenberger, Schreiner, and Baldwin argue that the Greek construction uses the correlative pairs "to teach" and "to exercise authority over" as synonyms or parallel words in a positive way (81-103). But as Belleville points out, there is a grammatical flaw in this approach since it is limited to formally equivalent constructions and excludes functionally equivalent ones (Belleville: 3-9). Thus it applies only to correlated verbs. Greek grammars define Greek infinities as verbal nouns. They carry both verbal and nominal functions. Here in 1 Timothy 2:12, the infinitive "to teach" and *authentein* function less as verbs and more as nouns in the sentence structure. The verb in the sentence is "I permit" (*epitrepō*) and is used in the present continual sense. By the tense of the verb, Paul does not mean "I will not ever permit." Rather, the verb tense suggests, "I am not [now] permitting," which does not imply perpetual action (Witherington 2006: 226-27). One interpretation of the grammar sees the verb as supplemented by two complementary infinitives. Another interpretation of the grammar sees the verb "I permit" as needing an infinitive to complete its meaning. But the use of the infinitive in this verse is restricted by the direct object of the verb (*woman*) and therefore ties into the noun more than the verb. So instead of reading, "I do not permit to teach a woman," Paul is saying, "I do not [now] permit a woman to teach."

Köstenberger, Schreiner, and Baldwin argue that the Greek infinitives (to teach, to exercise authority over) are to be interpreted positively, since the first infinitive (to teach) is positive. However, Towner says that Köstenberger's positive interpretation of the infinitive is too confident and artificial (Towner 2006: 223). Belleville says that the "neither-nor" language of 1 Timothy 2:12 pairs the two infinitives in a way that does not move from the general to the specific. In this case, instead of moving from "neither to exercise authority [general] nor to teach [particular]," the thought runs in the opposite direction. The emphasis is on the purpose or goal of teaching. Thus, a better translation is "I do not permit a woman to teach so as to gain mastery over a man," or "I do not permit a woman to teach with a view to dominate a man" (see TNIV footnote on 1 Tim 2:12). This way of translating the passage fits well with the second part of the verse: "I do not permit a woman to teach a man in a dominating way but to have a quiet demeanor." As I. H. Marshall says, "It is, therefore, more likely that the verb characterizes the nature of the teaching rather than the role of the women in church leadership in general" (1999: 460). In light of the grammar in 1 Timothy 2:12, it seems best to translate *authentein* as "to dominate" rather than "to rule over."

CHIASM A chiasm is a literary device in which an author arranges words, statements, or themes in an orderly way to move the reader "inward" through parallel phrases to the central theme, and then "outward" in reverse order by repeating the parallel phrases. The "X" shape of the chiasm comes from the Greek letter *chi*, from which we derive the word "chiasm," or *chiasmus*. A simple chiasm is an A-B-C-B′-A′ or A-B-C-C′-B′-A′ arrangement. The words, statements, or themes are arranged as follows:

A [item]
  B [item]
    C [item]
    C′ [omitted if no item for this]
  B′ [item]
A′ [item]

In this form of the chiasmus, C is the central theme. A is the beginning theme, which then moves inward through B to C. In the reverse order the thought pattern moves outward from C to B′ and finally to A′. Thus B and B′ represent parallel thought patterns, and A and A′ represent parallel thought patterns.

CHRISTOLOGY IN THE LETTERS TO TIMOTHY AND TITUS The name Jesus Christ or Christ Jesus occurs 32 times in the letters to Timothy and Titus. In this essay I am indebted to Fee's excellent work on Christology (Fee 2007: 418-72). Two themes emerge around Christology: salvation and epiphany. In these letters, *salvation* is used for the work of both God and Christ. In a general way, the title sets forth God as *Savior* in the sense of being the architect and initiator of the salvation plan (1 Tim 2:3; 4:10; Titus 1:3; 2:10, 13; 3:4). Christ is the means by which this salvation plan is implemented within history (2 Tim 1:10; Titus 3:6).

In 1 Timothy, Jesus Christ is presented as the incarnate Savior (Fee 2007: 422). Four major passages speak of the human work of Christ as Redeemer (1 Tim 1:11-17; 2:4-6; 3:16; 6:13-16). Two of these passages presuppose the preexistence of Christ and present his human life as a divine incarnation (1 Tim 1:15; 3:16). In 1 Timothy 1:11-17, Paul says that Jesus Christ was sent by God into the world to save sinners. Salvation originates in the Father's love and is made available through the incarnate Christ. Christ does not work independently from the Father, nor is his work done in isolation from what God is doing in the world (Fee: 2007: 429). In 1 Timothy 2:4-6, Christ Jesus is a human person who gave himself as a ransom for all. Christ, the divine mediator, was neither an angelic being nor some kind of divine visitation that appeared to be human. He was truly a human being who, though divine, provided ransom for sin.

The Christ hymn in 1 Timothy 3:16 also affirms the humanity of Christ. Christ, the divine one, was revealed in real human flesh. He received divine vindication by the Spirit and angels and by the subsequent proclamation of the early church. Jesus Christ received final vindication by being taken up into glory. In 1 Timothy 6:13-16, the work of Christ is presented within the eternal verity of God the Father (Fee 2007: 435). Timothy is charged by the living God and by the historical Christ, who gave an effective witness before his crucifixion. The goal of everything is the coming of Christ, and the source of all things is the eternal and only God (Fee 2007: 435). Thus 1 Timothy assumes a human trajectory. As such it connects with the Christology in the other Pauline letters. Christ also is the object of faith (3:13), the source of Paul's and Timothy's ministries (1:1; 4:6), and the source and content of sound instruction of the gospel (6:3).

In Titus, we see only four direct references to Christ and a different trajectory. Titus 1:1-4 presents Christ Jesus as *our Savior*. In 2:13, Christ manifests God's glory, and in 2:11, 14, Christ manifests God's grace. In 3:6, Christ gives the Holy Spirit. Thus, language that is ordinarily used with reference to the role of God the Father in our salvation is here attributed to Christ (Fee 2007: 449). The difference in trajectory is based on a different historical situation. Whereas the Christology in 1 Timothy emphasizes the incarnate Christ in response to the unhealthy teaching in Ephesus, the Christology in Titus is behavior- and salvation-centered, intended to correct the aberrations that had emerged within the churches of Crete (Fee 2007: 420). The Cretans believed that Zeus received divine status for his benefactions to humans. The Christology of Titus confronts the cultural myth by playing down the humanity of Christ and insisting that Christ appeared among humans from above and conferred the gift of salvation upon them. In the opening and closing texts, both God and Christ are cosharers in the title *Savior* (Titus 1:3-4; 3:4, 6). The themes of Savior and epiphany converge to describe Christ's historical ministry as the *epiphany* of God's grace (2:11 GNT), and Christ's eschatological return is described as the *epiphany of the glory of our great God and Savior* (2:13 GNT). In Titus 3:3-7 we see the same emphasis. Paul describes the Christ event in the language of divine epiphany, with Christ as a ruler, bestowing gifts of kindness and love onto his subjects (3:4). The benefactor is *God our Savior*, whose redemptive ministry resides in *Jesus Christ our Savior*. Instead of Zeus being the divine benefactor for the people, it is God and Christ who bring benefits. Thus Christology in Titus follows a higher divine trajectory, which sharpens the Christian message as it penetrates Cretan culture. It is the story of the elevated Christ, who in his divine past appearance is Savior, and in his future appearance is the glory of our great God and Savior.

Christology in 2 Timothy takes yet another direction. The title "Lord" (*kyrios*) occurs 17 times in 2 Timothy and 6 times in 1 Timothy, with no occurrences in Titus. Emphasis is placed on the resurrected Lord, who is a descendant of David (2 Tim 2:8). Located in Rome, Paul looked to Jesus Christ the Lord for his deliverance and strength (3:11; 4:17-18) and for his vindication (4:8, 14), precisely in the setting where the title *lord* was used for the Roman emperor. The themes of resurrection and vindication run throughout 2 Timothy. The epiphany of Christ in history is viewed from the results it has achieved. He destroyed death (2 Tim 1:10; cf. Rom 6:6, 10; 2 Cor 4:10; 1 Thess 5:10). And he *brought life and immortality to light* in the resurrection (2 Tim 1:10b), which opens the door to eternal life. In 2 Timothy, the Christology addresses both human suffering and vindication by the resurrection. Christology supports Paul's own testimony (1:8, 11-12) and assures Timothy that neither suffering nor death poses an ultimate threat to the gospel or its representative, despite the popular false belief that the Roman emperor is savior and lord. Finally, Christ will rule in his kingdom and vindicate his people (4:1, 8, 14). Thus Timothy is to fulfill his ministry (4:5). Paul's suffering is about to result in death, but his vindication through the coming bodily resurrection in Christ's second epiphany looms large in Paul's thinking. In like manner, Timothy will find encouragement to move forward in continuing the gospel ministry, which also follows the pattern of suffering, death, and vindication in the resurrection of Jesus.

The "epiphany" word group appears in all three letters. Both the noun *epiphaneia* (1 Tim 6:14; 2 Tim 1:10; 4:1, 8; Titus 2:13) and the verb *epiphainō* (Titus 2:11; 3:4) occur. In Hellenistic religious life, the terms described the appearance of a god on behalf of his worshipers. Throughout the Mediterranean world, it was used for the cult of Asclepius, the god of healing. Hellenistic Judaism (as in LXX) used the term to retell the stories of Yahweh's interventions in the world. The term was also used about 100 times in Hellenistic texts to speak about such deified political rulers (emperors) as Claudius, Caligula, Diocletian, and Valerian. Epiphany language was used to describe their births, their coming into power, their enthronement, their imperial visits, and their victories. Julius Caesar was described as a god made manifest. And an inscription found in the city of Ephesus identifies Caesar as "savior."

Thus, language used of Christ in the letters to Timothy and Titus parallels the ruler cult of the Roman Empire. As the emperor was god by being the son of a god or the manifestation of a god, so Christ is Lord and God. He is God's Son or God's manifestation. When Christ visits the earth, God appears. Given these parallels, it is not unreasonable to suggest that there is a deliberate placing of this Christ cult against the Caesar cult (Young: 65). In 2 Timothy 1:10, Caesar or some other emperor is clearly not savior; *Christ Jesus* is *Savior*. Christ Jesus, not Caesar, is the manifestation of divine benevolence. In making use of epiphany language as well as the term *Savior*, Paul expresses his gospel (1 Cor 15:1-2) in language that everyone in the Hellenistic world could understand.

In the letters to Timothy and Titus, the term *epiphany* (*appearing*) has two meanings. First, it refers to the future appearance of Christ. It is synonymous with the *parousia* of Christ in 1 Timothy 6:14 and 2 Timothy 4:1, 8. The noun form often refers to the historical appearance of Christ as Savior (2 Tim 1:10). The verb form sometimes refers to the appearances of God's grace (Titus 2:11; 3:4). God's grace has appeared in the epiphany of his Son. It is revealed in and through the proclamation of the gospel, and it will be fully revealed in the future appearance of Christ (Titus 2:13). Epiphany language underscores the deity of Christ in 1 Timothy 1:15 and 2 Timothy 1:9-10; 4:18. Epiphany terminology tells the story of God's salvation in Christ in the common religious-political language of discourse in the Hellenistic world. But the terminology applied to Christ goes beyond its use by the imperial cult. It refers to the past human experience of Christ coming into the world in the incarnation (2 Tim 1:10) as well as the future appearance of Christ. Though epiphany language called to mind imperial power and divine intervention in the Greco-Roman world, the letters to Timothy and Titus present Christ's power and presence in human weakness, his death on the cross, his resurrection by God, and his ultimate return in power. In short, epiphany language serves to present Christ in direct opposition to the emperor, who was considered savior and appeared before the people.

The three trajectories in the letters to Timothy and Titus present Christology in both a unified and diversified way. All three letters talk about Jesus Christ. But only as they are read separately does one find the richness of

Christology. Christology in 1 Timothy follows a human trajectory. In Titus, Christology subverts a Cretan cultural and religious story centered on Zeus. And in 2 Timothy, the lordship of Christ promises resurrection and vindication as it lays out the suffering and death of Christ. In a unified way Jesus Christ is presented in all three letters by use of the terms *Savior* and *epiphany* (*appearing*). In a diversified way, Jesus Christ is presented in each letter's historical, social, and cultural context to enhance the proclamation of the gospel.

In the letters to Timothy and Titus, Jesus Christ is a historical person. Jesus is a descendant of David (2 Tim 2:8), was revealed in flesh (1 Tim 3:16), made the great confession in his testimony before Pontius Pilate (1 Tim 6:13), was human and brought redemption through his death (1 Tim 2:5-6; Titus 2:14; 3:6-7), and *abolished death* by his work on the cross and resurrection (2 Tim 1:10). Jesus is also a divine person (Titus 2:13). And Jesus Christ will come again (2 Tim 4:1, 8).

In summary, the Christology in the letters to Timothy and Titus is Pauline in nature and is in keeping with the Christology found in the other Pauline letters. The way Christology is expressed in the letters to Timothy and Titus reflects the different historical situations and issues facing the church in Ephesus and Crete. The content, however, is in keeping with Pauline theology. (Cf. *ABD* 1:985; Young: 59-68; Towner 2006: 59-68; Collins: 202-9; I. H. Marshall 1999: 287-96; Fee 2007: 418-78.)

CONSCIENCE The term *conscience* (*syneidēsis*) occurs six times in the letters to Timothy and Titus. Four times it is used for Christian believers and is modified by the terms *good* or *clear* (1 Tim 1:5, 19; 3:9; 2 Tim 1:3). It refers twice to the opponents, whose conscience is *seared* (1 Tim 4:2) or *corrupted* (Titus 1:15). The term appears 14 times in all of Paul's other writings and 31 times in the entire NT. It is not found in the LXX, although it appears a few times in noncanonical Jewish wisdom writings. In secular writings, conscience is connected to consciousness, or lack thereof, when one has committed a negative action. In Philo and Josephus, the term sometimes is used as "good conscience," but only from the second century AD onward do we find the term used this way in secular Greek writings.

For Paul, conscience is a part of being human, whether Jew or Gentile. It has the function of bringing to consciousness one's conduct or that of other persons according to given and recognized norms. By itself, conscience is not the source of moral norms; rather, it acts on the basis of norms it receives. For Paul, the source of such norms is the mind. Conscience alone and by itself is not the voice of God. Greek culture emphasized the concept of a bad conscience, but Paul generally uses *conscience* to express freedom from guilt. For Paul, the conscience acts as a norm-based judge of behavior that brings its judgment—positive or negative—to the awareness of the individual through criticism or affirmation (Towner 2006: 117). When challenged, Paul insists that his conscience bears witness in the Holy Spirit that he is telling the truth (Rom 9:1), that he has acted in a holy and sincere manner (2 Cor 1:12), and that he has not acted deceitfully, but has faithfully proclaimed the word of God (2 Cor 4:2).

In the case of Corinthian believers who had differences of conscience regarding which foods to eat, Paul spoke of the need to respect the other person's "weak" conscience (1 Cor 8:7-12), but he did not equate a weak conscience with an evil conscience. The weak conscience is to be respected, while the evil conscience is to be condemned (I. H. Marshall 1999: 223).

In the letters to Timothy and Titus, the term *conscience* is an anthropological concept that functions in relation to norms and behavior. However, the ways the term is qualified (good, clear, defiled, seared) and its tie to how one responds to the Christian faith by belief or unbelief reflects a theological perspective not found earlier in Paul. The opponents who have rejected the gospel have defiled consciences or seared consciences (Titus 1:15; 1 Tim 4:2). Rejection of the faith tends to render the conscience ineffective and results in behavior that runs counter to godliness.

In contrast, persons who believe in the true apostolic gospel have a *good conscience* (1 Tim 1:5, 19) or a *clear conscience* (1 Tim 3:9; 2 Tim 1:3), which results in love and service. A distinction can be made between a good conscience and a clean conscience. A *good conscience* relates to the manner or process by which the conscience receives information on the norm of the right and good and acts on the basis of this information. Thus the process has been effective. A *clean or clear conscience* results from an assessment of one's actions that indicates innocence through the consistency of faith and the resulting action (Towner 2006: 118). This theological development suggests that, in the letters to Timothy and Titus, the term *conscience* functions more like the mind (*nous*) in Paul's other writings. As the heart and conscience are cleansed through Christian conversion (1 Tim 1:5), one senses little difference from what Paul calls the renewed mind in Romans 12:2. How one responds to the teaching of the apostolic gospel is highly important. The gospel has an educative role in training us to renounce impiety and worldly passions and to live lives that are self-*controlled, upright, and godly* (Titus 2:12). When the conscience is educated in the right way by the revelation of God's truth and grace, and one acts accordingly, the conscience is clear and good. But when one rejects the truth of the gospel and educates the conscience accordingly, the conscience becomes morally ineffective and cannot translate corrupt doctrine into godly conduct (I. H. Marshall 1999: 227). (Cf. *ABD* 1:1129-30; *DPL* 155-56; I. H. Marshall 1999: 217-27; Towner 2006: 117-19.)

CONTEXTUALIZING THE GOSPEL "Contextualizing the gospel" is terminology used in the missionary work of the Christian church to describe how the gospel communicates and takes root in a new culture. Missionaries try not to impose on one culture the moral and ethical norms considered "Christian" in another. When one keeps mission first, one can authentically make allowances for certain ethical practices until seasoned indigenous moral discernment can emerge. The author of the letters to Timothy and Titus indicates his contextualization of the gospel by the use of *hina* clauses and by borrowing terminology from contemporary culture and changing its content.

The Greek conjunction *hina* (*so that, then*) appears 15 times in 1 Timothy, 5 times in 2 Timothy, and 13 times in Titus. Certain behaviors are prescribed for the sake of the church and its mission. Apparently bad behavior on the part of some elicited negative reactions against the church in the pagan society. So the author of the letters to Timothy and Titus mutes the rights of Christians in their freedom in Christ for the sake of the gospel. By lessening freedom in some areas of behavior, the church was able to contextualize its life and message for a time and win over the unbelievers to Christ. The following teaching indicates this contextualizing process (with stress added for *so that* or *then*).

Teaching directed to slaves:

> Let all who are under the yoke of slavery regard their masters as worthy of all honor, *so that* the name of God and the teaching may not be blasphemed. (1 Tim 6:1)
>
> Tell slaves to be submissive in every respect; they are not to talk back, not to pilfer, but to show complete and perfect fidelity, *so that* in everything they may be an ornament to the doctrine of God our Savior. (Titus 2:9-10)

Teaching directed to bishops:

> Moreover, he must be well thought of by outsiders, *so that* he may not fall into disgrace and the snare of the devil. (1 Tim 3:7)

Teaching directed to young widows:

> Give these commands as well, *so that* they [the young widows] may be above reproach. (1 Tim 5:7)

Teaching directed to young women:

> being submissive to their husbands, *so that* the word of God may not be discredited. (Titus 2:5)

Teaching directed to young men:

> Likewise urge the younger men to be . . . a model of . . . sound speech that cannot be censured; *then* any opponent will be put to shame, having nothing evil to say of us. (Titus 2:6-8)

A second way the letters to Timothy and Titus contextualize the gospel is to fill terms used in the culture of the day with new Christian meaning. For example, Paul takes the terminology used in imperial religion and fills it with new meaning. For Paul, the gospel of Jesus Christ is God's saving action in history and thus discounts the claims of the false gods of the empire *[Names for God and the Imperial Cult, p. 357]*.

ECCLESIOLOGY In contrast to Paul's earlier writings, the phrase "body of Christ" is not used in the letters to Timothy and Titus (Rom 12:4-5; 1 Cor 12:12-27; Eph 2:16; 4:4, 12-16; 5:30). The gifts of the Holy Spirit in the body of Christ, as seen in the Corinthian church and in Ephesians 4:11-16, are not emphasized in the letters to Timothy and Titus, except for the gift given to Timothy for Christian ministry (1 Tim 4:14; 2 Tim 1:6). Noting the emphasis on church organization, household behavior, and how to relate to the social and cultural context, some scholars conclude that the letters to Timothy and Titus fit a setting similar to the letters of Ignatius in the second century (ca. 115). The adjustment of the church to live within its historical and cultural setting is further enhanced by the use of the term *household of God* (1 Tim 3:5; 15; cf. 2 Tim 2:20-21). However, Paul used two of these office titles (*bishop* and *deacon*) in his earlier epistles. So the assumption of a clean, linear progression in ecclesiology from charismatic leadership to hierarchical leadership should not be imposed upon the text. The concept of the church as household of God also occurs in Ephesians and Galatians (1 Cor 4:1-2; Gal 6:10; Eph 2:19-22). Furthermore, Paul and Peter use the term "people of God" (cf. Titus 2:14) for the church (Rom 9:25-26; 1 Pet 2:9-10).

By the time 1 Timothy was written, the Ephesian church had been in existence for some years. Leaders of the church are to be upright in moral behavior and able to teach sound doctrine. In Titus, the church is in its early stages of development, and elders need to be chosen to provide leadership for the new house fellowships of believers. The church is taking root in these new house fellowships, and new leaders are to guide new Christians in godly ways. In 2 Timothy, the leader of the church is to be dedicated and useful to the owner of the house. The idea of "house" is more in keeping with the Jewish tabernacle and temple than with the Greco-Roman household.

Paul uses the term *household of God* (1 Tim 3:15) as a way to communicate the gospel cross-culturally. On the one hand, the term picks up the idea of God's dwelling with his people in the ancient tabernacle and temple. Jesus called the temple "the house of God" (Mark 2:26; 11:17). Paul refers to the church as "God's building" and "God's temple" (1 Cor 3:9, 16), "the household of God" (Eph 2:19), "a holy temple in the Lord" (2:21), and "a dwelling place for God" (2:22). And in 1 Timothy 3:15, Paul calls this household *the church of the living God.* In the NT, the house is where church happens. The NT repeatedly talks about the church in someone's house (Rom 16:5; 1 Cor 16:19; Col 4:15; Philem 2). On the other hand, in the letters to Timothy and Titus, *household of God* recalls the household as a social unit within Hellenistic society. These households had a definite structure, as seen in the household codes of behavior. Household management was largely in the hands of the paterfamilias. When Paul talks about desired qualities in church leaders, one major concern is that the person chosen for bishop is to be a good household manager (1 Tim 3:4-5), and the persons chosen as deacons must manage their children and households well (3:12). In 2 Timothy 3:6, Timothy is warned about unhealthy teachers disturbing Christian households. Titus is to warn those who subvert whole households by teaching for financial gain (Titus 1:11). Church leaders are to exercise self-discipline.

Because the author of the letters to Timothy and Titus uses household language that is familiar in the Greco-Roman society, some NT scholars think Paul is affirming a new pattern of church order and offices for church structure as the church accommodates itself to living within the society around it. But this view is questionable. Witherington says, "It is simply incorrect to say that we have in the Pastorals a mere baptizing of the status quo of a bourgeois Greco-Roman ethic and calling of it good" (2006: 114). When Paul talks about the household of God, he is more likely speaking of God's dwelling in the church by combining the temple idea with the household idea, thus describing Christian truth in language that the Greco-Roman world could understand. The church as household of God has structure, with the bishop and elders giving leadership to the household of faith. But its foundation is the temple, the dwelling of God. Christian teaching is recast into language that is intelligible in the Hellenistic world. Because the church assembles in households, there are no lines between public and private, or between domestic and ecclesial. As non-Christians observe the conduct of Christians, they perceive that Christianity is not completely overturning traditional social and domestic values. The instructions that Paul gives have a larger agenda in mind: he wants to build bridges between the Christian culture and the larger society that will assist the church to win the battles it deems essential (de Silva: 749-50).

The idea that church order is the main emphasis in the letters to Timothy and Titus is also questionable. An organized church is emphasized, but details of the leaders' duties and functions are not stated. The right people are to be chosen as leaders, and these qualified leaders are to teach sound doctrine. Women also were involved in teaching. Action is to be taken against opponents of the true gospel. But the organizational structure in the letters to Timothy and Titus does not resemble the more rigid structure that we see in Ignatius's letters. It comes closer to the synagogue structure of Diaspora Judaism, which in turn resembles that in the Greco-Roman collegia (Johnson 2001: 75). As noted above, two of the three titles that Paul uses for church leaders in 1 Timothy and Titus also appear in the undisputed letters of Paul (Rom 16:1; Phil 1:1).

Church structure in the letters to Timothy and Titus is much looser and less official than some scholars imply. In light of the dangers of deviant teaching, the church is closely associated with the gospel and is the guardian of the true message of salvation. This message is contained in the teaching handed down by Paul and ultimately rests on Scripture. It requires that faithful people in the congregation teach it and take action against those who pervert it. The stress on "office" and "order" must be seen in its context. When this is done, the ecclesiology of the letters to Timothy and Titus emerges as being more akin to that reflected in Paul's other letters (I. H. Marshall 1999: 521). (Cf. I. H. Marshall 1999: 512-21; Collins: 102-6; Johnson 2001: 74-76; de Silva: 748-56.)

ESCHATOLOGY Some NT scholars see a major change in Paul's eschatology in the letters to Timothy and Titus when compared with his earlier writings. The normal Pauline term for the Lord's second coming is the Greek term *parousia,* which does not appear in the letters to Timothy and Titus. The church in the letters to Timothy and Titus is adjusting to the culture in which it finds itself, thereby suggesting that Paul's earlier emphasis on an imminent return of Christ has faded.

In the letters to Timothy and Titus, the term *appearance* (*epiphaneia*) occurs several times. In Greek-speaking Judaism, the term was used to discuss Yahweh's theophanic appearances to save God's people. In the literature of Judaism, the term sometimes means "revelation." Epiphany describes something that was hidden and is now appearing or arriving, such as the arrival of dawn or the appearance of gods. In Hellenism the term was used for ruler cults and was applied to kings who appeared at various cities and bestowed gifts upon the people. Given its use for the ruler cult, it is likely that Paul used it deliberately in the letters to Timothy and Titus to contrast the Christ cult with the Caesar cult. Christ is the true, universal Savior, manifested according to the providential plan of the universal God, who is Savior of all. His "epiphany" as the man Jesus Christ and his return as Lord and Judge rival the claims of lord Caesar (Young: 65).

Two epiphanies receive attention in the letters to Timothy and Titus. The first is Jesus' coming into the world in the flesh, as a human being. Second, Jesus Christ will "appear" at the end of time as judge. In using the term *epiphaneia* for the future appearance of Christ (1 Tim 6:14; 2 Tim 4:1, 8; Titus 2:13), the author is referring to the same event as *parousia* in Paul's earlier writings (1 Thess 5:23; 2 Thess 2:1). The noun *epiphaneia* refers to the historical appearance of Christ as Savior (2 Tim 1:10). The verb form refers to past appearances of God's grace (Titus 2:11; 3:4). God's grace *has appeared* in the epiphany of his Son. It is being revealed in and through the church's proclamation of the gospel. And it will be revealed finally and ultimately in the future epiphany of the Lord (Towner 2006: 417). The resurrection of Christ makes eternal life a reality for believers (1 Tim 1:16; 4:8; 6:12; 2 Tim 1:10; 2:8-13; Titus 1:2; 3:7). Faithfulness to Christ means that we will also reign with him (2 Tim 2:12) in his future kingdom (4:1, 18) and, like Paul, receive the crown of righteousness (4:8). This is possible because the work of Christ *abolished death and brought life and immortality to light through the gospel* (1:10). Thus, Paul speaks of *the blessed hope and the manifestation of the glory of our great God and Savior, Jesus Christ* (Titus 2:13). We can rest assured in Jesus Christ, who is *the righteous judge* (2 Tim 4:8). At his appearing, Christ is expected *to judge the living and the dead* (4:1).

Epiphany language in the letters to Timothy and Titus engages the dominant religious-political discourse. The imperial cult became the basis for communicating the political, social, and religious ideals of Rome. This imperial cult was present in Ephesus at all levels of society. Paul's use of epiphany language forced a rethinking of common cultural categories as it told God's story in Hellenistic terms. In popular Hellenistic usage, epiphany language called attention to power and divine intervention of the Greco-Roman gods and Roman emperors. Paul says that in the epiphany of Jesus Christ, divine power and presence are present in human weakness, suffering, and death. In this way the gospel was communicated in a thought-provoking way.

> By co-opting the term *epiphany* in reference to Christ (or in reference to the grace of God), Paul is challenging the local Ephesian association of protection, prosperity, and importance with Artemis and the imperial association of peace, power, security, and dignity with the emperor. Instead, he is proclaiming the superiority of the "epiphany" of Christ as Lord. (Towner 2006: 418)

Finally, the epiphany language identifies a relationship between eschatology and mission and ethics. Timothy lives between the past epiphany, which has introduced salvation, and the future epiphany, which will complete salvation. The present time is to be characterized by holy living and proclamation of the gospel, carrying out the mission of the church. Holy living enhances the witness of the gospel. The language of epiphany stresses the expectancy of a real and visible future event of divine intervention. With the uncertainty and an awareness of *the last days* (1 Tim 4:1; 2 Tim 3:1), Paul draws attention to the future return of Christ as "epiphany" and teaches that with his return, salvation will be completed. This gives ongoing meaning to living in the present time between the two epiphanies (Towner 2006: 419). In short, Paul presents a clear Christian eschatology in the letters to Timothy and Titus that includes an "already, but not yet" concept. Language for this eschatology centers on the term *epiphany* rather than *parousia*, but its content is similar to that in Paul's other writings. (Cf. Elias 2006: 479-99; Young: 70-72; Davies: 43-47; Collins: 202-9; Towner 2006: 416-20; Witherington 2006: 371-76.)

FAITHFUL SAYINGS The formula *faithful saying* (KJV), *sure saying* (NRSV), or *trustworthy saying* (TNIV) occurs five times in the letters to Timothy and Titus (1 Tim 1:15; 3:1; 4:9; 2 Tim 2:11; and Titus 3:8). Two times (1 Tim 1:15; 4:9) the phrase is enlarged by the words *and worthy of full acceptance* (NRSV) or *that deserves full acceptance* (TNIV). In shorter or longer form, the formula is not found elsewhere in the NT or in the Greek OT (LXX). Neither in secular Greek nor in Jewish writings is the exact formula used as it appears in Timothy and Titus. At most one can say that the author of the letters to Timothy and Titus is using language that reflects phraseology in current Hellenistic Greek, but the formula itself comes from the author of the letters to Timothy and Titus. When it is expanded into a longer formula, the author uses repetition for the sake of emphasis. At times the *sure saying* formula precedes the actual saying (1 Tim 1:15; 3:1; 2 Tim 2:11) and at other times it follows the actual saying (1 Tim 4:9; Titus 3:8).

The word *faithful*, *sure*, or *trustworthy* (*pistos*) has both an active and a passive meaning in its classical usage and in the NT. However, in the NT it generally has the passive sense of "faithful" (*TDNT* 6:204). God is faithful, as noted in 2 Timothy 2:13: *If we are faithless, he remains faithful—for he cannot deny himself.* In like manner the *word/saying* is faithful because it sets forth the truth of the one who is faithful (Knight 1979: 9). Since God cannot deny himself, the faithful word cannot be denied. Since God *never lies* (Titus 1:2), the faithful saying will never be untrue.

Is the formula a citation formula or a formula of emphasis? In using the formula, the author emphasizes that the content of his gospel corresponds with the apostolic tradition and asserts its authenticity. As a formula of emphasis, the sayings point to the object of the writer's exhortation. The formula is flexible enough to refer to teaching based on tradition, to salvation, and to practical behavior.

The first use of the formula, found in its longer expression, occurs in 1 Timothy 1:15: *Christ Jesus came into the world to save sinners.* The saying is applied to Paul's own life, but its content reaches to all. The content of this saying can be traced to the words of Jesus in Luke 19:10. It describes the condition of human persons and God's action in Jesus Christ in time and history to bring about salvation. With one verb, *to save*, the whole work of Christ Jesus and its effect upon humankind is set forth.

A second use of the formula is found in Titus 3:4-7. Here the formula appears after the saying. *But when the goodness and loving kindness of God our Savior appeared, he saved us, not because of any works of righteousness that we have done, but according to his mercy, through the water of rebirth and renewal by the Holy Spirit. This Spirit he poured out on us richly through Jesus Christ our Savior, so that, having been justified by his grace, we might become heirs according to the hope of eternal life.* The saying calls attention not only to what God did in Christ, but also to the action of the Holy Spirit within the Christian believer.

Third, the formula is found in 1 Timothy 4:9 in its longer expression. Here the saying appears *before* the formula and can be traced back to verse 8. *While physical training is of some value, godliness is valuable in every way, holding promise for both the present life and the life to come.* Scholars debate whether the saying precedes or follows the formula. It can be argued both ways, since verse 10 also speaks of God our Savior. In the larger context, it seems best to interpret the formula as applying to what precedes it, in verse 8. In this saying the author argues from the lesser value to the greater value. Though there is some value in physical training in the gymnasium for the Olympic contests, there is far greater value in godliness, which holds promise both for the present life and the life to come.

A fourth saying occurs in 2 Timothy 2:11-13, where the formula in its shorter wording appears before the saying. *If we have died with him, we will also live with him; if we endure, we will also reign with him; if we deny him, he will also deny us; if we are faithless, he remains faithful—for he cannot deny himself.* The saying focuses on salvation and faithful living. Though in the former sayings believers are passive, in 2 Timothy 2:11-13 they are active and responsible. Furthermore, the statements are conditional and move from the soteriological to the ethical and the experiential.

Finally, a fifth saying appears in 1 Timothy 3:1, which follows the shorter formula. *Whoever aspires to the office of bishop desires a noble task.* This faithful saying takes the reader beyond salvation and Christian living to the good work of leadership in the church. Here too scholars debate whether the formula points backward to salvation through childbirth (1 Tim 2:15) or whether it points forward to the good work of the bishop's function in the church. Given the content of 1 Timothy 2:8-15, it seems highly unlikely that the formula points in the direction of childbirth. Thus I interpret it as referring to the good work of leadership in the church.

These five sure sayings (NRSV) are rooted in traditional Christianity. Though the formula itself may have been created by the author of the letters to Timothy and Titus, the content of the sayings is tied to the apostolic message, and the formula emphasizes the importance of that apostolic message for the church. These five sure sayings, based on the faithfulness of God, move from salvation (1 Tim 1:15; Titus 3:4-7) to godly living (1 Tim 4:8; 2 Tim 2:11-13) and finally to church leadership (1 Tim 3:1). (Cf. Collins: 41-44; Dibelius and Conzelmann: 28-29; I. H. Marshall 1999: 326-30; Mounce: 48-49; Knight 1979; Quinn 1990: 230-32; Towner 2006: 143-48; Young: 56-57.)

GODLINESS *Godliness* (*eusebeia*) is a term that sets forth the author's view of the Christian life and ethics. It was a common term in the pagan world of the first century. According to Foerster in the *TDNT*, in popular usage this term came to refer to piety expressed in worship given to the gods in cultic acts. Such piety was both a virtue and a duty in Greek and Roman life. For the educated Greek, godliness was expressed through acts of worship and through respect for the order sustained by it (7:168-96).

In the LXX, the noun *eusebeia* occurs 59 times. It is typically translated "the fear of the LORD" in English translations. Its verb form is found only in the apocryphal books of the LXX. *Eusebeia* in the LXX gathers in one comprehensive idea the knowledge of God and the appropriate response (fear of the LORD; cf. I. H. Marshall 1999: 141). "The fear of the LORD is the beginning of knowledge" (Prov 1:7a). Both the Greco-Roman world and the Jewish Diaspora used the term *godliness* for daily conduct, but in different ways. The term offered the Hellenistic Jew a means for explaining and expressing oneself to contemporary society (Quinn 1990: 287ff.). Although in Greek thinking *godliness* was a virtue and was tied to cultic acts, it was large enough to communicate the necessary inner and outer dimensions and connotation of loyalty to God and to express adequately an OT Jewish concept of "piety" or spiritual life (I. H. Marshall 1999: 141).

In the letters to Timothy and Titus, the noun *godliness* describes the life—or in its adverb form, the manner of life—that is true Christianity (1 Tim 2:2; 3:16; 4:7-8; 6:3, 5-6, 11; 2 Tim 3:5, 12; Titus 1:1; 2:12). Godliness is rooted in the Christ event (1 Tim 3:16; 2 Tim 3:12; Titus 2:12) and is integrally related to the knowledge of God in the gospel and in the truth (1 Tim 6:3, 5-6, 11; Titus 1:1). In contrast to the superficial godliness of the unhealthy teachers (2 Tim 3:5), true godliness arises out of a commitment to God and the teaching of the faith. It goes beyond worship and includes both belief and behavior. Although the NRSV translates the word for *godliness* as "religion" in 1 Timothy 3:16, it is more than religion in that it defines the serious pursuit of God, Christian living, and Christian knowledge.

As used in the letters to Timothy and Titus, *godliness* is more than a polemic defense of Christianity. It also defines the Christian community as distinct from the Roman society in which it lived (Quinn 1990: 289). The use of the term *godliness* in Acts and in the letters to Timothy and Titus demonstrates how Christian missionaries can use a common term in contemporary society and fill it with new meaning that communicates the gospel and calls for faithful Christian living.

HAPAX LEGOMENA "Hapax legomena" is the plural form of a Greek literary term for a word or form occurring only once in the recorded corpus of a given body of literature. The term is used by scholars for 175 words in the letters to Timothy and Titus that do not occur elsewhere in the New Testament. Several NT scholars conclude, from the use of these hapax legomena in late first- and early second-century Greco-Roman literature, that Paul did not write the letters to Timothy and Titus. This is an important argument.

However, one can ask whether 175 words are enough to build a strong argument based on a literary analysis. I tend to agree with Metzger that it is too small a number of words on which to build a good argument (1958: 94).

Furthermore, many of the 175 hapax legomena are found in the first century before AD 50 (Guthrie 1990b: 224-40). According to one count, of the 175 hapax legomena, 80 appear in the LXX (Mounce: ciii). Thus, deciding on the date and authorship of 1 & 2 Timothy and Titus by using a literary analysis of these 175 hapax legomena seems to claim more than the evidence supplies.

HERMENEUTICAL ISSUES The Christian church's interpretation of the letters to Timothy and Titus includes several areas of disagreement. The authorship question was significant in the past 275 years. Some scholars hold to a post-Pauline period for these letters, when an unknown writer penned the letters to Timothy and Titus in the name of the apostle Paul. The view taken in this commentary is that these letters were written somewhere between AD 65 and 85. Though the letters reflect Pauline thought, their terminology may suggest a different writer than Paul, with Luke perhaps serving as secretary *[Authorship, p. 325]*.

A related issue is whether to read these letters as a unit, commonly known as the pastoral epistles, or as individual letters. Recent studies by Johnson (2001: 1-99) and Towner (2006: 1-89) favor seeing these as individual letters. I think the letters need to be read both vertically (examining each individual letter with its theology and ethical teaching) and horizontally (tracing theological and ethical themes through the three letters).

What about church governance? How are we to understand the role and function of bishop (*episkopos, overseer*)? Do these letters reflect the monarchical bishop of the second century? Can the interpreter simply exchange the word *bishop* for *elder?* The church has debated this for centuries, with believers churches rejecting the monarchical bishop but retaining the office of bishop (or something similar) along with elders and deacons.

How shall the church relate to the governing authorities? Titus 3:1 calls for submission to rulers and authorities, and 1 Timothy 2:2 calls for prayers for kings and all who are in high positions. At the same time 1 & 2 Timothy and Titus present the lordship of Christ and God as Savior over against Roman imperial religion, which assigned deity to the Roman emperor.

Good biblical interpretation demands that the interpreter begin with a search for the meaning of the text in its original historical context. Next, the interpreter can move to today's context and explain what the text means now. In this journey between two worlds, the interpreter moves from the *meaning* of the text within its historical context, to the *significance* of the text in today's context. As Paul applies the gospel in the letters to Timothy and Titus, the prevailing culture is not completely rejected, nor is it fully accepted. This change in context has important implications for the way the household behavior texts are applied today.

In the first century, the state ruled over its subjects in a monarchical or aristocratic system of government. The state could rule in peace (Rom 13:1-7) or as an evil tyranny (Rev 13). Today many countries have a democratic rule in which citizens can vote incompetent and unjust rulers out of office. This democratic context suggests that while obedience to the state (Rom 13:1-7; 1 Tim 2:2; Titus 3:1) is still important (Christians are not to be anarchists), the conditions for that obedience have changed, and the significance of the text for our day goes beyond the parameters of its first-century context.

In the first century, a high percentage of people were slaves. First-century culture accepted slaves. Today Christians recognize that slavery is not acceptable because all human beings are created in the image of God, and all persons are objects of Christ's redemption. Today slavery is seen as sinful and is rejected by all Christian groups in North America. Abolition of slavery has altered the way Christians understand the meaning of the texts regarding slaves in the household behavior texts of the NT. Today's employer-employee relationships have different dynamics. Though the employee will continue to give a good day's work to the employer, the employer must treat the employee with respect, justice, and honor, as expressed in a fair wage. In this new context, the meaning and significance of the household behavior texts on slaves are radically different.

Likewise, a major change in context has taken place between women and men in the modern world. In the first century, females in their early teens were typically married to males in their midtwenties. In that context it was necessary for older women to teach younger women to love their husbands and be good managers of the household (Titus 2:4-5). Not to teach younger women would have brought dishonor on the Christian household in Paul's day. Today Western women and men often marry at a similar age and often after each has completed college and started a profession. The context also has changed. No longer is the extended family living in the household. Though older women still have something to offer younger women, the nature and extent of that teaching has changed radically.

Moreover, the dynamics of the marriage relationship have changed since the first century. In the patriarchal system, the first-century husband had power over the wife simply because he was male. This was modified by the household behavior texts in the NT. Sadly, some persons have used these texts in support of male abuse by demanding female submission. Interpreting male-female roles in this way corresponds largely to the way some interpreters of these same texts justified slavery. Faithful Christians do not support slavery, nor do they support male abuse by demanding female submission. Marriage in today's context is characterized by a partnership of equals. In this partnership both husbands and wives often are employed and together supply the income for the family. No longer are children an economic necessity as they were in colonial America, with its agricultural economy. So the number of children born in present-day families is significantly reduced. Both husband and wife partner in rearing the children. Both husband and wife bring strengths and weaknesses to the marriage relationship. As each lovingly discerns their own strengths and weaknesses (Rom 12:3) as well as those of the other, they make adjustments in order to build their marriage on each other's strengths. Both husband and wife love as Christ loved, and both submit themselves to each other. Instead of exercising power over the other as a domineering husband or manipulative wife, power arises out of the equality of the relationship, which is sealed in a Christian marriage covenant. It is enhanced by God's grace, by speaking the truth in love to each other, and by an intimacy that seeks to honor the other person and strengthen the relationship. This Christian view of marriage assumes that God created male and female for the good of the other and not to compete with each other. It is a relationship of complementarity without hierarchy.

Whether one is talking about the citizen-state relationship, the slave-master relationship, the younger-older women relationship, or the husband-wife relationship, the new context in which Christians find themselves today alters the meaning of the household behavior texts.

However, some aspects of the relationship carry over from the first century. The qualities of character carry over. Self-control carries over for all persons, as do Christlike attitudes, thoughts, and behavior. Male and female traits carry over, though they also vary from culture to culture. The spiritual quality of life lived by members of the church within the household today enhances or detracts from the missionary witness of the church. Each generation must discern how best to apply the household behavior texts within its context.

HISTORY OF INTERPRETATION Polycarp, bishop of Smyrna, presents early evidence of the use of 1 and 2 Timothy. In his letter *To the Philippians* (4.1), written around 117, Polycarp cites 1 Timothy 6:10 and 6:7, indicating that he drew instructions from Paul's letters and shaped his language from them. Polycarp's letter (5.2; 11.4; 9.2) also alludes to 2 Timothy 2:11-12, 25 and 4:10. *First Clement* (61.2; 60.4; 2.7; written ca. 96) uses language similar to what we see in 1 Timothy 1:17; 2:7; and Titus 3:1. These early witnesses suggest that the letters to Timothy and Titus could not have been written in the middle of the second century, as F. C. Baur proposed in the nineteenth century. Irenaeus (d. ca. 202) attributes 1 Timothy to "the apostle." Clement of Alexandria (d. ca. 215) frequently used 1 and 2 Timothy, and Tertullian (d. ca. 220) also frequently cited them. Although Marcion (ca. 150) rejected the letters to Timothy and Titus, they were included in Syriac and Latin versions and eventually became part of the canon.

First and 2 Timothy and Titus were included in the Muratorian Canon, in which lines 59-63 read, "[Paul also wrote] out of affection and love one to Philemon, one to Titus, and two to Timothy; and these are held sacred in the esteem of the Church catholic for the regulation of ecclesiastical discipline" (Metzger 1987: 307). Although $\mathfrak{p}^{46}$, a papyrus manuscript listing the Pauline epistles (ca. 200), does not have the letters to Timothy and Titus, the last seven pages of the manuscript are missing. However, because this manuscript was known to consist originally of 104 leaves, scholars have determined that it could not originally have included the letters to Timothy and Titus.

From the fourth century onward, the church accepted the letters to Timothy and Titus as part of the NT canon and as authored by the apostle Paul. This combination of the early use of the letters to Timothy and Titus and their inclusion in the canon bear witness to their authenticity in the eyes of the church from the first to the fourth centuries.

Throughout the medieval period, commentaries written both in the Eastern and in the Western church readily included the letters to Timothy and Titus. Augustine emphasized love as the goal of the law, appealing to 1 Timothy 1:5. We see, however, a growing sexism in the medieval commentaries, which were written by monks. Thomas Aquinas (d. 1274), wrote negative comments about women in his exegesis of 1 Timothy 2:11-15. Thomas thought that men should be teachers because, as Aristotle noted, male is to reason as female is to sensuality. Thus, a rule by women is a corruption of the family as tyranny is of kingship (Johnson 2001: 35).

In the sixteenth to the eighteenth centuries, such church leaders as Martin Luther, John Calvin, Johann Albrecht Bengel, John Wesley, and a few Roman Catholic scholars wrote commentaries on the letters to Timothy and Titus. Calvin's work indicates rare insight into ancient rhetoric, but it is limited by his cultural and religious biases. Calvin not only repeatedly reacted to the papists; on the basis of 1 Timothy 2:11-12, he also declared that rule by women is a bad thing (Johnson 2001: 38). Johann David Michaelis's *Introduction to the New Testament* (1750) marks the beginning transition to criticisms of the nineteenth century. Until the nineteenth century, Pauline authorship of 1 & 2 Timothy and Titus was not challenged, and their status as canonical Scripture was never seriously questioned.

The term "pastoral epistles" was first used for Titus by D. N. Bardot in 1703 and for all three epistles by P. Anton in 1726. Eventually these three letters came to be referred to almost exclusively as pastoral epistles and were treated as a single corpus of writings. With this interpretation came also an assumption of their literary, historical, and theological consistency.

At the beginning of the nineteenth century, historical-critical analysis led scholars to question their authenticity—specifically whether they were written by Paul himself. This question of authenticity would dominate discussion for the next 200 years. Friedrich Schleiermacher (d. 1834) first questioned the authenticity of 1 Timothy in 1807. His analysis was largely linguistic: he discovered several words that occur only once in 1 Timothy when compared with 2 Timothy and Titus. Schleiermacher added that 1 Timothy does not fit the history recorded in the book of Acts, and he concluded that the church organization reflected there fits a development later than Paul. Schleiermacher concluded that 1 Timothy was written after the first century. He considered it a forgery, which rendered it suspect as Scripture (Johnson 2001: 43).

Johann Gottfried Eichhorn (d. 1827) identified all three letters as a group or special set of distinct writings, minimizing the differences between them. In 1812, Eichhorn said that the letters could not be Pauline because they do not fit Paul's career as we know it. A few years later, Ferdinand Christian Baur (d. 1860) also questioned the authenticity of the letters. Instead of concentrating primarily on literary style, Baur looked at history. As he studied second-century Gnosticism, Baur concluded that the teachers opposed in these letters must have been the Gnostics and that these letters must have come from the mid-second century. Baur said that 1 Timothy's instructions on women fit the second century and rejected the citations in Polycarp. He also noted the absence of the letters in Marcion's canon. Baur and his student Albert Schwegler said that the pastorals represented an attempt by early Catholicism to establish church order and repress diversity (Johnson 2001: 45). Baur compared the church order reflected in the three letters with that in the letters of Ignatius of Antioch (ca. 115), in which the monarchical episcopate and hierarchical order unified the churches against heterodoxy.

Since Baur, most New Testament introductions and commentaries have interpreted Timothy and Titus as one body of literature and have concluded that they are pseudonymous writings from the second century. Pseudonymity became the majority view of scholarly writing in the nineteenth and twentieth centuries *[Authorship, p. 325].*

This view was promoted by Martin Dibelius (d. 1947), whose scholarship dominated the discussion of Timothy and Titus since 1970 (Dibelius and Conzelmann 1972). At the center of the rejection of Pauline authorship are differences between the undisputed letters of Paul and the letters to Timothy and Titus. Dibelius emphasized an adjustment of the church in the direction of good Christian citizenship (*christliche Bürgerlichkeit*) so it would be accepted by the larger Roman society. In 1991 J. Christiaan Beker pointed out the continuing importance of Paul after his death and called attention to the need for Paul's authoritative voice in the church during the post-Pauline period and before the rise of the monarchical bishop (Beker 1991). According to Beker, these letters fit a late first- or early second-century setting, in which eschatology no longer influences life. This changing outlook forced the church to adjust to society in the postapostolic period while maintaining the continuity of the gospel and the authoritative voice of Paul. A few contemporary commentaries, such as Jouette M. Bassler (1996) and Collins (2002), accept pseudonymity as conventional wisdom.

However, conservative scholars, representing a minority view, have continued to defend Pauline authorship over the past 150 years. Studies by E. E. Ellis (1959: 343-54), C. F. D. Moule (1982: 113-32), and B. M. Metzger (1958: 91-94) and commentaries by D. Guthrie (1990b), J. N. D. Kelly (1960), G. D. Fee (1988), G. W. Knight (1992), and C. Spicq (1969) did not accept the letters' pseudonymity and held to Pauline authorship. Conservative NT introductions, such as by de Silva (2004: 733-48), continue to defend Pauline authorship. In 1994, Young pointed out that the relationship between the letters' value and authority on the one hand and their authorship on the other cannot be completely separated: "A new convergence of scholarly work is arriving at a more positive estimate of the value of the Pastorals over against an older view, which arose largely from the historical judgment that these texts were pseudonymous and secondary" (146).

Six major commentaries published since 1990 seriously challenge the pseudonymous view of authorship (Quinn 1990; I. H. Marshall 1999; Mounce 2000; Johnson 2001; Towner 2006; Witherington 2006). Though no one knows for sure who wrote 1 & 2 Timothy and Titus, the authorship question remains a live issue in the interpretation of these letters at the present time. (Cf. Dibelius and Conzelmann: 1-10; Johnson 2001: 1-99; Towner 2006: 1-89; Kümmel: 258-72; de Silva: 733-57; Young: 145-47; Witherington 2006: 23-75; Aageson 2008.)

HOLY SPIRIT IN THE LETTERS TO TIMOTHY AND TITUS Studies in the letters to Timothy and Titus tend to see institutional church order and ministerial offices as the means through which the Holy Spirit works. However, there is also a larger theology of the Holy Spirit in 1 & 2 Timothy and Titus. This theology, as expounded by Fee (1994: 755-94), relates the person and work of the Holy Spirit to Christ, salvation, and Christian living. It also emphasizes the relation of the Holy Spirit to ministry in the church. In addition, the Holy Spirit aids the church leader in perceiving unhealthy teachings and how to deal with them.

THE HOLY SPIRIT AND CHRIST We see a connection between the Holy Spirit and Christ in the hymn in 1 Timothy 3:16. The phrase *vindicated in spirit* ties into the previous phrase, *revealed in flesh*, which speaks of the incarnation of Jesus Christ. The phrase *vindicated in spirit* refers to the supernatural existence entered into by Christ through the resurrection. In this interpretation, the resurrection vindicated the humanity of Christ, including his experience of the cross. Just as Christ in the flesh ministered in the power of the Spirit, so now, through the resurrection, Christ has entered into the spiritual and supernatural realm. Though the unhealthy teachers in Ephesus tended to reject the flesh (1 Tim 4:1-4), the phrase *vindicated in spirit* affirms the created order.

A second passage showing the connection between the Holy Spirit and Christ is Titus 3:6. *This Spirit he* [God] *poured out on us richly through Jesus Christ our Savior*. Christ is the agent through whom God sends the Holy Spirit into the world. Thus, Christ's work of salvation is actualized in the Christian believer by the person of the Holy Spirit. It follows that the activity of Christ and the Holy Spirit are connected in a third passage (2 Tim 1:12, 14). Paul has put his trust in Jesus Christ, who is able to stand guard over his salvation. Similarly, Timothy is instructed to guard the treasure of the gospel of Christ entrusted to him, *with the help of the Holy Spirit living in us*. Though in verse 12 Christ is the agent of guardianship, in verse 14 guarding comes through the Spirit.

THE HOLY SPIRIT AND SALVATION Salvation is an important theme in the letters to Timothy and Titus (1 Tim 1:15; 2:3-7; 3:16; 4:10; Titus 2:11-14; 3:4-7; 2 Tim 1:8-14; 3:15). Salvation is emphasized in Titus 3:4-7, which says the Holy Spirit "washes" and thus brings about rebirth and renewal. Salvation comes through the regenerating work of the Spirit, who is the agent of rebirth and transformation. Because the Holy Spirit is lavishly poured out by God through Jesus Christ (Titus 3:6), there is no question regarding the Spirit's ability to bring salvation in the life of the believer.

THE HOLY SPIRIT AND CHRISTIAN LIVING In contrast to opponents, the author exhorts Christian believers in Ephesus and in Crete to practice good works. Christians are to live lives that are *godly and respectful in every way* (1 Tim 2:2 RSV). Although the lives of some are filled with evil, Christ gave himself to *redeem us from all iniquity and purify for himself a people of his own who are zealous for good deeds* (Titus 2:14). Christ's saving work, coupled with the work of the Holy Spirit in regeneration, transforms the believer, resulting in new ways of living. This newness is contrasted with the way people once lived in sin (3:3). It therefore follows that believers washed by the Spirit will avoid the actions of the opponents described in what follows in Titus 3:9-11.

THE HOLY SPIRIT AND MINISTRY In the letters to Timothy and Titus, the character of leaders is given major attention. Leaders are to be sound in teaching, to guard the deposit of the gospel of salvation, and to lead the household of God (1 Tim 3:1-5). In several passages, Timothy is reminded of the Holy Spirit's work in calling him to ministry and enabling him for the task (1 Tim 1:18; 4:14; 2 Tim 1:6-7). The gift of the Spirit is associated with the laying on of hands by the council of elders. Timothy is given the gift of teaching and preaching by the Holy Spirit. With this gift he is enabled to teach sound words that protect and guard the faith. Through the gift of prophecy, the church has identified Timothy and his ability to lead the congregation (1 Tim 1:18). The prophetic gift as office, however, is not identified in the letters to Timothy and Titus, nor is any church leader called a prophet. Only the pagan poet Epimenides is called a prophet (Titus 1:12). Both 1 Timothy 1:18 and 4:14 refer to the prophetic Spirit that directed Timothy on how to lead the community of faith in Ephesus. Thus, the Holy Spirit identified who was gifted for ministry, and the community first tested and then openly recognized this gifting by the laying on of hands (1 Tim 5:22; 2 Tim 1:6). Christian ministry is exercised in the power of the Spirit (2 Tim 1:7). Both the origin and strength for Timothy's ministry came from the Holy Spirit. Timothy is to remember the gift that the Holy Spirit gave him. He is not to neglect it (1 Tim 4:14), but to fan it into flame (2 Tim 1:6).

The Holy Spirit dwells in all Christian believers (Titus 3:6-7). All Christians are given the Spirit of power and of love and of self-discipline (2 Tim 1:7). Furthermore, the Spirit provides self-discipline. Not only are leaders called to self-discipline (Titus 1:8); the Holy Spirit also provides this discipline to leaders and all Christians.

Timothy is to remember that all Scripture is inspired—literally, *God-breathed*—and therefore useful for the preaching and teaching ministry (2 Tim 3:14-17 TNIV). The same Holy Spirit who called Timothy to ministry, who equips him for the task, was also at work in the process of divine revelation, transmission, and writing of the sacred Scriptures. These sacred Scriptures instruct one for salvation in Jesus Christ and equip church leaders for every good work.

THE HOLY SPIRIT IN PAUL AND IN THE PASTORALS Many aspects of the Holy Spirit mentioned in the other Pauline letters also appear in the letters to Timothy and Titus. These include the relation between the Holy Spirit and Christ (2 Tim 1:12-14; Titus 3:6-7), the role of the Holy Spirit in Christian conversion (Titus 3:5-6), the Holy Spirit and Christian living (Titus 3:1-8), the Holy Spirit's indwelling (2 Tim 1:6-7; Titus 3:5-6), the Holy Spirit and power (2 Tim 1:7), the Holy Spirit and love (2 Tim 1:7), and the Holy Spirit and eschatology (1 Tim 4:1; Titus 3:6-7).

Absent from the letters to Timothy and Titus is Paul's teaching on the contrast between the Spirit and the flesh (Rom 8:3-17; Gal 4:29; 5:13–6:10; Phil 3:3), the Spirit giving revelation and understanding (1 Cor 2:6-16), the Spirit and worship (Rom 12:1-2; 1 Cor 14:2, 6, 24, 26; Phil 3:3), and the Spirit and Christian unity (1 Cor 12:13; 2 Cor 13:13; Phil 2:1).

New aspects of the Holy Spirit's work include guarding the deposit of faith (2 Tim 1:14), providing self-discipline (2 Tim 1:7; but cf. Gal 3:23, 26), and giving the gift of ministry (1 Tim 4:14; 2 Tim 1:6-7; but cf. Rom 12:7). Thus the author of the letters to Timothy and Titus largely affirms what is said previously in Paul's epistles regarding the person and work of the Holy Spirit. At the same time, the letters to Timothy and Titus give additional insights into the Spirit's work that are relevant to the situation of the church at Ephesus and Crete when they were written (Fee 1994: 755-94; Treblico: 241-56; Young: 68-70).

HONOR AND SHAME Western culture is highly individualistic and places high value on personal freedom. Sin is defined in terms of personal *guilt*, which requires forgiveness and cleansing. More recently, sin is seen as alienation and meaninglessness.

Ancient cultures in the first century were characterized by honor and shame. Honor is a claim to worth along with the social acknowledgment of worth. In ancient cultures the group was more important than the individual. How one is viewed by the group is given highest importance. A person is who one is perceived to be by others in the culture (e.g., by one's family, clan, or the leaders of society). In first-century culture, honor was ascribed to a person or a group on the basis of public acknowledgment that one's family was honorable or had inherited honor, or that good deeds had been done. Other values, such as strength, courage, wisdom, and generosity, were associated with honor. In an honor-and-shame culture, interactions outside the family are important for the recognition of honor or the loss of honor. Gift giving, invitations to dinners, seating at dinners, marriage arrangements, business, and mutual help were all social interactions that contributed to or took away from honor. Thus acceptance by the group rose above all other considerations.

Shame is the absence of these virtues and the refusal of others to ascribe dignity to certain persons. Those without honor in the NT world included lepers, the poor, slaves, and women. Gentiles were considered without honor in the Jewish world, and Jews were considered without honor in the Gentile world. Dishonorable people were taken advantage of and had no way to gain honor. They were dependent on wealthy patrons to give them honor. Women depended on fathers and husbands to give them honor.

Gregory S. MaGee shows the connection between Paul's imprisonment and the shame and pain associated with it in the Roman world (338-53). According to MaGee's research, Greco-Roman sources pointed to the disgrace of imprisonment in three ways. First, they marked the general shame associated with being chained; second, they highlighted the particular affront of imprisonment to people of high status; and third, they saw shame reflected by the behavior of the prisoners' companions (343). Onesiphorus's lack of shame in visiting Paul was clearly countercultural (Collins: 217).

Paul was aware of the shame and reproach of his imprisonment. Suffering for the cause of the gospel was considered shameful by the cultured society of the Roman world. And Timothy faced shame by identifying himself with Paul and the gospel. In 2 Timothy, Paul exhorts Timothy to look at honor and shame from a different perspective. Paul reinterpreted the shame as honor because his imprisonment was for the sake of the gospel. He upended the honor and shame calculus by honoring the shame of the cross.

The gospel message of the crucified and resurrected Lord Jesus Christ gives new meaning and dignity to life. This gospel gives people worth and relationship with the risen and ascended Lord Jesus Christ. Though the gospel may appear as scandal to first-century culture, God's work of salvation actually gives dignity, purpose, and life to Christian believers. One finds honor by becoming part of the church, the new people of God. Shame is associated with walking in darkness and engaging in vices. By being adopted into God's family, receiving the promised inheritance, becoming citizens of heaven, and claiming victory in Jesus Christ, the early church defined itself as living in honor despite the shame ascribed to the death of Jesus, to the church, and to the good news of the gospel. (Cf. Toews: 385-86; Towner 2006: 463-64; MaGee: 338-53; Malina: 28-60; de Silva: 128-29, 754-56.)

HOUSEHOLD BEHAVIOR Household codes in the Greco-Roman world originated with Aristotle (*Politics* 1.2.1-2; *Great Ethics* 1:33.15-18; *Nicomachean Ethics* 8.10.4-6). Aristotle described a female as a deformed male and concluded that women are inferior to men (*Generation of Animals* 737a.28). In his writing about politics, Aristotle talked about the way the city is governed. In Aristotle's view, household management is a microcosm of the city and therefore has established a hierarchy for the larger household. Households consisted of a husband, a wife, children, slaves, and sometimes members of the extended family. The head of the household ruled over all other household members. Aristotle taught that some ethnic groups were by nature suited to be slaves (*Politics* 1.1255a.20; Bell: 193). He went so far as to define a slave as a living tool or living property (*Nicomachean Ethics* 8.11; de Silva: 142, 672). Slaves lived entirely under the authority of their master. Aristotle addressed four subtopics in his treatment of the household: master-slave relationships, husband-wife relationships, father-child relationships, and the art of acquiring wealth. These relationships were understood as the relationships of ruler and ruled, of superior and subordinate (Verner: 84). According to Aristotle, slaves and women were fit by nature to be ruled, not to rule (Osiek, MacDonald, and Tulloch: 95). Based on the premise that men are more rational and women less rational, children prerational (immature) and slaves irrational, these codes established an order of authority and submission for each of the classes (Achtemeier: 52).

Though Stoics encouraged more humane treatment, especially of slaves, the order of family life changed little from the time of Aristotle until the first century. Such Hellenistic Jewish writers as Philo (*Hypothetica* 7.14) and Josephus (*Against Apion* 2.23-29 [§§190-210]) used Aristotle's classic teaching on household codes to talk about household management. When Christianity arose, the Greco-Roman household was guided largely by this classical Greek teaching on household behavior.

Christianity changed household behavior. The Christian confession "Jesus is Lord" brought a new dimension to it. A complicating factor for women and slaves was the ancestral gods of the Roman world. When a woman married, she was supposed to accept the gods of her husband. And when one became a slave, one also accepted the master's gods. Female slaves were treated as property, and the master sometimes used them for sexual satisfaction. When slaves and women became Christians in the Roman household, they turned away from their husband's or master's gods and committed themselves to the lordship of Christ. When female slaves became Christians, they no longer offered their bodies to the sexual desires of their masters. New life and freedom in Christ (Gal 3:27-28) clashed with the household practices of the first-century world.

How did the NT church find its way between new life in Christ and the household codes of the Greco-Roman world? Since the church comprised God's household (1 Tim 3:15), how did Christian believers relate to their ruler within the household as understood in first-century Roman culture? David L. Balch suggests that the household behavior passage in 1 Peter 2:13–3:7 reflects the Aristotelian view and was adopted to defend the Christian community against accusations of improper household relationships (1981: 80-109). More recent study has questioned Balch's interpretation (cf., e.g., Bauman-Martin: 263). Feminist critics see a hidden agenda in the household behavior texts in the letters to Timothy and Titus, an agenda that wrongfully justifies men ruling over women in the church.

Schroeder argues that the household codes in the NT address how the new life in Jesus Christ is applied in the new Christian community (1959). Yoder follows Schroeder and interprets the household codes according to the suffering servant motif of Jesus. Yoder calls for "revolutionary subordination" (Yoder 1994: 163-92). Schroeder and Yoder note major differences between the prevailing Roman practice and the NT household behavior texts. First, the NT texts see a reciprocal relationship between husbands and wives, masters and slaves, fathers and children. Second, the NT texts address the customarily inferior person in the relationship first, thus giving them moral dignity. Third, the customarily superior person is also addressed and asked to treat the other person in the relationship in a Christlike manner. Thus, Christ is the model and motivator for a new understanding of relationships within the household (Yoder Neufeld: 276).

In the household codes, Christ models behavior for the husband and master. Christ is repeatedly appealed to as model with phrases "to the Lord," "just as Christ," "as you obey Christ." Christ is not only a model for the subordinates (wives, children, slaves); he is also a model especially for the superordinates (husbands, fathers, masters), according to Yoder Neufeld (281). Husbands are to reject the domineering style of their culturally accepted authority, and to love their wife as Christ loved the church. To carry out one's duty in mutual submission with the wife, sharing authority, indicates a radical departure from the traditional practice of household behavior in Paul's day. Likewise, the authority of the master changes, since both master and slave are accountable to Jesus Christ. As this new behavior takes place in the household, the rights of master over slave are greatly altered.

As members of the Roman household became Christians, revolutionary change took place. No longer did Christians serve the pagan gods of the head of the house. No longer did female slaves give in to the sexual advances of their male masters. No longer did the head of the house rule over the inferior ones. Surely there were conflicts along the way, especially when one or two of the household members became Christian and not the other members—especially the head of the house (Osiek, MacDonald, and Tulloch: 117). In Christ, household members found new freedom to love and serve each other. To a watching world, this was revolutionary—a cause for concern for those in power, and a cause for joy and liberation for those suffering abuse. In a society of honor and shame, such a drastic change in household behavior likely brought scorn upon the church. So Titus 2:1-10 calls for a balanced approach between the new freedom in Christ and a desire that the church not be thought of as a threat to the Roman state and culture. By briefly limiting freedom in Christ to contextualize mission efforts, the church was able to grow and promote equality and justice.

NAMES FOR GOD AND THE IMPERIAL CULT In the letters to Timothy and Titus, several distinctive terms for God and Christ are used: *Sovereign, King of the ages, blessed, Savior,* and *great God.* In addition, terms such as *blessed hope* and *appearance* (*epiphaneia*) occur. All of these terms were used in the imperial cult in the first and second centuries.

Imperial religion		**Christian gospel**
Roman emperor	*sōtēr*	God and Jesus Christ
Emperor's benevolence	*charis*	God's grace in Jesus Christ
Emperor's appearance	*epiphaneia*	Christ's first and second comings
Godliness as respect for the gods	*eusebeia*	Godliness as living by the gospel truth

Emperor worship (designating the political ruler a god) has a long history. It characterized ancient Egypt and Asia Minor. The Pharaohs in Egypt were traditionally deified. The Syrian Seleucid ruler Antiochus IV Epiphanes ([god] manifest) demanded that the Jews worship him (likely identified as Zeus), which led to the Maccabean revolt in 167 BC (1 Maccabees; 2 Macc 6 and 9). In his later years, Julius Caesar was planning to institute the cult of *Divus Julius.* This cult was used by his successors to ensure stability in Roman society and to instill loyalty to the empire in the various provinces. Some Roman emperors, such as Gaius, Nero, and Domitian, took their divinity seriously. During the last two years of Nero's life, he was described as "lord and savior of the world." Emperor Domitian demanded that he be addressed as *dominus et deus noster* (our lord and god).

Some Christians were persecuted during Nero's reign and some during Domitian's reign. During the reigns of Domitian, Nerva, and Trajan (AD 81-117), the imperial cult became a serious problem for Christians. When local authorities coordinated worship of these Roman emperors as divine, they claimed that the emperor as god had begun a new age for humankind.

In contrast, the letters to Timothy and Titus apply to Christ the terms used in the imperial cult. Paul was aware of the imperial cult. He calls Christ both Lord and Savior. For Paul, Caesar's empire is the parody; Jesus' empire is the reality (N. T. Wright 2000: 173, 183). Theologically, the author of the letters to Timothy and Titus presents Christ as the true Savior of the human race, over against the imperial cult of the Roman emperor (Hanson: 187). *Sōtēr* (Savior) is also used for God in the Septuagint (see BDAG).

The term *appear* (*epiphaneia*) was also used by the imperial cult. This term was used to describe the deified Roman emperor's birth, coming into power, enthronement, imperial visits, victories, and return from foreign lands (Collins: 203). But in the letters to Timothy and Titus, it is *Christ* who will appear as God and King, not the Roman emperor (1 Tim 6:14; 2 Tim 1:10; 4:1, 8; Titus 2:13). Moreover, 2 Timothy 1:10 speaks of a past appearance of *our Savior Christ Jesus*, who destroyed death and brought life. And Jesus Christ will appear again in the future to judge the living and the dead. In two doxologies Paul states:

> To the King of the ages, immortal, invisible, the only God be honor and glory forever and ever. Amen. (1 Tim 1:17)

> [God] is the blessed and only Sovereign, the King of kings and Lord of lords. It is he alone who has immortality and dwells in unapproachable light, whom no one has ever seen or can see; to him be honor and eternal dominion. Amen. (1 Tim 6:15-16)

In using the language of the emperor cult, the author of Timothy and Titus implies that Christ, not Caesar, is the true God (Hansen 1982: 5). In this way the early Christians denied the imperial cult its false status and declared their faith in God and in Jesus Christ as the only true Lord.

> From this point of view, therefore, this counter empire can never be merely critical, never merely subversive. It claims to be the reality of which Caesar's empire is the parody; it claims to be modeling the genuine humanness, not least the justice and peace, and the unity across traditional racial and cultural barriers, of which Caesar's empire boasted. (N. T. Wright 2000: 183)

(Cf. Young: 64-65; Hansen 1982: 5; Friesen: 34-49; Kraybill: 60; N. T. Wright 2000: 160-83.)

ORDER AND HISTORICAL SEQUENCE OF THE LETTERS TO TIMOTHY AND TITUS Traditionally, Paul's epistles were arranged in a sequence according to size (generally longest to shortest), with those addressed to churches first, and those addressed to individuals or co-workers second. Hebrews appears at different places in the canon since it was not clear who authored this letter. In the list of Paul's letters to churches, Galatians precedes Ephesians even though Ephesians is a little longer than Galatians. Philemon is included with the writings to individuals.

The letters to Timothy and Titus were arranged in the NT canon according to the following order, based on the number of lines in the manuscript, called "stichs":

1 Timothy	238 stichs
2 Timothy	182 stichs
Titus	100 stichs

Many persons assumed that the letters were written as a unified body of writing in this order. Recent scholars, such as Johnson, I. H. Marshall, Fee, and Towner, have called into question the unified "letters to Timothy and Titus" view and have directed attention to differences in these epistles. Most NT scholars agree that 2 Timothy is different in style and content from 1 Timothy and Titus. In 2 Timothy, Paul is in prison and facing death. He instructs Timothy to carry on the missionary task and leadership of the church at Ephesus and to follow his example of suffering for the gospel. First Timothy and Titus give more instructions on how to guide the church and deal with unhealthy teaching. Titus is written in the context of a young church that needs leaders who will give the church guidance as it grows. First Timothy is written to a church that is established and needs to replace some leaders because some have left the faith and have become part of a deviant teaching movement. Thus, 1 Timothy and Titus, though addressed to different churches in different stages of life, should be studied separately from 2 Timothy.

Which of the three letters was written first? Normally commentaries cover 1 Timothy first and then either 2 Timothy or Titus. Recently some NT scholars are asking whether Titus may have been written before 1 Timothy. It begins with a 66-word prologue (Titus 1:1-4), which is considerably longer than the prologues of 1 and 2 Timothy. Quinn argues that this longer prologue may well serve as a preface to the collection and that themes in Titus are expanded in 1 Timothy (1990: 20). Towner leans toward placing 1 Timothy before Titus (2006: 30). I. Howard Marshall places Titus first, followed by 1 Timothy and 2 Timothy. However, if Paul wrote 2 Timothy, and if Luke had a greater hand in writing 1 Timothy and Titus at a later date, then the order would be 2 Timothy, Titus, and 1 Timothy. As part of the Believers Church Bible Commentary series, this commentary follows the canonical order of 1 Timothy, 2 Timothy, and Titus. (Cf. Metzger 1987: 297-98; Quinn 1990: 19-20; Towner 2006: 30.)

ORDINATION AND THE LAYING ON OF HANDS In 1 Timothy 4:14, Paul says that the council of elders has laid hands on Timothy in recognition of his gift for leading the church. In 2 Timothy 1:6, Timothy is reminded that Paul laid hands on him in recognition of his gift.

In the OT, hands were laid on to convey a blessing. Jacob blessed his grandsons by laying his hands on them (Gen 48:17-20). Aaron lifted his hands toward the people and blessed them (Lev 9:22-23). At other times the laying on of hands passed authority to another person. Moses laid hands on Joshua (Num 27:18-23; Deut 34:9). Also, hands were laid on the head of a sacrificial animal to symbolize the transfer of sin to the animal (Lev 16:21-22).

In the NT, Jesus laid hands on the sick in some cases, though in other cases he did not do so. Christ commissioned his disciples but there is no mention of him laying hands on them (Matt 28:19-20; John 20:19-23; Acts 1:6-8). In the early church the apostles laid hands on seven persons for the task of mutual care when they recognized that these men were filled with the Holy Spirit and with wisdom (Acts 6:1-6). After fasting and praying, the church in Antioch recognized that two of their prophets and teachers had missionary gifts. So the church laid hands on Barnabas and Paul and commissioned them for missionary service (13:1-3).

When the council of elders laid hands on Timothy, his gift of leadership had already been recognized by the prophetic voice of the church. Laying on hands did not *confer* the gift of leadership; rather, it *affirmed* the gift that was already in evidence. Nothing is said about anyone laying hands on Titus.

The threefold order of ordained offices of bishop, elder, and deacon did not come into full usage until the time of Ignatius, about 115. Later, the offices of Christian ministry were sacramentalized. The church began to speak of "ordination," and the laying on of hands indicated apostolic succession. In the West, Roman Catholicism held that the authority of Christ was passed to Peter, then from Peter to popes and bishops; as vicars of Christ, they have wisdom and final authority in matters of faith (P. M. Miller: 207). The same can be said for the Orthodox Church in the East.

In a recently published Catechism (§1538), the Roman Catholic church states,

> Today the word "*ordination*" is reserved for the sacramental act which integrates a man into the order of bishops, presbyters, or deacons, and goes beyond a simple *election, designation, or institution* by the community, for it confers a gift of the Holy Spirit that permits the exercise of a "sacred power" (*sacra potestas*) which can come only from Christ himself through his Church. Ordination is also called *consecration*, for it is a setting apart and an investiture by Christ himself for his Church. The *laying on of hands* by the bishop, with the consecratory prayer, constitutes the visible sign of this ordination. (Ratzinger: 384)

The Anglican Church likewise holds to apostolic succession, but the authority resides not in one bishop—the pope—but in all bishops ordained by successors of the apostles. The Roman Catholic, Orthodox, and Anglican churches all hold to a sacramental theory of ordination. The laying on of hands indicates the passing of authority to the newly ordained person.

A study of the NT raises questions regarding apostolic succession and ordination as sacrament. No less than 13 different Greek words are used when the NT church chose leaders (Kauffmann and M. Miller: 34; Johns: 109). The King James Version translated all of these terms as "ordain," due largely to King James's own interest in maintaining order in the church. The English word "ordain" implies a sacramental meaning in the minds of many people. However, the use of many different terms in the NT may suggest that the term "making a minister" comes closer to the practice of the early church.

Recent study on ordination has led the Mennonite Church to the following (Thomas: 25-27):

> Ordination is an act of the church (congregation, conference, and denomination) which calls and appoints a member to ongoing leadership ministry in the life and mission of the church. The ordination rite includes the covenant between the church and the minister being ordained, the laying on of hands, and the prayer of ordination. When the church ordains a man or woman to ministerial leadership, it intends to say at least the following:
>
> 1. We confirm the call of God to the person being ordained for ministry within or on behalf of the church. . . .

2. We affirm the person for the unique leadership gifts the minister brings to the Christian community. . . .

3. We identify the person being ordained as one who in some way represents God in a "priestly" role within the community of faith, where all are priests of God. . . .

4. We entrust an office of ministry to the person being ordained. By this, we empower the person to act in a representative way on the church's behalf with both the privileges and responsibilities of this office. . . .

5. We call the person being ordained to particular tasks associated with this office: to preach and teach; to lead with vision and wisdom; to equip members to release their spiritual gifts; to provide pastoral care, to be responsible for the church's rites of marriage, baptism, observance of the Lord's table; and to help represent the church in the local community and in the conference of congregations.

6. We covenant between the congregation and the person ordained a mutual accountability of support, respect, and care. . . .

7. We declare our trust in the person being ordained by providing a *credential* for leadership ministry; the credential is primarily for service within the church, and, secondly, a credential is also acknowledged in society and by the state.

Believers churches do not follow a formal tradition of apostolic succession. But they recognize that those ordained need to preserve and propagate the apostolic faith. Orderly transmission of the ordained ministry symbolizes the continuity of the church and its faith through history. Therefore, no one ordains oneself; another ordained person, usually one given the ministry of oversight, leads the ordination ceremony (Thomas: 29).

In the ordination rite, the chosen candidate takes a vow before God and the people. A charge to carry out the Christian ministry is given, and there is a laying on of hands and a prayer of consecration. The laying on of hands in the ordination rite indicates that the prayers of the people in the congregation are focused on the person being ordained for the task of caring out the Christian ministry. It is a concrete symbol of God's action in setting apart the individual for ministry. Ordination focuses the prayers and charge of a congregation upon the head of one person at a particular point in time. It is an expression of solidarity in prayer and commitment between the congregation and the person being ordained. So important in the life of the congregation is the preaching and teaching of God's Word that ordination is an appropriate act of setting a person aside for the task. The laying on of hands is a gesture of intense intercession that focuses the prayers of the church upon the life of the person, who is charged with the awesome responsibility of giving his life to the ministry of the Word (P. M. Miller: 29).

PORTRAIT OF THE PASTOR In 2 Corinthians 4, Paul talks about the Christian minister and the work of ministry. A Christian minister's primary work is to present the gospel of Jesus Christ honestly, while recognizing one's own humanity and the need to rely on the power of God. The central task is to proclaim Jesus Christ.

In the letters to Timothy and Titus, Paul says that the Holy Spirit guides the church in selecting a gifted spiritual leader and lays hands on that leader, confirming the call of God (1 Tim 4:14; 2 Tim 1:6). This spiritual leader is entrusted with the standard of sound teaching, which the leader is to guard with the help of the Holy Spirit (2 Tim 1:13-14).

The central task of ordained leaders is to preach and teach. The gospel is committed to their trust (1 Tim 1:11), and they are to preach and teach it (4:13). If they preach and teach the gospel faithfully, they are worthy of double honor (5:17). If they put these instructions before the church, they are good ministers (4:6). Persons chosen for this role may not be novices; they must be people whose life and gifts are clearly visible, both in their homes and before persons outside the church (2 Tim 1:3-14). If called to the overseer role, they must be gifted in managing their own households and the church as the household of God (1 Tim 3:4-5).

In preaching and teaching, pastors gives themselves wholly to the Scriptures (1 Tim 4:15-16; Titus 1:9). Their attention is focused on the gospel entrusted to them (1 Tim 1:11) and on the faithful sayings (1:15; 4:8-10). The pastor's attention is directed to the truth (2:4), to the truth in Christ (2:7), to *the mystery of the faith* (3:9), *to the sound words of the Lord Jesus Christ and the teaching that is in accordance with godliness* (6:3).

Pastors are not to be ascetics (1 Tim 4:3-7), but are to discipline themselves in godliness more than athletes discipline themselves, since godliness holds promise both in this life and the life to come (4:7-8). Pastors are to be the Lord's servants as they maintain Christlike attitudes during difficult times (2 Tim 2:22-24). They test their ministry in the presence of the living God and the living Christ.

By faithfully preaching and teaching the Scriptures through sound doctrine, pastors help the congregation discern within their culture what to choose and what to reject. They reject the ascetic practices of the surrounding culture (1 Tim 4:1-6) but borrow from the athletic ideal (4:7-10). They borrow from the medical use of wine (5:23), but reject drunkenness (1 Tim 3:3, 8; Titus 1:7). They borrow from the household practices of caring and sharing (1 Tim 5:8), adjust slavery practice with the Christian gospel and the mission of the church (6:1-2), and reject the view that one can use religion to gain money (6:5, 9-10). Instead, they are to be content with what they have (6:6-7) and not be lovers of money (1 Tim 3:3, 8; 6:9; Titus 1:7).

Central in the pastor's work is the charge to *preach the word* (2 Tim 4:2 TNIV). Pastors give themselves *to the public reading of Scripture* (1 Tim 4:13), *do the work of an evangelist* (2 Tim 4:5), make use of Christian creeds and hymns (1 Tim 1:15, 17; 3:16; 6:15-16; Titus 2:11-13), and keep Christ's work on the cross before the people (1 Tim 1:11, 15; 2:3-6; 3:16; 4:8-10; 2 Tim 1:8-10; 2:8; 3:15; Titus 1:2-3; 2:11-14; 3:4-7). This kind of preaching and teaching will save both the preacher and the people (1 Tim 4:16).

Finally, preachers are to grow in this work so that the members of the congregation can observe their progress (1 Tim 4:15) and so that they may carry out this Christian ministry fully (2 Tim 4:5b).

SELF-CONTROL A group of words appear in the letters to Timothy and Titus around the theme of self-control. The "self-control" (*sōphrōn*) word group appears in the noun form and is translated as "modesty" or "decency" (1 Tim 2:9, 15) and "self-discipline" (2 Tim 1:7). In the verb form it is translated as "self-control" in Titus 2:4, 6. The adjective form, also translated as "*self-control,*" appears in 1 Timothy 3:2; Titus 1:8; 2:2, 5. The adverb, translated *self-control,* is found in Titus 2:12. In these occurrences, the word group ranges from moral and ethical control of the self regarding sexual purity, to sound or controlled thinking, to upright character. Self-control is a virtue expected of Timothy (2 Tim 1:7), of overseers (1 Tim 3:2; Titus 1:8), of young men (Titus 2:6), and of women (1 Tim 2:9, 15; Titus 2:4-5), and it characterizes the Christian life (Titus 2:12).

Of the 16 occurrences of the *sōphrōn* word group in the NT, 10 are in the letters to Timothy and Titus. In using this word group, the NT authors made contact with the Hellenistic worldview; self-control was one of the Greek virtues. Three of the virtues appear together in Titus 2:12 (self-control, upright, godly) and are linked to the work of God's grace, which results in authentic Christian living. Clearly, the author is engaging the Hellenistic culture by using these terms. In Hellenistic culture, the goal of education was to take on the cardinal virtues of Greek civilization. But Paul ties education to the grace of God in Christ. God's grace brings about moral change and the individual's response of faith to the gospel. The virtues described by "self-control" are products of faith and therefore components of authentic Christian existence (Witherington 2006: 208).

Other related terms are *disciplined* (Titus 1:8 TNIV) and *sobriety* or *temperate* (1 Tim 3:2, 11; Titus 2:2). Overseers and female deacons must be temperate (1 Tim 3:2, 11) as well as older men (Titus 2:2). Sobriety was commanded of all church leaders (1 Tim 3:2, 8; Titus 1:7; 2:3). *Dignity* is a related term (1 Tim 2:2; 3:4, 8; Titus 2:2, 7). In using these related terms with the *sōphrōn* word group, the author uses language familiar in the Hellenistic world, but fills that language with new meaning as a result of God's grace in Christ. Thus the gospel and Christian living are taken seriously and applied in the Hellenistic setting. (Cf. I. H. Marshall 1999: 182-91; Towner 2006: 206-8.)

TIMOTHY Timothy was a native of Lystra in Asia Minor, the son of a Jewish woman and a Greek father (Acts 16:1-2). Because of the Jewish matrilineal principle of descent, Timothy was considered a Jew. According to 2 Timothy 1:5, both his mother Eunice and his grandmother Lois were Christian believers. Timothy was converted to the Christian faith during the first missionary journey of Paul and Barnabas. At Lystra, during Paul's second missionary journey, Timothy was summoned to accompany Paul in mission work because "he was well spoken of by the believers in Lystra and Iconium" (Acts 16:2). Paul had Timothy circumcised to clarify his Jewish religious status and to make it easier for him to relate to the Jews in Paul's missionary endeavors. The noninterference of Timothy's Greek father with the circumcision rite could suggest that his father was deceased by this time. Timothy is named as Paul's co-worker in 8 other Pauline letters, in which his name appears 13 times.

Timothy accompanied Paul through Asia Minor to Troas and over to Macedonia. After facing conflict in Philippi, they passed through Amphipolis and Apollonia and eventually arrived at Thessalonica. Then Paul and Timothy went to Beroea and on to Athens. At Athens, Paul sent Timothy back to Thessalonica to establish the young Christians in the faith, to encourage them, and to report back on the welfare of this young Christian community (1 Thess 3:2, 5). After completing the mission to the Thessalonians, Timothy returned to Paul at Corinth and reported on his successful missionary work (Acts 18:5). At Corinth he joined Paul and Silvanus in preaching "the son of God, Jesus Christ" (2 Cor 1:19). Later, Timothy joined Paul in an extended Ephesian ministry. Hearing reports of difficulty in the Corinthian church, Paul sent Timothy to Corinth with a letter for the church. This letter introduced Timothy as a "beloved and faithful child in the Lord" (1 Cor 4:17). Paul told the Corinthians, "If Timothy comes, see that he has nothing to fear among you, for he is doing the work of the Lord just as I am; therefore let no one despise him. Send him on his way in peace, so that he may come to me; for I am expecting him with the brothers" (1 Cor 16:10-11). It is not clear how Timothy's work in Corinth turned out. Although Timothy is mentioned as a cosender of 2 Corinthians, Titus was Paul's emissary and carried that letter to the Corinthian church (cf. Shillington: 165-67).

When Paul left Corinth for Jerusalem, Timothy was among those who started out with him (Acts 20:4), but it is not known if Timothy traveled all the way to Jerusalem. At Rome, Timothy is mentioned as a cosender of three letters that Paul wrote during his first imprisonment in this capital city (Phil 1:1; Col 1:1; Philem 1).

Later Timothy returned to Ephesus and provided leadership for the Ephesian believers. Paul wrote two letters to Timothy, giving instructions on how to deal with deviant teaching and how to guide the church. The first letter suggests that Paul was released from Roman imprisonment and was on his way to the East when he appointed Timothy to remain in Ephesus (1 Tim 1:3). In the first letter, Paul calls Timothy *my loyal child in the faith* (1:2). The second letter was written at a later time, when Paul was arrested and placed in prison in Rome a second time. The second letter reflects a special relationship between Paul and Timothy. Paul encourages Timothy not to be ashamed of the Lord or of Paul, but rather to stir up the gift of God within him for church leadership (2 Tim 1:6-8). Paul asks Timothy to come and visit him soon—before winter, if possible (2 Tim 4:9, 21). Timothy is to bring Paul's cloak to protect the apostle from the cold weather—along with the books—and to come with Mark (2 Tim 4:13). According to later tradition recounted by Eusebius, Timothy, the disciple of Paul, was the first bishop of Ephesus. (See *ABD* 6:558-60.)

TITUS Titus was a Gentile Christian and one of Paul's travel companions (Gal 2:1, 3). He was a Greek and was not compelled to be circumcised to be a faithful missionary (2:3). It is likely that he accompanied Paul and Barnabas to the Jerusalem conference as a Gentile convert to the Christian faith (Gal 2:3; Acts

15:2). If so, as an uncircumcised believer, Titus became a test case for the church to discern whether Gentiles need to be circumcised in order to be Christians. Titus is identified as one of Paul's fellow workers (2 Cor 8:23) and Paul's trusted emissary for the Corinthian church (12:18). He assisted with the collection for the church in Jerusalem (8:6) and was the recipient of the letter bearing his name, in which Paul calls him *my loyal child in the faith we share* (Titus 1:4).

Titus played a prominent role in Paul's relationship to the Corinthian church, as indicated in 2 Corinthians. After Paul's initial visit to Corinth and a first letter, word came that some Corinthians had turned against him. Paul turned to Titus, who was a co-worker with proved pastoral skill, and sent him to Corinth to mediate the situation. After a failed attempt to meet Titus at Troas, which frustrated Paul (2 Cor 2:12-13), the two met later in Macedonia. In addition to the joy of meeting Titus again, Paul was comforted by the report of progress in the Corinthian church. Titus's mediating efforts paid off. The Corinthian church repented (7:10) and expressed a desire to see Paul again (7:7). So Paul sent Titus to Corinth a second time to assist in the collection for the saints in Jerusalem (8:6).

Two later references to Titus are found in the NT. Paul mentions that Titus had gone to Dalmatia (2 Tim 4:10). And Paul identifies Titus as *my loyal child in the faith we share* (Titus 1:4). The apostle trusted Titus with leadership in the church by leaving him in Crete to correct the church and to appoint elders. In the final instructions from Paul, Titus is urged to join Paul at Nicopolis (3:13) and to spend the winter with the apostle. Soon after the letter reached Titus, he was to be replaced by either Artemas or Tychicus (3:12).

Various scholars have tried to explain why Titus is not named in the book of Acts: he was not known well enough to be included, he was a relative or close friend of Luke, he was involved in the controversial events of Paul's life including the circumcision question, or he worked with the conflicting situation in the Corinthian community. The short book of Titus demonstrates Paul's admiration for his loyal child in the faith. Paul placed major leadership responsibility in Titus's hands and entrusted the future of the Cretan church to his wisdom and guidance. What better leader could Paul find for the church in pagan Crete than Titus? (See *ABD* 6:581-82.)

UNHEALTHY TEACHING I have used the words *unhealthy teaching, unhealthy* or *deviant teachers,* and *opponents* in this commentary in a general way to suggest opposition to the healthy teaching and Christian doctrine from the perspective of the author. I do not mean to imply that we see evidence in the letters to Timothy and Titus of the full-blown "orthodoxy" or "heterodoxy" that was to come in later centuries. The churches in Ephesus and Crete lived in the midst of religious syncretism and Roman imperial religion. Thus the church needed to clarify healthy, Christian teaching within its cultural context.

Opposition to Paul's teaching is referred to in all three pastoral letters. Apparently the opposition was successful, especially among women (2 Tim 3:6-9). The opponents taught in house churches and in private conversations in homes. These believers raised foolish controversies (1 Tim 6:3-5; Titus 1:10-11; 3:9; 2 Tim 2:14-16, 23) and deceived people (Titus 1:10; 2 Tim 3:13). Their teaching was unhealthy and led people astray (1 Tim 1:3-6; 4:1-2; 6:3-5; Titus 1:10-16; 3:9-11; 2 Tim 2:16-18). Hearing only Paul's side of the story makes it difficult for some interpreters to assess their statements.

When one reads each individual letter in sequence, one discovers several features in this unhealthy teaching. In 1 Timothy, these teachers follow speculative, allegorical interpretations of the OT law and thereby miss its true meaning (1:6-7). They occupy themselves with myths and endless genealogies (1:4). The names *Hymenaeus and Alexander* are specifically named as having rejected conscience and having suffered shipwreck to their faith (1:19-20). In 1 Timothy 4:1-3, the deviant teachers have renounced the Christian faith by turning to asceticism. They forbid marriage and demand abstinence from certain foods. In 1 Timothy 4:7 they are guilty of propagating *profane myths and old wives' tales.* Some women had yielded to this teaching and were turning away to Satan (5:15). Moreover, these teachers had rejected the sound words of the gospel of Christ and had a morbid craving for controversy and disputes about words (6:4). Their minds were depraved, and they were missing the truth (6:5a). They even used religion as a means of financial gain (6:5b). Timothy is instructed to avoid these teachers because they have missed the mark of the true Christian faith (6:20-21).

In Titus, the unhealthy teachers are a rebellious group (1:10). Unhealthy teachers had made more progress in Crete than in Ephesus; they were upsetting whole households (1:11). Some had to be silenced because they were a threat to Christian faith and taught for dishonest gain (1:10-11). Titus is instructed to *rebuke them sharply* in an attempt to bring them back to true faith (1:13). In Crete, the deviant teachers had also given in to Jewish myths. In fact, they had corrupt consciences and minds (1:15). They professed to know God, but their actions indicated that they denied God (1:16a). They were detestable, disobedient, and unfit for any good work (1:16b). Near the end of the letter, Titus is instructed to avoid controversy with the opponents and to have nothing to do with them, since they caused divisions (3:10). They were perverted, sinful, and self-condemned (3:11).

In 2 Timothy, Phygelus, Hermogenes, and Alexander had forsaken Paul's teaching and left the church (1:15; 4:14). Their unacceptable teaching is more openly identified. They had rejected a future bodily resurrection and taught that the resurrection had already taken place (2:18). The opponents' impiety and profane chatter were spreading like gangrene (2:17a). Hymenaeus and Philetus had turned away from the truth and were upsetting the faith of some in the church (2:17-18). On the one hand, Timothy is to have nothing to do with the opponents' stupid and senseless controversies because they only lead to quarrels (2:23). On the other hand, Timothy is to teach them carefully and treat them kindly so that perhaps some would *repent and come to know the truth* (2 Tim 2:25). As Titus is instructed in Crete, so Timothy is instructed to avoid the opponents (Titus 3:9; 2 Tim 3:5). As the OT characters Jannes and Jambres opposed Moses, so the opponents in Ephesus were now opposing the truth. They had corrupt minds and possessed a counterfeit faith (2 Tim 3:8).

In all three letters the opponents' teaching has a Jewish element, perhaps a kind of Hellenistic Judaism that allegorized the OT as did Philo, who regularly used Greek allegory in his interpretation of the OT. Nevertheless, the unhealthy teaching is not uniform in the letters to Timothy and Titus.

It consists of several parts, and we may conclude that several deviant teachings are at stake rather than a united unhealthy view.

The teaching that was threatening the church in Ephesus and in Crete had not yet become second-century Gnosticism. References to elements in the opponents' teaching can be found in Paul's earlier writings. For example, some form of resurrection misunderstanding was present in the Corinthian church. Judaizing tendencies were also present and dealt with in Paul's letters to Romans, Galatians, Philippians, and Colossians. Food restrictions are addressed in Romans, 1 Corinthians, and Colossians. And sexual asceticism is present in the Corinthian church. In the letters to Timothy and Titus, the following ingredients within the unhealthy teachings were present.

1. Paul implies that those promoting certain Jewish elements have departed from normative Judaism. The unhealthy teachers are called *teachers of the law* (1 Tim 1:7) and *those of the circumcision* (Titus 1:10). But the opponents held to Jewish myths and genealogies, which likely indicates allegorical interpretations of the OT.
2. The opposition had Hellenistic elements. The opponents claimed some special (false) knowledge of God.
3. Some opponents taught and encouraged ascetic practices. Ascetic practices became a problem for the Christian church prior to AD 50 (Acts 10:1-48; 11:1-18) and shortly thereafter (1 Cor 8:1-13; Col 2:16-17).
4. Some of the opponents taught that godliness was a means of financial gain (1 Tim 6:5; Titus 1:11).
5. Some opponents misunderstood the resurrection (2 Tim 2:18).
6. Some opponents had depraved minds (1 Tim 6:5; Titus 1:15; 2 Tim 3:8).
7. Some opponents were affected by the demonic (1 Tim 4:1).
8. Some opponents used ungodly speech. Their speech is described as profane chatter (1 Tim 6:10; 2 Tim 2:16), endless words (1 Tim 1:4), stupid or foolish controversies (Titus 3:9), meaningless talk (1 Tim 1:6), craving for controversy and dispute about words (1 Tim 6:4; 2 Tim 2:14), and useless quarrels (Titus 3:9; 2 Tim 2:23). Today the church would deal with this ungodly speech through conflict resolution, but in Titus and 1 & 2 Timothy, it is seen as unhealthy teaching.
9. Some opponents appealed to some women (1 Tim 5:11-15; 2 Tim 3:6).
10. Some opponents reject conscience and have a seared conscience (1 Tim 1:19, 4:2)

To combat the deviant teaching movements in both Ephesus and Crete, Timothy and Titus must give themselves to a teaching ministry that exhorts and clarifies sound doctrine. This emphasis on teaching healthy doctrine, modeling Christian living, and refuting the opposing views in Ephesus and Crete tells us that the opponents' teaching was a real threat to these growing congregations. In the later part of the first century, the church of Timothy and Titus was trying to find clarity on its theology and ethical instruction amid the Greco-Roman world. (Cf. Elias 2006: 476-77; Fee 1988: 7-11; Davies: 90-99, Johnson 2001: 145-46; I. H. Marshall 1999: 40-51; Mounce: lxix-lxxvi; Towner 2006: 41-50; Young: 74-84; Witherington 2006: 341-47.)

VICE LISTS Several virtue and vice lists are found in the NT. Virtue lists appear in Matthew 5:3-11; Galatians 5:22-23; 2 Corinthians 6:6-7; Ephesians 4:32; 6:14-17; Philippians 4:8; Colossians 3:12-14; 1 Timothy 3:2-3; 6:11; Titus 1:7-8; 3:1-2; James 3:17; 2 Peter 1:5-8. Vice lists include Matthew 15:19; Mark 7:21-22; Romans 1:18-32; 13:13; 1 Corinthians 5:10-11; 6:9-10; 2 Corinthians 12:20-21; Galatians 5:19-21; Ephesians 4:31; 5:3-7; Colossians 3:5-9; 1 Timothy 1:9-10; 6:4-5; 2 Timothy 3:2-5; Titus 3:3; 1 Peter 2:1; 4:3-4; and Jude 8-16. In the letters to Timothy and Titus, four vice lists appear (1 Tim 1:9-10; 6:4-5; 2 Tim 3:2-5; Titus 3:3). These lists differ enough to require individual attention rather than dealing with all of the vices in a single compilation.

The list in 1 Timothy 1:9-10 alludes to the precepts of the Decalogue. The list appears in the context of persons who desire to be teachers of the law but do not use the law legitimately. The first four commands in the Decalogue may serve as background to the vices, which appear in three couplets. The first couplet, *lawless and disobedient*, applies to persons who refuse the law and follow an independent attitude. The second couplet, *godless and sinful*, are persons who exhibit impiety, lack due respect for God, and live in offense to God. The third couplet, *unholy and profane*, designates the sinner in relationship to God. The sinner is not separated from evil or consecrated to God. Therefore the sinner is profane. After these three couplets come vices that stand in direct opposition to the other commands in the Decalogue. Those who kill fathers and mothers disobey the fifth commandment. Murderers disobey the sixth commandment. Those who practice sexual sins disobey the seventh commandment. Slave traders disobey the command not to steal. And liars disobey the command not to bear false witness.

The list in 1 Timothy 6:4-5 also applies to teachers who want to assert themselves by sowing discord:

> *Whoever teaches otherwise . . . is conceited, understanding nothing, and has a morbid craving for controversy and for disputes about words. From these come envy, dissension, slander, base suspicions, and wrangling among those who are depraved in mind and bereft of the truth, imagining that godliness is a means of gain.* (6:3-5)

The mistake of the unhealthy teachers consists of craving for controversy. They spend extraordinary time disputing about words. Inwardly they are filled with envy and dissension. They tear down others. More seriously, their minds are depraved. They use religion as a means of financial gain. The net result of their sin is serious dissension in the church.

The list in 2 Timothy 3:2-5 is a standard list of vices associated with the wicked. The closest parallel to this list is Romans 1:29-31. Four terms are used in both lists. However, 14 of the 18 vices in 2 Timothy 3:2-5 do not appear in Romans 1:29-31, and 17 vices in the Romans list do not appear in the 2 Timothy list. The list in 2 Timothy begins with *lovers of themselves* and ends with *lovers of pleasure rather than lovers of God*. Sinners in this vice list are *selfish, boasters, arrogant*, and *disobedient to parents*, which indicates a lack of respect for authority (cf. versions for these lists). The list includes a series of negative words: *ungrateful, unholy, unloving, irreconcilable*. The sinners lack sensitivity to other human persons. They are slanderers and lack self-control. They hate the good, are reckless, and are filled with conceit. The sinners described in this list are hedonists, who live for pleasure. They have an outward appearance of godliness but inwardly disown the power of God. Such a self-centered life not only rejects God in favor of the self, but also brings ruin to one's life.

A fourth list appears in Titus 3:3. In this list the author of Titus identifies himself with some of the vices before God's work of salvation in his life, as the author identifies the behavioral patterns of the Christians in Crete before their conversion to Christ. The vice list includes *foolishness* and *disobedience to God.* Thus they became enslaved in various lusts and pleasures. The second part of the list speaks of human relationships. Before becoming Christians, the sins of malice, envy toward others, and hatred characterized their lives.

Variations in these lists indicate that the writer does not draw from one background vice list. Instead, the literature of antiquity provides a larger background from which the author drew these lists. This background includes the Decalogue and other commands in the OT law, polemics against immoral pagan idolaters, Hellenistic concepts of vices, and inward moral degeneration that makes humans selfish and brutal.

We also find virtue lists in the letters to Timothy and Titus. Timothy is to flee certain vices and pursue healthy virtues (2 Tim 2:22-25). Elsewhere Paul enjoins his readers to "put off" vices and "put on" virtues (e.g., Eph 4:22-24). Desired qualities of bishops, deacons, and elders include vices to be avoided *and* virtues to be practiced (1 Tim 3:2-13; Titus 1:6-8). Virtues for persons in the Christian community are listed according to age groupings: older women (Titus 2:3-5), younger men (2:6-8), and slaves (2:9-10). Paul's lists of virtues have significant parallels in Greek literature. (See *ABD* 6:857-58; *DPL* 962-63; McEleny: 203-19.)

WOMEN IN MINISTRY Women were involved in the first-century church, with some taking active leadership roles (see Women in the Church in the TBC for 1 Tim 2:1-15). Throughout the history of the church, women have taken leadership roles. Evidence exists that the Eastern church ordained deaconesses. The strong reaction that developed to it at a later time confirms that this was the case (Madigan and Osiek 2005). In fourth-century Rome, two women assisted Saint Jerome. Marcella was a close associate, and Jerome referred people to her for counsel. When people debated Scripture, Jerome sent them to Marcella for correct interpretation. Another Christian woman—Paula—worked with Jerome in translating the Latin Vulgate, which was then used as *the* Bible in medieval Europe for more than 1,000 years. Women's monasticism arose in the fourth and fifth centuries and continued to grow for several hundred years. After some decline, it thrived again in the twelfth century. Susanna Wesley, mother of John and Charles Wesley, preached sermons to Anglican parishioners. She preached so well that there was standing room only in some settings as people came to hear her exposition of Scripture. John Wesley referred to her as a preacher of righteousness.

In the nineteenth and early twentieth centuries, Bible institutes led by A. B. Simpson of the Christian and Missionary Alliance Church and D. L. Moody's famous Moody Bible Institute promoted women in ministry. Many

Pentecostal and other evangelical women preached, served as pastors of churches, and taught the Bible during this period, believing that they were obedient to God's Word. A decline in women's ministry in the church developed between World War I and World War II, due to a separatist subculture and a Protestant backlash against changing social values.

In mainline Protestant denominations, women were regularly called and ordained to ministry around the middle of the twentieth century. From 1975 onward in the church, women in leadership became a growing movement known as the Second Wave of Renewal of women's ministry. From 1977 onward, evangelicals wrote and published a steady stream of quality biblical and theological studies that supported and encouraged women in ministry. In 1984, twenty-six evangelical leaders met for a colloquium on Women and the Bible. Following this meeting, conservative evangelical leader J. I. Packer said, "The burden of proof regarding the exclusion of women from the office of teaching and ruling within the congregation now lies on those who maintain the exclusion rather than on those who challenge it" (Mickelsen: 298). Some evangelicals disagreed with this assessment, and a backlash arose from a subculture that interpreted biblical feminism as an expression of unfaithful feminism in the culture at large.

At the annual Evangelical Theological Society meeting in the winter of 1986, the debate came to a head. Many evangelicals hoped for good dialogue and reconciliation between opposing views on the subject of women in leadership. Unfortunately, reconciliation between the opposing groups did not happen. Instead, a group of conservative evangelicals, known as the Council on Biblical Manhood and Womanhood, produced a statement and later published a book in strong opposition to women in leadership. Another study of 1 Timothy 2:9-15 was published in 1995 by conservative evangelicals opposed to women in leadership (Köstenberger, Schreiner, and Baldwin 1995). The debate continues among evangelicals.

In the patriarchal society of the sixteenth century, Anabaptist and Mennonite women shared more actively in church life than did women in Protestant and Roman Catholic groups of that time. Anabaptist women held worship services, taught the Scriptures, saw visions, distributed the sacraments, evangelized, prophesied, and debated with theologians (*ME* 5:933). A third or more of all Anabaptist martyrs were women. In some regions as many as 40 percent of Christian martyrs were women (Snyder 1996: 12). This large number of Anabaptist women martyrs indicates the major role these women took in the church's life and mission. In North America, the Church of the Brethren, Mennonite Brethren, and Mennonite Church worked at biblical and theological studies of women in ministry between 1950 and 2000. The Church of the Brethren officially granted ordination of women for pastoral ministry in 1958. Although as early as 1911 Ann Allebach was ordained as the first Mennonite woman pastor, not until 1980 did Mennonite congregations choose women as pastors with the blessing of their conferences and denominations. In its official polity, Mennonites affirm the ordination of women for pastoral ministry while respecting a minority who are not yet open to women in ministry (Thomas: 49-51).

Presently the debate over women in leadership in the church continues, with less rejection of women in ministry. Perhaps Bartlett goes too far when he says, "To deny ordained ministry to women does not come from faith but from fear, and whatever does not come from faith is sin" (Bartlett: 197; Rom 14:23). Much of the debate on women in ministry hinges on hermeneutics. Does one interpret the Bible by privileging a hierarchical view as some read in Genesis 2:18-25; 1 Corinthians 14:34-36; and 1 Timothy 2:9-15? Or does one privilege an egalitarian view as others read in Genesis 1:26-28 and Galatians 3:28 and as Jesus apparently did when he taught and responded to women? And how should the narrative evidence of women in leadership roles in the NT church affect one's hermeneutic? Should one use the ministry of Christ and the practice of the early church as a lens through which to read all of the relevant passages? If one interprets the Bible this way, the prohibition passages in 1 Corinthians 14:34-36 and 1 Timothy 2:9-15 appear to be exceptions due to the recipients' particular historical and cultural contexts. From my perspective, the biblical witness and the church's experience of the blessing of God on women's ministries place the burden of proof regarding the ordination of women on those who oppose women in leadership.

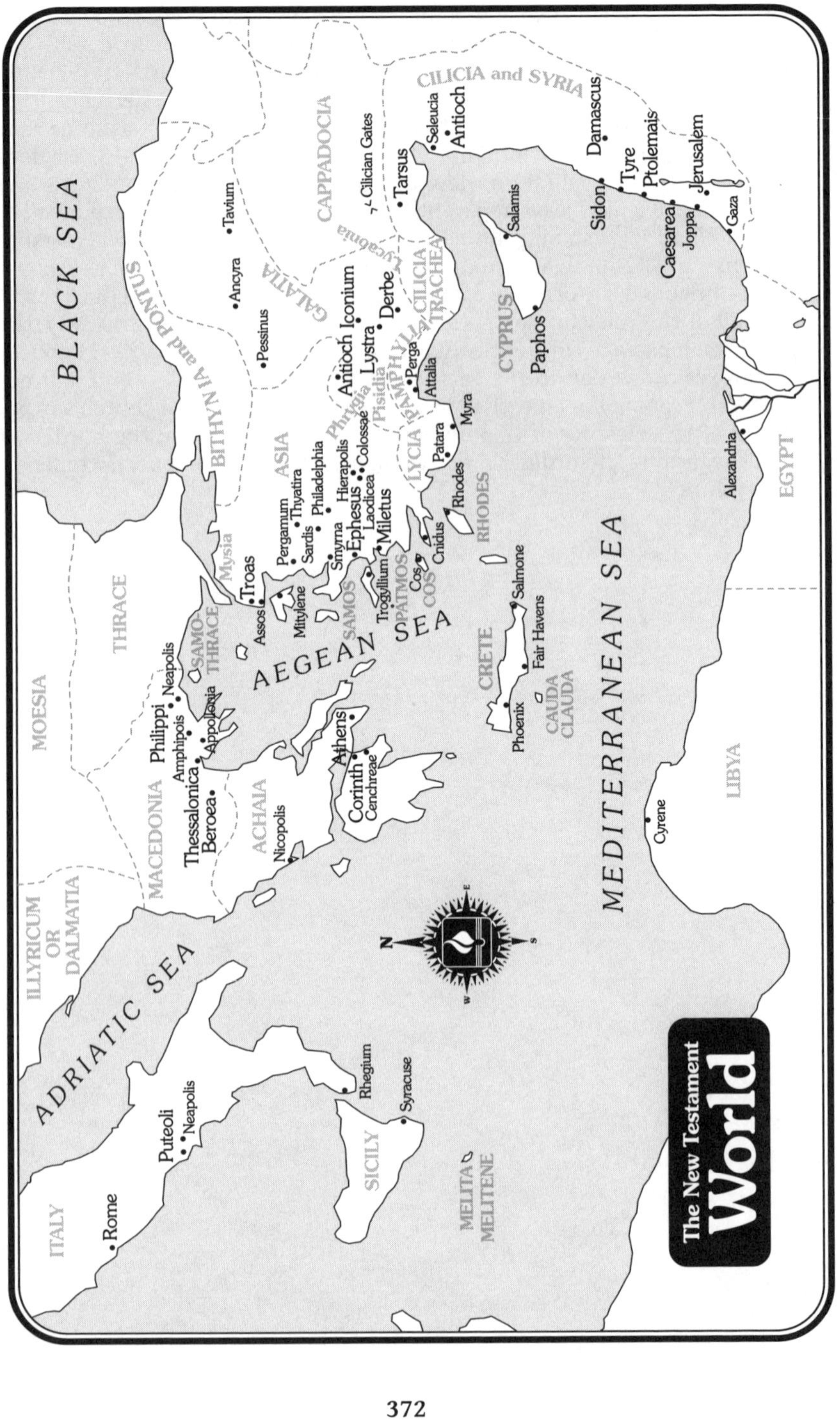
The New Testament
World
BLACK SEA
ADRIATIC SEA
AEGEAN SEA
MEDITERRANEAN SEA
ITALY
Rome
Puteoli
Neapolis
Rhegium
Syracuse
SICILY
MELITA
MELITENE
ILLYRICUM
OR
DALMATIA
MACEDONIA
MOESIA
THRACE
Thessalonica
Beroea
Amphipois
Appolonia
Philippi
Neapolis
SAMO-
THRACE
ACHAIA
Nicopolis
Corinth
Cenchreae
Athens
Troas
Assos
Mitylene
Mysia
BITHYNIA and PONTUS
ASIA
Pergamum
Thyatira
Sardis
Philadelphia
Smyrna
Ephesus
Hierapolis
Colossae
Laodicea
Miletus
Trogyllium
SAMOS
PATMOS
COS
Cos
Cnidus
Rhodes
RHODES
Phrygia
Pisidia
PAMPHYLIA
LYCIA
Patara
Myra
Attalia
Perga
Antioch
Iconium
Lystra
Derbe
Lycaonia
GALATIA
Pessinus
Ancyra
Tavium
CAPPADOCIA
Cilician Gates
Tarsus
CILICIA TRACHEA
CILICIA and SYRIA
Seleucia
Antioch
CYPRUS
Salamis
Paphos
Damascus
Sidon
Tyre
Ptolemais
Caesarea
Joppa
Jerusalem
Gaza
Alexandria
EGYPT
CRETE
Salmone
Fair Havens
Phoenix
CAUDA
CLAUDA
Cyrene
LIBYA
N
S
E
W

Bibliography

Aageson, James W.

1997 "2 Timothy and Its Theology: In Search of a Theological Pattern." Pages 693-714 in *Society of Biblical Literature 1997 Seminar Papers*. Atlanta: Scholars Press.

2008 *Paul, the Pastoral Epistles, and the Early Church*. Peabody, MA: Hendrickson.

Achtemeier, Paul J.

1996 *1 Peter*. Hermeneia. Minneapolis: Fortress.

Anselm

1962 *Saint Anselm: Basic Writings*. Translated by S. N. Deane. LaSalle, IL: Open Court Publishing.

Aristotle

1963 *Generation of Animals*. Translated by A. L. Peck. Loeb Classical Library. Cambridge, MA: Harvard University Press.

Augsburger, Myron S.

2000 *The Robe of God*. Scottdale, PA: Herald Press.

Bailey, James L., and Lyle D. Vander Broek

1992 *Literary Forms in the New Testament: A Handbook*. Louisville, KY: Westminster John Knox.

Baker, Mark D., ed.

2006 *Proclaiming the Scandal of the Cross: Contemporary Images of the Atonement*. Grand Rapids: Baker Academic.

Balch, David L.

1981 *Let Wives Be Submissive: The Domestic Code of 1 Peter*. Society of Biblical Literature Monograph Series 26. Chico, CA: Scholars Press.

1988 "Household Codes." Pages 25-50 in *Greco-Roman Literature and the New Testament*. Edited by David E. Aune. Atlanta: Scholars Press.

Balch, David L., and Carolyn Osiek

1997 *Families in the New Testament World: Households and House Churches*. Louisville, KY: Westminster John Knox, 1997.

2003 *Early Christian Families in Context: An Interdisciplinary Dialogue.* Grand Rapids: Eerdmans.

Banks, Robert J.
1994 *Paul's Idea of Community.* Rev. ed. Peabody, MA: Hendrickson.

Barclay, William
1960 *The Letters to Timothy, Titus and Philemon.* 2nd ed. Daily Study Bible. Edinburgh: Saint Andrew Press.

Barrett, C. K.
1963 *The Pastoral Epistles in the New English Bible.* New Clarendon Bible: New Testament. Oxford: Clarendon.
1987 *The New Testament Background: Selected Documents.* Rev. and expanded ed. San Francisco: Harper & Row.

Bartchy, S. Scott
1992 "Slavery (New Testament)." *ABD* 6:65-73.

Bartlett, David L.
1993 *Ministry in the New Testament.* Minneapolis: Fortress.

Bassler, Jouette M.
1984 "The Widow's Tale: A Fresh Look at 1 Tim. 5:3-16." *Journal of Biblical Literature* 103:23-41.
1996 *1 Timothy, 2 Timothy, Titus.* Abingdon New Testament Commentaries. Nashville: Abingdon.

Bauckham, Richard
1988 "Pseudo-Apostolic Letters." *Journal of Biblical Literature* 107:469-94.

Baugh, S. M.
1992 "Savior of All People: 1 Tim. 4:10 in Context." *Westminster Theological Journal* 54:335.

Bauman-Martin, Betsy J.
2004 "Women on the Edge: New Perspectives on Women in the Petrine Haustafel." *Journal of Biblical Literature* 123:253-79.

Beachy, Alvin J.
1977 *The Concept of Grace in the Radical Reformation.* Nieuwkoop: B. De Graf.

Beker, J. Christiaan
1980 *Paul the Apostle: The Triumph of God in Life and Thought.* Minneapolis: Fortress.
1991 *Heirs of Paul: Paul's Legacy in the New Testament and in the Church Today.* Minneapolis: Fortress.

Bell, Albert A., Jr.
1998 *Exploring the New Testament World.* Nashville: Thomas Nelson.

Belleville, Linda, Jon C. Laansma, J. Ramsey Michaels, and Philip W. Comfort
2009 *1 & 2 Timothy, Titus, Hebrews.* Carol Stream, IL: Tyndale House.

Bender, Harold S.
1961 "Walking in the Resurrection." *Mennonite Quarterly Review* 35:96-110.

Berge, Paul Stanton
1973 "'Our Great God and Savior': A Study of *Sōtēr* as a Christological Title in Titus 2:11-14." ThD diss., Union Theological Seminary in Virginia.

Bettenson, Henry
1963 *Documents of the Christian Church.* 2nd ed. New York: Oxford University Press.

Blough, Neal

1994 "The Holy Spirit and Discipleship in Pilgram Marpeck's Theology." In *Essays in Anabaptist Theology*. Edited by H. Wayne Pipkin. Text Reader Series 5. Elkhart, IN: Institute of Mennonite Studies.

Bratcher, Robert G.

1983 *A Translator's Guide to Paul's Letters to Timothy and to Titus*. New York: United Bible Societies.

Brown, Raymond E.

1997 *An Introduction to the New Testament*. New York: Doubleday.

Bruce, F. F.

1982 *The Epistle to the Galatians*. Grand Rapids: Eerdmans.

Brunk, George, III

1989 "The Exclusiveness of Jesus Christ." In *Jesus Christ and the Mission of the Church: Contemporary Anabaptist Perspectives*. Edited by Erland Waltner. Newton, KS: General Conference Mennonite Church; Elkhart, IN: Mennonite Church.

Calvin, John

1960 *Institutes of the Christian Religion*. Edited by John T. McNeill. Translated by Ford Lewis Battles. 2 vols., paginated continuously. Library of Christian Classics 20–21. Philadelphia: Westminster.

Campbell, R. A.

1994a *The Elders: Seniority Within Earliest Christianity*. Studies of the New Testament and Its World. Edinburgh: T&T Clark.

1994b "Identifying the Faithful Sayings in the Pastoral Epistles." *Journal for the Study of the New Testament* 54:73-86.

Collins, Raymond F.

2002 *1 and 2 Timothy and Titus: A Commentary*. New Testament Library. Louisville, KY: Westminster John Knox.

Cullmann, Oscar

1959 *The Christology of the New Testament*. Rev. ed. Philadelphia: Westminster.

Danby, Herbert, trans.

1933 *The Mishnah*. London: Oxford University Press.

Dandamayev, Muhammad A.

1992 "Slavery (Old Testament)." *ABD* 6:58-65.

Davies, Margaret

1996 *The Pastoral Epistles: I and II Timothy and Titus*. Sheffield: Sheffield Academic Press.

Dawn, Marva J., and Eugene H. Peterson

2000 *The Unnecessary Pastor: Rediscovering the Call*. Grand Rapids: Eerdmans.

De Silva, David A.

2004 *An Introduction to the New Testament: Contexts, Methods and Ministry Formation*. Downers Grove, IL: InterVarsity.

Denck, Hans

1956 *Religiöse Schriften*. Part 2 of *Schriften*. Edited by Walter Fellmann. Quellen zur Geschichte der Täufer 6. Gütersloh: Bertelsmann.

Dibelius, Martin, and Hans Conzelmann

1972 *The Pastoral Epistles: A Commentary on the Pastoral Epistles*.

Translated by P. Buttolph and A. Yarbro. Edited by H. Koester. Hermeneia. Philadelphia: Fortress.

Donelson, Lewis R.
1997 "Studying Paul: 2 Timothy as Remembrance." Pages 715-31 in *Society of Biblical Literature 1997 Seminar Papers*. Atlanta: Scholars Press.

Driver, John
1986 *Understanding the Atonement for the Mission of the Church*. Scottdale, PA: Herald Press.

Duff, Jeremy
1988 "𝔓46 and the Pastorals: A Misleading Comparison." *New Testament Studies* 44:578-90.

Dunn, James D. G.
1998 *The Theology of Paul the Apostle*. Grand Rapids: Eerdmans.

Durnbaugh, Donald F.
1968 *The Believers' Church: The History and Character of Radical Protestantism*. New York: Macmillan. Reprinted, Scottdale, PA: Herald Press, 1985.

Dyck, Cornelius J., William E. Keeney, and Alvin J. Beachy, trans. and eds.
1992 *The Writings of Dirk Philips*. Classics of the Radical Reformation 5. Scottdale, PA: Herald Press.

Elias, Jacob W.
1995 *1 and 2 Thessalonians*. Believers Church Bible Commentary. Scottdale, PA: Herald Press.
2006 *Remember the Future: The Pastoral Theology of Paul the Apostle*. Scottdale, PA: Herald Press.

Eller, David B.
1990 *Servants of the Word: Ministry in the Believers' Church*. Elgin, IL: Brethren Press.

Elliott, Elisabeth
1978 *The Journals of Jim Elliott*. Grand Rapids: Revell.

Elliott, J. H.
1970 "Ministry and Church Order in the NT: A Traditio-Historical Analysis." *Catholic Biblical Quarterly* 32:367-91.

Elliott, J. K.
1968 *The Greek Text of the Epistles to Timothy and Titus*. Studies and Documents 36. Salt Lake City: University of Utah Press.

Ellis, E. Earle
1959 "The Problem of the Authorship of First and Second Timothy." *Review and Expositor* 56:343-54.
1987 "Tradition in the Pastoral Epistles." Pages 237-53 in *Early Jewish and Christian Exegesis: Studies in Memory of William Hugh Brownlee*. Edited by Craig A. Evans and William F. Stinespring. Atlanta: Scholars Press.
1989 *Pauline Theology: Ministry and Society*. Grand Rapids: Eerdmans.

Esau, John A., ed.
1995 *Understanding Ministerial Leadership*. Occasional Papers 6. Elkhart, IN: Institute of Mennonite Studies.

Ewert, David
1983 *The Holy Spirit in the New Testament*. Scottdale, PA: Herald Press.

Faus, Nancy Rosenberger, and Nadine Pence Frantz, eds.
2005 "Voices of Women Preaching God's Word" (Issue Theme). *Brethren Life and Thought* 50, nos. 1–2.

Fee, Gordon D.
1987 *The First Epistle to the Corinthians*. Grand Rapids: Eerdmans.
1988 *1 and 2 Timothy, Titus*. New International Biblical Commentary. Peabody, MA: Hendrickson.
1994 *God's Empowering Presence: The Holy Spirit in the Letters of Paul*. Peabody, MA: Hendrickson.
1997 "Toward a Theology of 2 Timothy—from a Pauline Perspective." Pages 732-49 in *Society of Biblical Literature 1997 Seminar Papers*. Atlanta: Scholars Press.
2007 *Pauline Christology: An Exegetical-Theological Study*. Peabody, MA: Hendrickson.

Finger, Thomas N.
1985 *Christian Theology: An Eschatological Approach*. Vol. 1. Nashville: Thomas Nelson.
1989 *Christian Theology: An Eschatological Approach*. Vol. 2. Scottdale, PA: Herald Press.
2004 *A Contemporary Anabaptist Theology: Biblical, Historical, Constructive*. Downers Grove, IL: InterVarsity.

Fiore, Benjamin, SJ
2006 *Pastoral Epistles: First Timothy, Second Timothy, Titus*. Sacra pagina 12. Collegeville, MN: Liturgical Press.

Freeman, Curtis W., et al.
1999 *Baptist Roots: A Reader in the Theology of a Christian People*. Valley Forge, PA: Judson Press.

Friesen, Steven J.
1993 *Twice Neokoros: Ephesus, Asia and the Cult of the Flavian Imperial Family*. Leiden: E. J. Brill.

Gagnon, Robert A.
2001 *The Bible and Homosexual Practice: Texts and Hermeneutics*. Nashville: Abingdon.

Gehring, Roger W.
2004 *House Church and Mission: The Importance of Household Structures in Early Christianity*. Peabody, MA: Hendrickson.

Goppelt, Leonhard
1993 *A Commentary on 1 Peter*. Edited by Ferdinand Hahn. Translated and edited by John E. Alsup. Grand Rapids: Eerdmans.

Gorday, Peter
2000 *Colossians, 1–2 Thessalonians, 1–2 Timothy, Titus, Philemon*. Ancient Christian Commentary on Scripture 9. Downers Grove, IL: InterVarsity.

Green, Joel B., and Mark D. Baker
2000 *Recovering the Scandal of the Cross: Atonement in New Testament and Contemporary Contexts*. Downers Grove, IL: InterVarsity.

Greenleaf, Robert K.
1975 *Trustees as Servants*. Cambridge, MA: Center for Applied Studies.

2002 *Servant Leadership*. 25th anniversary ed. Mahwah, NJ: Paulist Press.

Greiser, David B., and Michael A. King

2003 *Anabaptist Preaching: A Conversation Between Pulpit, Pew, and Bible*. Scottdale, PA: Herald Press.

Grimsrud, Ted, and Mark T. Nation

2008 *Reasoning Together: A Conversation on Homosexuality*. Scottdale, PA: Herald Press.

Gritz, Sharon Hodgin

1991 *Paul, Women Teachers, and the Mother Goddess at Ephesus*. Landam, MD: University Press of America.

Guthrie, Donald

1990a *New Testament Introduction*. 4th ed. Downers Grove, IL: InterVarsity.

1990b *The Pastoral Epistles: An Introduction and Commentary*. Rev. ed. Tyndale New Testament Commentaries. Grand Rapids: Eerdmans.

Hagner, Donald A.

1998 "Titus as a Pauline Letter." Pages 546-58 in *Society of Biblical Literature 1998 Seminar Papers*. Atlanta: Scholars Press.

Hanson, A. T.

1982 *The Pastoral Epistles*. New Century Bible Commentary. Grand Rapids: Eerdmans.

Harder, Helmut

1990 "Salvation." *ME* 5:785-86.

Harder, Leland, ed.

1985 *Sources of Swiss Anabaptism: The Grebel Letters and Related Documents*. Classics of the Radical Reformation 4. Scottdale, PA: Herald Press.

Harding, Mark

2001 *What Are They Saying About the Pastoral Epistles?* New York: Paulist Press.

Harris, Murray J.

1980 "Titus 2:13 and the Deity of Christ." Pages 262-77 in *Pauline Studies: Essays Presented to F. F. Bruce on his 70th Birthday*. Edited by David A. Hagner and Murray J. Harris. Grand Rapids: Eerdmans.

Harrison, P. N.

1964 *Paulines and Pastorals*. London: Villiars Publications.

Hawthorne, Gerald F., and Ralph P. Martin, eds.

1993 *Dictionary of Paul and His Letters*. Downers Grove, IL: InterVarsity.

Hays, Richard B.

1986 "Relations Natural and Unnatural: A Response to John Boswell's Exegesis of Romans 1." *Journal of Religious Ethics* 14, no. 1:184-215.

1996 *The Moral Vision of the New Testament*. New York: Harper-SanFrancisco.

2002 *The Faith of Jesus Christ*. Rev. ed. Grand Rapids: Eerdmans.

Heidebrecht, Doug

2004 "Reading 1 Timothy 2:9-15 in Its Literary Context." *Direction* 33, no. 2:171-84.

Holmes, J. M.

2000 *Text in a Whirlwind: A Critique of Four Exegetical Devices at 1 Timothy*

2:9-15. Journal for the Study of the New Testament: Supplement Series 196. Sheffield: Sheffield Academic Press.

Holmes, Michael W.
2006 *The Apostolic Fathers: Greek Texts and English Translations*. 3rd ed. Grand Rapids: Baker Academic.

Horrell, David G.
2001 "From *Adelphoi* to *Oikos Theou*: Social Transformation in Pauline Christianity." *Journal of Biblical Literature* 120:293-311.

Houlden, J. L.
1989 *The Pastoral Epistles: I and II Timothy, Titus*. Philadelphia: Trinity Press International.

Jeschke, Marlin
1990 "Discipline, Church." *ME* 5: 239-40.

Jewett, Paul K.
1974 *Man as Male and Female: A Study of Sexual Relationships from a Theological Point of View*. Grand Rapids: Eerdmans.

Johns, Loren L.
2004 "*Ordination* in the King James Version of the Bible." Pages 105-17 in *The Heart of the Matter: Pastoral Ministry in Anabaptist Perspective*. Edited by Erick Sawatzky. Telford, PA: Cascadia Publishing House; Scottdale, PA: Herald Press.

Johnson, Luke Timothy
1996 *Letters to Paul's Delegates*. Philadelphia: Trinity Press International.
1999 *The Writings of the New Testament: An Interpretation*. Rev. ed. Minneapolis: Fortress.
2001 *The First and Second Letters to Timothy: A New Translation with Introduction and Commentary*. Anchor Bible 35A. New York: Doubleday.

Kauffman, Richard A.
1990 "Sin." *ME* 5:821-25.

Kauffmann, Ivan, ed., and Marlin Miller, writer for the task force
1981 *Leadership and Authority in the Life of the Church: A Summary Statement*. Scottdale, PA: Mennonite Publishing House.

Kelly, J. N. D.
1960 *The Pastoral Epistles*. Black's New Testament Commentary. Peabody, MA: Hendrickson.

Kidd, Reggie M.
1990 *Wealth and Beneficence in the Pastoral Epistles*. Society of Biblical Literature Dissertation Series 122. Atlanta: Scholars Press.

Kimberley, David R.
1992 "I Tim 2:15: A Possible Understanding of a Difficult Text." *Journal of the Evangelical Theological Society* 35:481-86.

Knight, George W., III
1979 *The Faithful Sayings in the Pastoral Letters*. Grand Rapids: Baker Book House.
1984 "*Authenteō* in Reference to Women in I Tim. 2:12." *New Testament Studies* 30:143-57.
1992 *The Pastoral Epistles: A Commentary on the Greek Text*. New International Greek Testament Commentary. Grand Rapids: Eerdmans.

Köstenberger, Andreas J., Thomas R. Schreiner, and Scott Baldwin
1995 *Women in the Church: A Fresh Analysis of I Timothy 2:9-15.* Grand Rapids: Baker Books.

Kraus, C. Norman
1993 *The Community of the Spirit: How the Church Is in the World.* Rev. ed. Scottdale, PA: Herald Press.

Kraybill, J. Nelson
1996 *Imperial Cult and Commerce in John's Apocalypse.* Journal for the Study of the New Testament: Supplement Series 132. Sheffield: Sheffield Academic Press.

Kroeger, Catherine C.
1989 "Women in the Church: A Classicist's View of 1 Tim 2:11-15." *Journal of Biblical Equality* 1:3-31.

Kroeger, Richard C., and Catherine C. Kroeger
1992 *I Suffer Not a Woman: Rethinking 1 Timothy 2:11-14 in Light of Ancient Evidence.* Grand Rapids: Baker.

Kümmel, Werner Georg
1966 *Introduction to the New Testament.* Translated by A. J. Mattill Jr. Nashville: Abingdon.

Lea, Thomas D., and Hayne P. Griffin Jr.
1992 *1, 2 Timothy, Titus.* New Broadman Commentary. Nashville: Broadman.

Lebold, Ralph
2006 *Strange and Wonderful Paths: The Memoirs of Ralph Lebold.* Kitchener, ON: Pandora Press.

Lebold, Ralph, and Luke L. Keefer Jr.
1990 "Pastoral Education." *ME* 5:676-78.

Lederach, Paul M.
1980 *A Third Way.* Scottdale, PA: Herald Press.

Lehman, Ruth Krady
1992 "A Century of Deaconesses in the Virginia Conference." *Mennonite Historical Bulletin* 53, no. 2:1-5.

Liefeld, Walter L.
1999 *1 and 2 Timothy, Titus. The NIV Application Commentary.* Grand Rapids: Zondervan.

Liefeld, W. L., D. Moo, and P. B. Payne
1986 *What Does Scripture Teach About the Ordination of Women?* Esp. 96-115. Minneapolis: Evangelical Free Church of America.

Louw, Johannes P., and Eugene A. Nida
1989 *Greek-English Lexicon of the New Testament: Based on Semantic Domains.* 2nd ed. 2 vols. New York: United Bible Societies.

MacDonald, Margaret Y.
1988 *The Pauline Churches: A Socio-Historical Study of Institutionalization in the Pauline and Deutero-Pauline Writings.* Society for New Testament Studies: Monograph Series 60. Cambridge: Cambridge University Press.

Madigan, Kevin, and Carolyn Osiek, eds.
2005 *Ordained Women in the Early Church: A Documentary History.* Baltimore: John Hopkins University Press.

MaGee, Gregory S.
2008 "Paul's Response to the Shame and Pain of Imprisonment in 2 Timothy." *Bibliotheca Sacra* 165 (July-September): 338-53.
Maier, Harry O.
2004 "Family Quarrels: The Politics of Discord and the Representation of Household Division in Greco-Roman Literature and the Pastoral Epistles." Paper presented at the Annual Meeting of the Society of Biblical Literature, San Antonio. November 20, 2004. Photocopy in writer's files.
Malherbe, A. J.
1986 *Moral Exhortation: A Greco-Roman Sourcebook.* Philadelphia: Westminster.
Malina, Bruce J.
1993 *The New Testament World: Insights from Cultural Anthropology.* Rev. ed. Louisville, KY: Westminster/John Knox.
Marshall, Christopher D.
2003 "Atonement, Violence and the Will of God: A Sympathetic Response to J. Denny Weaver's *The Nonviolent Atonement.*" In *Mennonite Quarterly Review* 77:69-92.
Marshall, I. Howard
1988 "The Christology of the Pastoral Epistles." *Studien zum Neuen Testament und seiner Umwelt* 13:157-77.
1996 "Salvation, Grace and Works in the Later Writings of the Pauline Corpus." *New Testament Studies* 42:339-58.
1999 *The Pastoral Epistles.* International Critical Commentary. Edinburgh: T&T Clark.
Martin, Ernest D.
1993 *Colossians, Philemon.* Believers Church Bible Commentary. Scottdale, PA: Herald Press.
McClendon, James William, Jr.
1994 *Systematic Theology.* Vol. 2, *Doctrine.* Nashville: Abingdon.
McDermott, J. S.
1991 "The Quest for Community Stabilization: A Social Science Interpretation of the Pastoral Epistles." PhD diss., Drew University.
McEleny, N. J.
1974 "The Vice Lists of the Pastoral Epistles." *Catholic Biblical Quarterly* 36:203-19.
Meeks, Wayne E.
1983 *The First Urban Christians: The Social World of the Apostle Paul.* New Haven: Yale University Press.
Mendelsohn, I.
1962 "Slavery in the OT." *IDB* 4:383-91. New York. Nashville: Abingdon.
Mennonite Church and General Conference Mennonite Church
1995 *Confession of Faith in a Mennonite Perspective.* Scottdale, PA: Herald Press.
Merkle, Benjamin L.
2003 *The Elder and Overseer: One Office in the Early Church.* Studies in Biblical Literature 57. New York: Peter Lang.

Metzger, Bruce M.
1958 "A Reconsideration of Certain Arguments Against the Pauline Authorship of the Pastoral Epistles." *Expository Times* 70:91-94.
1972 "Literary Forgeries and Canonical Pseudepigrapha." *Journal of Biblical Literature* 91:3-24.
1983 *The New Testament: Its Background, Growth, and Content*. 2nd ed. Nashville: Abingdon.
1987 *The Canon of the New Testament: Its Origin, Development, and Significance*. Oxford: Clarendon.
1994 *A Textual Commentary on the Greek New Testament*. 2nd ed. Stuttgart: Deutsche Bibelgesellschaft/German Bible Society.

Mickelsen, Alvera, ed.
1986 *Women, Authority, and the Bible*. Downers Grove, IL: InterVarsity.

Miller, James D.
1997 *The Pastoral Letters as Composite Documents*. Society for New Testament Studies: Monograph Series 93. Cambridge: Cambridge University Press.

Miller, Paul M.
1964 *Servant of God's Servants: The Work of a Christian Minister*. Scottdale, PA: Herald Press.

Moo, Douglas J.
1981 "The Interpretation of 1 Timothy 2:11-15: A Rejoinder." *Trinity Journal*, n.s. 2:198-222.

Morris, Leon
1955 *The Apostolic Preaching of the Cross*. Grand Rapids: Eerdmans.

Moule, C. F. D.
1965 "The Problem of the Pastoral Epistles: A Reappraisal." *Bulletin of the John Rylands University Library of Manchester* 47:430-52.
1982 "The Problem of the Pastoral Epistles: A Reappraisal." Pages 113-32 in *Essays in New Testament Interpretation*. Cambridge: Cambridge University Press.

Mounce, William D.
2000 *Pastoral Epistles*. Word Biblical Commentary 46. Nashville: Thomas Nelson.

Murphy-O'Conner, Jerome
1996 *Paul: A Critical Life*. Oxford: Oxford University Press.

Murray, Stuart
2000 *Biblical Interpretation in the Anabaptist Tradition*. Kitchener, ON: Pandora Press.

Oden, Thomas C.
1989 *First and Second Timothy and Titus*. Interpretation: A Bible Commentary for Teaching and Preaching. Louisville, KY: John Knox.

Osiek, Carolyn, and Margaret Y. MacDonald, with Janet H. Tulloch
2006 *A Woman's Place: House Churches in Earliest Christianity*. Minneapolis: Fortress.

Padgett, Alan
1987a "Wealthy Women at Ephesus: 1 Timothy 2:8-15 in Context." *Interpretation* 41:19-31.

1987b "The Pauline Rationale for Submission: Biblical Feminism and the *Hina* Clauses of Titus 2:1-10." *Evangelical Quarterly* 59:39-52.

Page, S.
1993 "Marital Expectations of Church Leaders in the Pastoral Epistles." *Journal for the Study of the New Testament* 50:105-20.

Payne, P. B.
1981 "Libertarian Women in Ephesus: A Response to Douglas J. Moo's Article '1 Timothy 2:11-15: Meaning and Significance.'" *Trinity Journal*, n.s. 2:169-97.
1986 "*Oude* in 1 Timothy 2:12." Paper presented at the Annual Meeting of the Evangelical Theological Society, Atlanta.
2008 "1 Tim 2:12 and the Use of *Oude* to Combine Two Elements to Express a Single Idea." *New Testament Studies* 54, no. 2:235-53.

Perriman, Andrew C.
1993 "What Eve Did, What Women Shouldn't Do: The Meaning of *Authenteō* in 1 Timothy 2:12." *Tyndale Bulletin* 44:129-42.

Pierce, Ronald W., and Rebecca Merrill Groothuis, eds.
2004 *Discovering Biblical Equality: Complementarity Without Hierarchy.* Downers Grove, IL: InterVarsity.

Pipkin, H. Wayne
1994 *Essays in Anabaptist Theology.* Text Reader Series 5. Elkhart, IN: Institute of Mennonite Studies.

Pipkin, H. Wayne, and John H. Yoder, trans. and eds.
1989 *Balthasar Hubmaier: Theologian of Anabaptism.* Classics of the Radical Reformation 5. Scottdale, PA: Herald Press.

Porter, Stanley E.
1993 "What Does It Mean to Be 'Saved by Childbirth' (I Timothy 2:15)?" *Journal for the Study of the New Testament* 49:87-102.

Prior, Michael
1989 *Paul the Letter Writer and the Second Letter to Timothy.* Journal for the Study of the New Testament: Supplement Series 23. Sheffield: JSOT Press.

Quinn, Jerome D.
1978 "The Last Volume of Luke: The Relation of Luke-Acts and the Pastoral Epistles." Pages 62-75 in *Perspectives on Luke-Acts.* Edited by Charles Talbert. Edinburgh: T&T Clark.
1990 *The Letter to Titus: A New Translation with Notes and Commentary and an Introduction to Titus, I and II Timothy, the Pastoral Epistles.* Anchor Bible 35. New York: Doubleday.

Quinn, Jerome D., and William C. Wacker
2000 *The First and Second Letters to Timothy.* Grand Rapids: Eerdmans.

Ratzinger, Joseph
1994 *Catechism of the Catholic Church.* English translation of the 1992 Latin original. Liguori, MO: Liguori Publications. Cf. 2nd ed., 1997, http://www.christusrex.org/www1/CDHN/ ccc.html.

Richards, William A.
2002 *Difference and Distance in Post-Pauline Christianity: An Epistolary Analysis of the Pastorals.* Studies in Biblical Literature 44. New York: Peter Lang.

Riedemann, Peter

1999 *Peter Riedemann's Hutterite Confession of Faith.* Translated and edited by John J. Friesen. Classics of the Radical Reformation 9. Scottdale, PA: Herald Press.

Sacks, Kenneth

1990 *Diodorus Siculus and the First Century.* Princeton, NJ: Princeton University Press.

Sawatzky, Erick, ed.

2004 *The Heart of the Matter: Pastoral Ministry in Anabaptist Perspective.* Scottdale, PA: Herald Press.

Schroeder, David

1959 "Die Haustafeln des Neuen Testaments: Ihre Herkunft und ihr theologischer Sinn." DTheol Diss., Hamburg University.

Selwyn, Edward G.

1981 *The First Epistle to Peter.* Reprinted, Grand Rapids: Baker Books.

Shenk, Wilbert R.

2000 *By Faith They Went Out: Mennonite Missions, 1850-1999.* Occasional Papers 20. Elkhart, IN: Institute of Mennonite Studies.

Shepherd, M. H., Jr.

1962 "Elder in the NT." *IDB* 2:73-75.

Shillington, V. George

1997 *2 Corinthians.* Believers Church Bible Commentary. Scottdale, PA: Herald Press.

Snyder, C. Arnold

1995 *Anabaptist History and Theology: An Introduction.* Kitchener, ON: Pandora Press.

1999 *From Anabaptist Seed.* Kitchener, ON: Pandora Press.

Snyder, C. Arnold, and Linda A. Huebert Hecht, eds.

1996 *Profiles of Anabaptist Women.* Waterloo, ON: Wilfrid Laurier University Press.

Sparks, Irving Allen

1985 *The Pastoral Epistles: Introduction and Commentary.* San Diego: Institute of Biblical Studies.

Spicq, Ceslaus

1969 *Les Épitres Pastorales.* 4th ed. Paris: Gabalda.

Stambaugh, John E., and David L. Balch

1986 *The New Testament in Its Social Environment.* Philadelphia: Westminster.

Steifel, J. H.

1995 "Women Deacons in I Timothy: A Linguistic and Literary Look at 'Women Likewise . . . ' (I Tim. 3:11)." *New Testament Studies* 41:442-57.

Stuckey, Anne

2004 *Training Ministry Teams: A Manual for Elders and Deacons.* Scottdale, PA: Faith & Life Resources.

Sumney, Jerry L.

1998 "'God Our Savior': The Theology of I Timothy." *Lexington Theological Quarterly* 33, no. 3:151-61.

Swartley, Willard M.

1983 *Slavery, Sabbath, War, and Women: Case Studies in Biblical Interpretation.* Scottdale, PA: Herald Press.

2003 *Homosexuality: Biblical Interpretation and Moral Discernment.* Scottdale, PA: Herald Press.

Thiselton, Anthony C.

2000 *The First Epistle to the Corinthians.* New International Greek New Testament Commentary. Grand Rapids: Eerdmans.

Thomas, Everett J., ed.

1996 *A Mennonite Polity for Ministerial Leadership.* Newton, KS: Faith & Life Press.

Thurston, B. B.

1989 *The Widows: A Women's Ministry in the Early Church.* Minneapolis: Fortress.

Toews, John E.

2004 *Romans.* Believers Church Bible Commentary. Scottdale, PA: Herald Press.

Towner, Philip H.

1989 *The Goal of Our Instruction: The Structure of Theology and Ethics in the Pastoral Epistles.* Journal for the Study of the New Testament: Supplement Series 34. Sheffield: Sheffield Academic Press.

1994 *1–2 Timothy and Titus.* The IVP New Testament Commentary Series. Downers Grove, IL: InterVarsity.

1995 "Pauline Theology or Pauline Tradition in the Pastoral Epistles: The Question of Method." *Tyndale Bulletin* 46, no. 2 (November): 287-314.

2006 *The Letters to Timothy and Titus.* New International Commentary on the New Testament. Grand Rapids: Eerdmans.

Treblico, Paul

2004 "The Significance and Relevance of the Spirit in the Pastoral Epistles." Pages 241-56 in *The Holy Spirit and Christian Origins: Essays in Honor of James D. G. Dunn.* Edited by Graham N. Stanton, Bruce W. Longenecker, and Stephen C. Barton. Grand Rapids: Eerdmans.

Verner, David C.

1983 *The Household of God: The Social World of the Pastoral Epistles.* Society of Biblical Literature Dissertation Series 71. Chico, CA: Scholars Press.

Vincent, Mark

1997 *A Christian View of Money: Celebrating God's Generosity.* Scottdale, PA: Herald Press.

Von Campenhausen, H.

1969 *Ecclesiastical Authority and Spiritual Power in the Church of the First Three Centuries.* Translated by J. Baker. Stanford: Stanford University Press.

Von Dehsen, Christian D.

1984 "Hymnic Forms in the New Testament." *Reformed Liturgy and Music* 18, no. 1 (Winter): 7-11.

Waltner, Erland, and J. Daryl Charles
1999 *1–2 Peter, Jude.* Believers Church Bible Commentary. Scottdale, PA: Herald Press.

Ward, R. A.
1974 *Commentary on 1 and 2 Timothy and Titus.* Waco, TX: Word Books.

Waters, Kenneth L., Sr.
2004 "Saved Through Childbearing: Virtues as Children in 1 Timothy 2:11-15." *Journal of Biblical Literature* 123:703-35.

Weaver, J. Denny
2001 *The Nonviolent Atonement.* Grand Rapids: Eerdmans.

Wenger, John C.
1956 *Introduction to Theology.* Scottdale, PA: Herald Press.

Wilder, Terry L.
2003 "A Brief Defense of the Pastoral Epistles' Authenticity." *Midwestern Journal of Theology* 2, no. 1 (Fall): 38-42.

Wilshire, Leland Edward
1988 "The TLG Computer and Further Reference to αὐθεντέω [*authenteō*] in 1 Timothy 2:12." *New Testament Studies* 34:120-34.

Wilson, Steven G.
1976 "The Portrait of Paul in Acts and the Pastorals." Pages 397-411 in *Society of Biblical Literature 1976 Seminar Papers.* Edited by George W. MacRae. Missoula, MT: Scholars Press.

Winter, Bruce W.
1988 "*Providentia* for the Widows of I Timothy 5:3-16." *Tyndale Bulletin* 39:83-99.
2003 *Roman Wives, Roman Widows: The Appearance of New Women and the Pauline Communities.* Grand Rapids: Eerdmans.

Witherington, Ben, III
1988 *Women in the Earliest Churches.* Cambridge: Cambridge University Press.
2006 *Letters and Homilies for Hellenized Christians: A Socio-Rhetorical Commentary on Titus, 1–2 Timothy and 1–3 John.* Downers Grove, IL: IVP Academic.

World Council of Churches
1982 *Baptism, Eucharist and Ministry.* Faith and Order Paper No. 111. Geneva: World Council of Churches. http://www.oikoumene.org/en/resources/documents/wcc-commissions/faith-and-order-commission/i-unity-the-church-and-its-mission/baptism-eucharist-and-ministry-faith-and-order-paper-no-111-the-lima-text.html.

Wright, David F.
1984 "Homosexuals or Prostitutes? The Meaning of *Arsenokoitai* (I Cor. 6:9; I Tim. 1:10)." *Vigiliae christianae* 38:125-53.

Wright, N. T.
1996 *Jesus and the Victory of God.* Minneapolis: Fortress.
2000 "Paul's Gospel and Caesar's Empire." Pages 160-83 in *Paul and Politics: Ekklēsia, Israel, Imperium, Interpretation; Essays in Honor of Krister Stendahl.* Edited by Richard A. Horsley. Harrisburg, PA: Trinity Press International.

2003 *The Resurrection of the Son of God.* Minneapolis: Fortress.
2005 *Paul: In Fresh Perspective.* Minneapolis: Fortress.

Yoder, John H.
1977 *The Schleitheim Confession.* Scottdale, PA: Herald Press.
1992 *Body Politics: Five Practices of the Christian Community Before the Watching World.* Nashville, Discipleship Resources. Reprinted, Scottdale, PA: Herald Press, 2001.
1994 *The Politics of Jesus: Vicit Agnus Noster.* 2nd ed. Grand Rapids: Eerdmans.

Yoder, John H., trans. and ed.
1973 *The Legacy of Michael Sattler.* Classics of the Radical Reformation 1. Scottdale, PA: Herald Press.

Yoder Neufeld, Thomas R.
2002 *Ephesians.* Believers Church Bible Commentary. Scottdale, PA: Herald Press.

Young, Frances
1994 *The Theology of the Pastoral Letters.* Cambridge: Cambridge University Press.

Selected Resources

Bassler, Jouette M. *1 Timothy, 2 Timothy, Titus.* Abingdon New Testament Commentaries. Nashville: Abingdon, 1996. A good, easy-to-read commentary written by a woman scholar. Does not accept Pauline authorship. Moves the reader quickly into the main themes of the books. Helpful for the busy pastor who does not have time to read an extensive commentary.

Collins, Raymond F. *I and II Timothy and Titus: A Commentary*. New Testament Library. Louisville, KY: Westminster John Knox, 2002. A recent work in a classic series of commentaries by a Catholic scholar. Draws heavily from Greco-Roman literature and rejects Pauline authorship. This commentary has several helpful articles on important themes in the books. Recommended for the reader who wants up-to-date scholarship.

Fee, Gordon D. *1 and 2 Timothy, Titus*. New International Biblical Commentary. Peabody, MA: Hendrickson, 1988. An excellent commentary for the pastor, written by a highly respected evangelical scholar. Comments are based on good research. Not extensive, but enough is said for the pastor to gain a good understanding of these books. Holds to Pauline authorship. Highly recommended.

Johnson, Luke Timothy. *The First and Second Letters to Timothy: A New Translation with Introduction and Commentary*. Anchor Bible 35A. New York: Doubleday, 2001. A companion volume to Quinn's work on Titus. Excellent work on both 1 and 2 Timothy. Questions the reasoning of those who reject Pauline authorship. Historical and literary analyses give new insights into the thought of these two books. Highly recommended.

Kelly, J. N. D. *The Pastoral Epistles.* Black's New Testament Commentary. Peabody, MA: Hendrickson, 1960. Older but excellent work by a good scholar. Reads easily and gives good insight into the biblical text. Favors Pauline authorship. Though this work is not up-to-date, the pastor will find this commentary helpful. Recommended.

Knight, George W. *The Pastoral Epistles: A Commentary on the Greek Text.* New International Greek Testament Commentary. Grand Rapids: Eerdmans, 1992. A comprehensive analysis of the Greek text by a conservative scholar. This commentary is useful for the reader who seeks the shades of meaning in Greek grammar. Strongly supports Pauline authorship. Recommended for the person who wants to work in Greek exegesis.

Marshall, I. Howard. *The Pastoral Epistles.* International Critical Commentary. Edinburgh: T&T Clark, 1999. A detailed and thorough commentary based on up-to-date research. Makes extensive analysis of the Greek text, lists possible interpretations of difficult passages, and gives his own views. A major work by an evangelical scholar from England. Highly recommended for the person who has time for extensive reading and detailed analysis of the Greek text.

Mounce, William D. *Pastoral Epistles.* Word Biblical Commentary 46. Nashville: Thomas Nelson, 2000. Written by an American conservative evangelical scholar. Extensive analysis based on the Greek text. Holds to Pauline authorship. Interprets controversial sections in a conservative manner. Tends to rely on Fee's work. Recommended.

Quinn, Jerome D. *The Letter to Titus.* Anchor Bible 35B. New York: Doubleday, 1990. The most comprehensive commentary on Titus available in the English language. Written by a Catholic scholar after many years of research. Rejects Pauline authorship in favor of Luke. Quinn's extensive research into both Jewish and Greco-Roman resources enhances exposition of Greek words and their meanings in the context of the late first-century world. Highly recommended.

Quinn, Jerome D., and William C. Wacker. *The First and Second Letters to Timothy.* Eerdmans Critical Commentary. Grand Rapids: Eerdmans, 2000. A comprehensive commentary on the two letters to Timothy that largely follows the style of Quinn's commentary on Titus. Recommended for the reader who wants an in-depth commentary.

Towner, Philip P. *1–2 Timothy and Titus.* IVP New Testament Commentary Series. Downers Grove, IL: InterVarsity, 1994. Written by an evangelical scholar from Scotland for the lay reader and the pastor who does not know Greek. Reads easily and gives helpful insights. Affirms Pauline authorship. Recommended for lay teachers and pastors who want an easy-to-read commentary. Good overview of 1 and 2 Timothy and Titus.

Towner, Philip P. *The Letters to Timothy and Titus.* New International Commentary on the New Testament. Grand Rapids: Eerdmans, 2006. The best recent commentary on the letters to Timothy and Titus written by an evangelical scholar from Scotland. Towner follows and builds on the work of I. Howard Marshall. He affirms Pauline authorship. While making excellent use of Greek exegesis, Towner relegates his extensive Greek analysis to the footnotes. Makes use of the latest insights into the literary and historical approaches to these books. Highly recommended.

Witherington, Ben, III. *Letters and Homilies for Hellenized Christians.* Vol. 1, *A Socio-Rhetorical Commentary on Titus, 1–2 Timothy and 1–3 John.* Downers Grove, IL: IVP Academic, 2006. Witherington uses insights from studies in ancient rhetoric and sociology to interpret the letters to Timothy and Titus. An American evangelical scholar, Witherington vigorously and extensively defends Pauline authorship and Luke as secretary in writing 1 and 2 Timothy and Titus. Highly recommended.

Index of Ancient Sources

John

Acts

1 Corinthians

2 Corinthians

Galatians

Ephesians

The Author

Paul M. Zehr was born in Croghan, New York, where he grew up on a farm and attended local public schools. He graduated from Eastern Mennonite College in 1962 and from Eastern Mennonite Seminary in 1965. Paul served as pastor at First Mennonite Church of St. Petersburg, Florida, from 1965 to 1973. Following this eight-year experience of pastoring an urban church, he attended Princeton Theological Seminary, where he earned a ThM in biblical studies in 1975.

Paul then served as pastor at a small church and began teaching biblical and theological courses in the Lancaster, Pennsylvania, area. His teaching ministry reached several in-service pastors, which led to his appointment as director of external programs for Eastern Mennonite Seminary. It also created within him a greater awareness of the person, role, and function of the pastor.

In 1980, Paul was ordained bishop and supervised pastors in five congregations, a position he held for twenty-five years. In 1987, he graduated from The Eastern Baptist Theological Seminary with a DMin. A major part of this doctoral study was the preparation of a philosophy of Mennonite pastoral education and a curriculum guide for Mennonite conference-based pastoral education. For more than 20 years Paul worked in supervised pastoral education. His interest in biblical studies continued in teaching classes and in chairing the editorial council for the Believers Church Bible Commentary series.

Paul and his wife, Mary, are active members of Witmer Heights Mennonite Church. Now in their retirement years, Paul and Mary have more time to relax, travel, and give themselves to the comings and goings of their four adult children (Karen, Marcia, Timothy, Daniel), their spouses, and six grandchildren.